# Ocean
# Navigator

OTHER TITLES OF INTEREST

*Ocean Yachtmaster* Pat Langley-Price and Philip Ouvry
ISBN 7136-3596-7

The ideal classroom course textbook for the thousands who embark each year on the most advanced RYA grade – the Yachtmaster Ocean Certificate. Using this book and its exercises, the student will be able to study from home.

*Ocean Yachtmaster Exercises* Pat Langley-Price and Philip Ouvry
ISBN 0-229-11792-9

Companion volume to *Ocean Yachtmaster* for those taking the Yachtmaster Ocean Certificate and for navigators' revision.

*Using Loran* Conrad Dixon
ISBN 0-7136-3567-3

This book aims to help owners get the best from their sets and make full use of the facilities offered, from position fixing to waypoint navigation, anchor watch to racing starts, and cross track error to the man overboard facility.

*Using GPS* Conrad Dixon
ISBN 0-7136-3952-0

Unravelling the jargon associated with instruction manuals, this book will help owners make full use of the facilities available, whether simply position fixing and course setting or interfacing with radar, Loran, autopilots, logs, chart plotters, video sounders and fish finders.

*Atlantic Crossing Guide* 3rd edition: RCC Pilotage Foundation. Revised by Anne Hammick
ISBN 0-7136-3599-1

This established reference work for all those planning an Atlantic crossing is packed with advice on choosing equipment and a suitable boat, provisioning, navigation, safety, route planning, landfalls and port details.

*Atlantic Pilot Atlas* James Clark
ISBN 0-7136-3640-8

A complete guide to the weather of the North and South Atlantic, the Mediterranean, and the Caribbean, this is an ideal volume for anyone planning an Atlantic crossing. The Atlas contains monthly pilot charts for all these oceans, information on cyclones and regional weather patterns.

Sixth edition

# Ocean Navigator

Kenneth Wilkes
Revised by Pat Langley Price
and Philip Ouvry

ADLARD COLES NAUTICAL
London

Sixth edition
Published in 1994 by Adlard Coles Nautical
an imprint of A & C Black (Publishers) Ltd
35 Bedford Row, London WC1R 4JH

First edition published by Nautical Books 1975
Second edition 1976
Reprinted 1977, 1980
Third edition 1982
Fourth edition 1985
Fifth edition 1987
Sixth edition published by Adlard Coles Nautical 1994

ISBN 0-7136-3924-5

A CIP catalogue record for this book is available from the
British Library.

Typeset by August Filmsetting, Haydock, St Helens
Printed and bound in Great Britain by Butler and Tanner
Ltd, Frome and London

## Acknowledgements

The Publishers would like to thank the following
organisations, companies and individuals for their
contributions to this edition:

The Controller of HM Stationery Office for
permission to reproduce extracts from AP3270 *Sight
Reduction Tables for Air Navigation* and from the
*Nautical Almanac*.

The Hydrographer of the Navy for permission to
reproduce portions of Plotting Sheet 5333A and
extracts from NP401.

Imray, Laurie, Norie and Wilson Ltd for permission
to reproduce extracts from *Norie's Nautical Tables*.

Brookes and Gatehouse Ltd        Tamaya & Co Ltd
Ebbco Ltd                        Bill Streets
ICS Electronics Ltd              D J Butler
Raytheon Marine Ltd

*Note from the publishers*
The publishers grant permission for the reproduction
of the forms in Appendix 4 on pages 167–73 of the b

# Contents

# Introduction

Years ago a deck officer in the merchant navy never went to sea without his own sextant and a copy of Nautical Tables (Nories, Burtons or Inmans). At noon every day at sea he would complete his daily sights then use his Tables to plot the ship's position and work out the distance run from noon the previous day. It was part of the professionalism of an officer of the merchant navy. Following the classic voyages of Joshua Slocum and Francis Chichester, small craft sailors began making increasingly longer ocean passages basing their navigation on the traditions of the merchant navy. Nowadays, it seems that every year there is yet another race or rally taking small craft around the world or across the oceans. The fear of making a long distance ocean passage has gone, though seafarers should never lose their respect for the sea.

With the advent of modern technology, today's navigators have many aids at their disposal. Clocks are accurate to within one second a month; and there is no shortage of time signals. The Global Positioning System appears to have made obsolete all other methods of long distance navigation. In the United Kingdom, however, the Royal Yachting Association issues a Yachtmaster Ocean Certificate of Competency, with the requirement for a qualifying passage based on the traditional methods of navigation. The Royal Institute of Navigation has recently introduced the International Oceanic Award to encourage amateur small craft navigators to practice *traditional* ocean navigation which is still regarded as an essential back-up system for satellite navigation.

In 1975 Kenneth Wilkes wrote *Ocean Yacht Navigator*. Since then very many small craft have set sail across the oceans with this book as the principal guide to the navigation. It included many examples and exercises to act as refreshers both for the first timer and for the out-of-practice navigator. Kenneth Wilkes emphasised the golden rule for every navigator to **check** every figure, check every addition or subtraction and every name (N or S, E or W) and every sign (+ or −) and **tick** every item checked . . . and then to **have confidence** in the final result.

In this new edition, now re-titled *Ocean Navigator*, we have followed the pattern set by Kenneth Wilkes, but simplified many of the examples and exercises to make them easier to understand. A wide selection of sight reduction forms are included which we hope will make the checking of preparatory data and the working of the sights a straightforward operation.

Let us not forget that satellite position finding systems are aids to navigation, not a means of navigation. It is to be expected that any long distance navigator will be prepared to use the traditional methods even though they could become very much out of practice. It is even more important, therefore, to have to hand, a complete reference to traditional navigation just in case the electronics systems should fail.

Pat Langley-Price
Philip Ouvry
May 1994

# 1 Where Are We?

The weather has been clear for the most of the ocean passage, but for the past two days the sky has been overcast and it is now blowing quite hard. Evening is approaching and you estimate that your position is about 50 miles off the coast, which the chart shows as rocky. It is also a lee shore. The position is by no means certain as there has been some instrument failure and the last reliable sights were taken three days ago. Is it safe to stand on, or should you heave-to and wait for daylight?

Whilst you consider the problem there is a brief clearing in the sky, and the moon, a planet and a couple of stars become visible.

Out with the sextant and in a short time you obtain an up-to-the-minute observed position. As all four position lines form only a small 'cocked hat' on the chart the position appears to be reliable. A course can now be shaped to the destination and a fairly accurate prediction made of the time and position of landfall. The navigator can now get his head down for a few hours, safe in the knowledge that the boat will not finish up on the rocks in the middle of the night.

This is the sort of situation every navigator faces from time to time, but the more you know about deep sea navigation, the safer and quicker the passage.

Safe navigation depends upon the navigator knowing the boat's position at any time. When within sight of landmarks these can be used to fix the position. When no such landmarks are available the boat's position can be estimated by taking into account the distance run, allowing for wind and tidal stream or current. If radio navigational aids are available these will, of course, give an absolute fix of position.

When making an ocean passage, we use celestial navigation. This means finding the position by the observation of heavenly bodies. Let us consider how this is done.

It is no exaggeration to say that a long offshore passage should not be attempted without someone aboard with the equipment and the ability to take celestial sights, and the sextant is the traditional instrument used for such sights.

Many years ago the tables and books available and the methods used needed much study and a fair knowledge of trigonometry. Now, the use of a 'rapid sight reduction' table has vastly simplified the necessary work. No knowledge of trigonometry is required: simply the ability the follow a set pattern of work, to look up a few figures in tables, to add and subtract, and to plot the resultant position.

The best approach to deep sea navigation is to learn how to work out sights in comfort at home, working with exercises and then to practise taking sights with the sextant from a known position so that the accuracy of the results can be checked. Sights taken from the beach can be most useful for this purpose.

There is really nothing difficult about taking celestial sights but initially it is all too easy to make mistakes. Taking and working out sights is like riding a bicycle: anyone can do it, but not the first time. As with most things, what seems difficult at first soon becomes simplicity itself after a little practice.

In the explanations that follow, a number of examples are given and practice exercises provided. We strongly recommend that these are worked through and the figures checked with the answers at the end of the book. Extracts to enable you to complete these exercises are provided in Appendices 5 and 6.

All celestial sights rely upon the solution of a spherical triangle on the surface of the earth, commonly called the PZX triangle. For those interested, an explanation of the solution of such a triangle is given in Appendix 2. It is stressed that it is not necessary to study the theory of the PZX triangle in order to be able to use the sextant and the relevant tables to obtain a position anywhere in the world.

## Nautical Almanac

For a navigator on the surface of the earth using celestial bodies to determine position, the first information required is the knowledge at any instant of time of the position in space of datum points on the earth's surface. This is found by referring to an almanac such as the *Nautical Almanac*, published jointly by HM Stationery Office in London, and the US Government Printing Office; or the small craft navigator's version in *Reed's Nautical Almanac*.

Extracts used in this book are from the *Nautical Almanac* which gives details of the datum constellation Aries, four planets, 57 stars, the sun and the moon, together with the times of twilight, sunrise and sunset.

## Sight reduction

Data from the *Nautical Almanac* is used to extract further information from sight reduction tables to enable a sight taken with the sextant to be plotted. Sights can be worked out by various methods:

- *Sight Reduction Tables for Air Navigation*, AP 3270 (UK), HO 249 (US). *Volume 1* covers rapid sight reduction of selected stars (7 at any one time). *Volume 2*, latitudes 0°–39°, and *Volume 3*, latitudes 40°–89°, cover all tabulated heavenly bodies. Extracts from these tables for use with the exercises in this book are given in Appendix 6.
- *Sight Reduction Tables for Marine Navigation*, NP 401 (UK), HO 229 (US): six volumes in 16 latitude bands cover all heavenly bodies. The information contained is similar to that in *Volumes 2* and *3* of AP3270. An example of a sight worked out from these tables is given in Appendix 1.
- *Norie's Tables*. These contain tables for solving the PZX triangle for any heavenly body by using the Haversine formula. An example is given in Appendix 3. They also contain many other useful tables, such as Traverse Tables, an example of which is shown in Chapter 11.

Other items and instruments required are:

Sextant
Reliable watch which can be taken on deck
Reliable clock (chronometer) for use below deck
Radio able to receive time signals
Parallel rule or course plotter
Square protractor
Dividers
Pencil compass
Graph paper
Plotting sheet
2B pencils

Perhaps, rather surprisingly, the most difficult part of celestial navigation is the need for accuracy. Detailed sight reduction forms contain all the steps necessary in the procedure for converting the sights into a format ready for plotting; a simple headed form is shown in Appendix 4. Inevitably a number of figures have to be looked up, written down, added or subtracted. The mistakes occur in simple arithmetic. There is a golden rule for every navigator whether novice or experienced: *Check* every figure, every addition or subtraction, every 'name' (N or S, E or W), every sign ( + or − ) and tick every item as it is checked. Do not use the answer until everything has been checked. This may sound tedious, but it only takes a few moments if done while the book or table is open. It is maddening when a sight makes nonsense and it is found to be due to a simple mistake right at the beginning. Further points worth making are:

- Write all figures down. Do not rely on memory or attempt mental arithmetic. What is easy at home is not quite so easy at sea.
- Be methodical and follow a regular sequence of working. Do not try short cuts. Always insert a caption or label against a figure and put in the 'name' (N or S, E or W); for example: 10h 25m 18s GMT, 24° 48'.0N. This greatly helps checking.
- Write all figures boldly and clearly so that there is no risk of them being misread. Write figures directly beneath each other, so that adding or subtracting is made easier.
- Check all subtraction by adding up backwards:

- If a mistake is made, do not try to write over a figure. Cross it out and put in the new corrected figure.
- Having done a calculation, whenever possible 'stand back' and see whether it *looks* sensible. If it does not, it is almost certain to be wrong and needs re-checking.
- If the above advice has been followed, *have confidence* in the result.

*Example 1a*

```
 − 35° 05'     Check by adding 10' to 34° 55'
   34° 55'     ensuring it makes 35° 05'
       10'
```

# 2 Signposts in the Sky

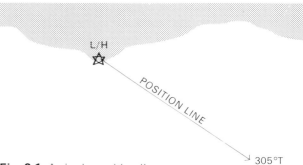

**Fig. 2.1** A single position line.

When in coastal waters, the boat's position can usually be fixed by reference to landmarks. When crossing an ocean, the boat will be out of sight of land for several weeks so such landmarks are not available. However, there are other objects that can be used for position finding, such as the sun, moon, planets and stars.

In coastal navigation a single observation of a landmark provides a single position line along which, at some point, is the boat's position (Fig 2.1). A suitably situated second landmark, observed simultaneously, provides a second position line which intersects the first to fix the boat's position, (Fig 2.2).

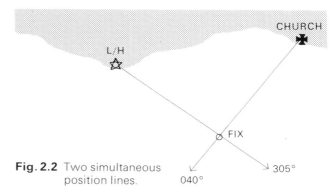

**Fig. 2.2** Two simultaneous position lines.

When only one landmark is available, a fix can be obtained as follows: take a bearing and plot the resultant position line. The boat then runs on a suitable distance when a second bearing of the same landmark is obtained. The distance and direction the boat has run between the two position lines is plotted, starting at any convenient point on the first position line. The first position line is transferred to the end of the run so that it intersects the second position line. The point of intersection is the boat's position (Fig. 2.3). This construction is called a running fix or a transferred position line.

In celestial navigation observations of the sun can be used in the same way. The construction is not, however, called a transferred position line, it is called a sun-run-sun sight.

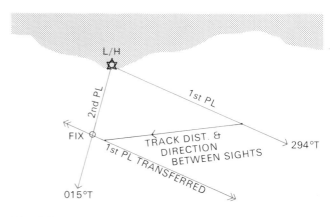

**Fig. 2.3** A transferred position line.

If two or more heavenly bodies can be seen at the same time, then simultaneous sights may be taken:

- by day, when both sun and moon are visible
- occasionally by day when a planet is visible and can be used together with the sun or moon
- at dawn and dusk when stars, planets and the moon are visible together with a clear horizon
- at night if the horizon is well lit and defined.

The explanations that follow refer to the sun, though the principles can be applied to any heavenly body. Data about the position of heavenly bodies is contained in the *Nautical Almanac*. This data makes it possible to find the point on the earth's surface which is directly beneath the body's position in the sky and to deduce the boat's position relative to that point. Before considering celestial co-ordinates, let us revise a few general principles.

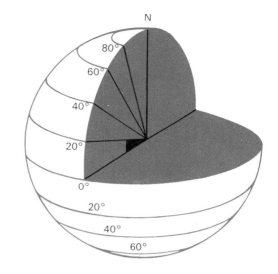

**Fig. 2.4** Parallels of latitude.

### Angles and circles
There are 360 degrees (360°) in a circle and 60 minutes (60′) in a degree. A fraction of a minute of arc is recorded in decimals of a minute, for example: 50° 25′.5.

### Parallels of latitude
The equator is a great circle girdling the earth exactly midway between the north and south poles, the plane of which passes through the centre of the earth. A parallel of latitude is a small circle girdling the earth parallel to the equator. Latitude is 0° at the equator, increasing to 90° north and south of the equator (Fig 2.4).

### Meridians of longitude
Any straight line between the north pole and the south pole is a meridian. It crosses the equator at right angles. A meridian is half a great circle. The meridian which passes through Greenwich, London, is 0°. To the east and west of Greenwich, meridians increase up to 180° (Fig 2.5).

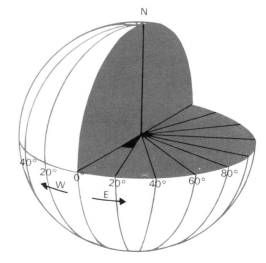

**Fig. 2.5** Meridians of longitude.

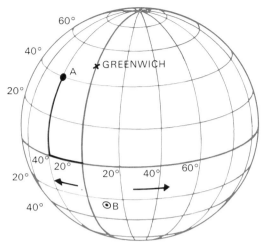

**Fig. 2.6** Defining position: A is 40°N 20°W; B is 25°S 10°E.

## Position
A position on the surface of the earth is defined by the co-ordinates of latitude and longitude (Fig 2.6).

## Nautical mile
A nautical mile (M) is defined as the distance between two points on the earth's surface which subtend an angle of one minute at the centre of the

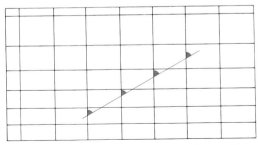

**Fig. 2.7** Mercator projection. Longitude is equally spaced, but latitude is spaced further apart nearer the poles.

earth. On a mercator projection chart (Fig 2.7) the latitude scale level with the area of interest is used to measure nautical miles, one minute of latitude being equivalent to one nautical mile. A cable is a tenth of a nautical mile. A speed measurement of one nautical mile per hour is called a knot.

## Geographical position
The earth revolves around its axis (which is between the north and south poles) completing one revolution every 24 hours. The earth itself travels around the sun once a year. For navigational purposes it is simpler to assume that the centre of the earth is the centre of the universe with the sun travelling around the earth from east to west.

At any instant there is a point on the earth's surface where the sun is exactly overhead. An imaginary line drawn from the centre of the earth to the centre of the sun would cut the earth's surface at this point which is called the sun's geographical position (GP) (Fig 2.8).

The geographical position is constantly changing as the sun moves from east to west around the earth, making one complete circuit (360°) every twenty-four hours (Fig 2.9). Throughout the year, the sun's geographical position also changes in a north-south direction, but very much more slowly. This is because the earth is tilted on its axis which is the reason that different seasons occur. At the spring equinox, 21 March, the sun's daily track is around the equator. Until the middle of the northern summer, 22 June, it slowly spirals northwards when it is tracking around approximately in latitude 23° N. It then starts southwards, recrossing the equator at the autumnal equinox on 23 September, and continuing southwards until it reaches latitude 23° S on 22 December.

The sun's geographical position is thus moving in an east-west direction extremely quickly (approximately one nautical mile every 4 seconds), and in a north-south or south-north direction much more slowly.

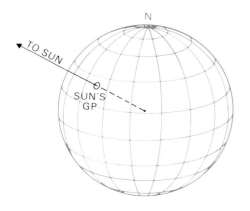

Fig. 2.8 Geographical position.

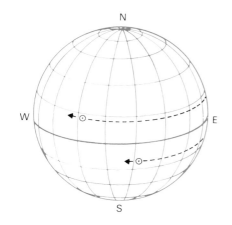

Fig. 2.9 The sun's geographical position is constantly changing as the earth rotates.

### Observer's zenith

The point in the heavens exactly over the observer's head is called his zenith: it is the point vertically above him. An observer standing on the sun's geographical position would see the sun directly overhead on his zenith (Fig 2.10). However, the observer is rarely on the sun's geographical position but some distance away from it. The angular difference, subtended at the centre of the earth, between the observer's zenith and the sun's geographical position is called the zenith distance (ZD) (Fig 2.11). This angular difference is, of course, the same as that between the observer's position and the sun's geographical position.

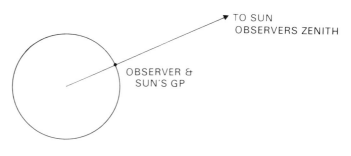

Fig. 2.10 Observer's zenith.

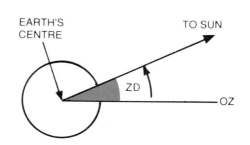

Fig. 2.11 Zenith distance.

Suppose that the angular measurement of zenith distance was 10°. One minute of arc at the earth's centre is equal to one nautical mile on the earth's surface, so the observer would be 600 miles away from the sun's geographical position (10 × 60).

However, the observer's position would not be known. Imagine a ring of people standing in a circle with a radius of 600 miles around the sun's geographical position. Each would find that the sun's zenith distance at that point was 10°. They would all be on a *circle* of position. Without further information their position on the circle would not be known. They would only know that they were 600 miles from the sun's geographical position.

If the sun's geographical position could be marked on the chart, and the circle of position drawn around it, the boat would be somewhere on that circle. This is not practical as the sun's geographical position could be over 4000 miles away from the observer's position. So the problem has to be tackled in a different way.

### Altitude
The exact point in space which is the observer's zenith cannot be accurately measured, so zenith distance has to be found another way. At 90° to the zenith is the horizon. It is fairly easy to measure in degrees the sun's height above the horizon, which is the sun's altitude. 90° minus altitude will give zenith distance. For example if the altitude was 20°, the zenith distance would be 70° (Fig 2.12).

### Intercept and azimuth
If the positions of two points on the earth's surface are known, the distance between them can be found by calculation or by using a table. The examples in this book use tabulated altitude from which the zenith distance is readily deduced (as one is the complement of the other, this is not important).

A latitude and longitude somewhere near the boat's actual position, such as a dead reckoning (DR) position, is required for use with the table. The table will give the altitude of the sun from the DR position, from which is deduced the size of the position circle around the sun's geographical position. If the tabulated altitude was 29° 40'.0 (ZD 60° 20'.0), the radius of the position circle would be 3620 miles (60 × 60 + 20). This circle would pass through the DR position. However, the boat will be *near* but *not on* the position circle as it was calculated from a DR position. Even if it were practicable, it is not necessary to draw this position circle.

At any specific time, by using a sextant to measure the altitude of the sun, the observer's true distance from the sun's geographical position can be found. Suppose this true altitude was 29° 48'.0 (ZD 60° 12'.0). The observer would be on a true position circle with a radius of 3612 miles. When the sextant sight is taken, the exact time is recorded which is then used for entry to the tables.

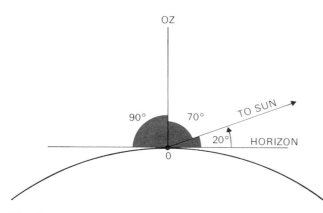

**Fig. 2.12** 90° − altitude = zenith distance.

By comparison of the tabulated altitude (calculated from the DR position) and the true altitude (measured by using the sextant from the true position), the distance of the true position circle from the DR position can be determined and part of it plotted. In the example, the boat's true position circle is smaller than the tabulated position circle so it will be nearer to the sun's GP. The difference between the two (29° 48'.0 − 29° 40'.0) is 8'.0 which is equivalent to 8 miles:

| | |
|---|---|
| True altitude | 29° 48'.0 |
| Tabulated altitude | 29° 40'.0 |
| Difference | 8'.0 = 8 miles |

The difference of 8 miles is called the *intercept*.

The table used to find tabulated altitude also gives the bearing or azimuth of the sun's GP; in other words the centre of the position circle. For the example this is 220° T.

If the DR position is plotted, and a line drawn in the direction of 220° T for 8 miles, this will intersect the true position circle. A small part of this circle can be plotted (as a straight line) at right angles to the line of azimuth (Fig 2.13).

The observer's position will be on this small part of the true position circle but not necessarily on the end of the line of azimuth, as the azimuth was for the dead reckoning position and represents an angular measurement from the sun's GP which is not sufficiently accurate. A second position line from another observation is required to fix the position.

The azimuth found from the tables is always given as a bearing towards the sun's GP. In the example, because the true position circle was smaller than the tabulated one, the intercept was plotted *towards* the sun's GP in the direction of 220° T. In the following example, the true position circle is larger than the tabulated one. The intercept will still be plotted along the line of azimuth but in the opposite direction *away* from the sun's GP.

| | |
|---|---|
| Tabulated altitude | 47° 16'.1 |
| True altitude | 47° 10'.0 |
| Difference | 6'.1 = 6.1 M |

Azimuth 120° T (plot in the direction of 300° T). See Fig 2.14.

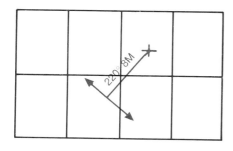

**Fig. 2.13** Intercept *towards*.

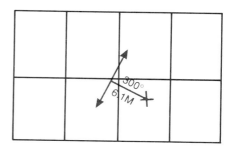

**Fig. 2.14** Intercept *away*.

The following mnemonic may help in deciding whether to plot along the line of azimuth *towards* or *away* from the geographical position. It refers to altitude:

Tabulated Tiny Towards.

If the *tabulated* altitude is *smaller* than the true altitude then the line is drawn *towards* the GP, in other words in the direction shown in the tables.

If the *tabulated* altitude is *larger* than the true altitude then the line is drawn *away* from the GP, which is the reciprocal to that shown in the tables. (See Fig 2.15).

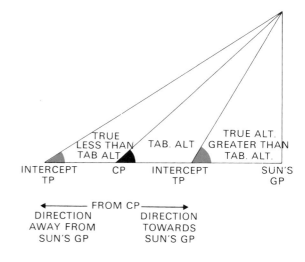

**Fig. 2.15** Direction to plot the intercept.

# 3 How the Sextant Works

The sextant does something quite simple. It is an instrument designed to measure the angle subtended at the observer's eye between two objects. In celestial navigation this angle is between the horizon and the heavenly body (Fig 3.1).

Although simple in principle, the sextant has to be extremely accurate and is made to very fine limits. It is a delicate instrument and its accuracy may be impaired by rough handling.

The sextant consists of a triangular frame to which

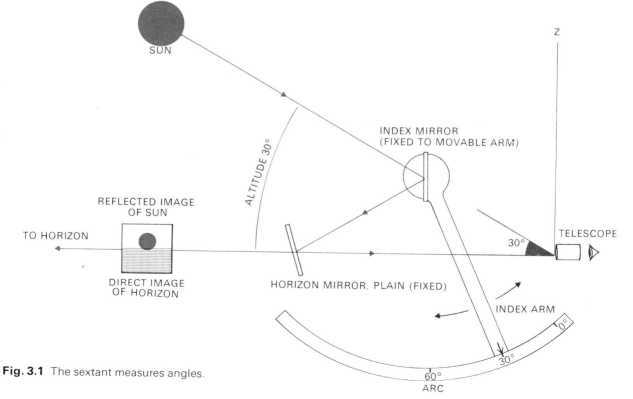

**Fig. 3.1** The sextant measures angles.

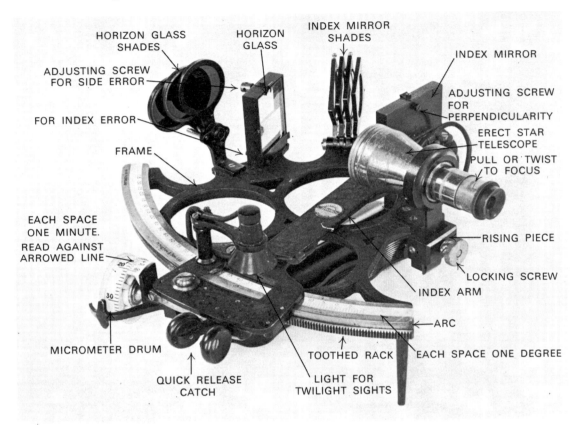

Parts of a sextant.

is fixed a telescope, two mirrors, shades, and a movable arm. The curved part or arc of the sextant is inscribed with a degree scale. At the end of the movable arm there is a fine tuning device called a micrometer which is used to measure minutes and decimal points of a minute.

The mirrors are so arranged that a reflected image of the sun can be viewed through the telescope at the same time as the actual horizon.

The shades in front of the mirror at the top of the index arm are to filter light received from the sun to a suitable brilliance. The shades behind the other mirror reduce the light from the sea cutting out excessive sparkle. The photograph above shows the parts of a sextant.

### Sextant adjustment

The sextant is a well-made instrument which, with reasonable care, will last a lifetime. However, the mirrors, upon which the accuracy depends, are mounted so that their rake and angle can be adjusted should they accidentally be slightly

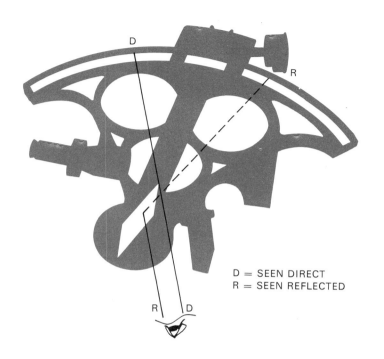

D = SEEN DIRECT
R = SEEN REFLECTED

AS SEEN WHEN CHECKING

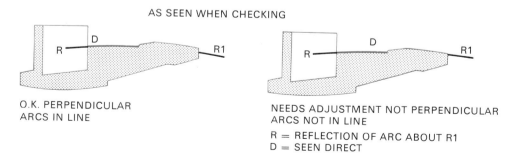

O.K. PERPENDICULAR
ARCS IN LINE

NEEDS ADJUSTMENT NOT PERPENDICULAR
ARCS NOT IN LINE
R = REFLECTION OF ARC ABOUT R1
D = SEEN DIRECT

**Fig. 3.2** Sextant error – perpendicularity.

Checking a sextant for perpendicularity. Hold the sextant
so that it faces this way.

Perpendicularity. Line up in the index mirror both the
reflected and direct image of arc. In this picture they are
both in line so that there is no error.

displaced. Apart from focusing the telescope, these are the only parts which may need adjustment.

Checks for accuracy are easy to do and should be made periodically. The errors and corrections are as follows:

**Perpendicularity** The index mirror should be perpendicular to the plane of the instrument. To check, remove the telescope. Set the index arm at about 45°. With the sextant in the horizontal plane hold it up to the eye. Look in the index mirror and move the sextant slightly until both the actual arc and the reflected image of the arc can be seen. (See Fig 3.2, and photographs on page 22.) Unless these are level, the index mirror is not vertical. Adjustment is done by fractionally turning a screw at the back of the index mirror.

**Side error** The horizon mirror should be perpendicular to the plane of the instrument. To check for side error, replace the telescope and set the index arm and the micrometer to zero. Hold the sextant in the vertical position. Sight any distant clearly defined object which has a vertical edge, such as a chimney, flagstaff or building. If there is no side error, the actual and reflected image will coincide.

Side error can also be checked by sighting a star. When there is an error present, the actual and reflected images will be seen side by side (Fig. 3.3). Adjustment is done by fractionally turning one of the screws at the back of the horizon mirror.

**Index error (IE)** Both mirrors should be parallel to each other when the index arm is set to zero. To check, set the sextant to zero, sight any sharp distant object more than about 3 miles away. The line of a clear horizon is excellent for this. Adjust the sextant until actual and reflected images coincide (Fig 3.4).

Sextant held vertically

**Fig. 3.3** Sextant error – side error.

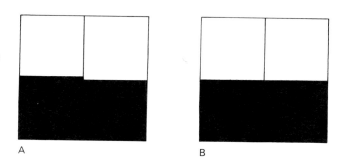

A                                    B

**Fig. 3.4** Sextant error – index error.

Look at the reading on the scale. If the arrow on the index arm is to the left of 0°, the error is *on* the arc, the sextant is over reading and the amount indicated must be *subtracted* from all sights. If on the other hand the arrow is to the right of 0°, then the error is *off* the arc, the sextant is under reading and the amount indicated must be *added* to all sights taken (Fig 3.5).

Adjustment is made by fractionally turning one of the screws at the back of the horizon mirror. If index error is small, for example less than 4'.0, it is usually left and allowed for when working out sights. The sextant should always be checked for index error before taking a sight.

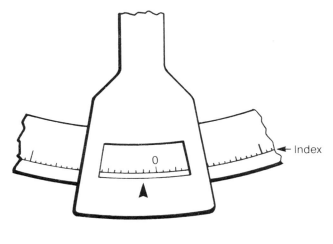

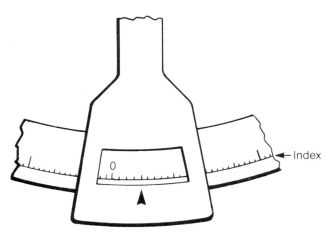

Fig. 3.5 Index error *on* and *off* the arc.

### Taking a sight

Before taking a sight of the sun, it is essential to move one or more protective shades into place so that the sun's rays viewed through the telescope do not blind the observer.

Having done this, set the arrow on the movable arm and the micrometer to zero and point the telescope at the sun. If the movable arm is now disengaged and the sextant frame swung slightly downwards, a reflected image can be seen underneath the sun's true image. The reflected image is moved downwards until near the horizon. The micrometer is used for fine tuning to set the sun's lower or upper edge on the horizon. (See Fig 3.6 and photographs opposite.)

To ensure that the sextant is being held vertically, it should be rocked laterally so that it pivots around the telescope and the sun appears to swing like a pendulum. The sextant is vertical at the lowest point of the swing (Fig 3.7). The required angle is read in two stages:

1. First the number of degrees of arc, by noting where the arrow on the index arm touches the scale. If this is between two degree marks, the lower is used.
2. Next the number of minutes on the micrometer edge. Decimal points of a minute are either interpolated to the nearest 0'.2 or there may be a small scale adjacent to an engraved arrow for this purpose (Fig 3.8).

Sights of the moon and the four navigation planets (Jupiter, Venus, Saturn and Mars) can be taken in the same way. For a star, because it is a small point of light, it is easier to work out (from sight reduction tables) its approximate angle (altitude) and its bearing (azimuth). This angle is set on the sextant which is pointed at the horizon in the direction of the bearing. The star should be seen

THE SUN

**Fig. 3.6** The sun's lower limb is on the horizon.

The author, Kenneth Wilkes, taking a sight. Here the quick release catch is used to 'find' the sun.

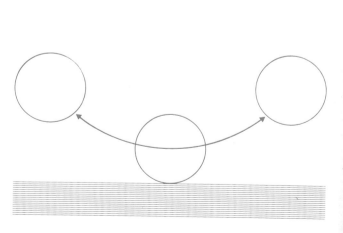

**Fig. 3.7** Swinging the sextant.

The next stage in taking a sight. An exact coincidence is obtained by using the micrometer drum.

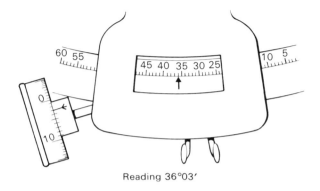

Reading 36°03′

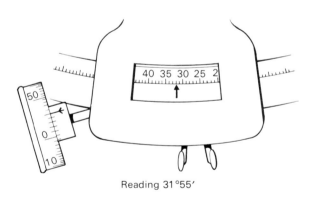

Reading 31°55′

either slightly above or below the horizon. The micrometer can then be used to bring it into co-incidence with the horizon.

### Time
All observations of heavenly bodies require the Greenwich Mean Time to be recorded at the time of the sight. The time must be accurate to within two seconds. The only exceptions to this are midday sights of the sun and sights of the pole star.

### Care of the sextant
When not being used, the sextant should always be kept in its box in a secure position below deck so that it is not thrown about when the sea is rough. Ideally the stowage should be so arranged that the sextant can be taken out of the box and the box left in place. Immediately after use the sextant should be replaced in the box. If it is accidentally dropped, there is a risk of irreparable damage.

Always remove it from the box using the left hand, with the fingers through the frame and transferring to the right hand. Replace in the reverse manner. A cord attached to the sextant and passed around the user's neck will save loss overboard.

The mirrors, shades and telescope lenses should be kept clean by lightly rubbing with a soft cloth. Occasionally the gears and teeth on the scale should be lubricated with a small amount of light oil and the scale wiped over with a lightly oiled cloth. *Never* polish the scale. Should the sextant get completely covered in salt water, it should be washed off with fresh water and dried with a soft cloth.

**Fig. 3.8**  Reading the angle on the sextant.

## Types of sextant

There are many good types of sextant available, some of which are shown in the photographs opposite and page 28. The plastic sextant shown is a useful addition to the boat's equipment. It is accurate to within 2'.0 of arc and very competitively priced. If not used as the main instrument it is invaluable as a back up for emergencies.

When buying a second-hand sextant, care must be taken to check that it is functioning accurately. The following points are worth remembering:

- Only buy from a reputable instrument supplier.
- Check that the scale is still visible and not worn through repeated polishing.
- See that the mirrors are unblemished, that they are firm and the adjustment screws are not too loose or seized up.
- Inspect the frame for signs of distortion.
- Make sure the telescope can be focused.
- Run through the checks for perpendicularity, side error and index error, but do not condemn unless these cannot be removed.

A Tamaya MS 933 Univision sextant.

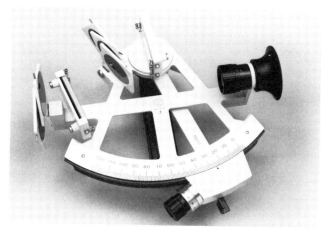

A sextant of German manufacture.

The Ebbco plastic sextant.

# 4 True Altitude

The first step in using a sextant observation of a heavenly body is to determine the body's true altitude. The altitude read on the sextant is the sextant altitude which has to have some corrections made to it before it becomes the true altitude. The corrections which have to be made are:

**1 Index error** This is found by the observer for the particular sextant being used. It can be either plus or minus.

**2 Dip** This is found by reference to the *Nautical Almanac*. Dip is always subtracted.

**3 Semi-diameter/Refraction/Parallax** These are combined as a single correction which is found in the *Nautical Almanac*.

The Apparent Altitude is the Sextant Altitude corrected for Index error and Dip.

### Index error
Few sextants have no index error (IE), any more than a watch corresponds exactly with Greenwich Mean Time. Every reading of the sextant must be corrected for index error if the sight is to be accurate. As indicated in the previous chapter it can be subtracted or added dependent upon whether it is on or off the arc.

### Dip
This is the angle between the horizontal plane through the observer's eye and the visible horizon

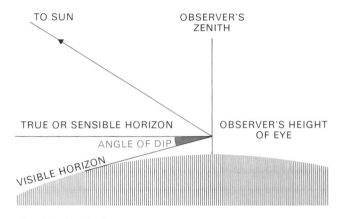

**Fig. 4.1** Dip is determined by height of eye.

(Fig 4.1). It occurs because the eye is always above sea level so that the observed altitude is always greater than the altitude as measured from a point at sea level, where theoretically the horizon would be in a true horizontal plane.

The amount of correction depends upon the height of eye (HE) of the observer above sea level. This correction is always subtracted. A correction table in the *Nautical Almanac* shows the corrections, in minutes of arc, to be applied for various heights of eye. Fig 4.2 shows a small portion of this table.

In the left-hand column the height of eye is tabulated in metres from 2.4 metres to 21.4 metres.

| DIP | | | | | |
|---|---|---|---|---|---|
| Ht. of Eye | Corrⁿ | Ht. of Eye | Ht. of Eye | Corrⁿ |
| m | | ft. | m | |
| 2·4 | −2·8 | 8·0 | 1·0 — 1·8 | |
| 2·6 | | 8·6 | 1·5 — 2·2 | |
| 2·8 | −2·9 | 9·2 | 2·0 — 2·5 | |
| 3·0 | −3·0 | 9·8 | 2·5 — 2·8 | |
| 3·2 | −3·1 | 10·5 | 3·0 - 3·0 | |
| 3·4 | −3·2 | 11·2 | See table | |
| 3·6 | −3·3 | 11·9 | | |
| 3·8 | −3·4 | 12·6 | | |
| 4·0 | −3·5 | 13·3 | m | |
| 4·3 | −3·6 | 14·1 | 20 — 7·9 | |

**Fig. 4.2** *Nautical Almanac* extract: altitude correction table showing dip.

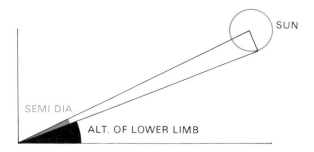

**Fig. 4.3** Semi-diameter.

The table is so arranged that the correction for a tabulated height of eye is diagonally to the right. For example, for a height of eye of 2.8 metres, the correction would be − 2.9. This correction would also apply to a height of eye of 2.7 metres. For a height of eye of 2.6 metres the correction would be − 2.8.

Heights of eye not included in the main table are shown in small tables to the right. In these tables the correction for a given height of eye is alongside; for example: the correction for 3.0 metres is − 3′.0. When taking a sight it is sufficient to gauge height of eye to the nearest quarter of a metre.

## Semi-diameter

The true altitude is the angle between the true horizon and the *centre* of the observed body (Fig 4.3). Stars have no visible diameter but both the sun and the moon have appreciable diameters. It is much more accurate to measure the angle of the sun or the moon by sighting the upper or lower edge or limb on the horizon and making a correction for half the body's diameter than it is to guess when the centre of the body is on the horizon.

## Refraction

This is caused by light rays bending as they pass from one medium to another of different density. The phenomenon of the stick which appears to be bent when part of it is placed in water at an angle is well known (Fig 4.4). Light passing from outer

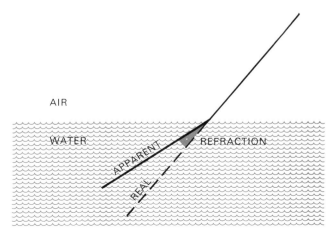

**Fig. 4.4** Refraction – the stick appears bent.

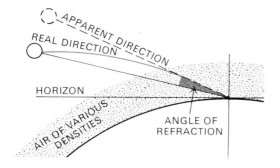

**Fig. 4.5** Refraction – the heavenly body's altitude appears to be higher than it actually is.

space into the earth's atmosphere is similarly refracted (Fig 4.5). Refraction is at a maximum when the body viewed is low down near the horizon, diminishing to zero when the body is overhead.

## Parallax

The altitude of a body as measured from the surface of the earth differs from that which would be found if it were measured from the centre of the earth, which is the condition required for true altitude. The difference is called parallax (Fig 4.6).

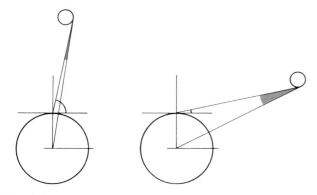

**Fig. 4.6** Parallax is greater when altitude is low.

Parallax is greatest when the altitude is low and diminishes gradually to zero when the body is overhead. Parallax also varies as the distance between the body and the earth changes. The moon's parallax can be up to 61' in arc because it is relatively near to the earth. The amount, therefore, depends upon the moon's altitude and distance from the earth, which varies during the year. The sun's parallax is fractional, never exceeding 0'.15. Parallax of all other heavenly bodies is so small it can be regarded as negligible.

## Total correction

Semi-diameter, refraction and parallax are combined in a single total correction which is found in the *Nautical Almanac* for the observed body's particular altitude. In the case of the sun, there is a separate table for summer and winter. The table is entered with apparent altitude. If the apparent altitude of the

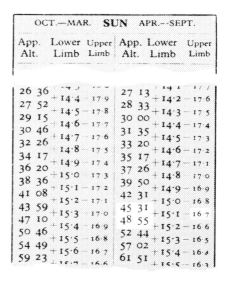

**Fig. 4.7** *Nautical Almanac* extract: altitude correction table – sun's total correction.

sun's upper limb (UL) was 46° 10'.1, and the observation was made in June, then the correction to apply would be − 16'.7 (Fig 4.7). This correction applies to all apparent altitudes between the tabulated figures of 45° 31'.0 and 48° 55'.0. The correction for the sun's upper limb is subtracted and that for the lower limb added.

The moon's parallax changes so markedly that it is given as a separate correction according to the changing apparent diameter of the moon. The simple correction table to be used for the moon is fully explained in Chapter 10.

### Application of corrections to sextant altitude

**Application of corrections to sextant altitude** The example below shows how the corrections should be applied to convert sextant altitude to true altitude.

*Example 4a*
An observation of the sun's lower limb taken in November, gave a sextant reading of 34° 25'.0. Height of eye 2.5 metres. Index error − 2'.0. Refer to Figs 4.2 and 4.7.

| | |
|---|---|
| Sextant altitude (SA) | 34° 25'.0 |
| Index error (IE) | − 2'.0 (on the sextant) |
| Dip (HE 2.5 metres) | − 2'.8 (from the almanac) |
| Apparent altitude (AA) | 34° 20'.2 |
| corrn (lower limb (LL) Nov) | |
| | + 14'.9 (from the almanac) |
| True altitude | 34° 35'.1 |

### Exercise

**Exercise**
*Answers and extracts are at the back of the book.*
Find the sun's true altitude.

| | Date | Sextant Altitude | Index Error | Height of Eye |
|---|---|---|---|---|
| **4.1** | 31 August | LL 20° 43'.6 | − 1'.9 | 2.5 metres |
| **4.2** | 17 February | LL 19° 57'.2 | − 3'.0 | 2.5 metres |
| **4.3** | 20 May | LL 28° 51'.4 | + 2'.0 | 2.0 metres |
| **4.4** | 30 August | UL 20° 54'.1 | − 2'.6 | 2.0 metres |
| **4.5** | 30 August | LL 48° 31'.8 | − 2'.6 | 2.6 metres |

# 5 Tabulated Altitude

Extracts from the *Nautical Almanac* and from sight reduction tables which will be required for this chapter are at the back of the book (Appendices 5 and 6).

## Altitude and azimuth from a chosen position

From Chapter 2 it will be recalled that finding a position line from a sight is achieved by making a simple comparison between two angles. The altitude of the sun at the true position which is measured by using the sextant, and the altitude of the sun at a position close to the true position which is found from tables. In Chapter 2, a DR position was used, but, as will be explained later, it is more convenient to use an alternative position near the DR position called a chosen position (CP).

The first step is to find the sun's geographical position at the moment the sextant sight was taken. This data is obtained from the *Nautical Almanac*. Refer to the extracts for May. Pages are in pairs, comprising a left-hand and a right-hand page. They are divided horizontally into three, covering three consecutive days. The left-hand page tabulates information for Aries, the four navigational planets (Venus, Mars, Jupiter and Saturn), and 57 stars. The right-hand page covers the sun, the moon and the times of twilight.

The daily panel shows the date and is divided into 24 hours. The layout of every page throughout the year is identical.

## The sun's position

Position on the earth or on the chart is expressed in terms of latitude and longitude (Fig 5.1). The terms used to define the sun's position in the heavens, and hence its geographical position on earth, are Declination (Dec) and Greenwich Hour Angle (GHA).

To explain, imagine that the earth is surrounded by a celestial sphere of infinite size with its centre at the centre of the earth. This sphere has a celestial equator directly above the terrestrial equator and celestial north and south poles directly above the terrestrial poles. It has celestial meridians but, because of the earth's rotation, these are continuously changing relative to the terrestrial meridians.

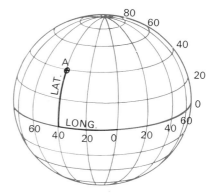

**Fig. 5.1** Position A is latitude 40°N longitude 40°W.

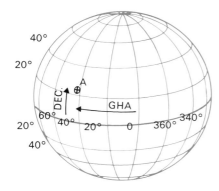

**Fig. 5.2** At A, GHA is 40° declination N20°.

| G.M.T. | SUN | | | G |
|---|---|---|---|---|
| | G.H.A. | | Dec. | |
| **19** 00 | 180 54.3 | N19 | 35.1 | 81 |
| 01 | 195 54.2 | | 35.6 | 95 |
| 02 | 210 54.2 | | 36.2 | 110 |
| 03 | 225 54.2 | ·· | 36.7 | 124 |
| 04 | 240 54.2 | | 37.3 | 139 |
| 05 | 255 54.1 | | 37.8 | 153 |
| 06 | 270 54.1 | N19 | 38.4 | 168 |
| 07 | 285 54.1 | | 38.9 | 182 |
| 08 | 300 54.1 | | 39.4 | 197 |
| M 09 | 315 54.0 | ·· | 40.0 | 211 |
| O 10 | 330 54.0 | | 40.5 | 226 |
| N 11 | 345 54.0 | | 41.1 | 240 |
| D 12 | 0 53.9 | N19 | 41.6 | 255 |
| A 13 | 15 53.9 | | 42.1 | 269 |
| Y 14 | 30 53.9 | | 42.7 | 284 |
| 15 | 45 53.9 | ·· | 43.2 | 298 |
| 16 | 60 53.8 | | 43.8 | 313 |
| 17 | 75 53.8 | | 44.3 | 327 |
| 18 | 90 53.8 | N19 | 44.8 | 342 |
| 19 | 105 53.8 | | 45.4 | 356 |
| 20 | 120 53.7 | | 45.9 | 1( |
| 21 | 135 53.7 | ·· | 46.4 | 25 |
| 22 | 150 53.7 | | 47.0 | 39 |
| 23 | 165 53.6 | | 47.5 | 54 |

**Fig. 5.3** *Nautical Almanac* extract: GHA and declination.

Declination is measured north or south from the celestial equator. It is the angle subtended at the centre of the celestial sphere between the equator and the sun's position in the celestial sphere (Fig 5.2).

The Greenwich Hour Angle is measured from the Greenwich meridian projected on to the celestial sphere. Unlike longitude, it is measured only in a westerly direction, starting at 0° on the meridian and increasing through 360° during 24 hours (Fig 5.2).

The Greenwich Hour Angle of the sun at any instant of time is the angular distance at either celestial pole between the Greenwich meridian and the meridian passing through the sun.

The geographical position of the sun (on the earth) will be directly beneath the point of intersection on the celestial sphere between declination and Greenwich Hour Angle.

The *Nautical Almanac* gives the sun's position in terms of its GHA and declination at any required time.

*Example 5a*
Use Fig 5.3.
Find the sun's GHA and Dec on 19 May at 07h 52m 15s GMT.

GHA and Dec for 07h for 19 May will be found on the daily panel for 19 May under the column headed 'Sun'.

| | | GHA | Dec |
|---|---|---|---|
| 19 May | 07h | 285° 54'1 | N19° 38'.9 |

The tabulations are for hourly intervals and a separate table, called an increments table, is used for intervals between each hour.

At the bottom of the declination column there is a small 'd' with a figure alongside it: in this case 0.5 (Fig 5.4). This figure is the amount the declination is changing each hour and it will be needed later to find the correction to apply to declination for 52m (seconds are ignored).

The GHA increases throughout the day, but declination can either increase or decrease dependent upon the time of year. The extract Fig 5.3 shows that declination at 07h on 19 May is N19° 38′.9, whereas at 08h it is N19° 39′.4. In this case declination is increasing. Now look at Fig 5.5 which shows declination for 15 February. At 11h

declination is S12° 48′.4 but at 12h it is S12° 47′.5, so declination is decreasing. The table also shows whether declination is north or south.

So five things have been extracted from the daily page: GHA, Dec, whether declination is N or S, whether it is increasing or decreasing, and the hourly rate of change (d) .

The GHA and Dec above are for 07h. The 52m 15s still has to be allowed for. This is done by referring to an increments and corrections table which follows the daily page tabulations in the almanac. Fig 5.6 shows a small portion of the table for 52m.

| | | |
|---|---|---|
| 19 | 105 52.1 | 10.4 |
| 20 | 120 52.1 | 10.9 |
| 21 | 135 52.0 ·· | 11.5 |
| 22 | 150 52.0 | 12.0 |
| 23 | 165 52.0 | 12.5 |
| | S.D. 15.8 | *d* 0.5 |

**Fig. 5.4** *Nautical Almanac* extract: 'd'.

## SUN

| G.M.T. | G.H.A. | Dec. | G. |
|---|---|---|---|
| d h | ° ′ | ° ′ | |
| 15 00 | 176 26.7 | S12 57.8 | 139 |
| 01 | 191 26.7 | 56.9 | 154 |
| 02 | 206 26.8 | 56.1 | 169 |
| 03 | 221 26.8 ·· | 55.2 | 183 |
| 04 | 236 26.8 | 54.4 | 198 |
| 05 | 251 26.8 | 53.5 | 212 |
| 06 | 266 26.9 | S12 52.7 | 227 |
| 07 | 281 26.9 | 51.8 | 241 |
| S 08 | 296 26.9 | 51.0 | 256 |
| A 09 | 311 27.0 ·· | 50.1 | 271 |
| T 10 | 326 27.0 | 49.3 | 285 |
| U 11 | 341 27.0 | 48.4 | 300 |
| R 12 | 356 27.0 | S12 47.5 | 314 |
| D 13 | 11 27.1 | 46.7 | 329 |
| A 14 | 26 27.1 | 45.8 | 343 |
| Y 15 | 41 27.1 ·· | 45.0 | 358 |
| 16 | 56 27.1 | 44.1 | 12 |
| 17 | 71 27.2 | 43.3 | 27 |
| 18 | 86 27.2 | S12 42.4 | 42 |
| 19 | 101 27.2 | 41.5 | 56 |
| 20 | 116 27.3 | 40.7 | 71 |
| 21 | 131 27.3 ·· | 39.8 | 85 |
| 22 | 146 27.3 | 39.0 | 100 |
| 23 | 161 27.4 | 38.1 | 114 |

**Fig. 5.5** *Nautical Almanac* extract: sun's GHA and Dec.

## 52ᵐ

| 52 | SUN PLANETS | ARIES | MOON | v or Corrⁿ d | | v or Corrⁿ d | | v or Corrⁿ d | |
|---|---|---|---|---|---|---|---|---|---|
| s | ° ′ | ° ′ | ° ′ | ′ | ′ | ′ | ′ | ′ | ′ |
| 00 | 13 00·0 | 13 02·1 | 12 24·5 | 0·0 | 0·0 | 6·0 | 5·3 | 12·0 | 10·5 |
| 01 | 13 00·3 | 13 02·4 | 12 24·7 | 0·1 | 0·1 | 6·1 | 5·3 | 12·1 | 10·6 |
| 02 | 13 00·5 | 13 02·6 | 12 24·9 | 0·2 | 0·2 | 6·2 | 5·4 | 12·2 | 10·7 |
| 03 | 13 00·8 | 13 02·9 | 12 25·2 | 0·3 | 0·3 | 6·3 | 5·5 | 12·3 | 10·8 |
| 04 | 13 01·0 | 13 03·1 | 12 25·4 | 0·4 | 0·4 | 6·4 | 5·6 | 12·4 | 10·9 |
| 05 | 13 01·3 | 13 03·4 | 12 25·7 | 0·5 | 0·4 | 6·5 | 5·7 | 12·5 | 10·9 |
| 06 | 13 01·5 | 13 03·6 | 12 25·9 | 0·6 | 0·5 | 6·6 | 5·8 | 12·6 | 11·0 |
| 07 | 13 01·8 | 13 03·9 | 12 26·1 | 0·7 | 0·6 | 6·7 | 5·9 | 12·7 | 11·1 |
| 08 | 13 02·0 | 13 04·1 | 12 26·4 | 0·8 | 0·7 | 6·8 | 6·0 | 12·8 | 11·2 |
| 09 | 13 02·3 | 13 04·4 | 12 26·6 | 0·9 | 0·8 | 6·9 | 6·0 | 12·9 | 11·3 |
| 10 | 13 02·5 | 13 04·6 | 12 26·9 | 1·0 | 0·9 | 7·0 | 6·1 | 13·0 | 11·4 |
| 11 | 13 02·8 | 13 04·9 | 12 27·1 | 1·1 | 1·0 | 7·1 | 6·2 | 13·1 | 11·5 |
| 12 | 13 03·0 | 13 05·1 | 12 27·3 | 1·2 | 1·1 | 7·2 | 6·3 | 13·2 | 11·6 |
| 13 | 13 03·3 | 13 05·4 | 12 27·6 | 1·3 | 1·1 | 7·3 | 6·4 | 13·3 | 11·6 |
| 14 | 13 03·5 | 13 05·6 | 12 27·8 | 1·4 | 1·2 | 7·4 | 6·5 | 13·4 | 11·7 |
| 15 | 13 03·8 | 13 05·9 | 12 28·0 | 1·5 | 1·3 | 7·5 | 6·6 | 13·5 | 11·8 |
| 16 | 13 04·0 | 13 06·1 | 12 28·3 | 1·6 | 1·4 | 7·6 | 6·7 | 13·6 | 11·9 |
| 17 | 13 04·3 | 13 06·4 | 12 28·5 | 1·7 | 1·5 | 7·7 | 6·7 | 13·7 | 12·0 |
| 18 | 13 04·5 | 13 06·6 | 12 28·8 | 1·8 | 1·6 | 7·8 | 6·8 | 13·8 | 12·1 |
| 19 | 13 04·8 | 13 06·9 | 12 29·0 | 1·9 | 1·7 | 7·9 | 6·9 | 13·9 | 12·2 |

**Fig. 5.6** *Nautical Almanac* extract: increments table for 52m.

First, GHA for 52m 15s is found under 'Sun – Planets'. The 52m is at the top of the panel and the 15s down the side. The additional amount of GHA is 13° 03'.8. This is applied to the GHA already found for 07h. The increment is always added, because GHA is constantly increasing throughout the day.

The correction to declination is also found in the block headed 52m under the heading 'v or d Corr$^n$' The correction to apply to declination is alongside the d factor (0.5) in the table: it is 0.4, which is added to declination because declination is increasing. It can also be calculated without reference to the table:

$$\text{Corrn} = \frac{\text{minutes of GMT}}{1 \text{ hour}} \times \text{d factor}$$

$$= \frac{52'.25}{60'} \times 0.5 = 0.4$$

|        | GHA          |       | Dec        |
|--------|--------------|-------|------------|
| 07h    | 285° 54'.1   |       | N19° 38'.9 |
| 52m 15s| + 13° 03'.8  | d 0.5 | + 0'.4     |
| 07h 52m 15s | 298° 57'.9 |    | N19° 39'.3 |

Here are two further examples, using the extracts at the back of the book:

*Example 5b*
What are the GHA and Dec of the Sun on 17 February at 18h 55m 50s GMT?

|          | GHA         |       | Dec        |
|----------|-------------|-------|------------|
| 18h      | 86° 29'.0   |       | S12° 00'.8 |
| 55m 50s  | 13° 57'.5   | d 0.9 | − 0'.8     |
| 18h 55m 50s | 100° 26'.5 |    | S12° 00'.0 |

*Example 5c*
What are the GHA and Dec of the Sun on 30 August at 10h 53m 38s GMT?

|          | GHA         |       | Dec        |
|----------|-------------|-------|------------|
| 10h      | 329° 48'.3  |       | N9° 09'.5  |
| 53m 38s  | 13° 24'.5   | d 0.9 | − 0'.8     |
| 10h 53m 38s | 343° 12'.8 |    | N9° 08'.7  |

## Local Hour Angle

Local Hour Angle (LHA) is the angle at either pole between the meridian passing through the chosen position and the meridian passing through the sun's geographical position (Fig 5.7). It is always measured westwards. From the sun's GHA and the longitude of the chosen position, LHA can be deduced.

Suppose the Sun's GHA was 60° and the chosen position longitude 40° W. The LHA would be 20° (Fig 5.8). If the GHA was 60° and the chosen position longitude 20° E, then the LHA would be 80° (Fig 5.9).

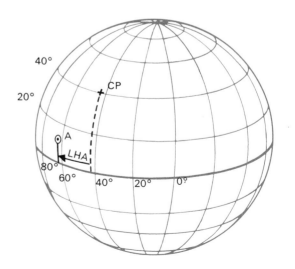

**Fig. 5.7** Local Hour Angle (LHA).

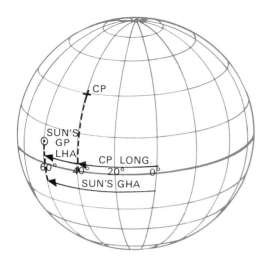

**Fig. 5.8** GHA − long W = LHA.

So the formula is:

GHA + E long or
 − W long = LHA

Sometimes it is necessary to either add or subtract 360° to carry out the calculation. Fig 5.10, which represents a satellite view of the earth from over the north pole, will clarify this.

The following rhyme is helpful when deciding how to apply longitude to GHA:

Longitude *east*, Greenwich *least*; Longitude *west*, Greenwich *best*.

This means that in longitude east GHA is less than LHA and in longitude west GHA is greater than LHA.

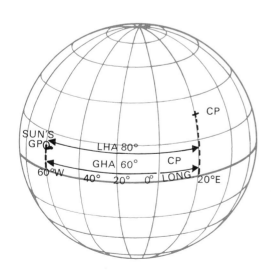

**Fig. 5.9** GHA + long E = LHA.

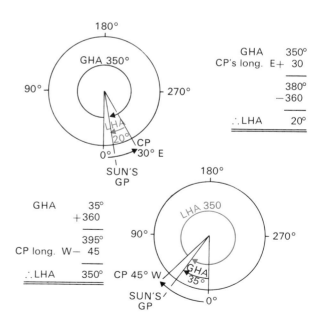

**Fig. 5.10** Applying 360° to find LHA.

## Chosen position

The tables used to find tabulated altitude use whole degrees of latitude and LHA. A DR position would normally be shown in degrees and minutes, such as 48° 10'N 5° 35'W. To be compatible with the tables an alternative position is chosen (CP) so that a whole degree of latitude and a whole degree of LHA can be used.

Latitude presents no problem. A round degree of latitude nearest to the DR latitude is chosen:

DR latitude 50° 10'.4 = CP latitude 50°

The CP longitude is chosen such that, when it is added to or subtracted from the GHA, a whole degree of LHA is the result. The chosen longitude should be within 30' of the DR longitude.

For westerly longitude, minutes of longitude are made the same as the minutes of GHA:

DR long 21° 34'.0W

| | |
|---|---|
| GHA | 93° 45'.0 |
| CP long W | − 21° 45'.0 |
| LHA | 72° |

For easterly longitude the minutes of longitude are made the complement of the minutes of GHA:

DR long 33° 18'.0E

| | |
|---|---|
| GHA | 284° 45'.0 |
| CP long E | + 33° 15'.0 |
| LHA | 318° |

Sometimes it may be necessary to change the degrees as well as the minutes to keep the CP longitude within 30' of the DR longitude:

DR long 22° 50'.0W

| | |
|---|---|
| GHA | 86° 15'.0 |
| CP long W | − 23° 15'.0 |
| LHA | 63° |

DR long 43° 10'.0E

| | |
|---|---|
| GHA | 286° 11'.0 |
| CP long E | + 42° 49'.0 |
| LHA | 329° |

## Using the sight reduction tables

The tables used to find the sun's tabulated altitude are *Sight Reduction Tables for Air Navigation*, AP3270, Volumes 2 and 3. The co-ordinates required for their use are:

1 A whole degree of latitude.
2 A whole degree of LHA.
3 Declination.

*Example 5d*
Use Fig 5.11.
Chosen latitude 50° N, LHA 60°, Declination N3° 07'.3. (Use the nearest minute of declination, N3° 07'.)

First the tables for latitude 50° are found. These are arranged in blocks as follows:

| | |
|---|---|
| Declination 0°–14° | *Same* name as latitude. |
| Declination 0°–14° | *Contrary* name to latitude |
| Declination 15°–29° | *Same* name as latitude |
| Declination 15°–29° | *Contrary* name to latitude |

In the example latitude and declination are both north and the value of the declination is 3° 07', so the 0°–14° **same** table is required. LHA is tabulated down both sides of the table.

The headings at the top of each column are:
**Hc = altitude, d = factor, Z = azimuth angle.**

In the column for 3° declination, opposite 60° LHA, the following information will be found:

| Hc | d | Z |
|---|---|---|
| 21° 10' | + 48 | 112 |

| LHA | Hc | d | Z | Hc | d | Z | Hc | d | Z | Hc | d | Z | Hc | d | Z | Hc | d | Z | Hc | d | Z |
|---|---|---|---|---|---|---|---|---|---|---|---|---|---|---|---|---|---|---|---|---|---|
| 0 | 40 00 | +60 | 180 | 41 00 | +60 | 180 | 42 00 | +60 | 180 | 43 00 | +60 | 180 | 44 00 | +60 | 180 | 45 00 | +60 | 180 | 46 00 | +60 | 180 |
| 55 | 21 38 | +50 | 118 | 22 28 | +49 | 118 | 23 17 | +49 | 117 | 24 06 | +49 | 116 | 24 55 | +49 | 116 | 25 44 | +48 | 115 | 26 32 | +49 | 114 |
| 56 | 21 04 | 49 | 117 | 21 53 | 49 | 117 | 22 42 | 49 | 116 | 23 31 | 49 | 116 | 24 20 | 48 | 115 | 25 08 | 49 | 114 | 25 57 | 48 | 114 |
| 57 | 20 30 | 49 | 116 | 21 19 | 48 | 116 | 22 07 | 49 | 115 | 22 56 | 49 | 115 | 23 45 | 48 | 114 | 24 33 | 48 | 113 | 25 21 | 48 | 113 |
| 58 | 19 55 | 49 | 116 | 20 44 | 48 | 115 | 21 32 | 49 | 114 | 22 21 | 48 | 114 | 23 09 | 49 | 113 | 23 58 | 48 | 112 | 24 46 | 48 | 112 |
| 59 | 19 20 | 49 | 115 | 20 09 | 48 | 114 | 20 57 | 49 | 114 | 21 46 | 48 | 113 | 22 34 | 48 | 112 | 23 22 | 48 | 112 | 24 10 | 48 | 111 |
| 60 | 18 45 | +48 | 114 | 19 33 | +49 | 113 | 20 22 | +48 | 113 | 21 10 | +48 | 112 | 21 58 | +48 | 111 | 22 46 | +48 | 111 | 23 34 | +47 | 110 |
| 61 | 18 09 | 49 | 113 | 18 58 | 48 | 112 | 19 46 | 48 | 112 | 20 34 | 48 | 111 | 21 22 | 48 | 111 | 22 10 | 47 | 110 | 22 57 | 48 | 109 |
| 62 | 17 34 | 48 | 112 | 18 22 | 48 | 112 | 19 10 | 48 | 111 | 19 58 | 48 | 110 | 20 46 | 47 | 110 | 21 33 | 48 | 109 | 22 21 | 47 | 108 |
| 63 | 16 58 | 48 | 111 | 17 46 | 48 | 111 | 18 34 | 48 | 110 | 19 22 | 47 | 109 | 20 09 | 48 | 109 | 20 57 | 47 | 108 | 21 44 | 47 | 108 |
| 64 | 16 22 | 48 | 111 | 17 10 | 48 | 110 | 17 58 | 47 | 109 | 18 45 | 48 | 109 | 19 33 | 47 | 108 | 20 20 | 47 | 107 | 21 07 | 47 | 107 |
| 65 | 15 46 | +48 | 110 | 16 34 | +47 | 109 | 17 21 | +48 | 108 | 18 09 | +47 | 108 | 18 56 | +47 | 107 | 19 43 | +47 | 106 | 20 30 | +47 | 106 |
| 66 | 15 09 | 48 | 109 | 15 57 | 47 | 108 | 16 44 | 48 | 108 | 17 32 | 47 | 107 | 18 19 | 47 | 106 | 19 06 | 47 | 106 | 19 53 | 47 | 105 |
| 67 | 14 33 | 47 | 108 | 15 20 | 48 | 107 | 16 08 | 47 | 107 | 16 55 | 47 | 106 | 17 42 | 47 | 105 | 18 29 | 47 | 105 | 19 16 | 46 | 104 |
| 68 | 13 56 | 47 | 107 | 14 43 | 48 | 107 | 15 31 | 47 | 106 | 16 18 | 47 | 105 | 17 05 | 46 | 105 | 17 51 | 47 | 104 | 18 38 | 47 | 103 |
| 69 | 13 19 | 47 | 106 | 14 06 | 47 | 106 | 14 53 | 47 | 105 | 15 40 | 47 | 105 | 16 27 | 47 | 104 | 17 14 | 47 | 103 | 18 01 | 46 | 103 |
| | **0°** | | | **1°** | | | **2°** | | | **3°** | | | **4°** | | | **5°** | | | **6°** | | |

## DECLINATION (0°-14°) SAME NAME AS LATITUDE

**Fig. 5.11** *AP3270 Volume 3* extract: Hc, d and Z.

The azimuth angle (Z) is measured from the north or south pole from 0° to 180°. As an azimuth (Zn), which is a bearing in 360° notation, is required an adjustment has to be made. The simple calculation used is tabulated in the top left-hand corner of the table for north latitudes and in the bottom left-hand corner for south latitudes (Fig 5.12).

As the LHA in the example is less than 180°, azimuth (Zn) will be 360°−Z which is 360°−112° = 248°.

So far the tabulated altitude for 3° of declination only has been found. To find the additional correction for 07' a supplementary table, *Table 5: Correction to Tabulated Altitude for Minutes of Declination*, is used. Table 5 is entered along the top with factor d +48 and down the side with extra minutes of declination 07'. It can be seen from the table that the altitude has changed by 06' for 07' of declination (Fig 5.13). This 06' is now applied to Hc. It is added because there was a + sign by the d factor (+48).

| N. Lat | | | | | | |
|---|---|---|---|---|---|---|

LHA greater than 180° ...... Zn=Z
LHA less than 180° ........ Zn=360−Z

| LHA | Hc | d | Z | Hc | d | Z | Hc | d | Z |
|---|---|---|---|---|---|---|---|---|---|
| | **0°** | | | **1°** | | | **2°** | | |
| 0 | 40 00 | +60 | 180 | 41 00 | +60 | 180 | 42 00 | +60 | 180 |
| 1 | 40 00 | 60 | 179 | 41 00 | 60 | 179 | 42 00 | 60 | 179 |

**Fig. 5.12** *AP3270 Volume 3* extract: converting Z to Zn.

| | Hc | d | Z | Zn |
|---|---|---|---|---|
| | 21° 10' | +48 | 112° | 360°−112° |
| | + 06' | | | |
| Tab Alt | 21° 16' | | | Azimuth 248° |

## Exercise

*Answers and extracts are at the back of the book.*

**5.1** Find the Sun's GHA and Dec

|   | Date | Time GMT |
|---|------|----------|
| **a** | 20 May | 08h 53m 15s |
| **b** | 31 August | 20h 55m 40s |
| **c** | 17 February | 19h 52m 32s |
| **d** | 16 February | 05h 55m 25s |
| **e** | 20 May | 15h 54m 40s |

**5.2** Find chosen position latitude, longitude and LHA. Use the answers from question 5.1.

|   | DR position | |
|---|------|------|
| **a** | 50° 15'.1 N | 18° 25'.0 W |
| **b** | 49° 45'.7 S | 165° 05'.2 E |
| **c** | 50° 25'.3 S | 41° 50'.9 W |
| **d** | 49° 36'.0 S | 165° 30'.9 E |
| **e** | 49° 50'.8 N | 127° 40'.0 W |

**5.3** Find the tabulated altitude and azimuth for answers **a** to **e** in the previous questions. Use the answers from questions 5.1 and 5.2.

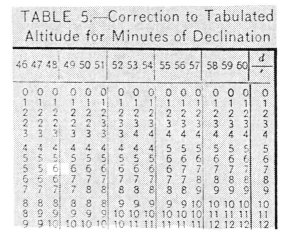

Fig. **5.13** *AP3270 Volume 3* extract: Table 5.

# 6 Plotting a Sight

Both true and tabulated altitude have now been determined. By comparing them, the intercept, which is the distance of the true position line from the chosen position, can also be determined:

True altitude        34° 45′
Tabulated altitude  34° 30′
Intercept                15′ Towards

The azimuth will also have been found. In the example this is 095° T. The sight is now ready to be plotted. This is done as follows:

*Example 6a*
Chosen position 50°N 2° 15′W.
Intercept 15M Towards; azimuth 095°T.

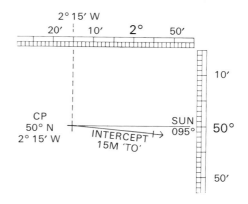

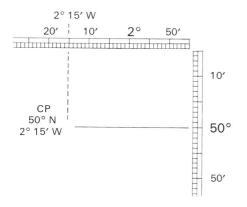

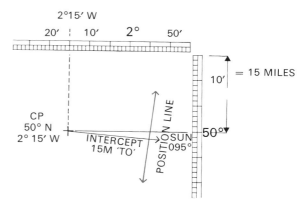

**Figs 6.1a, 6.1b, 6.1c** Plotting a position line – intercept *towards*.

1  Mark the chosen position on the chart (Fig 6.1a).
2  From this position draw a line in the direction of 095°T, which is *towards* the sun's geographical position, and mark 15 miles (intercept 15′ = 15M) along that line (Fig 6.1b).
3  At this point, draw a straight position line at right angles to the intercept (Fig 6.1c).
4  This position line is part of the true position circle on which the boat lies.

In Example 6a the intercept was *towards* the sun's GP so it was plotted in the direction of 095°T. In the following example, the intercept is *away*.

*Example 6b*
Chosen position 50°N 3° 53′ E. Intercept 8M Away; azimuth 175°T.

The bearing of the sun's geographical position is 175°T. The intercept is still plotted from the chosen position along the line of azimuth but *away* from the geographical position in the direction of 355°T (Fig 6.2).

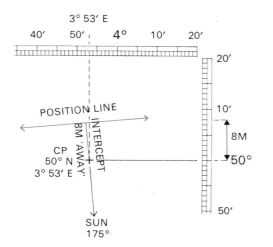

**Fig. 6.2** Plotting a position line – intercept *away*.

**A complete sight**
The next example shows how to work out a complete sight. To ensure accuracy the figures should be written down in a consistent order and for this purpose it pays to use a prepared form, called a sight reduction form, which lists the necessary entries. Examples are shown in Appendix 4.

*Example 6c*
*Use the extracts at the back of the book.*
On the morning of 19 May at 07h 52m 05s DWT (Deck Watch Time) in DR position 50° 15′N 9° 40′W, a sight was taken of the sun's lower limb giving a sextant altitude of 27° 01′.4. Index error 2′.0 on the arc, height of eye 2.0 metres. The DWE (Deck Watch Error) was 10s slow.

1  Enter all known data on the form.
2  Correct the DWT.
3  From the *Nautical Almanac* daily page, find the GHA and Dec and d factor for 07h. Write a + or − sign by declination to show whether it is increasing or decreasing.
4  From the increments table for 52m find the increment to add to GHA for 07h.
5  From the 'v or d Corrⁿ' table for 52m find the correction to apply to declination.
6  Select a chosen longitude to apply to the GHA which will give a whole degree of LHA.
7  Using the LHA and Dec with the chosen latitude, 50°N, find a **same** table which has a LHA of 289° and a Dec of 19°. Extract Hc, d, and Z. Refer to the rule for north latitude for converting Z to Zn.
8  Using Table 5, find the correction to apply to Hc for 39′ of declination.
9  Write the tabulated altitude and azimuth on the form.
10  Correct sextant altitude: apply index error, dip, and altitude correction for May for the lower limb.

11 Compare the true and tabulated altitude to find the intercept and label away or towards.
12 Plot the chosen position on the chart.
13 Plot the intercept from the chosen position and draw the position line (Fig 6.3).

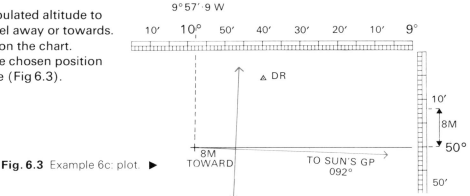

Fig. 6.3 Example 6c: plot. ▶

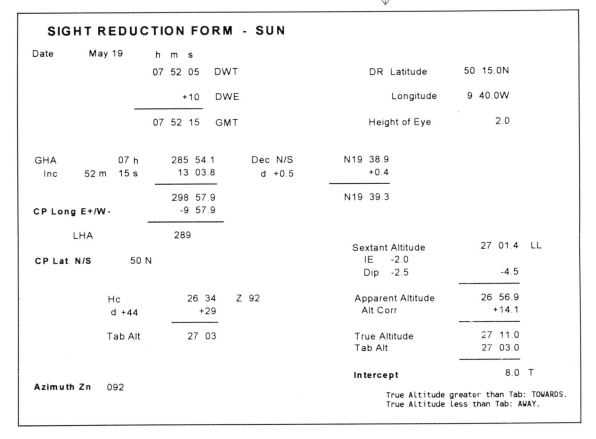

**SIGHT REDUCTION FORM  -  SUN**

| Date | May 19 | h m s | | | | | |
|---|---|---|---|---|---|---|---|
| | | 07 52 05 | DWT | | DR Latitude | 50 15.0N | |
| | | +10 | DWE | | Longitude | 9 40.0W | |
| | | 07 52 15 | GMT | | Height of Eye | 2.0 | |

| GHA | 07 h | 285 54.1 | Dec N/S | N19 38.9 |
|---|---|---|---|---|
| Inc | 52 m  15 s | 13 03.8 | d +0.5 | +0.4 |
| | | 298 57.9 | | N19 39.3 |
| **CP Long E+/W-** | | -9 57.9 | | |
| LHA | | 289 | | |

| | | | Sextant Altitude | 27 01.4  LL |
|---|---|---|---|---|
| **CP Lat N/S** | 50 N | | IE    -2.0 | |
| | | | Dip  -2.5 | -4.5 |
| Hc | 26 34 | Z 92 | Apparent Altitude | 26 56.9 |
| d +44 | +29 | | Alt Corr | +14.1 |
| Tab Alt | 27 03 | | True Altitude | 27 11.0 |
| | | | Tab Alt | 27 03.0 |
| | | | **Intercept** | 8.0  T |

Azimuth Zn    092

True Altitude greater than Tab: TOWARDS.
True Altitude less than Tab: AWAY.

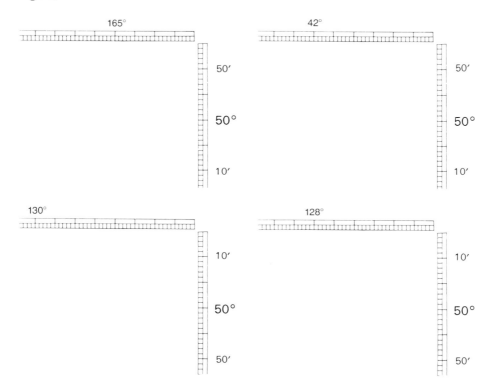

**Fig. 6.4** Portions of chart for questions 6.1 to 6.4.

## Exercise

Plot the intercept, azimuth and position line from the following information. Use the small portions of the chart provided (Fig 6.4).

**6.1** CP 50°S   165° 10'.0E,   intercept 12.0A, azimuth 060°T

**6.2** CP 50°S   41° 37'.0W,   intercept 21.0T, azimuth 280°T

**6.3** CP 50°N   129° 50'.0W,   intercept 11.5T, azimuth 134°T

**6.4** CP 50°N   127° 33'.0W,   intercept 18.0A, azimuth 100°T

# 7  Latitude by the Sun and Pole Star

**Latitude by the sun's meridian altitude**
A sextant sight of the sun taken at local noon
provides latitude with very little calculation.

*Meridian passage*  By definition when the sun is
on the observer's meridian (either due north or due
south) it is noon or midday local mean time (LMT).
As the bearing of the sun is due north or due south,
the position line obtained from a sight is east-west,
ie latitude, and, as the sun's meridian and the
observer's meridian are coincident, the local hour
angle (LHA) is 0°. The moment that the sun transits
(crosses) the observer's meridian is called *meridian
passage*. At this time the sun will be at its highest
altitude.

The approximate time of meridian passage can be
deduced from data in the *Nautical Almanac*:

*Example 7a*
Refer to Fig 7.1

**Fig. 7.1**  *Nautical Almanac* extract: sun meridian passage.

Find the time of meridian passage of the sun on
17 February in DR position 37° 15'.0N 27° 30'.0E.

1  The time of meridian passage of the sun is at the
   bottom right-hand corner of the right-hand daily
   page in the almanac. It is tabulated for three
   consecutive dates, in this case 15, 16 and 17
   February. Meridian passage for 17 February is
   shown as 12h 14m, which is local mean time on
   the Greenwich meridian. It can also be regarded
   as local mean time on all other meridians.
   Greenwich Mean Time of meridian passage at the
   DR position is required and this is found by
   correcting for the DR longitude.
2  Convert the DR longitude to time by using the
   conversion of arc to time table, Fig 7.2.

   27° 30' = 1h 50m.

3  Apply the converted longitude to the time of
   meridian passage:

   |  | h  m |  |
   |---|---|---|
   | LMT MP | 12 14 | |
   | DR long E | −1 50 | (subtract for E long) |
   | GMT MP | 10 24 | |

This is the approximate Greenwich Mean Time of
meridian passage. It is only as accurate as the
estimate of the DR longitude. In practice, this would
be used only as a guide when estimating the time to
take the sight.

## CONVERSION OF ARC TO TIME

| | 0°–59° | | 60°–119° | |
|---|---|---|---|---|
| ° | h m | ° | h m | |
| 0 | 0 00 | 60 | 4 00 | |
| 1 | 0 04 | 61 | 4 04 | |
| 2 | 0 08 | 62 | 4 08 | |
| 3 | 0 12 | 63 | 4 12 | |
| 4 | 0 16 | 64 | 4 16 | |
| 5 | 0 20 | 65 | 4 20 | |
| 6 | 0 24 | 66 | 4 24 | |
| 7 | 0 28 | 67 | 4 28 | |
| 8 | 0 32 | 68 | 4 32 | |
| 9 | 0 36 | 69 | 4 36 | |
| 10 | 0 40 | 70 | 4 40 | |
| 11 | 0 44 | 71 | 4 44 | |
| 12 | 0 48 | 72 | 4 48 | |
| 13 | 0 52 | 73 | 4 52 | |
| 14 | 0 56 | 74 | 4 56 | |
| 15 | 1 00 | 75 | 5 00 | |
| 16 | 1 04 | 76 | 5 04 | |
| 17 | 1 08 | 77 | 5 08 | |
| 18 | 1 12 | 78 | 5 12 | |
| 19 | 1 16 | 79 | 5 16 | |
| 20 | 1 20 | 80 | 5 20 | |
| 21 | 1 24 | 81 | 5 24 | |
| 22 | 1 28 | 82 | 5 28 | |
| 23 | 1 32 | 83 | 5 32 | |
| 24 | 1 36 | 84 | 5 36 | |
| 25 | 1 40 | 85 | 5 40 | |
| 26 | 1 44 | 86 | 5 44 | |
| 27 | 1 48 | 87 | 5 48 | |
| 28 | 1 52 | 88 | 5 52 | |
| 29 | 1 56 | 89 | 5 56 | |

| ′ | 0′·00 | 0′·25 | 0′·50 |
|---|---|---|---|
| | m s | m s | m s |
| 24 | 1 36 | 1 37 | 1 38 |
| 25 | 1 40 | 1 41 | 1 42 |
| 26 | 1 44 | 1 45 | 1 46 |
| 27 | 1 48 | 1 49 | 1 50 |
| 28 | 1 52 | 1 53 | 1 54 |
| 29 | 1 56 | 1 57 | 1 58 |
| 30 | 2 00 | 2 01 | 2 02 |
| 31 | 2 04 | 2 05 | 2 06 |
| 32 | 2 08 | 2 09 | 2 10 |
| 33 | 2 12 | 2 13 | 2 14 |
| 34 | 2 16 | 2 17 | 2 18 |
| 35 | 2 20 | 2 21 | 2 22 |

**Fig. 7.2** *Nautical Almanac* extract: arc to time.

The next step is to take the sight and record the time. This is then used to find latitude:

1 Observe the sun's altitude at meridian passage. This is done by taking a series of sights before the expected time of meridian passage until the altitude stops increasing. The sun may appear to be stationary at this time and there will be two identical readings or two readings which are very similar. Altitude will decrease after meridian passage.
2 Correct the sextant altitude to true altitude.
3 Subtract the true altitude from 90° to obtain true zenith distance (TZD).
4 Reverse the name of the sun's bearing (S to N or N to S)
5 Extract the sun's declination from the almanac.
6 Combine TZD with declination: same names add, contrary names subtract the smaller from the greater.
7 The result is the latitude at the time of the sight.

Refer to the following examples and use the extracts from the *Nautical Almanac*.

*Example 7b*
On 20 May in DR position 51° 30'.0N, 9° 10'.0W, the sextant altitude of the sun's lower limb taken at 12h 33m GMT (meridian passage) was 57° 50'.6 bearing south, index error − 2'.0. Height of eye 2.0 metres. Find the latitude.

| | | | | |
|---|---|---|---|---|
| SA LL | 57° 50'.6 bearing S | Dec 12h | N 19° 54'.4 | |
| IE − 2'.0) | | d + 0.5 | + 0'.3 | |
| Dip − 2'.5) | − 4'.5 | | N 19° 54'.7 | |
| AA | 57° 46'.1 | | | |
| corrn | + 15'.4 | | | |
| TA | 58° 01'.5 | | | |
| from | 90° | | | |
| TZD | 31° 58'.5 N (bearing reversed) | | | |
| Dec | 19° 54'.7 N | | | |
| Latitude | 51° 53'.2 N | | | |

*Example 7c*
On 17 February in DR position 32° 55'.1 N, 27° 30'0E, the sextant altitude of the sun's lower limb taken at 10h 24m 30s was 44° 57'.5, bearing south. Index error − 2'.4, height of eye 2.5 metres. What was the latitude?

| SA LL | 44° 57'.5 bearing S | Dec 10h | S12° 07'.8 |
|---|---|---|---|
| IE − 2'.4) | | d − 0'.9 | − 0'.4 |
| Dip − 2'.8) | − 5'.2 | | S12° 07'.4 |
| AA | 44° 52'.3 | | |
| corrn | + 15'.3 | | |
| TA | 45° 07'.6 | | |
| from | 90° | | |
| TZD | 44° 52'.4 N (bearing reversed) | | |
| Dec | − 12° 07'.4 S | | |
| Latitude | 32° 45'.0 N | | |

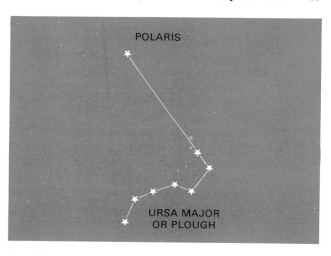

**Fig. 7.3** Ursa Major and Polaris.

## Latitude by the pole star (Polaris or the North Star)

The earth, spinning on its axis, behaves as a gyroscope. The axis of the earth points in a constant direction in space. Hence the north pole of the celestial sphere remains exactly above the north pole on earth. If we could identify the exact position of the celestial north pole, then its altitude would be equivalent to the observer's latitude.

Polaris is nearly but not exactly above the north pole. To an observer on earth it is almost due north and its altitude is approximately equivalent to the observer's latitude. It is important to the navigator because, like the sun, it can be used to find latitude. It is, however, only visible from the northern hemisphere. It is observed at dawn or dusk twilight and can be used together with other star sights to provide the observed position.

As Polaris is not a very bright star it is necessary to identify it with reference to the constellation Ursa Major, also called the Plough or Big Dipper (Fig 7.3). The two stars in line at the end of Ursa Major,

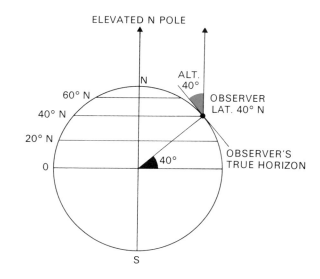

**Fig. 7.4** If Polaris bore exactly north, altitude would equal latitude.

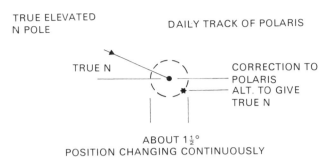

TRUE ELEVATED
N POLE

DAILY TRACK OF POLARIS

TRUE N

CORRECTION TO
POLARIS
ALT. TO GIVE
TRUE N

ABOUT 1½°
POSITION CHANGING CONTINUOUSLY

**Fig. 7.5** Polaris describes a small circle around the celestial north pole.

called the pointers, indicate the direction of Polaris. It is most easily seen just before dawn because, at that time, the sky is still dark and, by looking towards the north, it can be identified. The sight is taken immediately the horizon is visible, before the star becomes indistinct.

Before taking a sight, it is worth setting the approximate altitude of Polaris (the DR latitude) on the sextant. It can then be viewed through the magnifying telescope and the micrometer used for fine adjustment.

If Polaris was exactly above the north pole, its altitude would be equal to the observer's latitude (Fig 7.4). In fact, Polaris describes a small circle around the north pole of about 1½° in diameter, Fig 7.5. A small correction dependent on the time of the sight has to be made to its true altitude.

The necessary adjustment is found in the Polaris table in the *Nautical Almanac* (Fig 7.6). To use the table two inputs are needed:

1  LHA Aries at the time of the sight.
2  DR latitude.

Aries is a point in the heavens chosen by astronomers as a datum for defining the position of stars. On earth Greenwich is the datum point for

## POLARIS TABLES

| L.H.A. ARIES | 240°–249° | 250°–259° |
|---|---|---|
|  | $a_0$ | $a_0$ |
|  | ° ′ | ° ′ |
| 0 | 1 43·8 | 1 39·1 |
| 1 | 43·4 | 38·5 |
| 2 | 43·0 | 38·0 |
| 3 | 42·5 | 37·4 |
| 4 | 42·1 | 36·8 |
| 5 | 1 41·6 | 1 36·2 |
| 6 | 41·1 | 35·6 |
| 7 | 40·6 | 35·0 |
| 8 | 40·1 | 34·4 |
| 9 | 39·6 | 33·8 |
| 10 | 1 39·1 | 1 33·1 |
| Lat. | $a_1$ | $a_1$ |
|  | ′ | ′ |
| 0 | 0·5 | 0·4 |
| 10 | ·5 | ·4 |
| 20 | ·5 | ·5 |
| 30 | ·5 | ·5 |
| 40 | 0·6 | 0·5 |
| 45 | ·6 | ·6 |
| 50 | ·6 | ·6 |
| 55 | ·6 | ·6 |
| 60 | ·7 | ·7 |
| 62 | 0·7 | 0·7 |
| 64 | ·7 | ·7 |
| 66 | ·7 | ·8 |
| 68 | 0·7 | 0·8 |
| Month | $a_2$ | $a_2$ |
|  | ′ | ′ |
| Jan. | 0·4 | 0·4 |
| Feb. | ·3 | ·3 |
| Mar. | ·3 | ·3 |

**Fig. 7.6** *Nautical Almanac* extract: Polaris.

longitude. For the purpose of explanation, Aries can be thought of as an invisible star.

The GHA of Aries is obtained from the left-hand daily page of the almanac. The first column on this page is headed *Aries*, which can also be represented by the sign $\gamma$. The column is tabulated in the same way as that for the sun, except there is only GHA for hourly increments and no declination. The GHA for minutes and seconds is found, under the heading Aries, from the increments table.

The GHA is converted to LHA by application of longitude. A chosen longitude is not required, the DR longitude is used.

*Example 7d*
What is the LHA of Aries on 17 February at 06h 55m in DR position 50° 20'N, 8° 40'W ?

| GHA Aries 06h | 236° 35'.9 |
|---|---|
| Incr 55m | +13° 47'.3 |
| | 250° 23'.2 |
| DR long W | −8° 40'.0 |
| LHA Aries | 241° 43'.2 |

The next step is to convert the sextant altitude to true altitude.
Sextant altitude 49° 50'.6, index error −2'.0, height of eye 2.0 metres.

| SA Polaris | 49° 50'.6 |
|---|---|
| IE −2.0) | |
| Dip −2.5) | −4'.5 |
| AA | 49° 46'.1 |
| star corrn | −0'.8 |
| TA | 49° 45'.3 |

The star correction is found in the Altitude Correction Tables under the heading *Stars and Planets*.

A correction is now made to allow for the small amount that the position of Polaris differs from true north. For this the Polaris table is used (Fig 7.6).

True altitude 49° 45'.3, LHA 241° 43'.2.

1 The correction, which is applied to true altitude, is in three parts called: $a_0$, $a_1$ and $a_2$. Enter the table with LHA 241° 43'.2. The first column, headed 240°−249°, is the required one. Against the units of degrees shown to the left, interpolate between 1° and 2° for the required 43'.2 which gives a figure of 1° 43'.1 which is the $a_0$ correction.

2 Staying in the same column, move down to the next table for latitude and extract the $a_1$ correction opposite latitude 50°: this is 0'.6.

3 Finally, still in the same column, move down to the block for month of the year opposite February and extract the $a_2$ correction: 0'.3.

4 All the corrections, $a_0$, $a_1$, and $a_2$, are added to true altitude.

5 A value of 1° has been added to the table to simplify calculation. This means that all parts of the correction are *always* additive. To allow for this, 1° must be subtracted from the corrected true altitude to give latitude.

| TA | 49° 45'.3 |
|---|---|
| $a_0$ | +1° 43'.1 |
| $a_1$ | 0'.6 |
| $a_2$ | 0'.3 |
| | 51° 29'.3 |
| −1° | 1° |
| Latitude | 50° 29'.3 |

**Setting the approximate angle on the sextant**
As previously mentioned, if the approximate angle, corresponding to the DR position latitude, is set on the sextant and the sextant pointed towards the north horizon, location of Polaris is straightforward.

For this, the DR latitude can be used, or the angle can be made a little more accurate by subtracting the $a_0$ part of the correction from DR latitude and adding 1°. The GMT of twilight is used to find the LHA of Aries for the $a_0$ correction.

*Example 7e*
*Use the Polaris table at the back of the book.*
What is the approximate angle to set on the sextant for a dusk twilight sight of Polaris on 30 August in DR position 49° 45'N, 7° 21'W?

|  | h  m |  |
|---|---|---|
| Dusk twilight 50° N | +19 24 | LMT |
| DR long as time | 29 |  |
|  | 19 53 | GMT |
| GHA Aries 19h | 263° 20'.8 |  |
| Incre 53m | +13° 17'.2 |  |
|  | 276° 38'.0 |  |
| DR long W | −7° 21'.0 |  |
| LHA Aries | 269° 17'.0 |  |
| $a_0$ | 1° 26'.7 |  |
| DR Latitude | 49° 45'.0N |  |
| -$a_0$ | −1° 26'.7 |  |
|  | 48° 18'.3 |  |
| +1° | +1° |  |
|  | 49° 18'.3 | approximate sextant angle |

## Exercise

**7.1** What is the time of the meridian passage of the sun on 16 February in DR position 49° 40'.0S, 165° 00'.0E?

**7.2** On 20 May in DR position 49° 50'.0N, 127° 40'.0W, a sight of the sun's LL taken at 20h 27m GMT gave a sextant altitude of 60° 11'.9 bearing south. Index error +2'.0, height of eye 2.0 metres. What was the latitude at this time?

**7.3** On 30 August in DR position 50° 27'.0N, 6° 00'.0W, a sight of the sun's UL taken at 12h 25m GMT, gave a sextant altitude of 49° 00'.2 bearing south. Index error 1'.0 *off* the arc, height of eye 2.5 metres. What was the observed latitude?

**7.4** On 19 May in DR position 49° 40'.0N, 6° 25'.0W, a sight was taken of Polaris at 03h 54m 08s GMT. At this time the sextant altitude was 49° 29'.3. Index error −2'.6, height of eye 1.5 metres. What was the latitude?

**7.5** On 31 August in DR position 29° N 45° W, Polaris was observed at 21h 53m GMT when the sextant altitude was 28° 18'.1, index error 3.0' *off* the arc, height of eye 2.5 metres. Find the latitude.

# 8  Where on the Chart?

## Plotting the position from sun sights

The sun is the heavenly body most commonly used for navigation. In clear weather it is visible from dawn to dusk and needs no identification. Sights can be taken at any time during the day preferably when the sun's altitude is greater than 15°.

We have already seen that a single sight of any heavenly body only provides a single position line. However, a single sight of the sun can be combined with a second sight taken when the sun's position has changed significantly. This method is called a *transferred position line, running fix, or sun-run-sun sight*. An allowance is made on the plot for the boat's ground track and distance run between the times of the two sights.

*Example 8a*

On 8 August a morning sun sight was taken at 07h 50m GMT which gave an intercept of 6 miles away and an azimuth of 096°T. The chosen position was 50° N 2° 15′ W. The boat then steered a course of 220°T for a distance of 21 miles when a meridian altitude sight gave a latitude of 49° 41′.0N. Plot the boat's position.

**1** Plot the chosen position on the chart and from this position plot the intercept for 6 miles away from 096°T. At the end of the intercept plot the position line (Fig 8.1).

**2** From any point on the first position line, plot the boat's course and distance run and transfer the first position line to the end of the run. The transferred position line is marked with double arrows (Fig 8.2).
**3** Plot the position line of latitude.
**4** The fix of position is at the intersection of the position line of latitude and the transferred position line (Fig 8.3).

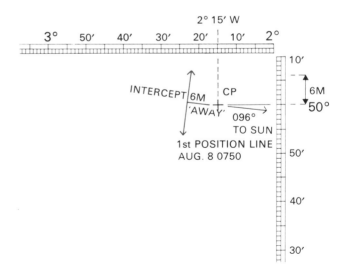

**Fig. 8.1**  Sun-run-sun sight – first position line.

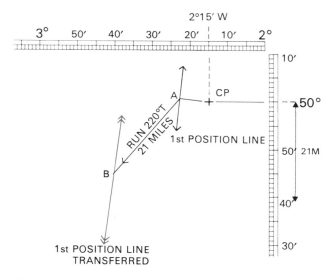

**Fig. 8.2** Sun-run-sun sight – transferring the position line.

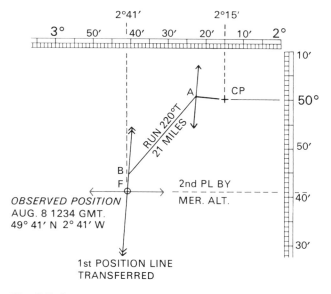

**Fig. 8.3** Sun-run-sun sight – the finished plot.

It must be remembered that the position line only indicates that the boat's position lies somewhere along it. It is more likely to be in the area of the DR position than anywhere else, unless the DR position is significantly inaccurate.

The accuracy of a sun-run-sun sight, or any sight involving a transferred position line, relies upon the accuracy of the course steered and the distance run, the correct assessment of tidal stream or current, the correct estimate of leeway, as well as the accuracy of both sights. A short run of a few hours should not normally be much in error, but if sights cannot be taken for a day or more, the rate and direction of the current are doubtful or for any reason the accuracy of the run between sights is suspect, a position depending upon a transferred position line should be treated with caution and only accepted as approximate. The strength of ocean currents, particularly running along coastlines, can be quite variable and a large margin for error should be allowed.

***Closing dangers*** When in DR position 53° 15'N 9° 55'W, a morning sun sight gave the following results: CP 53° N 10° 05'W, intercept 6M towards 102°T. The boat's course is 230°T.

For a sun-run-sight any point on the first position line can be chosen to lay off the boat's course. It could be plotted from point A (Fig 8.4), in which case the course of 230°T would appear to clear the rocks to the north west. However, further consideration of the DR position would suggest otherwise. If the boat is anywhere near the DR position then a course of 230°T passes dangerously close to the rocks. The complete plot (Fig 8.5), shows that the boat was at A2 when the morning sight was taken. However, it could have been at A1 in which case the course would have passed directly over the danger area.

This type of construction does not, therefore,

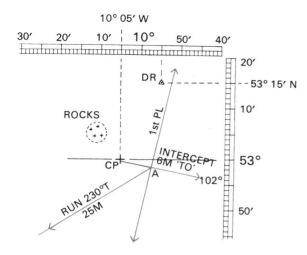

**Fig. 8.4** The run can be plotted from any point on the position line.

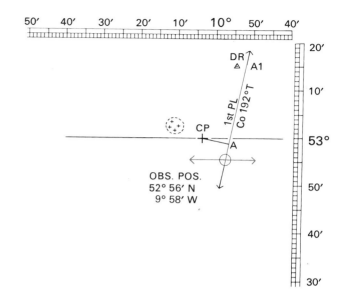

**Fig. 8.6** Steering along the first position line.

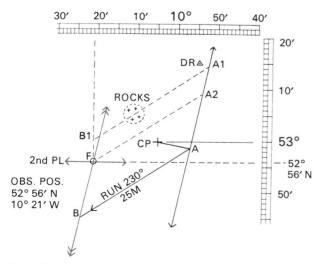

**Fig. 8.5** The plot shows the boat was at A when the first sight was taken.

show the presence of dangers along the track until the second position line is plotted. If there are any dangers present, the procedure should be to drop a perpendicular from the DR position to the first position line and use this as a tentative starting point; and also to allow a suitable margin for safety. Had this been done initially the danger would have been apparent.

In the above situation, the prudent action following the morning sight would be to alter course to steer along the position line (192°T) until the noon sight gave the latitude (Fig 8.6).

### Simultaneous sights

If simultaneous sights can be used, these are far more accurate. They can be taken:

● By day when the sun and moon are visible

- At dawn and dusk twilight when stars, planets and the moon are visible
- After dark stars and planets can be observed when the moon illuminates the horizon.

Sights can be regarded as simultaneous when they are taken within a few minutes of each other. The exact GMT of *each* sight must be recorded. It is best to take sights of at least three stars, any planets and the moon if visible. If all the position lines cross or nearly cross at the same point, each observation tends to confirm the others, giving a high degree of confidence in the resulting observed position. On the other hand, if the position lines do not cross each other near the same point, and there are several cocked hats, one or more of the sights must be incorrect and all should be re-checked. The ideal is to observe four or more stars or planets at altitudes between 20° and 50° located so that two are between 60° and 120° (ideally 90°) apart in azimuth in one direction, and two or more similarly apart in the opposite direction. This will show up any error due to abnormal refraction, or index error.

When simultaneous sights are taken, the latitude of all the chosen positions will be the same, since a whole degree of latitude nearest to the DR latitude is used. However, chosen position longitudes will differ because each depends upon the LHA for the sight concerned.

### Plotting simultaneous sights

*Example 8b*
Four star sights were taken at twilight, giving the following results:
Chosen latitude 40°N

| Star | CP long | Intercept | Azimuth |
|------|---------|-----------|---------|
| A | 19° 05'.0W | 8M away | 173°T |
| B | 18° 47'.0W | 12M away | 238°T |
| C | 18° 51'.0W | 12M towards | 083°T |
| D | 19° 00'.0W | 14M towards | 011°T |

What is the observed position?

1 Plot the chosen latitude as a position line opposite 40° on the latitude scale.
2 Mark the four chosen longitudes along this line.
3 From each chosen longitude, plot the intercept and azimuth.
4 Plot the position line at the end of each intercept.
5 Draw a small circle around the intersection point of the position lines.

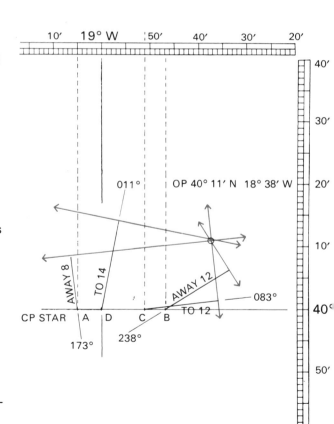

**Fig. 8.7** Plotting simultaneous sights.

**6** Find the observed position of the centre of this small circle by reference to the latitude and longitude scales.

Fig 8.7 shows the complete plot. Two pairs of stars have been chosen. One pair (A and B) is to the south of the observer, and the other pair (C and D) to the north. The position lines in each pair of stars make a good angle of cut with each other.

***Slow 'simultaneous' sights*** If two or more stars are taken with an appreciable time interval between them, an adjustment should be made to bring the position lines to a common time.

*Example 8c*
A boat travelling at 12 knots and steering a course of 045°T, takes three star sights at the following times:

Star A 19h 45m 15s GMT.
Star B 19h 51m 23s GMT. Distance run 2.2M, time taken 11m.
Star C 19h 56m 12s GMT. Distance run 1.0M, time taken 5m.

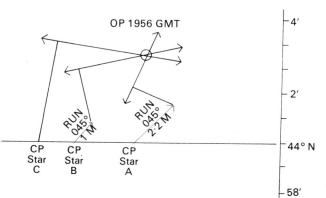

**Fig. 8.8** Allowing for distance run between sights.

**1** Using the elapsed time between sights, work out the distance run.
**2** Plot the chosen latitude and chosen longitudes on the chart in the usual way.
**3** From the chosen longitude for star A, plot the distance run between sights of stars A and B: 2.2M, course 045°T. Do the same between stars B and C: 1.0M, course 045°T.
**4** For stars A and B, plot the intercept, azimuth and position line from the end of the distance run.
**5** Plot the intercept, azimuth and position line for star C in the usual way.
**6** The observed position is at the intersection of the three position lines (Fig 8.8).

**Exercise**
*Use the portion of the chart provided in Figs 8.9 a and b.*

**8.1** On 16 February, in DR position 50° 04′N 6° 30′W, a morning sun sight gave a chosen position, 50°N 6° 21′.0W, intercept 3′.5 away, azimuth 101°T. The boat then travelled 23.7 M on a course of 038°T when the latitude by meridian altitude sight was determined as 50° 25′.5N. Find the observed position at the time of the meridian altitude sight.

**8.2** A boat in DR position 49° 45′N 126° 10′W takes three star sights which give the following results:

|  | Mirfak | Altair | Arcturus |
|---|---|---|---|
| CP Lat 50°N |  |  |  |
| CP long | 125° 45′.1W | 125° 54′.2W | 126° 02′.2W |
| Intercept | 0.9M away | 6.9M away | 1.0M away |
| Azimuth | 026°T | 143°T | 257°T |

Plot the observed position.

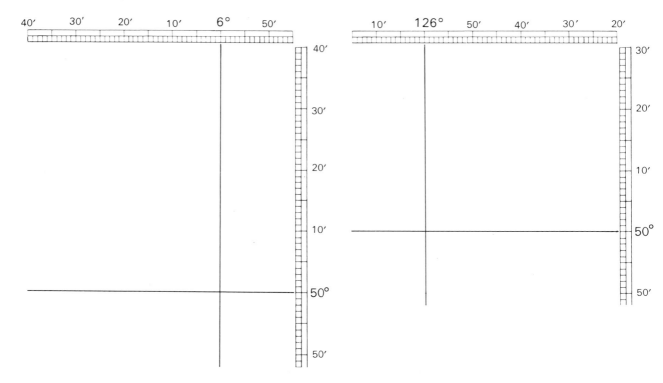

**Figs 8.9a, 8.9b** Portion of chart for questions 8.1 and 8.2.

# 9 Keeping Tabs on Time

The circumference of the earth is 21,600 miles. The sun effectively moves around the earth once every 24 hours, so its geographical position (GP) moves 21,600 miles in 24 hours or 900 miles an hour or 15 miles a minute or one mile every four seconds.

To achieve a positional accuracy of less than half a mile, time by Greenwich Mean Time (GMT) to an accuracy of less than two seconds is necessary for working out celestial sights. For this purpose a chronometer, which is a very precise timepiece, is used. A chronometer always shows GMT. Any reliable quartz clock will suffice. The chronometer should be kept below deck in a secure stowage. To avoid taking it on deck for the timing of sights, a deck watch, which also shows GMT, is used. This can be any accurate quartz watch, which can also act as a back up to the chronometer.

The errors of both chronometer and deck watch are checked by listening to radio time signals. Errors should be logged daily and applied to the time shown by the chronometer or deck watch. Constant small alterations are not made to timepieces used to show GMT as the less they are disturbed the more accurate they will be. Additionally, if the daily error is known and the time signal is not obtained, the correct time can easily be calculated:

*Example 9a*
On 26 June the deck watch showed 8h 48m 16s when a sight was taken. Earlier time checks showed the following deck watch error (DWE):

    3 June    2m 30s fast
    13 June   4m 10s fast

No more time checks were obtained. What was the correct GMT on June 26th?

| | |
|---|---|
| DWE 3 June | 2m 30s fast |
| DWE 13 June | 4m 10s fast |
| Difference 10 days | 1m 40s gained |
| Daily rate = 10s gain | |
| June 13th to 26th = 13 days; at 10s per day = 130s | |
| | |
| DWE June 13th | 4m 10s fast |
| Gain in 13 days | + 2m 10s |
| DWE June 26th | 6m 20s fast |
| | |
| Deck watch time June 26th | 8h 48m 16s |
| DWE | − 6m 20s |
| Correct GMT | 08h 41m 56s |

The chronometer or deck watch is not normally used for everyday purposes on a boat. It is more usual to have a separate clock fixed in a safe position below deck, which shows local time. This clock, called the ship's clock, is used for such purposes as meal times and watchkeeping.

Local time is derived from the sun's position. Approximate local noon occurs when the sun is on the observer's meridian when it will be bearing due north or south. Ashore, each country keeps its own standard time. Standard times for all countries are shown in the *Nautical Almanac*. Local Mean Time (LMT) is the theoretical time such that noon will coincide with the time of the sun's meridian passage.

## Time zones

The sun is a relatively good time keeper. It circles the earth travelling through 360° every 24 hours, so it moves through 15° each hour or 1° every four minutes. To keep the ship's clock roughly to the time by the sun, it has to be altered as the boat moves east or west. To avoid frequent alterations Time Zones have been devised.

The world has been divided into 24 zones of longitude each 15° wide; the same number of zones as hours in the day. Time in each zone differs by one hour (Fig 9.1). Zone 0 extends from 7° 30′ E, through 0°, to 7° 30′W. The zone time in zone 0 will be Greenwich Mean Time (GMT) as it straddles the Greenwich Meridian.

Zone +1 extends from 7° 30′ W to 22° 30′ W. In zone +1, zone time will be one hour earlier than GMT.

Zone −1 extends from 7° 30′ E to 22° 30′ E. In zone −1, zone time will be one hour later than GMT.

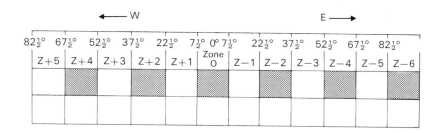

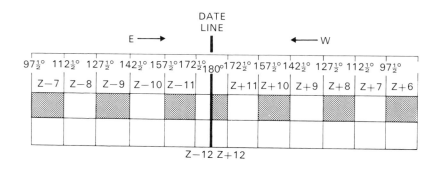

**Fig. 9.1** Time zones.

To find GMT given zone time, apply the zone number to zone time and obey the sign:

*Example 9b*

**1** The local time in zone $+5$ is 07h 00m. What is the GMT?

| | | h m |
|---|---|---|
| West of Greenwich | Zone Time | 07 00 |
| | Zone +5 | +5 |
| | GMT | 12 00 |

**2** The local time in zone $-3$ is 14h 00m. What is the GMT?

| | | h m |
|---|---|---|
| East of Greenwich | Zone Time | 14 00 |
| | Zone −3 | −3 |
| | GMT | 11 00 |

The following rhyme may be a useful aid to memory:

Longitude *east*, Greenwich *least* (less than zone time)

Longitude *west*, Greenwich *best* (more than zone time)

Whenever a passage may take a boat much beyond 8° E or 8° W, the zone number to which the ship's clock is set should be clearly written at the top of the time column in the deck log. Normally as the boat approaches a different zone the ship's clock is altered one hour, preferably at midnight, although this is not essential. A line is drawn across the deck log and the zone number altered by one hour to correspond.

*Example 9c*

On passage westwards:

In longitude west (Z+), the clock is put back 1 hour and the zone number increased by 1.
In longitude east (Z−), the clock is put back 1 hour and the zone number reduced by 1.

On passage eastwards:

In longitude west (Z+), the clock is advanced 1 hour and the zone number reduced by 1.
In longitude east (Z−), the clock is advanced 1 hour and the zone number increased by 1.

It is not essential for the clock and zone number to be altered when the boat crosses a zone boundary, it is merely convenient. If for example the clock and zone number were not changed for, say, 10° of longitude, all that would happen is that the sun would rise or set about half an hour earlier or later than usual, according to the time by the ship's clock. It is important that the deck log always indicates, by the zone number and sign at the head of the time column, the number of hours by which the local time differs from GMT as shown by the chronometer.

If the longitude is anything more than 10° east or west, the chronometer will read a different time to the ship's clock, the difference being the zone number in use. In longitude 30° W the time column in the deck log will be headed Z+2. If the ship's clock reads 6h, the chronometer will read 8h. This is quite straightforward, but remember that many clocks only register 12 hours, not 24 hours, and do not indicate whether the time shown is am or pm. In the morning in zone +7 if the ship's clock showed 8h, the chronometer would show 3h. However, the application of the zone number to zone time would immediately show that it was 3 pm or in nautical time 1500. On the other hand, in the evening, if the working clock showed 8h, the nautical time would be 0300 the next morning. In this case the date in zone 0 which straddles the Greenwich meridian would be a day later than the local date. So by application of the zone number, GMT and Greenwich Date (GD) can be checked. GMT and GD are required to obtain correct data from the *Nautical Almanac*.

*Example 9d*

On 10 June (local date) an evening star sight was taken at 4h 13m 20s by the chronometer. The boat was in zone +10 and the zone time was 6h 15m. What was the Greenwich Date and the Greenwich Mean Time to use for the sight.

As it was evening local time the zone time of 6h 15m is taken as 18h 15m.

|  |  | h m |
|---|---|---|
| June 10th |  | 18 15 Zone Time |
| Zone +10 |  | +10 |
| GD 11th |  | 04 15 GMT |

The correct Greenwich Date is 11 June and the correct GMT taken from the chronometer is 4h 13m 20s.

The Greenwich Date and Time can also be checked by application of DR longitude converted to time:

*Example 9e*

The DR position is 20°S 155°E and the local date 20 May. A morning twilight sight was taken when the chronometer showed 7h 35m 45s. What was the Greenwich Date and the Greenwich Mean Time to use for the sight?

Morning civil twilight for 20 May for latitude 20°S is found from the *Nautical Almanac* in the top right-hand panel (the bottom panel is for evening twilight) on the right-hand daily page (Fig 9.2).

|  |  | h m |  |
|---|---|---|---|
| Civil twilight am | 20d | 05 59 | LMT |
| Long 155° E |  | −10 20 |  |
| Greenwich Date | 19d | 19 39 | GMT |

The chronometer time must, therefore, be 19h 35m 45s and not 7h 35m 45s, and the Greenwich Date differs from the local date.

| H.P. | Lat. | Twilight Naut. | Twilight Civil | Sunrise | Moonrise 19 | Moonrise 20 | Moonrise 21 | Moonrise 22 |
|---|---|---|---|---|---|---|---|---|
|  |  | h m | h m | h m | h m | h m | h m | h m |
|  | N 72 | ▢ | ▢ | ▢ | 12 37 | 14 40 | 16 47 | 19 05 |
| 59.4 | N 70 | ▢ | ▢ | ▢ | 12 40 | 14 35 | 16 32 | 18 35 |
| 59.4 | 68 | //// | //// | 01 21 | 12 42 | 14 30 | 16 21 | 18 13 |
| 59.4 | 66 | //// | //// | 02 05 | 12 44 | 14 27 | 16 11 | 17 56 |
| 59.4 | 64 | //// | 00 27 | 02 34 | 12 45 | 14 24 | 16 03 | 17 43 |
| 59.4 | 62 | //// | 01 32 | 02 55 | 12 47 | 14 21 | 15 56 | 17 31 |
| 59.4 | 60 | //// | 02 05 | 03 13 | 12 48 | 14 19 | 15 50 | 17 21 |
| 59.4 | N 58 | 00 24 | 02 29 | 03 27 | 12 49 | 14 17 | 15 45 | 17 13 |
| 59.4 | 56 | 01 23 | 02 48 | 03 40 | 12 50 | 14 15 | 15 40 | 17 05 |
| 59.4 | 54 | 01 54 | 03 04 | 03 50 | 12 51 | 14 13 | 15 36 | 16 59 |
| 59.4 | 52 | 02 16 | 03 17 | 04 00 | 12 52 | 14 12 | 15 33 | 16 53 |
| 59.4 | 50 | 02 34 | 03 28 | 04 09 | 12 53 | 14 11 | 15 29 | 16 47 |
| 59.4 | 45 | 03 07 | 03 52 | 04 27 | 12 54 | 14 08 | 15 22 | 16 36 |
| 59.4 | N 40 | 03 32 | 04 10 | 04 41 | 12 55 | 14 05 | 15 16 | 16 26 |
| 59.4 | 35 | 03 51 | 04 25 | 04 53 | 12 57 | 14 03 | 15 11 | 16 18 |
| 59.4 | 30 | 04 06 | 04 38 | 05 04 | 12 58 | 14 02 | 15 06 | 16 11 |
| 59.4 | 20 | 04 30 | 04 59 | 05 22 | 12 59 | 13 59 | 14 58 | 15 59 |
| 59.5 | N 10 | 04 49 | 05 16 | 05 38 | 13 01 | 13 56 | 14 52 | 15 48 |
| 59.5 | 0 | 05 05 | 05 31 | 05 53 | 13 02 | 13 54 | 14 45 | 15 39 |
| 59.5 | S 10 | 05 19 | 05 45 | 06 07 | 13 04 | 13 51 | 14 39 | 15 29 |
| 59.5 | 20 | 05 33 | 05 59 | 06 23 | 13 06 | 13 49 | 14 32 | 15 18 |
| 59.5 | 30 | 05 46 | 06 15 | 06 40 | 13 07 | 13 46 | 14 25 | 15 07 |
| 59.5 | 35 | 05 52 | 06 23 | 06 50 | 13 08 | 13 44 | 14 21 | 15 00 |
| 59.5 | 40 | 06 00 | 06 33 | 07 02 | 13 10 | 13 42 | 14 16 | 14 52 |
| 59.5 | 45 | 06 07 | 06 43 | 07 16 | 13 11 | 13 40 | 14 10 | 14 43 |
| 59.5 | S 50 | 06 16 | 06 56 | 07 32 | 13 13 | 13 38 | 14 04 | 14 33 |
| 59.5 | 52 | 06 20 | 07 02 | 07 40 | 13 13 | 13 36 | 14 01 | 14 28 |
| 59.5 | 54 | 06 24 | 07 08 | 07 49 | 13 14 | 13 35 | 13 57 | 14 22 |
| 59.5 | 56 | 06 29 | 07 15 | 07 58 | 13 15 | 13 34 | 13 54 | 14 16 |
| 59.5 | 58 | 06 33 | 07 23 | 08 10 | 13 16 | 13 32 | 13 50 | 14 10 |
| 59.5 | S 60 | 06 39 | 07 31 | 08 22 | 13 17 | 13 31 | 13 45 | 14 02 |

**Fig. 9.2** *Nautical Almanac* extract: twilight.

## The Date Line

The Date Line is an arbitrary line in the vicinity of the 180° meridian. On either side of this line the date and day of the week differ by one day. The date on the eastern side is one day behind the date on the western side of the line.

*Example 9f*

A boat is travelling westward and approaching the Date Line. DR longitude is about 179° W. The deck log will be headed Z + 12. It is not essential to change the zone time on the exact date that the boat crosses the date line, but it is best to do so at midnight about that date. Just before midnight the deck log might show the following entries:

### Deck Log

| Local date | Time Z +12 | 15d | 2355 local time |
|---|---|---|---|
| | | | +12 |
| 15 July | 2355 | GD 16d | 1155 approx GMT |

Ten minutes later date and zone sign have altered but the clock showing zone time is left *unchanged*.

### Deck Log

| Local date | Time Z −12 | 17d | 0005 local time |
|---|---|---|---|
| | | | −12 |
| 17 July | 0005 | GD 16d | 1205 approx GMT |

The GMT has changed by the correct amount, 10 minutes, but the local date has changed a whole day.

In the next example the boat is travelling eastward across the Date Line:

*Example 9g*
### Deck Log

| Local date | Time Z −12 | 16d | 2355 local time |
|---|---|---|---|
| | | | −12 |
| 16 July | 23 55 | GD 16d | 1155 approx GMT |

Ten minutes later only the zone sign has altered

### Deck Log

| Local date | Time Z +12 | 16d | 0005 local time |
|---|---|---|---|
| | | | +12 |
| 16 July | 0005 | GD 16d | 1205 approx GMT |

The GMT has changed by the correct amount, 10 minutes, but the date is unchanged.

## Exercise

*Answers and extracts at the back of the book.*

**9.1** On August 10th the error on the chronometer was 3m 42s slow. On 14 August it was 3h 34m slow. On 21 August, a sight was taken when the chronometer read 16h 43m 18s. What was the correct GMT?

**9.2** Near Vancouver in Canada a local time signal gave the time as 1200 midday. Zone time was Z + 8. What was the GMT?

**9.3** An evening twilight sight was taken on 20 May in DR position 50°N 128°W. The deck watch showed 4h 54m 13s. What was the Greenwich Date and the Greenwich Mean Time to use for the sight.

**9.4** A morning twilight sight was taken on 15 February when in DR position 22°S 100°E. The deck watch, which was 1m 32s fast, showed 10h 48m 20s. What was the Greenwich Date and Greenwich Mean Time to use for the sight?

# 10 Planet, Star and Moon Sights

## Planets

The four planets used for navigation, Venus, Mars, Jupiter and Saturn, are easily identified and, when visible, provide good sights. If observed simultaneously with one or more stars, an observed position can be obtained. This should be more accurate than a position found by only observing the sun.

The *Nautical Almanac* provides data about the planets to aid identification, with notes and accompanying chart to indicate when each planet will be above the horizon.

A planet is more easily observed at morning or evening twilight when the sky is dark enough for it to show up, but with the horizon still clearly defined.

The left-hand daily page of the almanac tabulates the GHA and the Declination for the four planets. Each page covers three days. At the foot of the GHA column there is a factor v. The movement of the planets is not exactly 15° every hour so an additional small correction is required which is given by the value of v. It is always added except occasionally for Venus when it is accompanied by a minus sign (Fig 10.1). At the foot of the declination column is a factor d. The value of d is the hourly difference of declination.

The method of working is similar to that for a sun sight, except for the v factor applied to GHA. The v correction is found in the increments table for minutes of GHA under the heading 'v or d Corrections'. A chosen longitude is applied to GHA to give LHA.

Sextant altitude is corrected for index error and height of eye, and the middle column in the *Altitude Correction Table* headed '*Stars and Planets*' is used for their apparent altitude correction. For Venus and Mars there is a small additional correction based upon the month of the year and altitude.

Once the LHA and Declination have been found, tabulated altitude and azimuth are obtained by reference to AP3270 Volume 2 or 3 in a similar manner to that used for sun sights. Tabulated and true altitude are compared to find the intercept.

*Example 10a*
*Use the extracts at the back of the book.*
On 15 February in DR position 50° 10'N 15° 20'W an evening sight of Venus was taken. The deck watch, which was 2m 15s slow, read 6h 50m 09s. The sextant altitude was 14° 12'.7, index error 3'.0 *on* the arc, height of eye 2.0 metres.

| DWT | 18 50 09 | | | |
|-----|----------|---|---|---|
| DWE | +2 15 | | | |
| GMT | 18 52 24 | | | |
| | | | | |
| GHA | 18h | 63° 19'.2 | Dec | S4° 56'.6 |
| Incre | 52m 24s | +13° 06'.0 | d − 1.3 | −1'.1 |
| v | −0.4 | −0'.4 | | |
| | | | | − S4° 55'.5 |
| GHA | | 76° 24'.8 | | |
| CP long W | | −15° 24'.8 | | |
| | | | | |
| LHA | | 61° | | |

| G.M.T. | VENUS −3.7 | | MARS +1.0 | | JUPITER −1.7 | | SATURN +0.4 | |
|---|---|---|---|---|---|---|---|---|
| d h | G.H.A. | Dec. | G.H.A. | Dec. | G.H.A. | Dec. | G.H.A. | Dec. |
| 21 00 | 134 13.5 | N25 25.1 | 237 36.6 | S 1 35.0 | 224 09.2 | N 4 41.2 | 130 54.5 | N22 23.2 |
| 01 | 149 13.0 | 24.8 | 252 37.3 | 34.2 | 239 11.2 | 41.4 | 145 56.7 | 23.1 |
| 02 | 164 12.4 | 24.6 | 267 38.1 | 33.5 | 254 13.2 | 41.6 | 160 58.9 | 23.1 |
| 03 | 179 11.9 ·· | 24.3 | 282 38.8 ·· | 32.8 | 269 15.1 ·· | 41.8 | 176 01.1 ·· | 23.1 |
| 04 | 194 11.3 | 24.1 | 297 39.5 | 32.0 | 284 17.1 | 42.0 | 191 03.3 | 23.1 |
| 05 | 209 10.7 | 23.8 | 312 40.3 | 31.3 | 299 19.1 | 42.1 | 206 05.5 | 23.0 |
| 06 | 224 10.2 | N25 23.6 | 327 41.0 | S 1 30.6 | 314 21.1 | N 4 42.3 | 221 07.7 | N22 23.0 |
| 07 | 239 09.6 | 23.4 | 342 41.7 | 29.8 | 329 23.1 | 42.5 | 236 09.8 | 23.0 |
| 08 | 254 09.1 | 23.1 | 357 42.5 | 29.1 | 344 25.1 | 42.7 | 251 12.0 | 23.0 |
| 09 | 269 08.5 ·· | 22.9 | 12 43.2 ·· | 28.3 | 359 27.1 ·· | 42.9 | 266 14.2 ·· | 22.9 |
| 10 | 284 08.0 | 22.6 | 27 44.0 | 27.6 | 14 29.1 | 43.1 | 281 16.4 | 22.9 |
| 11 | 299 07.4 | 22.4 | 42 44.7 | 26.9 | 29 31.1 | 43.3 | 296 18.6 | 22.9 |
| 12 | 314 06.9 | N25 22.1 | 57 45.4 | S 1 26.1 | 44 33.1 | N 4 43.5 | 311 20.8 | N22 22.8 |
| 13 | 329 06.3 | 21.9 | 72 46.2 | 25.4 | 59 35.0 | 43.7 | 326 23.0 | 22.8 |
| 14 | 344 05.7 | 21.6 | 87 46.9 | 24.7 | 74 37.0 | 43.9 | 341 25.1 | 22.8 |
| 15 | 359 05.2 ·· | 21.4 | 102 47.6 ·· | 23.9 | 89 39.0 ·· | 44.1 | 356 27.3 ·· | 22.8 |
| 16 | 14 04.6 | 21.1 | 117 48.4 | 23.2 | 104 41.0 | 44.2 | 11 29.5 | 22.7 |
| 17 | 29 04.1 | 20.8 | 132 49.1 | 22.4 | 119 43.0 | 44.4 | 26 31.7 | 22.7 |
| 18 | 44 03.5 | N25 20.6 | 147 49.8 | S 1 21.7 | 134 45.0 | N 4 44.6 | 41 33.9 | N22 22.7 |
| 19 | 59 03.0 | 20.3 | 162 50.6 | 21.0 | 149 47.0 | 44.8 | 56 36.1 | 22.7 |
| 20 | 74 02.4 | 20.1 | 177 51.3 | 20.2 | 164 49.0 | 45.0 | 71 38.3 | 22.6 |
| 21 | 89 01.9 ·· | 19.8 | 192 52.1 ·· | 19.5 | 179 51.0 ·· | 45.2 | 86 40.4 ·· | 22.6 |
| 22 | 104 01.3 | 19.5 | 207 52.8 | 18.8 | 194 53.0 | 45.4 | 101 42.6 | 22.6 |
| 23 | 119 00.8 | 19.3 | 222 53.5 | 18.0 | 209 55.0 | 45.6 | 116 44.8 | 22.6 |
| | $v$ −0.6 $d$ 0.2 | | $v$ 0.7 $d$ 0.7 | | $v$ 2.0 $d$ 0.2 | | $v$ 2.2 $d$ 0.0 | |

**Fig. 10.1** *Nautical Almanac* extract: planets.

CP latitude N 50°

Dec S 4° 55'

Lat and Dec **contrary**

Hc 14° 55'
d −49 −45'

Tab alt 14° 10'

360°
Z −116°

Zn 244° Azimuth

| | |
|---|---|
| Sextant altitude | 14° 12'.7 |
| IE −3'.0 | |
| Dip −2'.5 | −5'.5 |
| Apparent altitude | 14° 07'.2 |
| corrn | −3'.8 |
| add.corrn | +0'.1 |
| True alt | 14° 03'.5 |
| Tab alt | 14° 10'.0 |
| Intercept | 6'.5A |

The star correction for apparent altitude is always subtracted and the additional correction for planets is added.

**Stars**

Stars are extremely valuable for position finding. They are not visible by day, but at dawn or dusk twilight when the sky is clear, any number of stars can be used for observations. Sometimes, when the horizon is well defined, star sights can be taken in full darkness. The great value of star sights is that a number of stars can be observed almost simultaneously which enables a position to be established without the possible inaccuracy caused by using a run between sights.

When multiple star sights have been taken, the proximity of the resulting position lines to an intersection or small cocked hat gives an excellent guide as to the accuracy of each sight and so the reliability of the position found.

Many navigators are put off from attempting star sights because they feel that it is difficult to identify individual stars. A little practice will quickly enable a small number of brighter stars to be identified. It helps to first identify the major constellations such as Ursa Major (the Plough), Orion, Cassiopeia, Pegasus, the Southern Cross, and so on. Having done this, pick out prominent stars in or near a constellation. Star charts are included in the *Nautical Almanac* to aid identification. There are also many excellent star chart diagrams available.

The 57 stars suitable for observation are tabulated on the left-hand daily page of the almanac. These vary in brightness or magnitude. Magnitude is shown as a number which is sometimes accompanied by a minus sign. The larger the minus number, the brighter the star: Acamar (mag 3.1) is very dim; whereas Sirius (mag −1.6) is the brightest star in the heavens.

The quickest and easiest way to work out star sights is by using a sight reduction table based upon the position of Aries. This is AP3270 *Sight Reduction Tables for Air Navigation* Volume 1.

The tables are entered with a whole degree of LHA of Aries at the time of the sight, and a whole degree of latitude.

*Example 10b*
On 31 August in DR position 49° 40′N 7° 20′W at 19h 53m 50s GMT a sight of Arcturus was taken. The sextant altitude 36° 07′.3, index error −3′.0, height of eye 2.5 metres. Find the intercept and azimuth.

The GHA of Aries for 19h and the increment for 53m 50s is found:

| | |
|---|---|
| GHA Aries 19h | 264° 19′.9 |
| Incre 53m 50s | +13° 29′.7 |
| GHA | 277° 49′.6 |
| CP long W | −7° 49′.6 |
| LHA Aries | 270° |

CP latitude N50°

Use the extract from AP3270 Vol 1 for 50°N (Fig 10.2). Find the local hour angle, 270°, down the side of the table. Under the heading *Arcturus* will be found altitude and azimuth (Hc and Zn).

Hc 36° 06′   Zn 257°T

There are no corrections to be applied to altitude and azimuth.

Correct the sextant altitude to true altitude, using the star correction column in the *Altitude Correction Tables*. Compare with the tabulated altitude and find the intercept.

| | | |
|---|---|---|
| SA | 36° 07′.3 | |
| IE −3′.0 | | |
| Dip −2′.8 | −5′.8 | |
| AA | 36° 01′.5 | |
| Star corrn | −1′.3 | |
| True alt | 36° 00′.2 | |
| Tab alt | 36° 06′.0 | |
| Intercept | 5′.8A | Azimuth 257°T |

The table in AP3270 Volume 1 lists the seven most suitable stars available for a given latitude and LHA of Aries. Those printed in capital letters are the brightest. Those marked with a diamond will give a good intersection of position lines.

The table can only be used for the stars listed. If a sight is taken of a star not tabulated in Volume 1, then Hc and Zn can be found from AP3270 Volume

## AP 3270 Sight reduction tables

| LHA ϒ | Hc | Zn | Hc | Zn | Hc | Zn | Hc | Zn | Hc | Zn | Hc | Zn | Hc | Zn |
|---|---|---|---|---|---|---|---|---|---|---|---|---|---|---|
| | ◆Mirfak | | Alpheratz | | ◆ALTAIR | | Rasalhague | | ◆ARCTURUS | | Alkaid | | Kochab | |
| 270 | 15 18 | 025 | 20 42 | 069 | 42 56 | 142 | 52 12 | 190 | 36 06 | 257 | 50 18 | 295 | 58 49 | 337 |
| 271 | 15 35 | 026 | 21 18 | 070 | 43 20 | 143 | 52 04 | 192 | 35 29 | 257 | 49 43 | 295 | 58 34 | 337 |
| 272 | 15 52 | 026 | 21 54 | 071 | 43 43 | 144 | 51 55 | 194 | 34 51 | 258 | 49 08 | 295 | 58 19 | 337 |
| 273 | 16 09 | 027 | 22 31 | 071 | 44 05 | 145 | 51 46 | 195 | 34 13 | 259 | 48 33 | 296 | 58 04 | 337 |
| 274 | 16 27 | 028 | 23 07 | 072 | 44 27 | 147 | 51 35 | 197 | 33 35 | 260 | 47 59 | 296 | 57 49 | 337 |
| 275 | 16 45 | 028 | 23 44 | 073 | 44 48 | 148 | 51 24 | 198 | 32 57 | 261 | 47 24 | 297 | 57 33 | 336 |
| 276 | 17 03 | 029 | 24 21 | 073 | 45 08 | 149 | 51 11 | 200 | 32 19 | 262 | 46 50 | 297 | 57 18 | 336 |
| 277 | 17 22 | 029 | 24 58 | 074 | 45 27 | 151 | 50 58 | 201 | 31 41 | 262 | 46 15 | 298 | 57 02 | 336 |
| 278 | 17 41 | 030 | 25 35 | 075 | 45 45 | 152 | 50 43 | 203 | 31 03 | 263 | 45 41 | 298 | 56 47 | 336 |
| 279 | 18 00 | 031 | 26 12 | 075 | 46 03 | 153 | 50 28 | 204 | 30 24 | 264 | 45 07 | 299 | 56 31 | 336 |
| 280 | 18 20 | 031 | 26 50 | 076 | 46 20 | 155 | 50 11 | 206 | 29 46 | 265 | 44 34 | 299 | 56 15 | 336 |
| 281 | 18 40 | 032 | 27 27 | 077 | 46 36 | 156 | 49 54 | 207 | 29 08 | 266 | 44 00 | 299 | 55 59 | 336 |
| 282 | 19 01 | 032 | 28 05 | 077 | 46 51 | 157 | 49 36 | 209 | 28 29 | 266 | 43 26 | 300 | 55 43 | 336 |
| 283 | 19 21 | 033 | 28 42 | 078 | 47 06 | 159 | 49 17 | 210 | 27 51 | 267 | 42 53 | 300 | 55 27 | 335 |
| 284 | 19 42 | 033 | 29 20 | 079 | 47 19 | 160 | 48 57 | 211 | 27 12 | 268 | 42 20 | 301 | 55 11 | 335 |

**Fig. 10.2** *AP3270 Volume 1* extract: selected stars.

2 or 3 in a similar manner to sun sights. GHA of stars is not tabulated, but it is easily found by:

SHA of star + GHA Aries = GHA of star

See Fig 10.3.

The Sidereal Hour Angle (SHA) of a star is fairly constant and is tabulated on the left-hand daily page of the almanac together with declination.
The GHA of Aries is for the time of the sight.

*Example 10c*
On 29 August in DR position 36° 10'N 71° 20'W a sight of Rigel was taken at 09h 52m 48s GMT. What was the LHA of the star? Use almanac extract Appendix 5 for August.

| | | |
|---|---|---|
| SHA Rigel | +281° 39'.4 | Dec S8° 13'.6 |
| GHA Aries 9h | 111° 57'.0 | |
| Incre 52m 48s | 13° 14'.2 | |
| GHA Rigel | 406° 50'.6 | |
| CP long W | 70° 50'.6 | |
| LHA Rigel | 336° | |

**Working out a plan** It is best to find out, well in advance, which stars will be available and the approximate time that sights can be taken. Additionally, the approximate altitude and azimuth of each star can be estimated. This not only aids identification, but if the approximate altitude of the required star is set on the sextant and it is pointed in the direction of the azimuth, the star should appear near the horizon and only fine tuning with the micrometer is necessary to bring it to the horizon.

The time of morning or evening twilight, the expected DR longitude expressed as time, and AP3270 Volume 1 is all that is required for such a plan.

*Example 10d*
It is proposed to take star sights at evening twilight on 30 August. The approximate DR position will be 49° 45'N 127° 30'W. List the stars available with their altitudes and azimuths. Which are the brightest? Which give the best angle of cut if three are used?

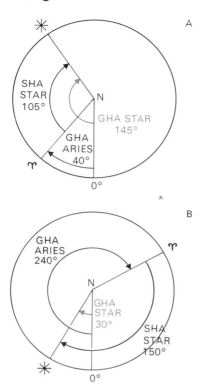

**Fig. 10.3** Sidereal Hour Angle (SHA) of a star.

Check for GD and GMT:

| | | | |
|---|---|---|---|
| Civil twilight dusk 50°N | 19 24 | LMT | 30d |
| Long 127° 30'W as time | +8 30 | | |
| | 03 54 | GMT | 31d |

| | |
|---|---|
| GHA Aries 31d 03h | 23° 40'.5 |
| Incre 54 m | 13° 32'.2 |
| GHA | 37° 12'.7 |
| | +360° |
| | 397° 12'.7 |
| DR long W | −127° 30'.0 |
| LHA | 269° 42'.7 (use 270°) |
| Chosen latitude 50°N | |

It is not necessary to use a chosen position longitude when working out a plan as the position is not plotted. The nearest whole degree of LHA in the answer is used.

Enter AP3270 Volume 1 with 50°N and LHA 270°:

| Star | Hc | Zn |
|---|---|---|
| *Mirfak | 15° 18' | 025° |
| Alpheratz | 20° 42' | 069° |
| *ALTAIR | 42 ° 56' | 142° |
| Rasalhague | 52° 12' | 190° |
| *ARCTURUS | 36° 06' | 257° |
| Alkaid | 50° 18' | 295° |
| Kochab | 58° 49' | 337° |

Brightest stars: Altair and Arcturus. *The three with the best angle of cut: Mirfak, Altair, Arcturus.

***Taking simultaneous star sights*** The plan is only to give a guide as to the availability of stars, the approximate time when they will be visible, their approximate altitudes and azimuths. When the sights are actually taken, the *exact time of each* sight must be used when working out the LHA *not* the time in the plan.

*Example 10e*
This example follows the previous plan. The check for the Greenwich Date and Time has already been done.

On 30 August in DR position 49° 45'N 126° 10'W, with an index error − 2'.0 and height of eye 2.5 metres, the following star sights were taken:

| Star | DWT | Sextant Alt |
|---|---|---|
| Mirfak | 03 48 38 | 15° 42'.3 |
| Altair | 03 49 14 | 43° 18'.9 |
| Arcturus | 03 49 46 | 35° 34'.2 |

The deck watch was 3m 32s slow.

|  | Mirfak | | Altair | | Arcturus |
|---|---|---|---|---|---|
| DWT | 03 48 38 | | 03 49 14 | | 03 49 46 |
| DWE | + 3 32 | | + 3 32 | | + 3 32 |
| GMT | 03 52 10 | | 03 52 46 | | 03 53 18 |
| GHA Aries 31d 03h | 23° 40′.5 | | 23° 40′.5 | | 23° 40′.5 |
| Incre   (52 10) | 13° 04′.6 | (52 46) | 13° 13′.7 | (53 18) | 13° 21′.7 |
|  | 36° 45′.1 | | 36° 54′.2 | | 37° 02′.2 |
|  | + 360° | | + 360° | | + 360° |
|  | 396° 45′.1 | | 396° 54′.2 | | 397° 02′.2 |
| CP long W | − 125° 45′.1 | | − 125° 54′.2 | | − 126° 02′.2 |
| LHA Aries | 271° | | 271° | | 271° |
| Chosen latitude 50°N | | | | | |
| Hc | 15° 35′ | | 43° 20′ | | 35° 29′ |
| Zn | 026° | | 143° | | 257° |
| Sextant altitude | 15° 42′.3 | | 43° 18′.9 | | 35° 34′.2 |
| IE − 2′.0 | | | | | |
| Dip − 2′.8 | − 4′.8 | | − 4′.8 | | − 4′.8 |
| Apparent altitude | 15° 37′.5 | | 43° 14′.1 | | 35° 29′.4 |
| Corrn | − 3′.4 | | − 1′.0 | | − 1′.4 |
| True alt | 15° 34′.1 | | 43° 13′.1 | | 35° 28′.0 |
| Tab alt | 15° 35′.0 | | 43° 20′.0 | | 35° 29′.0 |
| Intercept | 0′.9A | | 6′.9A | | 1′.0A |
| Azimuth | 026° | | 143° | | 257° |

Observed position: 50° 05′N 126° 02′W. See plotted answer 8.2 at the back of the book.

***Precession and Nutation*** We have, for practice purposes, regarded the stars as fixed points in the heavens. This is not strictly true. The earth spins on its axis like a gyro and, like a top, the axis moves slightly, causing the projected axes to describe small circles. This is called precession. The end of each axis also oscillates about this circular path. This is nutation. Precession and nutation are caused by the varying attractions of the sun, moon and planets and also because the earth is not a perfect sphere.

Precession and nutation do not affect AP3270 Volumes 2 or 3 or NP 401. However AP3270 Volume 1 tabulates information in relation to Aries and is affected. The data has been computed for a particular year, called an epoch, which is the middle year of a five year span.

If any but the middle year is used a slight correction should be applied, which is found at the back of the tables. Unless very strict accuracy is required, this can be ignored for the five year span as any error involved will not exceed two miles. Volume 1 tables are re-issued every five years.

## Moon

For long periods during the month the moon is visible and sufficiently high in altitude to provide excellent sights. There are times during the day when the moon can be used at the same time as the sun. At other times the moon may be available at dawn or dusk twilight and used together with stars for simultaneous sights.

Moon sights are worked out in a similar manner to sun sights, but as the moon is relatively near the earth and its distance is not constant, parallax is significant. This varies with altitude and with the moon's distance from the earth. It is tabulated hourly as horizontal parallax (HP) on the right-hand daily

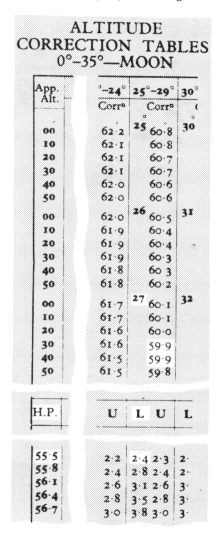

| G.M.T. | MOON | | | | |
|---|---|---|---|---|---|
| | G.H.A. | v | Dec. | d | H.P. |
| 22 | 89 30.8 | 13.2 | 14 13.7 | 8.8 | 55.1 |
| 23 | 104 02.8 | 13.2 | 14 22.5 | 8.7 | 55.1 |
| **17** 00 | 118 35.0 | 13.1 | N14 31.2 | 8.7 | 55.2 |
| 01 | 133 07.1 | 13.0 | 14 39.9 | 8.7 | 55.2 |
| 02 | 147 39.1 | 12.9 | 14 48.6 | 8.5 | 55.2 |
| 03 | 162 11.0 | 12.9 | 14 57.1 | 8.5 | 55.2 |
| 04 | 176 42.9 | 12.8 | 15 05.6 | 8.5 | 55.2 |
| 05 | 191 14.7 | 12.8 | 15 14.1 | 8.4 | 55.3 |
| 06 | 205 46.5 | 12.7 | N15 22.5 | 8.3 | 55.3 |
| 07 | 220 18.2 | 12.6 | 15 30.8 | 8.2 | 55.3 |
| 08 | 234 49.8 | 12.6 | 15 39.0 | 8.2 | 55.3 |
| M 09 | 249 21.4 | 12.5 | 15 47.2 | 8.2 | 55.4 |
| O 10 | 263 52.9 | 12.4 | 15 55.4 | 8.0 | 55.4 |
| N 11 | 278 24.3 | 12.3 | 16 03.4 | 8.0 | 55.4 |
| D 12 | 292 55.6 | 12.3 | N16 11.4 | 7.9 | 55.4 |
| A 13 | 307 26.9 | 12.2 | 16 19.3 | 7.9 | 55.5 |
| Y 14 | 321 58.1 | 12.2 | 16 27.2 | 7.8 | 55.5 |
| 15 | 336 29.3 | 12.1 | 16 35.0 | 7.7 | 55.5 |
| 16 | 351 00.4 | 12.0 | 16 42.7 | 7.6 | 55.6 |
| 17 | 5 31.4 | 11.9 | 16 50.3 | 7.6 | 55.6 |
| 18 | 20 02.3 | 11.9 | N16 57.9 | 7.5 | 55.6 |
| 19 | 34 33.2 | 11.7 | 17 05.4 | 7.4 | 55.6 |
| 20 | 49 03.9 | 11.8 | 17 12.8 | 7.3 | 55.7 |
| 21 | 63 34.7 | 11.6 | 17 20.1 | 7.3 | 55.7 |
| 22 | 78 05.3 | 11.6 | 17 27.4 | 7.1 | 55.7 |
| 23 | 92 35.9 | 11.5 | 17 34.5 | 7.2 | 55.7 |
| | S.D. | 14.8 | 15.0 | | 15.1 |

**Fig. 10.4** *Nautical Almanac* extract: moon's GHA and Dec.

## ALTITUDE CORRECTION TABLES 0°–35°—MOON

| App. Alt. | °–24° | 25°–29° | 30° |
|---|---|---|---|
| | Corrⁿ | Corrⁿ | |
| 00 | 62·2 | **25** 60·8 | **30** |
| 10 | 62·1 | 60·8 | |
| 20 | 62·1 | 60·7 | |
| 30 | 62·1 | 60·7 | |
| 40 | 62·0 | 60·6 | |
| 50 | 62·0 | 60·6 | |
| 00 | 62·0 | **26** 60·5 | **31** |
| 10 | 61·9 | 60·4 | |
| 20 | 61·9 | 60·4 | |
| 30 | 61·9 | 60·3 | |
| 40 | 61·8 | 60·3 | |
| 50 | 61·8 | 60·2 | |
| 00 | 61·7 | **27** 60·1 | **32** |
| 10 | 61·7 | 60·1 | |
| 20 | 61·6 | 60·0 | |
| 30 | 61·6 | 59·9 | |
| 40 | 61·5 | 59·9 | |
| 50 | 61·5 | 59·8 | |

| H.P. | U | L | U | L |
|---|---|---|---|---|
| 55·5 | | 2·2 | 2·4 2·3 | 2· |
| 55·8 | | 2·4 | 2·8 2·4 | 2· |
| 56·1 | | 2·6 | 3·1 2·6 | 3· |
| 56·4 | | 2·8 | 3·5 2·8 | 3· |
| 56·7 | | 3·0 | 3·8 3·0 | 3· |

**Fig. 10.5** *Nautical Almanac* extract: moon altitude correction tables.

page of the almanac, under the heading *Moon*. Factors v and d are also tabulated hourly together with GHA and declination (Fig 10.4).

There is also a separate altitude correction table for the moon (Fig 10.5).

As for the sun, either the upper or lower limb is used for the sight. The following example shows the procedure for a moon sight:

*Example 10f*

On 17 February at 13h 54m 20s GMT in DR position 50° 10′ N 25° 15′ W the sextant altitude of the moon's lower limb was 27° 40′.2. Index error − 2′.0, height of eye 2.0 metres. What is the intercept and azimuth?

Using the moon column for 17 February, write down GHA and Dec for 13h together with v and d and also HP (Fig 10.4).

Proceed as for a sun sight but use the moon column in the increments table. Find Hc and Zn from AP 3270 Volume 3.

| GHA | 13h | 307° 26′.9 | Dec | N16° 19′.3 | HP 55.5 |
|---|---|---|---|---|---|
| Incre | 54m 20s | +12° 57′.9 | d +7.9 | +7′.2 | |
| v 12.2 | | 11′.1 | | − N16° 26′.5 | |
| | | 320° 35′.9 | | | |
| CP long W | | 25° 35′.9 | | | |
| LHA | | 295° | | | |

| | | |
|---|---|---|
| Hc | 28° 11′ | |
| d + 45 | + 20′ | |
| Tab alt | 28° 31′ | |
| Z = 99°, Zn = 099° T | | |

Correct the sextant altitude as far as apparent altitude:

| Sextant altitude lower limb | 27° 40′.2 | |
|---|---|---|
| IE − 2′.0 | | |
| Dip − 2′.5 | | − 4′.5 |
| Apparent altitude (AA) | | 27° 35′.7 |

Refer to the top left-hand block of the *Altitude Correction Tables* for the moon (Fig 10.5). Apparent altitude is tabulated down each column in degrees, with minutes marked in tens down the sides of the table. The top of each column is marked for every 5° for example 0°–4°.

The correction for an apparent altitude of 27° 35′.7 will be in the column headed 25°–29° under 27° between 30′ and 40′ (shown at the side of the table). A little interpolation is necessary to find the correction which is 59′.9.

The correction for horizontal parallax (HP) is found in the same column further down the table under the heading L or U (lower or upper limb). As the lower limb was observed, the correction will be under L opposite HP 55.5. The correction is 2′.4.

These two corrections are always added to apparent altitude, but if the upper limb has been used for the sight, 30′ is subtracted.

Tabulated altitude is compared with true altitude to find the intercept.

| Sextant altitude lower limb | 27° 40′.2 | |
|---|---|---|
| IE dip | | − 4′.5 |
| AA | | 27° 35′.7 |
| corrn | | +59′.9 |
| HP corrn | | 2′.4 |
| True alt | | 28° 38′.0 |
| Tab alt | | 28° 31′.0 |
| Intercept | | 7′.0T Azimuth 099°T |

**Latitude by meridian altitude of the moon** There are a number of days during a lunar month when a meridian altitude of the moon can be observed during daylight hours. As with the sun, this will provide latitude, and if a simultaneous sight of the sun is taken, the boat's observed position can be found. The procedure is as follows:

*Example 10g*

Find the time of the moon's meridian passage on 30 August in DR position 50° 25′N 27° 00′W.

The local mean time (LMT) of meridian passage

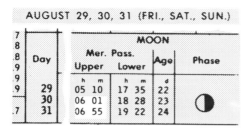

AUGUST 29, 30, 31 (FRI., SAT., SUN.)

| Day | MOON | | | |
|-----|------|------|-----|-------|
| | Mer. Pass. | | Age | Phase |
| | Upper | Lower | | |
| | h m | h m | d | |
| 29 | 05 10 | 17 35 | 22 | |
| 30 | 06 01 | 18 28 | 23 | |
| 31 | 06 55 | 19 22 | 24 | |

**Fig. 10.6** *Nautical Almanac* extract: moon meridian passage.

of the moon is shown on the daily page next to meridian passage of the sun. Upper and lower passage is shown, upper passage being the one used to find latitude. It is tabulated for three days on each page (Fig 10.6).

The tabulated time of 06h 01m is the local time on the Greenwich Meridian. Unlike meridian passage for the sun, it cannot be regarded as local time on every meridian because the moon takes in excess of 24 hours to complete one circuit of the earth. To find the local time of transit on other meridians, a proportion of the daily time difference is used:

| | |
|---|---|
| Moon meridian passage 30 August | 06h 01m |
| Moon meridian passage 31 August | 06h 55m |
| Daily difference | 54m |

Proportion of the daily difference for longitude 27°W $\frac{27}{360} \times 54m = 4m$

| | |
|---|---|
| Moon meridian passage 30 August | 06h 01m LMT at 0° |
| Difference for long 27°W | +04m |
| Moon meridian passage 30 August | 06h 05m LMT at 27°W |

Longitude is applied to LMT to find GMT:

| | |
|---|---|
| Moon meridian passage 30 August | 06h 05m LMT at 27°W |
| Longitude as time | +1h 48m |
| Moon meridian passage 30 August | 07h 53m GMT at 27°W |

In the above example, the day following 30 August was used to find the daily difference, because longitude was west. For longitude east the previous day is used:

*Example 10h*
*Use the extracts at the back of the book.*
On 16 February in DR position 48° 15′S 120° 00′E, what is the time of meridian passage of the moon?

| | |
|---|---|
| Meridian passage 16 February | 15 51 |
| Meridian passage 15 February | 15 07 |
| Daily difference | 44 |

$$\frac{120}{360} \times 44 = 15m$$

| | |
|---|---|
| | 15 51 |
| | −15 |
| | 15.36 LMT at DR |
| Long in time | −8 00 |
| Meridian passage 07 36 GMT at DR | |

As with the sun, the moon is observed a little before the calculated time of meridian passage and the time of the greatest altitude recorded.

When GMT of meridian passage has been found, the procedure is the same as for the sun:

*Example 10i*
On 15 February in DR position 48° 15′S, 120° 03′E a meridian altitude sight of the moon's lower limb taken at 06h 52m 10s gave a sextant altitude of 33° 09′.3 bearing north. Index error −2′.0, HE 2.5 metres. Find the latitude.

| | | | |
|---|---|---|---|
| SA moon's LL | 33° 09′.3N | | |
| IE −2′.0 | | | |
| Dip −2′.8 | −4′.8 | Dec | 7° 43′.1 |
| AA | 33° 04′.5 | d +10.5 | +9′.2 |
| corrn | 57′.4 | | 7° 52′.3 |
| HP 54.4 | 1′.3 | | |
| TA | 34° 03′.2N | | |
| From 90° | 90° | | |
| TZD | 55° 56′.8S (bearing reversed) | | |
| Dec | 7° 52′.3N | | |
| Latitude | 48° 04′.5S | | |

# Exercise

*Use extracts at the back of the book.*

**10.1**  On 20 May at 20h 53m 55s GMT in DR position 49° 40'N 3° 40'W the sextant altitude of Venus was 23° 02'.5, IE − 2.6, HE 2.0 metres. Find the chosen position, intercept and azimuth.

**10.2**  On 15 February at 17h 53m 15s GMT in DR position 49° 50'N 130° 00'W the sextant altitude of Mars was 17° 12'.5, IE − 2'.1, HE 2.5 metres. Find the chosen position, intercept and azimuth.

**10.3**  a) On 19 May in DR position 49° 40'N 6° 25'W dawn twilight sights are planned. Select the three best placed stars and give their approximate altitudes and azimuths.

b)  The following observations were made later. Find the chosen positions, intercepts and azimuths ready for plotting:

| GMT | Star | Sextant altitude |
|---|---|---|
| 03 54 42 | Altair | 48° 35'.9 |
| 03 55 10 | Mirfak | 21° 04'.9 |
| 03 55 50 | Arcturus | 24° 18'.8 |

IE − 2'.6, HE 2.0 metres.

**10.4**  On 31 August (GD) at 20h 54m 50s GMT in DR position 49° 45'S 165° 00'E, the sextant altitude of the moon's LL was 18° 28'.7, IE − 1'.9, HE 2.5 metres. Find the chosen position, intercept and azimuth.

**10.5**  a) On 16 February in DR position 56° 00'S 44° 30'W find the GMT of the moon's meridian passage.

b) A sight was taken at 18h 55m 20s giving a sextant altitude of the moon's LL of 18° 49'.5 bearing north. IE − 1'.9, HE 2.5 metres. What was the observed latitude?

# 11 Position without a Chart

## Plotting sheet

Charts are not produced for the middle of the ocean. A plotting sheet, a portion of which is shown in Fig 11.1, is an effective substitute. This plotting sheet, which is published by the Hydrographic Office, consists of a large blank area which is bordered with latitude and longitude scales similar to a chart. Several latitude scales are shown which are based on mercator projection, so it is essential that the correct scale for the latitude concerned is used when plotting on the sheet. The longitude scale shows minutes of longitude with a degree sign marked every 60 minutes. The longitude can be entered as required by the navigator.

The plotting sheet is used in the same way as a chart. The whole degree of longitude nearest to the chosen longitude is written next to the degree sign on the longitude scale (Fig 11.2). Any part of the longitude scale can be used. A horizontal line represents latitude (Fig 11.3). The latitude scale is used for measuring distance. Fig 11.4 shows a plot using simultaneous star sights. Three plotting sheets are available:

Chart 5331 for latitudes 0° to 30°
Chart 5332 for latitudes 30° to 48°
Chart 5333 for latitudes 48° to 60°

Charts with the same numbers but suffixed with the letter A have the useful addition of a key central parallel of latitude, meridians of longitude and two compass roses.

## Squared paper

Plotting can be done on squared paper which has the advantage that plots can be expanded. Squares are used to represent latitude. An adjustment has to be made to longitude. On the earth's surface meridians of longitude converge at the poles. The angular difference between them, difference of longitude (D Long), remains the same, but the actual distance in miles, known as departure (Dep), decreases as latitude increases.

The relationship between D Long and Dep can be calculated arithmetically:

$$Dep = D \ Long \times cos \ lat$$

$$D \ Long = \frac{Dep}{cos \ lat}$$

It can also be found by reference to the traverse tables found in Norie's Tables and similar publications.

## Using traverse tables

*Example 11a*

When in latitude 40°N it is required to know the departure for a difference of longitude of 7'.0.

1  Firstly find the page in the tables which corresponds to latitude. The latitude is

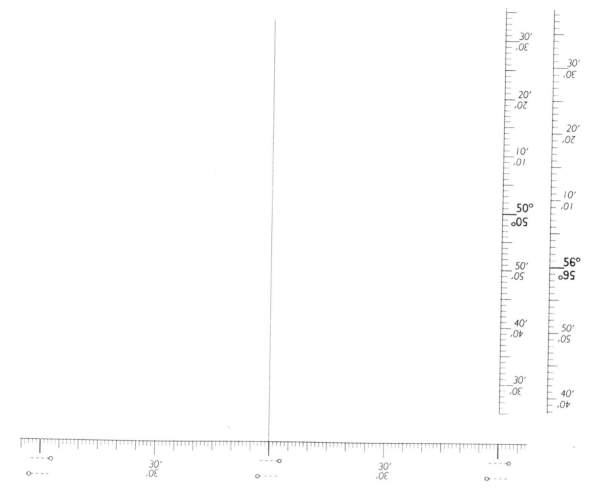

**Fig. 11.1** Part of a plotting sheet.

represented by bold figures at the top or bottom of the table. Refer to Fig 11.5 which is an extract from *Norie's Tables*.

2 Each page covers two latitudes, one tabulated at the top of the page and one at the bottom.

Latitude 40° is at the top of the page. The headings to the columns referring to this latitude are also at the *top* of the page. The headings in italics '*D Lon*' and '*Dep*' are the ones required (Fig 11.6). (For the time being ignore the

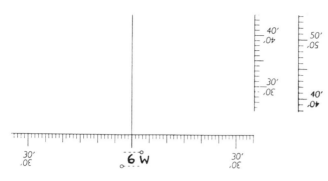

**Fig. 11.2** Using the longitude scale.

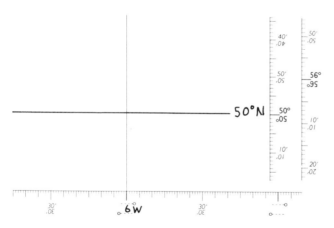

**Fig. 11.3** Plotting chosen latitude.

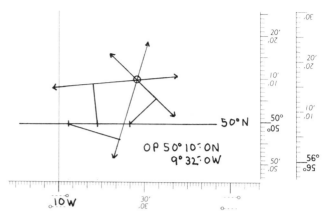

**Fig. 11.4** A simultaneous sight.

OP 50° 10′·0N
9° 32′·0W

In the following example the required latitude is at the bottom of the page (Use extract 11.5.):

*Example 11b*
When in DR latitude 50°N it is required to know the difference in longitude for a departure of 37.9M.

**1** The latitude is found at the bottom of the page so the headings at the bottom of the page apply. There is no heading for the middle column which is not used.
**2** The departure of 37.9M is found in the *Dep* column. The D Long, which is 59′.0, is to the left in the column labelled *D Lon*.

**Finding DR position after a run**
Traverse tables can also be used to find a DR position after a distance run between two points.

*Example 11c*
At morning twilight, a boat steering a course of 130°T, established her position as 49° 55′.6N 7° 15′.2W. She continued to sail on the same course

headings in bold type underneath.) Under the D Lon column, find 7′.0. The Dep of 5.4 miles is next to it. This would represent 5.4 squares on the paper (Fig 11.7). When latitude is at the top of the page, the third column (which had no heading) is not used.
**3** If it is required to know the difference of longitude given the departure, the procedure is reversed.

**40°**

# TRAVERSE TABLE
### 40 Degrees

320° / 220° ↑     040° / 140°    2h 40m

| Dist. | D. Lat. | Dep. | Dist. | D. Lat. | Dep. | Dist. | D. Lat. | Dep. | Dist. | D. Lat. | Dep. | Dist. | D. Lat. | Dep. |
|---|---|---|---|---|---|---|---|---|---|---|---|---|---|---|
| 1 | 00 8 | 00 6 | 61 | 46 7 | 39 2 | 121 | 92 7 | 77 8 | 181 | 138 7 | 116 3 | 241 | 184 6 | 154 9 |
| 2 | 01 5 | 01 3 | 62 | 47 5 | 39 9 | 122 | 93 5 | 78 4 | 182 | 139 4 | 117 0 | 242 | 185 4 | 155 6 |
| 3 | 02 3 | 01 9 | 63 | 48 3 | 40 5 | 123 | 94 2 | 79 1 | 183 | 140 2 | 117 6 | 243 | 186 1 | 156 2 |
| 4 | 03 1 | 02 6 | 64 | 49 0 | 41 1 | 124 | 95 0 | 79 7 | 184 | 141 0 | 118 3 | 244 | 186 9 | 156 8 |
| 5 | 03 8 | 03 2 | 65 | 49 8 | 41 8 | 125 | 95 8 | 80 3 | 185 | 141 7 | 118 9 | 245 | 187 7 | 157 5 |
| 6 | 04 6 | 03 9 | 66 | 50 6 | 42 4 | 126 | 96 5 | 81 0 | 186 | 142 5 | 119 6 | 246 | 188 4 | 158 1 |
| 7 | 05 4 | 04 5 | 67 | 51 3 | 43 1 | 127 | 97 3 | 81 6 | 187 | 143 3 | 120 2 | 247 | 189 2 | 158 8 |
| 8 | 06 1 | 05 1 | 68 | 52 1 | 43 7 | 128 | 98 1 | 82 3 | 188 | 144 0 | 120 8 | 248 | 190 0 | 159 4 |
| 9 | 06 9 | 05 8 | 69 | 52 9 | 44 4 | 129 | 98 8 | 82 9 | 189 | 144 8 | 121 5 | 249 | 190 7 | 160 1 |
| 10 | 07 7 | 06 4 | 70 | 53 6 | 45 0 | 130 | 99 6 | 83 6 | 190 | 145 5 | 122 1 | 250 | 191 5 | 160 7 |
| 11 | 08 4 | 07 1 | 71 | 54 4 | 45 6 | 131 | 100 4 | 84 2 | 191 | 146 3 | 122 8 | 251 | 192 3 | 161 3 |
| 12 | 09 2 | 07 7 | 72 | 55 2 | 46 3 | 132 | 101 1 | 84 8 | 192 | 147 1 | 123 4 | 252 | 193 0 | 162 0 |
| 13 | 10 0 | 08 4 | 73 | 55 9 | 46 9 | 133 | 101 9 | 85 5 | 193 | 147 8 | 124 1 | 253 | 193 8 | 162 6 |
| 14 | 10 7 | 09 0 | 74 | 56 7 | 47 6 | 134 | 102 6 | 86 1 | 194 | 148 6 | 124 7 | 254 | 194 6 | 163 3 |
| 15 | 11 5 | 09 6 | 75 | 57 5 | 48 2 | 135 | 103 4 | 86 8 | 195 | 149 4 | 125 3 | 255 | 195 3 | 163 9 |
| 16 | 12 3 | 10 3 | 76 | 58 2 | 48 9 | 136 | 104 2 | 87 4 | 196 | 150 1 | 126 0 | 256 | 196 1 | 164 6 |
| 17 | 13 0 | 10 9 | 77 | 59 0 | 49 5 | 137 | 104 9 | 88 1 | 197 | 150 9 | 126 6 | 257 | 196 9 | 165 2 |
| 18 | 13 8 | 11 6 | 78 | 59 8 | 50 1 | 138 | 105 7 | 88 7 | 198 | 151 7 | 127 3 | 258 | 197 6 | 165 8 |
| 19 | 14 6 | 12 2 | 79 | 60 5 | 50 8 | 139 | 106 5 | 89 3 | 199 | 152 4 | 127 9 | 259 | 198 4 | 166 5 |
| 20 | 15 3 | 12 9 | 80 | 61 3 | 51 4 | 140 | 107 2 | 90 0 | 200 | 153 2 | 128 6 | 260 | 199 2 | 167 1 |
| 21 | 16 1 | 13 5 | 81 | 62 0 | 52 1 | 141 | 108 0 | 90 6 | 201 | 154 0 | 129 2 | 261 | 199 9 | 167 8 |
| 22 | 16 9 | 14 1 | 82 | 62 8 | 52 7 | 142 | 108 8 | 91 3 | 202 | 154 7 | 129 8 | 262 | 200 7 | 168 4 |
| 23 | 17 6 | 14 8 | 83 | 63 6 | 53 4 | 143 | 109 5 | 91 9 | 203 | 155 5 | 130 5 | 263 | 201 5 | 169 1 |
| 24 | 18 4 | 15 4 | 84 | 64 3 | 54 0 | 144 | 110 3 | 92 6 | 204 | 156 3 | 131 1 | 264 | 202 2 | 169 7 |
| 25 | 19 2 | 16 1 | 85 | 65 1 | 54 6 | 145 | 111 1 | 93 2 | 205 | 157 0 | 131 8 | 265 | 203 0 | 170 3 |
| 26 | 19 9 | 16 7 | 86 | 65 9 | 55 3 | 146 | 111 8 | 93 8 | 206 | 157 8 | 132 4 | 266 | 203 8 | 171 0 |
| 27 | 20 7 | 17 4 | 87 | 66 6 | 55 9 | 147 | 112 6 | 94 5 | 207 | 158 6 | 133 1 | 267 | 204 5 | 171 6 |
| 28 | 21 4 | 18 0 | 88 | 67 4 | 56 6 | 148 | 113 4 | 95 1 | 208 | 159 3 | 133 7 | 268 | 205 3 | 172 3 |
| 29 | 22 2 | 18 6 | 89 | 68 2 | 57 2 | 149 | 114 1 | 95 8 | 209 | 160 1 | 134 3 | 269 | 206 1 | 172 9 |
| 30 | 23 0 | 19 3 | 90 | 68 9 | 57 9 | 150 | 114 9 | 96 4 | 210 | 160 9 | 135 0 | 270 | 206 8 | 173 6 |
| 31 | 23 7 | 19 9 | 91 | 69 7 | 58 5 | 151 | 115 7 | 97 1 | 211 | 161 6 | 135 6 | 271 | 207 6 | 174 2 |
| 32 | 24 5 | 20 6 | 92 | 70 5 | 59 1 | 152 | 116 4 | 97 7 | 212 | 162 4 | 136 3 | 272 | 208 4 | 174 8 |
| 33 | 25 3 | 21 2 | 93 | 71 2 | 59 8 | 153 | 117 2 | 98 3 | 213 | 163 2 | 136 9 | 273 | 209 1 | 175 5 |
| 34 | 26 0 | 21 9 | 94 | 72 0 | 60 4 | 154 | 118 0 | 99 0 | 214 | 163 9 | 137 6 | 274 | 209 9 | 176 1 |
| 35 | 26 8 | 22 5 | 95 | 72 8 | 61 1 | 155 | 118 7 | 99 6 | 215 | 164 7 | 138 2 | 275 | 210 7 | 176 8 |
| 36 | 27 6 | 23 1 | 96 | 73 5 | 61 7 | 156 | 119 5 | 100 3 | 216 | 165 5 | 138 8 | 276 | 211 4 | 177 4 |
| 37 | 28 3 | 23 8 | 97 | 74 3 | 62 4 | 157 | 120 3 | 100 9 | 217 | 166 2 | 139 5 | 277 | 212 2 | 178 1 |
| 38 | 29 1 | 24 4 | 98 | 75 1 | 63 0 | 158 | 121 0 | 101 6 | 218 | 167 0 | 140 1 | 278 | 213 0 | 178 7 |
| 39 | 29 9 | 25 1 | 99 | 75 8 | 63 6 | 159 | 121 8 | 102 2 | 219 | 167 8 | 140 8 | 279 | 213 7 | 179 3 |
| 40 | 30 6 | 25 7 | 100 | 76 6 | 64 3 | 160 | 122 6 | 102 8 | 220 | 168 5 | 141 4 | 280 | 214 5 | 180 0 |
| 41 | 31 4 | 26 4 | 101 | 77 4 | 64 9 | 161 | 123 3 | 103 5 | 221 | 169 3 | 142 1 | 281 | 215 3 | 180 6 |
| 42 | 32 2 | 27 0 | 102 | 78 1 | 65 6 | 162 | 124 1 | 104 1 | 222 | 170 1 | 142 7 | 282 | 216 0 | 181 3 |
| 43 | 32 9 | 27 6 | 103 | 78 9 | 66 2 | 163 | 124 9 | 104 8 | 223 | 170 8 | 143 3 | 283 | 216 8 | 181 9 |
| 44 | 33 7 | 28 3 | 104 | 79 7 | 66 8 | 164 | 125 6 | 105 4 | 224 | 171 6 | 144 0 | 284 | 217 6 | 182 6 |
| 45 | 34 5 | 28 9 | 105 | 80 4 | 67 5 | 165 | 126 4 | 106 1 | 225 | 172 4 | 144 6 | 285 | 218 3 | 183 2 |
| 46 | 35 2 | 29 6 | 106 | 81 2 | 68 1 | 166 | 127 2 | 106 7 | 226 | 173 1 | 145 3 | 286 | 219 1 | 183 8 |
| 47 | 36 0 | 30 2 | 107 | 82 0 | 68 8 | 167 | 127 9 | 107 3 | 227 | 173 9 | 145 9 | 287 | 219 9 | 184 5 |
| 48 | 36 8 | 30 9 | 108 | 82 7 | 69 4 | 168 | 128 7 | 108 0 | 228 | 174 7 | 146 6 | 288 | 220 6 | 185 1 |
| 49 | 37 5 | 31 5 | 109 | 83 5 | 70 1 | 169 | 129 5 | 108 6 | 229 | 175 4 | 147 2 | 289 | 221 4 | 185 8 |
| 50 | 38 3 | 32 1 | 110 | 84 3 | 70 7 | 170 | 130 2 | 109 3 | 230 | 176 2 | 147 8 | 290 | 222 2 | 186 4 |
| 51 | 39 1 | 32 8 | 111 | 85 0 | 71 3 | 171 | 131 0 | 109 9 | 231 | 177 0 | 148 5 | 291 | 222 9 | 187 1 |
| 52 | 39 8 | 33 4 | 112 | 85 8 | 72 0 | 172 | 131 8 | 110 6 | 232 | 177 7 | 149 1 | 292 | 223 7 | 187 7 |
| 53 | 40 6 | 34 1 | 113 | 86 6 | 72 6 | 173 | 132 5 | 111 2 | 233 | 178 5 | 149 8 | 293 | 224 5 | 188 3 |
| 54 | 41 4 | 34 7 | 114 | 87 3 | 73 3 | 174 | 133 3 | 111 8 | 234 | 179 3 | 150 4 | 294 | 225 2 | 189 0 |
| 55 | 42 1 | 35 4 | 115 | 88 1 | 73 9 | 175 | 134 1 | 112 5 | 235 | 180 0 | 151 1 | 295 | 226 0 | 189 6 |
| 56 | 42 9 | 36 0 | 116 | 88 9 | 74 6 | 176 | 134 8 | 113 1 | 236 | 180 8 | 151 7 | 296 | 226 7 | 190 3 |
| 57 | 43 7 | 36 6 | 117 | 89 6 | 75 2 | 177 | 135 6 | 113 8 | 237 | 181 6 | 152 3 | 297 | 227 5 | 190 9 |
| 58 | 44 4 | 37 3 | 118 | 90 4 | 75 8 | 178 | 136 4 | 114 4 | 238 | 182 3 | 153 0 | 298 | 228 3 | 191 6 |
| 59 | 45 2 | 37 9 | 119 | 91 2 | 76 5 | 179 | 137 1 | 115 1 | 239 | 183 1 | 153 6 | 299 | 229 0 | 192 2 |
| 60 | 46 0 | 38 6 | 120 | 91 9 | 77 1 | 180 | 137 9 | 115 7 | 240 | 183 9 | 154 3 | 300 | 229 8 | 192 8 |
| Dist. | Dep. | D. Lat. | Dist. | Dep. | D. Lat. | Dist. | Dep. | D. Lat. | Dist. | Dep. | D. Lat. | Dist. | Dep. | D. Lat. |

**50°**

310° / 230°    50 Degrees    050° / 130°    3h 20m

**Fig. 11.5** *Norie's Tables* extract.

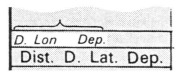

**Fig. 11.6** Use *italic* headings.

| D. Lon | Dep. | |
|---|---|---|
| **Dist.** | **D. Lat.** | **Dep.** |
| 1 | 00·8 | 00·6 |
| 2 | 01·5 | 01·3 |
| 3 | 02·3 | 01·9 |
| 4 | 03·1 | 02·6 |
| 5 | 03·8 | 03·2 |
| 6 | 04·6 | 03·9 |
| 7 | 05·4 | 04·5 |
| 8 | 06·1 | 05·1 |
| 9 | 06·9 | 05·8 |
| 10 | 07·7 | 06·4 |

**Fig. 11.7** A difference of longitude of 7'.0 = 5.4M of departure.

for a further 25M. What was the DR position at that time?

1 Ignore the large figures on each page which represent latitude. Find the boat's course in one of the boxes in the corners at the top or bottom of the page (Fig 11.8). In this case, the course of 130°T is in the bottom right-hand corner of the page.

2 The boxes represent quadrants of the compass, so 130° is in the south east quadrant. This means that the latitude will change in a southerly direction and the longitude in an easterly direction.

3 Refer to the headed columns. Ignore the italic headings on the column and concentrate on the bold headings: **Dist, D. Lat, Dep** on the top and **Dist, Dep, D. Lat** on the bottom. If the course is at the top of the page, then the top headings apply. If, as in the case of the example, 130° is at the bottom of the page, then the bottom headings apply. Distance travelled was 25M. Find 25.0 in the Dist column. The bottom headings apply so departure (Dep) will be 19.2M and difference of latitude (D Lat ) 16'.1.

4 Difference of latitude can be applied immediately:

| Latitude at twilight | 49° 55'.6N |
|---|---|
| D Lat south | −16'.1S |
| DR latitude | 49° 39'.5N |

5 Departure has to be converted to difference of longitude before it can be applied. The page for latitude 50° has been used but if strict accuracy is required, an interpolation should be done between latitudes 49° and 50°:

Latitude 50° Departure 19.2 = D Long 30'.0

| Longitude at twilight | 7° 15'.2W |
|---|---|
| D Long East | −30'.0E |
| DR longitude | 6° 45'.2W |

Plot the following on squared paper:

*Example 11d*
*Sun-run-sun sight. Use extract 11.5.*
In a DR position 50° 10'N 6° 35'W, a morning sight of the sun gave the following results:

CP 50°N 6° 06'W; intercept 20M away; azimuth 096°T

The boat then sailed on a course of 041°T for 24 miles when a midday sight of the sun gave the latitude as 50° 28'.0N.

1 Draw a horizontal line across the paper to represent the CP latitude (50°N). Somewhere along this line mark the CP longitude (6° 06'W).

| | Dist. | Dep. | D. Lat. | Dist. | Dep. | D. Lat. | Dist. | Dep. | D. Lat. | Dist. | Dep. | D. Lat. | Dist. | Dep. |
|---|---|---|---|---|---|---|---|---|---|---|---|---|---|---|
| | 21 | 16.1 | 13.5 | 81 | 62.0 | 52.1 | 141 | 108.0 | 90.6 | 201 | 154.0 | 129.2 | 261 | 19.9 |
| | 22 | 16.9 | 14.1 | 82 | 62.8 | 52.7 | 142 | 108.8 | 91.3 | 202 | 154.7 | 129.8 | 262 | 20.0 |
| | 23 | 17.6 | 14.8 | 83 | 63.6 | 53.4 | 143 | 109.5 | 91.9 | 203 | 155.5 | 130.5 | 263 | 20.1 |
| | 24 | 18.4 | 15.4 | 84 | 64.3 | 54.0 | 144 | 110.3 | 92.6 | 204 | 156.3 | 131.1 | 264 | 20.2 |
| | 25 | 19.2 | 16.1 | 85 | 65.1 | 54.6 | 145 | 111.1 | 93.2 | 205 | 157.0 | 131.8 | 265 | 20.3 |
| | 26 | 19.9 | 16.7 | 86 | 65.9 | 55.3 | 146 | 111.8 | 93.8 | 206 | 157.8 | 132.4 | 266 | 20.3 |
| | 27 | 20.7 | 17.4 | 87 | 66.6 | 55.9 | 147 | 112.6 | 94.5 | 207 | 158.6 | 133.1 | 267 | 20.4 |
| | 28 | 21.4 | 18.0 | 88 | 67.4 | 56.6 | 148 | 113.4 | 95.1 | 208 | 159.3 | 133.7 | 268 | 20.5 |
| | 29 | 22.2 | 18.6 | 89 | 68.2 | 57.2 | 149 | 114.1 | 95.8 | 209 | 160.1 | 134.3 | 269 | 20.6 |
| | 30 | 23.0 | 19.3 | 90 | 68.9 | 57.9 | 150 | 114.9 | 96.4 | 210 | 160.9 | 135.0 | 270 | 20.6 |
| | 57 | 43.7 | 36.6 | 117 | 89.6 | 75.2 | 177 | 135.6 | 113.8 | 237 | 181.6 | 152.3 | 297 | 22.7 |
| | 58 | 44.4 | 37.3 | 118 | 90.4 | 75.8 | 178 | 136.4 | 114.4 | 238 | 182.3 | 153.0 | 298 | 22.8 |
| | 59 | 45.2 | 37.9 | 119 | 91.2 | 76.5 | 179 | 137.1 | 115.1 | 239 | 183.1 | 153.6 | 299 | 22.9 |
| | 60 | 46.0 | 38.6 | 120 | 91.9 | 77.1 | 180 | 137.9 | 115.7 | 240 | 183.9 | 154.3 | 300 | 22.9 |
| Dist. | Dep. | D. Lat. | Dist. | Dep. | D. Lat. | Dist. | Dep. | D. Lat. | Dist. | Dep. | D. Lat. | Dist. | De. | |
| D. Lon | | Dep. | D. Lon | | Dep. | D. Lon | | Dep. | D. Lon | | Dep. | D. Lon | | |

310° / 230°     50 Degrees     050° / 130°

**Fig. 11.8** Finding position after a run.

From the chosen position, lay off a line in the direction of 276° (the direction of the intercept away from the azimuth 096°).

2 Assuming each square on the paper represents 1M, measure 20 squares across or down the paper (not diagonally) and mark this distance along the line of azimuth. Plot the position line at a right angle to the direction of azimuth. *In Fig 11.9 the squares are 10M.*

3 From any point on this position line, plot the course and distance run, which is 041°T, for 24M. For the 24M, measure 24 squares either across or down the paper and then mark the distance off along the course.

4 Transfer the first position line to the end of the distance run.

5 Plot the second position line at 50° 28'.0N by counting 28 squares from the 50°N datum line.

6 Draw a circle around the intersection of the two position lines. This is the observed position at midday.

7 Latitude can be read off directly, 50° 28'.0N.

8 Longitude has to be found by converting to departure. This is done by counting the number of squares horizontally, between the chosen position longitude and the observed position. There appear to be about 3.2 small squares, which is 3.2 miles of departure, to the west of the chosen position. Using latitude 50°, the departure is converted to D long:

Dep 3.2M = D Long 5'.0

9 Apply D Long to the chosen longitude:

| Chosen longitude | 6° 06'.0W |
|---|---|
| difference of long | + 5'.0W |
| Observed longitude | 6° 11'.0W |

10 Observed position at midday 50° 28'.0N 6° 11'.0W

See Fig 11.9.

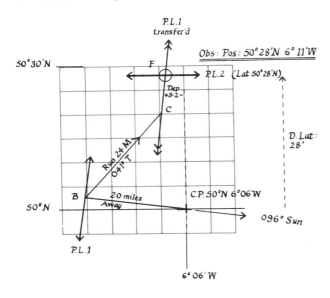

**Fig. 11.9** Plotting a sun-run-sun sight on squared paper. One square equals 5 miles.

*Example 11e*
Two simultaneous sights.

When in DR position 40° 20'N 18° 30'W, the following sights were taken:

| Body | Chosen Lat | Chosen Long | Intercept | Azimuth |
|------|-----------|-------------|-----------|---------|
| Sun | 40°N | 18° 28'.0W | 18M Towards | 113°T |
| Moon | 40°N | 18° 53'.0W | 27M Away | 195°T |

What is the observed position?

1  Mark the datum latitude (40°N) across the paper.
2  At any point along this line mark the sun's chosen position (A).

3  Work out the D Long between the sun and the moon:

| | |
|---|---|
| Sun | 18° 28'.0W |
| Moon | 18° 53'.0W |
| D Long | 25'.0W |

4  Using the page in the traverse tables for 40° latitude and the top italic headings, convert D Long to Dep:

D Long 25'.0 = Dep 19.2M

5  From the sun's position at A, count 19.2 squares to the west and mark the moon's chosen position (B).

6  Plot the intercepts and azimuths as before and mark the observed position (F).

7  Measure the difference of latitude in minutes from the 40°N latitude. There are 15 squares, which equals 15'.0, in a northerly direction:

| | |
|---|---|
| Sun CP latitude | 40° 00'.0N |
| D Lat | +15'.0N |
| Observed latitude | 40° 15'.0N |

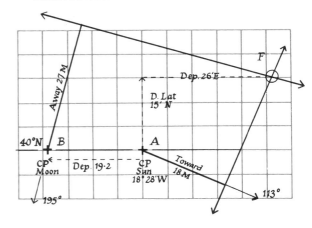

**Fig. 11.10** Plotting two simultaneous sights on squared paper. One square equals 5 miles.

**8** As F is to the east of the sun's position A, departure and hence D Long will be east. The number of squares of departure between A and F is 26. This is converted to D Long by using the latitude 40° page, top italic headings:

Dep 26.0M = D Long 34'.0E

**9** Apply D Long to the sun's chosen longitude to find the observed longitude:

| | |
|---|---|
| Sun's CP long | 18° 28'.0W |
| D Long | 34'.0E |
| Observed longitude | 17° 54'.0W |

**10** Observed position: 40° 15'.0N, 17° 54'.0W. See Fig 11.10.

*Example 11f*
Multiple simultaneous sights.

Any number of simultaneous sights can be plotted on squared paper. The previous method of calculating the moon's position along the latitude datum line by reference to the sun can be used. Another method is to plot the latitude datum line for the chosen latitude as before, but to chose a longitude datum line, preferably a whole degree, which is near to the chosen longitudes of all sights. The following example illustrates this:

| Star | Chosen longitude | Intercept | Azimuth |
|---|---|---|---|
| A | 19° 05'.0W | 8.0A | 173° |
| B | 18° 48'.0W | 12.0A | 238° |
| C | 18° 52'.0W | 12.0T | 083° |
| D | 19° 00'.0W | 14.0T | 011° |

Chosen latitude 40°N

**1** The datum lines will be latitude 40°N and longitude 19°W. These are plotted on the paper.

**2** The difference of longitude between the stars and the datum line is worked out and converted to departure:

| Star | D Long | Dep |
|---|---|---|
| A | 5'.0 W | 3.8 W |
| B | 12'.0 E | 9.2 E |
| C | 8'.0 E | 6.1 E |
| D | – | – |

**3** The chosen position of the four stars is plotted along the latitude datum line.
**4** Intercepts and azimuths are laid off from the chosen positions and the observed position found.
**5** The observed latitude is found by counting the number of squares between the datum line for latitude and the observed position.
**6** The departure of the observed position is found by counting the number of squares between the longitude datum line and the observed position, and then converting them to difference of longitude and applying to the datum longitude:

| | |
|---|---|
| Datum latitude | 40° 00'.0N |
| D Lat | +11'.0N |
| Observed latitude | 40° 11'.0N |
| Datum longitude | 19° 00'.0W |
| D Long | 22'.0E  Dep 17.0E |
| Observed longitude | 18° 38'.0W |

**7** Observed position: 40° 11'.0N, 18° 38'.0W. See Fig 11.11.

*Example 11g*
Finding a Estimated Position (EP) without plotting.

After fixing its position at 36° 05'.0N 25° 14'.0W, a boat travelled 24M on a course of 210°T. There was a current setting in a direction 146°T with a drift of 5M during this period. What was the estimated position at the end of the run?

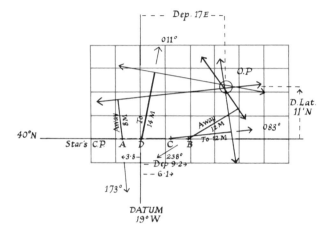

```
                    FROM
                   DATUM
         C.P        19°W
                   D.Lon.   Dep.        DATUM    40°00'N 19°00W
STAR A   19° 05'    5 'W  = 3·8 W       To O.P   D.Lat.   11'N
     B   18°48'    12' E  = 9·2 E       Dep 17 E , in M. Lat 40°
     C   18 52'     8' E  = 6·1 E                 = D.Lon      22'E
     D   19° 00      —       —          ∴ O.P is   40°11'N  18°38'W
```

**Fig. 11.11**  Plotting multiple sights on squared paper.

|                          | Lat         | Long        |
|--------------------------|-------------|-------------|
| Observed position        | 36° 05'.0N  | 25° 14'.0W  |
| Run: 24M on course 210°. | D Lat  20'.8S |           |
|   Dep 12.0M west         |             | D Long 14'.8W |
| Current: 5M in direction 146°. | D Lat  4'.1S |      |
|   Dep 2.8M east          |             | D Long  3'.5E |
| New EP                   | 35° 40'.1N  | 25° 25'.3W  |

*Example 11h*

Finding the Estimated Position (EP) without plotting after several course changes.

A boat's observed position was established as 49° 41'.0N, 17° 24'.0W. She then continued as shown:

| Course | Distance |
|--------|----------|
| 040°T  | 19M      |
| 310°T  | 29M      |
| 040°T  | 18M      |
| 320°T  | 26M      |

During this period the current was estimated at:

| Direction | Speed     | Time    |
|-----------|-----------|---------|
| 140°T     | 1.0 knots | 8 hours |
| 130°T     | 0.5 knots | 6 hours |

What was the EP at the end of the run?

|                       |       | D. Lat |      | Dep  |      |
|-----------------------|-------|--------|------|------|------|
| Course                | Dist  | N      | S    | W    | E    |
| 040° N40°E            | 19M   | 14.6   | —    | —    | 12.2 |
| 310° N50°W            | 29M   | 18.6   | —    | 22.2 | —    |
| 040° N40°E            | 18M   | 13.8   | —    | —    | 11.6 |
| 320° N40°W            | 26M   | 19.9   | —    | 16.7 | —    |
| *Current*             |       |        |      |      |      |
| 140°S 40°E 8 h 1.0k=8M |      | —      | 6.1  | —    | 5.1  |
| 130°S 50°C 6h 0.5k=3M |       | —      | 1.9  | —    | 2.3  |
|                       |       | 66.9   | 8.0  | 38.9 | 31.2 |
|                       |       | −8.0   |      | −31.2 |     |
| D Lat                 |       | 58.9N  |      |      |      |
| Dep                   |       |        |      | 7.7W |      |

Dep 7.7 in mean latitude 50° = D Long 12'.0

|        | Lat         |        | Long        |
|--------|-------------|--------|-------------|
| OP     | 49° 41'.0N  |        | 17° 24'.0W  |
| D Lat  | +58'.9N     | D Long | +12'.0W     |
| New EP | 50° 39'.9N  |        | 17° 36'.0W  |

## Exercise

**11.1** From a given DR position calculate the new DR position after the run shown by using traverse tables:

| | DR Position | | True course | Run Distance in miles |
|---|---|---|---|---|
| a) | 39° 50′.0N | 3° 25′.0E | 040° | 25 |
| b) | 40° 10′.0N | 6° 24′.0W | 140° | 24 |
| c) | 40° 15′.0S | 12° 30′.0E | 230° | 21 |
| d) | 50° 10′.0S | 18° 20′.0W | 130° | 30 |
| e) | 49° 45′.0N | 175° 25′.0E | 310° | 67 |

*Plot the following questions either on squared paper or on the portion of the plotting sheet Fig 11.1.*

**11.2** Approaching Vancouver Island in a DR position 50°N 129°W, a morning sun sight gave a chosen position 50°N 128° 55′.6W, intercept 3.7M towards, azimuth 093°T. The boat then steered a course of 120°T for 18M when a sight of the sun at its meridian passage gave the latitude as 49° 36′.0N. What was the observed position at the time of the meridian passage?

**11.3** Approaching South Island, New Zealand, in DR position 49° 48′S 159° 20′E, a meridian altitude of the sun gave the latitude as 49° 44′.0S. The boat then steered a course of 080°T for 21M when an afternoon sun sight gave the following results: chosen position 50°S 159° 49′.0E, intercept 11.0M towards, azimuth 282°T. What was the observed position at the time of the afternoon sight?

**11.4** When in DR position 50° 15′.0N 38° 39′.9W, evening twilight sights gave:

| Body | Chosen longitude | Intercept | Azimuth |
|---|---|---|---|
| Moon | 38° 39′.9W | 8.3A | 182°T |
| Venus | 37° 55′.5W | 23.5T | 280°T |
| Spica | 37° 50′.6W | 15.5A | 161°T |
| Arcturus | 38° 17′.5W | 11.5A | 132°T |

Find the observed position.

# 12  The Navigator at Work

## Practical application of celestial sights

Good navigation starts with good records. Written records are clearly necessary for a number of purposes. For navigation, accurate details of courses steered, times and distances, altitudes and azimuths, and so on, are needed. For historic record, broader details of passages, times of departure and arrival, names of crew and similar details are wanted. To attempt to incorporate all this in a single book would be cumbersome and confusing. It is better to have more than one record, each for a specific purpose.

The recommended records are:

- A deck log in which the watch leader records all events as they occur.
- A navigator's log in which the navigator records all the information from the deck log and elsewhere, which is necessary to plot the boat's position and progress.
- A boat log in which the skipper records a narrative of each passage, listing the crew, ports visited, times of arrival and departure, interesting occurrences and so on.
- A note book for recording all sights worked, calculations of heights of tides, radio time checks, and so on.

## Deck log

This will often be written up and referred to on deck, so a stout waterproof notebook is advisable. A recommended ruling is given in Fig 12.1.

*Time recorded*  This will normally be time by the ship's clock. If this differs from GMT, then the zone number should be noted on every page. At midnight each day a line is drawn across the page and the date of the following day is inserted.

*Log reading*  The log reading is an accurate record of the distance run through the water and should be recorded at regular intervals. When ocean currents are difficult to estimate, a comparison of the DR position (from course steered and log reading) and the observed position provides a good guide.

*Course required*  This should be entered by the navigator before the watch takes over, to eliminate any risk of error or misunderstanding which can easily occur if the course is passed on by word only.

*Course steered*  The helmsman decides upon the average or mean course steered since the last entry.

*Wind*  An estimate of wind strength and direction should be kept as this can help in predicting the future weather and wind direction.

*Barometer*  Regular recording of barometric reading is essential. Barometric trend is a good

**Deck log book**

| DATE | TIME Z + 1 | LOG READING | COURSE REQ'D | COURSE STEERED | WIND | BARO. | REMARKS |
|---|---|---|---|---|---|---|---|
| Aug 28 | 1200 | 648 | 065° | 065° | SW 4 | 1004 | Mer. Alt. Sight |
| | 1400 | 659 | " | " | WSW5 | 1006 | |
| | 1600 | 671 | " | " | W6 | 1008 | Reefed Main, No 2 jib |
| | 1800 | 682 | " | " | W5 | 1010 | |
| | 2000 | 694 | " | " | NW4 | 1006 | Unreefed, No 2 genoa |
| | 2200 | 704 | " | " | W4 | 1004 | |
| | 2400 | 715 | " | " | W 3 | 1004 | Set No 1 genoa |
| Aug 29 | | | Similar entries | | | | |
| Aug 30 | 0400 | 863 | 065° | 065° | SW4 | 996 | |
| | 0600 | 875 | " | " | " | 994 | |
| | 0655 | 888 | " | " | " | 994 | a.m. Sight   A |
| | 1000 | 906 | " | " | WSW3 | 998 | |
| | 1145 | 916 | " | " | SW4 | 1000 | Mer. Alt. Sight   B |
| | 1400 | 923 | " | " | " | 1004 | Saw tanker. 5M to S |
| | 1800 | 945 | " | " | " | 1004 | |
| | 2400 | 977 | " | " | W5 | 1008 | |
| Aug 31 | 0400 | 999 | 065° | 065° | NW4 | 1008 | |
| | 0600 | 016 | " | " | NW3 | 1002 | |
| | 0750 | 023 | " | " | W4 | 1002 | DR worked up for a.m. sight   C |

**Fig. 12.1** Deck log.

**Navigator's log book**

| DATE Z + 1 TIME 1975 | LOG READ'G | LOG MILES SINCE LAST PLOT | COURSE Co C° | DEV | VAR. | T° | LEE WAY | WATER TRACK | STREAM DIR | RATE | DRIFT | POSITION |
|---|---|---|---|---|---|---|---|---|---|---|---|---|
| Aug 28 1200 | 648 | | | | | | | | | | | O.P. 47° 50′ N   17° 30′ W |
| 30 0655 | 888 | 240 | 065° | E + 4 | W − 12 | 057° | + 5 | 062° | 090° | ½ k | 21·5 | D.R. 49° 43′ N   11° 41′ W   A   a.m. sight |
| 1145 | 916 | 28 | 065° | + 4 | − 12 | 057° | + 5 | 062° | 090° | ½ k | 2·5 | Mer. Alt   B   O.P. 49° 53′ N   10° 48′ W |
| 31 0750 | 23 | 107 | 065° | + 4 | −12 | 057° | + 5 | 062° | 090° | ½ | 10 | D.R. 50° 43′ N   8° 05′ W   C |

**Fig. 12.2** Navigator's log.

weather indicator, especially in the tropics in latitudes below 30° where a pressure fall may herald the approach of a tropical revolving storm.

***Frequency of entries***　The deck log should be written up at regular intervals and at the time of any occurrence. Every entry must start with time and log reading. The intervals prescribed will depend upon the circumstances. When ocean racing or on short passages or when approaching any dangers, entries every half hour are advisable. On a long passage, entries every hour would suffice.

Patent logs often get fouled up by weed and either stop or under-register. Regular log readings ensure that any fault is detected.

## The navigator's log
It is unlikely that a printed log book will be found which has captions and rulings for all the information that should be included for navigational purposes. No two navigators will agree on the precise format required, so it is best that the navigator rules and heads his log to his personal requirements. An example of the navigator's log is shown in Fig 12.2.

A fresh entry is necessary to record every alteration of course, significant alteration of tidal stream or current or leeway and whenever a new EP is to be plotted or calculated. Observed positions obtained by fixes of landmarks or by celestial navigation should be recorded. There should be provision for noting variation and deviation.

***Notebooks***　One notebook should be reserved for recording and working out all celestial sights. One with squared paper one side of the page and plain on the other is useful. An example of a sight book is shown in Fig 12.3. A separate book to record time checks should be kept.

## Frequency of sights
The frequency of celestial observations will depend upon the circumstances and the location. A point to bear in mind is that the last sight taken could be the last sight for several days, so it is best to take advantage of everything available at a particular time. On long passages many navigators take sights at regular intervals but only plot the observed positions once a day; so some sets of sights may never be plotted. It is useful to work out each day the run from noon to noon.

When in the open ocean, the daily routine should be: observations at morning twilight, a forenoon sun sight, a meridian altitude sun sight, an afternoon sun sight, evening twilight sights, plus observations of the moon when available. Occasionally when the horizon is bright enough, sights can also be taken after dark.

It is best to take the morning and afternoon sun sights when the sun's altitude is greater than 15°.

## Compass check
On a long voyage it is advisable to do a compass check to see whether there has been an alteration in the boat's deviation. When out of sight of land it is possible to use the sun at sunrise or sunset for this purpose.

The sun does not rise or set exactly due east or west every day. It varies north or south from these points according to its declination. This variation is called amplitude. Tables giving the sun's true bearing at sunrise and sunset are given in publications such as *Norie's Tables*, *Burton's Tables* or *Reed's Nautical Almanac*. The procedure for using the True Amplitudes table from Norie's Tables is given below. The information required for entry to the table is:

**1**　DR latitude at the time of the observation, to the nearest 1°.

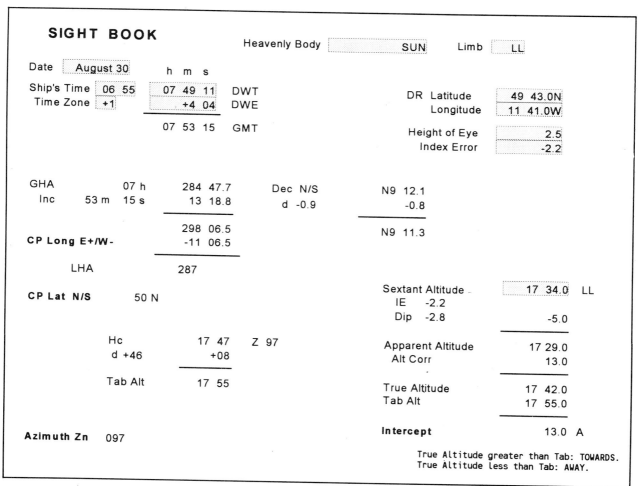

**SIGHT BOOK**

Heavenly Body [ SUN ]     Limb [ LL ]

Date [ August 30 ]

|  | h  m  s |  |
|---|---|---|
| Ship's Time [ 06  55 ] | 07  49  11 | DWT |
| Time Zone [ +1 ] | +4  04 | DWE |
|  | 07  53  15 | GMT |

DR  Latitude [ 49  43.0N ]
    Longitude [ 11  41.0W ]

Height of Eye [ 2.5 ]
Index Error [ -2.2 ]

| GHA | 07 h | 284  47.7 | Dec N/S | N9 12.1 |
|---|---|---|---|---|
| Inc | 53 m  15 s | 13  18.8 | d  -0.9 | -0.8 |
|  |  | 298  06.5 |  | N9  11.3 |
| **CP Long E+/W-** |  | -11  06.5 |  |  |
| LHA |  | 287 |  |  |

**CP Lat  N/S**   50 N

Sextant Altitude [ 17  34.0 ] LL
IE   -2.2
Dip  -2.8          -5.0

| Hc | 17  47 | Z 97 |
|---|---|---|
| d +46 | +08 |  |
| Tab Alt | 17  55 |  |

Apparent Altitude     17 29.0
Alt Corr              13.0

True Altitude         17 42.0
Tab Alt               17 55.0

**Azimuth Zn**   097

**Intercept**         13.0  A

True Altitude greater than Tab: TOWARDS.
True Altitude less than Tab: AWAY.

**Fig. 12.3** Sight records.

2  Declination to the nearest 0.5° which is found from the *Nautical Almanac* for the time of the compass check.

*Example 12a*
On 30 August in DR position 43°N 18°W the sun's bearing by compass at sunrise was 096°C. The variation was 12°W. What was the compass error? What was the deviation?

DR latitude 43° (it is immaterial whether this is N or S).

Declination N9°.

# TRUE AMPLITUDES

| Lat. | 1° | 2° | 3° | 4° | 5° | 6° | 7° | 8° | 9° | 10° | 11° | 12° | 13° | 14° | 15° |
|---|---|---|---|---|---|---|---|---|---|---|---|---|---|---|---|
| 2 | 1·0 | 2·0 | 3·0 | 4·0 | 5·0 | 6·0 | 7·0 | 8·0 | 9·0 | 10·0 | 11·0 | 12·0 | 13·0 | 14·0 | 15·0 |
| 4 | 1·0 | 2·0 | 3·0 | 4·0 | 5·0 | 6·0 | 7·0 | 8·0 | 9·0 | 10·0 | 11·0 | 12·0 | 13·0 | 14·0 | 15·0 |
| 6 | 1·0 | 2·0 | 3·0 | 4·0 | 5·0 | 6·0 | 7·1 | 8·1 | 9·1 | 10·1 | 11·1 | 12·1 | 13·1 | 14·1 | 15·1 |
| 8 | 1·0 | 2·0 | 3·0 | 4·1 | 5·1 | 6·1 | 7·1 | 8·1 | 9·1 | 10·1 | 11·1 | 12·1 | 13·1 | 14·1 | 15·2 |
| 10 | 1·0 | 2·0 | 3·1 | 4·1 | 5·1 | 6·1 | 7·1 | 8·1 | 9·2 | 10·2 | 11·2 | 12·2 | 13·2 | 14·2 | 15·3 |
| 12 | 1·0 | 2·1 | 3·1 | 4·1 | 5·1 | 6·1 | 7·2 | 8·2 | 9·2 | 10·2 | 11·3 | 12·3 | 13·3 | 14·3 | 15·4 |
| 14 | 1·0 | 2·1 | 3·1 | 4·1 | 5·2 | 6·2 | 7·2 | 8·3 | 9·3 | 10·3 | 11·3 | 12·4 | 13·4 | 14·4 | 15·5 |
| 16 | 1·1 | 2·1 | 3·1 | 4·2 | 5·2 | 6·2 | 7·3 | 8·3 | 9·4 | 10·4 | 11·5 | 12·5 | 13·5 | 14·6 | 15·6 |
| 18 | 1·1 | 2·1 | 3·2 | 4·2 | 5·3 | 6·3 | 7·4 | 8·4 | 9·5 | 10·5 | 11·6 | 12·6 | 13·7 | 14·7 | 15·8 |
| 20 | 1·1 | 2·1 | 3·2 | 4·3 | 5·3 | 6·4 | 7·5 | 8·5 | 9·6 | 10·7 | 11·7 | 12·8 | 13·9 | 14·9 | 15·9 |
| 22 | 1·1 | 2·2 | 3·2 | 4·3 | 5·4 | 6·5 | 7·6 | 8·6 | 9·7 | 10·8 | 11·9 | 13·0 | 14·1 | 15·1 | 16·2 |
| 24 | 1·1 | 2·2 | 3·3 | 4·4 | 5·5 | 6·6 | 7·7 | 8·8 | 9·9 | 11·0 | 12·1 | 13·2 | 14·3 | 15·4 | 16·5 |
| 26 | 1·1 | 2·2 | 3·4 | 4·5 | 5·6 | 6·7 | 7·8 | 8·9 | 10·0 | 11·2 | 12·3 | 13·4 | 14·5 | 15·6 | 16·8 |
| 28 | 1·1 | 2·3 | 3·4 | 4·5 | 5·7 | 6·8 | 7·9 | 9·1 | 10·2 | 11·4 | 12·5 | 13·6 | 14·8 | 15·9 | 17·1 |
| 30 | 1·2 | 2·3 | 3·5 | 4·6 | 5·8 | 6·9 | 8·1 | 9·3 | 10·4 | 11·6 | 12·7 | 13·9 | 15·1 | 16·2 | 17·4 |
| 31 | 1·2 | 2·3 | 3·5 | 4·7 | 5·8 | 7·0 | 8·2 | 9·4 | 10·5 | 11·7 | 12·9 | 14·0 | 15·2 | 16·4 | 17·6 |
| 32 | 1·2 | 2·4 | 3·6 | 4·7 | 5·9 | 7·1 | 8·3 | 9·5 | 10·6 | 11·8 | 13·0 | 14·2 | 15·4 | 16·6 | 17·8 |
| 33 | 1·2 | 2·4 | 3·6 | 4·8 | 6·0 | 7·2 | 8·4 | 9·6 | 10·8 | 12·0 | 13·2 | 14·4 | 15·6 | 16·8 | 18·0 |
| 34 | 1·2 | 2·4 | 3·6 | 4·8 | 6·0 | 7·3 | 8·5 | 9·7 | 10·9 | 12·1 | 13·3 | 14·5 | 15·8 | 17·0 | 18·2 |
| 35 | 1·2 | 2·5 | 3·7 | 4·9 | 6·1 | 7·3 | 8·6 | 9·8 | 11·0 | 12·2 | 13·5 | 14·7 | 16·0 | 17·2 | 18·4 |
| 36 | 1·2 | 2·5 | 3·7 | 5·0 | 6·2 | 7·4 | 8·7 | 9·9 | 11·2 | 12·4 | 13·7 | 14·9 | 16·2 | 17·4 | 18·7 |
| 37 | 1·3 | 2·5 | 3·8 | 5·0 | 6·3 | 7·5 | 8·8 | 10·0 | 11·3 | 12·6 | 13·8 | 15·1 | 16·4 | 17·6 | 18·9 |
| 38 | 1·3 | 2·5 | 3·8 | 5·1 | 6·4 | 7·6 | 8·9 | 10·2 | 11·4 | 12·7 | 14·0 | 15·3 | 16·6 | 17·9 | 19·2 |
| 39 | 1·3 | 2·6 | 3·9 | 5·2 | 6·4 | 7·7 | 9·0 | 10·3 | 11·6 | 12·9 | 14·2 | 15·5 | 16·8 | 18·1 | 19·5 |
| 40 | 1·3 | 2·6 | 3·9 | 5·2 | 6·5 | 7·9 | 9·2 | 10·5 | 11·8 | 13·1 | 14·4 | 15·8 | 17·1 | 18·4 | 19·8 |
| 41 | 1·3 | 2·7 | 4·0 | 5·3 | 6·6 | 8·0 | 9·3 | 10·6 | 12·0 | 13·3 | 14·7 | 16·0 | 17·4 | 18·7 | 20·1 |
| 42 | 1·4 | 2·7 | 4·0 | 5·4 | 6·7 | 8·1 | 9·4 | 10·8 | 12·2 | 13·5 | 14·9 | 16·3 | 17·6 | 19·0 | 20·4 |
| 43 | 1·4 | 2·7 | 4·1 | 5·5 | 6·9 | 8·2 | 9·6 | 11·0 | 12·4 | 13·7 | 15·1 | 16·5 | 17·9 | 19·3 | 20·7 |
| 44 | 1·4 | 2·8 | 4·2 | 5·6 | 7·0 | 8·4 | 9·8 | 11·2 | 12·6 | 14·0 | 15·4 | 16·8 | 18·2 | 19·7 | 21·1 |
| 45 | 1·4 | 2·8 | 4·3 | 5·7 | 7·1 | 8·5 | 9·9 | 11·4 | 12·8 | 14·2 | 15·7 | 17·1 | 18·6 | 20·0 | 21·5 |
| 46 | 1·4 | 2·9 | 4·3 | 5·8 | 7·2 | 8·7 | 10·1 | 11·6 | 13·0 | 14·5 | 16·0 | 17·4 | 18·9 | 20·4 | 21·9 |
| 47 | 1·5 | 2·9 | 4·4 | 5·9 | 7·4 | 8·8 | 10·3 | 11·8 | 13·3 | 14·8 | 16·3 | 17·8 | 19·3 | 20·8 | 22·3 |
| 48 | 1·5 | 3·0 | 4·5 | 6·0 | 7·5 | 9·0 | 10·5 | 12·0 | 13·5 | 15·1 | 16·6 | 18·1 | 19·7 | 21·2 | 22·8 |
| 49 | 1·5 | 3·1 | 4·6 | 6·1 | 7·6 | 9·2 | 10·7 | 12·3 | 13·8 | 15·4 | 16·9 | 18·5 | 20·1 | 21·6 | 23·2 |
| 50 | 1·6 | 3·1 | 4·7 | 6·2 | 7·8 | 9·4 | 10·9 | 12·5 | 14·1 | 15·7 | 17·3 | 18·9 | 20·5 | 22·1 | 23·8 |
| 50½ | 1·6 | 3·1 | 4·7 | 6·3 | 7·9 | 9·5 | 11·0 | 12·6 | 14·2 | 15·8 | 17·5 | 19·1 | 20·7 | 22·4 | 24·0 |
| 51 | 1·6 | 3·1 | 4·8 | 6·4 | 8·0 | 9·6 | 11·2 | 12·8 | 14·4 | 16·0 | 17·7 | 19·3 | 21·0 | 22·6 | 24·3 |
| 51½ | 1·6 | 3·2 | 4·8 | 6·4 | 8·0 | 9·7 | 11·3 | 12·9 | 14·6 | 16·2 | 17·8 | 19·5 | 21·2 | 22·9 | 24·6 |
| 52 | 1·6 | 3·3 | 4·9 | 6·5 | 8·1 | 9·8 | 11·4 | 13·1 | 14·7 | 16·4 | 18·1 | 19·7 | 21·4 | 23·2 | 24·9 |
| 52½ | 1·6 | 3·3 | 4·9 | 6·6 | 8·2 | 9·9 | 11·5 | 13·2 | 14·9 | 16·6 | 18·3 | 20·0 | 21·7 | 23·4 | 25·2 |

Fig. 12.4 *Norie's Tables* extract: true amplitudes.

Using the table (Fig 12.4) the figure at the intersection of latitude and declination is 12 .4°, which can be rounded to 12°.

The table tabulates degrees in 4 quadrants:

From east to north − 090°T to 000°T.
From east to south − 090°T to 180°T.
From west to north − 270°T to 000°T.
From west to south − 270°T to 180°T

In the example, declination is north and the sun is rising, so the bearing of the sun is 12° from east towards north, that is 090° − 12° = 078°T.

| True bearing | 078°T |
|---|---|
| Compass bearing | 096°C |
| Compass error | 18°W |
| Variation | 12°W |
| Deviation | 6°W |

*Example 12b*
On 17 February in DR position 13°S 164°E the sun's compass bearing at sunset was 256°C. Variation was 15°E. What was the compass error and deviation? Use table (Fig 12.4).

DR latitude 13°, sun's declination S12°

| Amplitude W12°S | 258°T |
|---|---|
| Compass bearing | 256°C |
| Compass error | 2°E |
| Variation | 15°E |
| Deviation | 13°W |

The sun's bearing should ideally be observed when its lower limb is about half the sun's visible diameter above the visible horizon, as, due to refraction at this time, its centre is on the true horizon.

It is difficult to take a bearing of the sun with the steering compass if it does not have an all round view of the horizon and an azimuth ring and prism.

A method which can be used if the course is roughly east or west, is to steer towards the sun lining up the fore and aft parts of the boat with the sun. It may also be possible if the course is roughly north or south to line the sun up with parts of the boat amidships. In this case the course will differ by 90°.

Alternatively the deviation of the steering compass, but not the compass error, can be found by taking a bearing of the boat's head with a hand-bearing compass held well away from all magnetic influences and comparing it with the reading on the steering compass. This method is not ideal on a steel-hulled boat.

If the true bearing of the sun is required at times other than sunrise or sunset, it can be found for the DR position by using AP3270 which is entered with Latitude, Local Hour Angle and Declination of the sun in the normal manner.

**Exercise**
Use Fig 12.4
Find the compass error and deviation:

**12.1** Sunrise 17 February DR position 18°N 48°W. Sun's bearing 114°C, variation 17°W.
**12.2** Sunrise August 30th DR position 49°S 165°E. Sun's bearing 050°C, variation 19°E.

# 13 Some Useful Tips

**Taking sights**

When visibility is good, sights should be taken from as high a position as can be conveniently arranged. The horizon seen then will be as far off as possible and so least affected by wave or swell tops forming a false horizon. In poor visibility when the distant horizon is indistinct or invisible in mist, sights should be taken from as low as possible so that the close horizon is used.

When using a sextant in a seaway it is advisable to wear a safety harness and be clipped on to a strong point on the boat. When busy taking sights it is easy to be distracted and not notice a large wave which may cause the boat to pitch or roll suddenly. Except in calm seas it is not advisable to take sights when standing. Adopt a position where the lower part of the body is well anchored and the upper part free to sway with the motion of the boat. The sextant must always be rocked to ensure that it is vertical.

During the period when multiple sights are taken, at dawn and dusk twilight, it may be easier to steer a course directly across or directly along the swell. It is simpler to take a sight when the boat has a steady roll rather than a corkscrew motion. To guard against losing the sextant overboard, or damaging it by dropping, a lanyard should be fitted to it which can then be slipped over the user's head.

Sight-taking is much easier if a second person is available to record the time and the sextant angle. This is particularly helpful when it is desired to take simultaneous sights or a series of sun sights in rapid succession.

Always use a shade before viewing the sun. Locating the sun is sometimes easier with a pale shade, but this should be replaced by a suitably dark one for final coincidence adjustment. If the horizon sparkles or is very bright, use a horizon mirror shade as well. At twilight, a bright moon sight may be improved by using a pale shade on the index mirror.

Try to establish coincidence quickly, then take the time at once. Do not spend minutes striving for perfection, the result will not be as good as a sight taken carefully but smartly.

If the sea is rough and the boat is pitching or rolling heavily, perfect sights are impossible. It then pays to take a series of sights over a short period and either take the average of these or plot the results as a graph.

*Example 13a*

The following sun sights were taken:

| GMT<br>h m s | Sextant altitude |
|---|---|
| 17 09 03 | 16° 43′.8 |
| 17 09 33 | 16° 39′.0 |
| 17 10 06 | 16° 37′.9 |
| 17 10 31 | 16° 30′.5 |
| 17 10 48 | 16° 27′.0 |
| 17 11 30 | 16° 21′.9 |

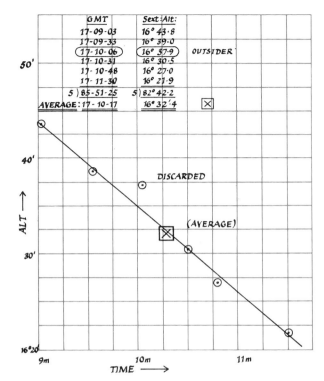

| GMT | Sext Alt: | |
|---|---|---|
| 17-09-03 | 16° 43·8 | |
| 17-09-33 | 16° 39·0 | |
| (17-10-06) | (16° 37·9) | OUTSIDER |
| 17-10-31 | 16° 30·5 | |
| 17-10-48 | 16° 27·0 | |
| 17-11-30 | 16° 21·9 | |
| 5 ) 85-51-25 | 5 ) 82° 42·2 | |
| AVERAGE : 17-10-17 | 16° 32′4 | ⊠ |

**Fig. 13.1** Averaging sights on graph paper.

1 Mark altitude intervals at the side of the graph.
2 Mark time intervals along the bottom.
3 Mark the position of the sun at each sight on the graph.
4 It should be possible to draw a line through most of the sights, discarding any which are obviously out of line.
5 Any convenient point along the line can be selected, or the altitudes and times can be averaged by adding up and dividing the total by the number of sights (Fig 13.1).

## Easy way to plot the intercept

The following method, using a square protractor and a pencil compass, shows a quick way to plot intercepts and position lines:

1 Set the pencil compass to the length of the intercept.
2 Place the centre of the protractor over the chosen position with the protractor lined up with meridians of longitude or parallels of latitude.
3 If the intercept is *towards*, position the protractor's north point upward. If *away* position the north point downward.
4 Find the required azimuth on the outer scale of the protractor and place the point of the compass on the chart in this position. Hold the compass point steady and swivel any straight edge of the protractor round the compass point to align on the chosen position.
5 Hold the protractor steady and transfer the compass so that one point is on the chosen position and the other along the line of azimuth. Mark the end of the intercept close to the protractor edge.
6 Still holding the protractor in place, draw the intercept from the chosen position to the mark made by the compasses.

## Spurious accuracy

It is seldom possible to take sextant sights to an accuracy of better than 1′ or 2′ from a boat in a seaway. It may, therefore, be considered a waste of time to worry about decimals of a minute of arc in GHA or declination. It is recommended that, initially at least, all figures are worked out as accurately as the tables permit for two reasons:

● Errors due to working only to whole numbers may happen to be all in the same direction resulting in an unacceptable compound error.
● If it becomes a habit to be meticulous with

decimals, the tens and units which do matter are more likely to be accurate.

The thoroughly experienced navigator knows when to take short cuts and whether a possible error is acceptable, but this practice is not recommended.

### Sights for latitude in the tropics

When sailing in the tropics there may be occasions when the sun passes almost exactly overhead at midday local time. This will occur when latitude is almost the same as declination and of the same name, both north or both south. The sun then rises almost due east, remains east until midday, suddenly becomes west and sets almost due west. It may then be difficult to obtain the sun's altitude when it is exactly on the meridian as it will be overhead at an altitude of nearly 90°. If the latitude of the DR position is within 2° of the sun's declination and the same name, both north or both south, a special technique is necessary.

The sun's declination and GHA represent the latitude and longitude of the sun's GP. If at midday, the sun's GP is exactly on the observer's position, then the observer's latitude will be equal to the sun's declination and longitude will be the same as GHA. Therefore:

Observer's latitude = GP latitude.
Observer's longitude = GP longitude.

The LHA will then be 0°.

When the sun's GP at meridian passage is not exactly, but very near to the observer's position, the technique is to take three observations of the sun, the first a few minutes before the expected time of meridian passage, the second at about the time of meridian passage and the third a few minutes later. The sun's GP when each sight was taken can be plotted. The true altitudes found from the observations subtracted from 90° will provide the

respective true zenith distances. A circle round each GP, the radius being the sun's true zenith distance, can be drawn and the intersection of the three circles will be the boat's position.

If, as is likely to be the case on an ocean passage, only a small scale chart is available, the plotting may be done on squared paper, changing D Long to Dep by using traverse tables.

### Procedure

1 Calculate the time of meridian passage at the DR position.
2 Take the first sight between 4 and 10 minutes before the approximate time of meridian passage, the second sight at meridian passage, and the third sight 4 to 10 minutes after meridian passage. Record the exact time of each sight.
3 Find the GHA, declination and TZD for each sight using the *Nautical Almanac*.
4 Plot the sun's GP when each sight was taken. Latitude = sun's declination. Longitude = sun's GHA (in east longitude subtract GHA from 360°).
5 With each GP as the centre and each TZD expressed in minutes of arc as the radius, describe three arcs. These should intersect at a common point which is the observed position.

**To plot on squared paper**  Any horizontal line can be used to represent the latitude of the sun's GP (lat = dec). The GHA of each sight will represent the longitude of the sun's GP at the time of each sight.

GHA less than 180°    GHA = long W
GHA more than 180°    360° − GHA = long E

On the horizontal line mark a middle point to represent the sun's GP at the second sight and mark it with the longitude. Compare the first and the third sights' GP with the GP of the second sight. The difference will give the D Long of sights 1 and 3 from sight 2. Convert these to Dep by using traverse tables.

Measure off the Dep of the first and third sights from the second sight and plot the resultant GP. Sight 1 will be to the right of the plot, sight 2 in the middle and sight 3 to the left, because the sun travels from east to west.

The GP for each sight has now been plotted. This is the centre of a position circle the radius of which is the zenith distance expressed as minutes or miles. The arcs of the circles can now be plotted. If at the second sight the sun bore north, describe the arcs on the south side of the line and vice versa. The observed position is where the three arcs intersect.

Measure the latitude and departure from the GP of the second sight to the observed position. Convert departure to D Long.

*Example 13b*

On passage to Barbados, the latitude is required on 20 May. The DR position is 21° 00'N 59° 30'W. Index error −2'.0, height of eye 2.0 metres.

|  | h m |  |  |
|---|---|---|---|
| Meridian passage | 11 56 | LMT | 20d |
| DR Long W | +3 58 |  |  |
| Meridian passage | 15 54 | GMT at DR | 20d |

|  | First sight | Second sight | Third sight |
|---|---|---|---|
|  | h m s | h m s | h m s |
| GMT | 15 52 10 | 15 55 40 | 15 58 35 |
| GHA | 45° 53'.1 | 45° 53'.1 | 45° 53'.1 |
| incr | +13° 02'.5 | +13° 55'.0 | +14° 38'.8 |
|  | 58° 55'.6 | 59° 48'.1 | 60° 31'.9 |
| Dec | N19° 56'.0 |  |  |
| d+0.5 | +0'.5 |  |  |
|  | N19° 56'.5 | = Latitude of GP |  |

GHA of the sun (above) = longitude of the sun's GP:

|  |  |  |
|---|---|---|
| 58° 55'.6 | 59° 48'.1 | 60° 31'.9 |

D Long between sights 1 and 2 = 52'.5E; Dep 49.0 miles.

D Long between sights 2 and 3 = 43'.8W; Dep 40.9 miles.

|  |  |  |  |
|---|---|---|---|
| SA LL | 88° 43'.6 | 88° 56'.6 | 88° 36'.6 |
| IE |  |  |  |
| Dip | −4'.5 | −4'.5 | −4'.5 |
| AA | 88° 39'.1 | 88° 52'.1 | 88° 32'.1 |
| corrn | +15'.9 | +15'.9 | +15'.9 |
| TA | 88° 55'.0 | 89° 08'.0 | 88° 48'.0 |
| from | 90° | 90° | 90° |
| TZD | 1° 05'.0 | 52'.0 | 1° 12'.0 |
|  | 65M | 52M | 72M |

Plot the arcs of the circles on the squared paper (Fig 13.2). The observed position is at the intersection between the three arcs.

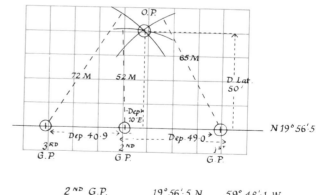

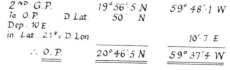

**Fig. 13.2** Latitude in the tropics.

Find the latitude of the observed position by counting vertically, the number of squares between the second sight and the intersection of the arcs.

Find the departure of the observed position by counting the number of squares between the second sight and the intersection of the arcs. Convert the departure to D Long.

| | | | |
|---|---|---|---|
| Second GP | 19° 56'.5N | | 59° 48'.1W |
| D Lat | 50'.0N | D Long | 10'.7E* |
| OP | 20° 46'.5N | | 59° 37'.4W |

*(Dep 10E = D Long 10'.7E)

Where there is difficulty in obtaining a sun meridian altitude sight, it is preferable to use some other body which is on the observer's meridian to find latitude, or to use multiple morning or evening sights to find observed position.

### Altitude and accuracy

The importance of rocking the sextant from side to side to ensure that it is vertical has been stressed. If a sight is taken when the sextant is not vertical, the altitude measured will always be greater than the real altitude. The amount of this error depends on:

- The angle the sextant is out of the perpendicular.
- The altitude of the body being observed. The larger the altitude the greater the error. On the other hand refraction is greater at lower altitudes and any abnormal refraction due to temperature or pressure is greater at very low altitudes. The following figures give an idea of the errors which can arise:

| *Sextant tilt* | *Altitude* | | | |
|---|---|---|---|---|
| | 10° | 25° | 50° | 89° |
| 2° | 0'.4 | 0'.9 | 1'.8 | 3'.2 |
| 5° | 2'.3 | 5'.7 | 11'.4 | 20'.2 |
| 10° | 9'.2 | 23'.1 | 46'.2 | 82'.2 |

Look at the extract from the *Nautical Almanac* 'Additional Correction Table for non-standard Conditions' and see how these vary:

| *App Alt* | *Between* |
|---|---|
| 2° 30' | − 2'.5 and + 2'.5 |
| 5° | − 1'.5 and + 1'.5 |
| 10° | − 0'.8 and + 0'.8 |
| 20° | − 0'.4 and + 0'.4 |
| 50° | − 0'.1 and + 0'.1 |

Experience has shown that the most reliable sights are taken when the body is not less than about 15° and not more than 45° altitude. When there is any option the bodies selected and times of sights should be chosen with this in mind. The meridian altitude of the sun, particularly when in the tropics, will often be far greater than 45° and special care should be taken to ensure that the sextant is vertical.

### Sights in heavy weather

If sights are essential at a time when seas are rough, special care of both the sextant and the observer is essential. Wear a safety harness and clip on with a short scope. Wrap a dry towel loosely around the sextant whilst carrying it to and from below deck to protect it from knocks. Keep a dry soft cotton cloth in a pocket to wipe lens or mirrors should they get covered with salt spray. If possible take a series of sights calling them to a writer below and later average out or graph the sights as previously shown. Clean the sextant when possible in fresh water, paying particular attention to the mirrors, before stowing.

# 14 Planning an Ocean Voyage

The speed and the comfort of an ocean passage will largely depend on the winds encountered and the currents prevailing. The choice of best route is of considerable importance. Many ocean areas are subject to hurricanes or typhoons at certain times of the year. The name varies according to the area, but all are classified as Tropical Revolving Storms, and can be called hurricanes. Of course, these must be avoided at all costs. Small craft have survived them, but even large liners take great pains to avoid them. The operative word for any small vessel is survival, bearing in mind that the winds may exceed 120 knots.

Clearly, a route on which mainly favourable winds of average strength not above force 6 can be expected is far preferable to one where mainly head winds, or winds from forward of abeam, or gales, prevail. Ocean currents too may affect the duration of a passage. A modest current of only half a knot in the wrong direction means that the small craft has to make good 12 extra miles each day. This soon mounts up on, say, a 20 day passage.

Planning the route should begin with a careful study of the Routeing or Pilot Charts of the ocean involved for the month(s) over the time of the proposed passage. For each ocean 12 routeing charts are published, one for each month of the year.

These are:

| | |
|---|---|
| Chart 5124 | North Atlantic Ocean |
| Chart 5125 | South Atlantic Ocean |
| Chart 5126 | Indian Ocean |
| Chart 5127 | North Pacific Ocean |
| Chart 5128 | South Pacific Ocean |

These Routeing charts contain information of vital interest to the mariner, and particularly the small craft navigator, who is more dependent on wind than his commercial counterpart. They show:

- Winds
- Currents
- Ice and fog limits
- Air and sea temperatures and dew points
- Tracks of tropical revolving storms over past years
- Steamer tracks (great circles) between principal ports

Winds are indicated by wind 'roses' placed all around the chart. Each shows the percentage of winds from various directions and their strengths. The general direction and average rate of ocean currents are shown by green arrows. Ice and fog areas and limits are marked. Small chartlets show sea and air temperature contours, and mean barometric pressure in millibars.

The first consideration in planning an ocean passage is to seek to avoid periods when tropical revolving storms may be expected. These are:

| | | |
|---|---|---|
| **North Atlantic, western side** | June to November | Hurricanes |
| **South Indian Ocean** | December to April | Cyclones |

| Arabian Sea and Bay of Bengal | June and November | Cyclones |
| North Pacific, eastern side | June to November | Hurricanes |
| North Pacific, western side | All year, but most frequently June to November | Typhoons |
| South Pacific, western side | December to April | Hurricanes |

## Route choices

Having settled on the months when there is least likelihood of tropical storms, the next step is to choose the best route. This may be influenced by the relative importance of speed or of pleasure and comfort; and on the windward ability of the small craft. The shortest distance between two places is a straight line but often this will not be the best route. For example, the direct route from the United Kingdom to the West Indies passes through large areas of contrary or light winds. A more southerly route will lead through the belt of Northeast Trade Winds where for days on end a good steady sailing wind from well abaft the beam can almost be guaranteed.

Where the Routeing Charts show that there is nothing to be gained by taking a more roundabout route, then a straight line course may be the best. On a sphere, and on the earth's surface, a straight line, and therefore the shortest distance, is a portion of a great circle passing through both the departure and the destination. A piece of string stretched taut between two points on a globe is part of a great circle. Except when stretched exactly N and S (forming a meridian), or along the equator (the only parallel which is a great circle), the string will cross each meridian at a different angle; the bearing of the string changes along its length. This is why a great circle track on a Mercator projection chart appears as a curve bowed away from the equator. A straight line on a Mercator chart (such as a Routeing Chart) is called a rhumb line because it crosses each meridian at the same angle; its bearing remains constant. Thus a rhumb line is always longer than part of a great circle drawn between two places (except when the two places are on the same meridian or both are on the equator).

However the difference in the length of a rhumb line and that of a great circle between two places is insignificant if the distance is only a few hundred miles and the latitudes are below 60° N or S. On ocean crossings of several thousand miles a great circle route can be appreciably shorter than a rhumb line. This is why commercial vessels tend to follow great circle tracks. The case is different for small craft depending on whether they are under sail or under power. A sailing vessel usually shapes a course which will take her through areas where winds and currents are most likely to be favourable, avoiding areas where bad weather can be expected. The moderate sized power craft also is interested in hospitable seas and winds. Both types will probably reach their destination more rapidly, and certainly more comfortably, by selecting courses based on the expectations of winds, weather, currents and sunshine, as indicated by Routeing Charts and Pilot books.

Some idea of the difference in distance between a rhumb line and a great circle course may be seen on page 95.

There is little advantage when the course is mainly N–S, such as: Lizard to Azores and Vancouver Island to Honolulu. The maximum saving of a great circle against a Mercator or rhumb line track occurs when the course is mainly in an E–W or W–E direction and when the passage is in a high latitude (N or S); for example Yokohama to Vancouver Island. Here a great circle course would take the small craft north of the Aleutian Islands, a quite impractical route. This is a case where the shortest practical route would be a great circle up to the highest possible

| | Rhumb line | Great circle | Difference |
|---|---|---|---|
| Orkney Isles to Stavanger | 92.7 | 91.5 | Negligible |
| Lizard (UK) to Azores | 1128 | 1123 | 5 |
| Vancouver Island to Honolulu | 2201 | 2186 | 15 |
| Yokohama to Vancouver Island | 4345 | 4080 | 265 |
| Durban to Melbourne | 5710 | 5296 | 414 |
| Hobart to Cape Town | 6097 | 5409 | 688 |

latitude, say 50° N, the second leg sailing due east along the 50° parallel, and a third leg another great circle to the destination.

The great circle route between two places is found by examination of the appropriate gnomonic or great circle chart. These are:

| Chart 5095 | North Atlantic |
|---|---|
| Chart 5096 | South Atlantic |
| Chart 5097 | North Pacific |
| Chart 5098 | South Pacific and southern oceans |
| Chart 5099 | Indian and southern oceans |

Fig 14.1 shows a portion of Chart 5099 on which the great circle track for a passage from Hobart to Cape Town has been plotted. That area of ocean is known for occasional icebergs. The great circle track reaches nearly to 62° S. It may be prudent to make a composite great circle track going no further than 50° S. A tangential line is drawn to the 50th parallel of latitude from both Hobart and Cape Town. The composite track consists of a great circle track from Hobart (42° 53'S 147° 20'E) to latitude 50°S at a longitude of 110°E, a parallel sailing track to 070°E,

and finally a great circle track to Cape Town (33° 54' S 18° 25'E).

Alternatively the Kerguelen Islands could become an intermediate waypoint. The great circle distance from Hobart to the Kerguelen Islands is 3130 miles and from Kerguelen to Cape Town 2422 miles totalling 5552 miles which compares with the direct route distance of 5409 miles.

Having decided on the great circle track or tracks, intermediate points are selected at intervals of 600 miles or so which are then transposed on to a mercator chart to determine the course alterations necessary. For the passage via the Kerguelen Islands, these intermediate points could be:

```
50° S 130° E
52° 20' S 120° E
53° 30' S 110° E
54° S 100° E
53° 30' S 90° E
52° 15' S 80° E
48° 30' S 69° 40' E (Kerguelen)
49° 10' S 60° E
47° 30' S 50° E
44° 50' S 40° E
40° 55' S 30° E.
```

**Measuring distances**
Neither a rhumb line nor a great circle distance can be measured on a small scale Mercator projection chart, such as a routeing chart, except very roughly and over short distances. To find the rhumb line distance between two places over, say, 500 miles apart with any accuracy, the tables of trigonometrical functions must be used.

There are several methods of calculating great circle distances. The easiest is by use of a navigational calculator (see Chapter 15). The Haversine formula used with *Norie's Tables* involves some arithmetic; or the NP 401 or AP3270 tables can be used by transposing inputs.

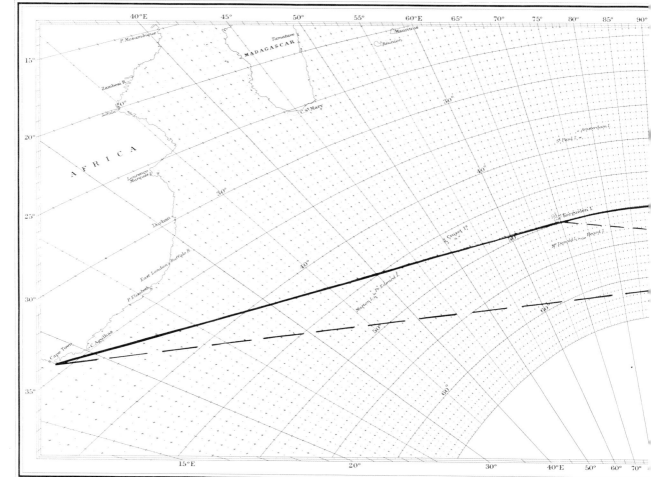

**Fig. 14.1** Great circle chart 5099.

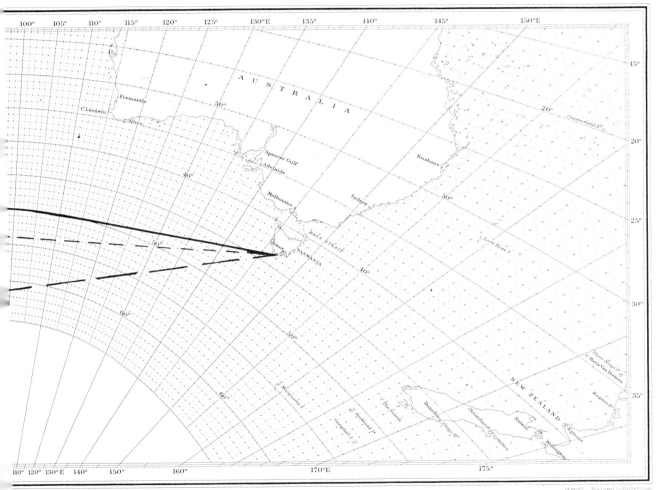

NOTE

This chart is not corrected for dangers or other information
received after the date of publication and should be used
in conjunction with Navigational charts (1924).

100° 105° 110° 115° 120° 125° 130°E 135° 140° 145° 150°E

15°

A   U   S   T   R   A   L   I   A

Fremantle

C.Leeuwin

Albany

30°

20°

Chesterfield Rf.

20°

Spencer Gulf

Adelaide

40°

Brisbane

30°

25°

Melbourne

Sydney

30°

BASS STRAIT

TASMANIA

40°

50°

25°

50°

30°

60°

50°

NEW ZEALAND

Three Kings Is.

C.Maria Van Diemen

35°

60°

Macquarie I.

Kaipara Hr.

The Snares

Auckland Is.

Campbell I.

Dunedin, Otago Hr.

Christchurch, Lyttelton

Nelson

C.Egmont

Wellington

110° 120° 130°E 140° 150° 160° 170°E 175°

ce of Rear Admiral H.E.Purey Cust, C.B. Hydrographer.

**5099**

**Great circle distance and initial course** Any tables which solve a spherical triangle can be used to find the great circle distance and initial course. The three methods illustrated are: Haversine and ABC Tables from *Norie's Tables, Sight Reduction Tables for Marine Navigation* (NP 401) and *Sight Reduction Tables for Air Navigation* (AP3270 Volumes 2 or 3).

Examples of the method of using NP401 and the Haversine formula are given in Appendices 1 and 3.

AP 3270 is limited because it only tabulates declinations to 29° which means that if the latitude of the destination is greater that 29°, these tables cannot be used.

All three tables are entered with LHA, Latitude and Declination in the usual way, but substituting the terms as follows:

Difference of longitude between two ports = LHA
Latitude of departure point
Latitude of destination point

For example consider a passage from Vancouver to Honolulu.

*Example 14*
*Use extracts provided in Figs 14.2, 14.3 and 14.4.*
What is the great circle distance and initial course from [A] Vancouver (49° 18′ N 123° 07′W) to [B] Honolulu (21° 18′N 157° 52′W)?

| | | |
|---|---|---|
| D Long | 34° 45′.0 | (LHA) |
| Lat A | 49° 18′.0 N | (LAT) |
| Lat B | 21° 18′.0 N | (DEC) |

**Haversine method**

| | | | |
|---|---|---|---|
| LHA | LH | 8.95025 | |
| LAT | LC | +9.81431 | |
| DEC | LC | +9.96927 | |
| | LH | 8.73383 | *convert to natural* |
| | NH | 0.05418 | *Haversine* |
| Diff Lat (28° 00′.0) | NH | +0.05853 | |
| | NH | 0.11271 | = 39° 14′.0 = 2354M |

| 34° | HAVERSINES | | | | | | | | | | | | |
|---|---|---|---|---|---|---|---|---|---|---|---|---|---|
| → | .0 | | .2 | | .4 | | .6 | | .8 | | | | |
| | Log. | Nat. | Log. | Nat. | Log. | Nat. | Log. | Nat. | Log. | Nat. | Log. | Nat. | |
| ′ | 2.or(8.) | 0. | 2.or(8.) | 0. | 2.or(8.) | 0. | 2.or(8.) | 0. | 2.or(8.) | 0. | 2.or(8.) | 0. | ′ |
| 00 | 93187 | 08548 | 93195 | 08550 | 93204 | 08551 | 93212 | 08553 | 93220 | 08555 | 93228 | 08556 | 59 |
| 01 | 93228 | 08556 | 93237 | 08558 | 93245 | 08560 | 93253 | 08561 | 93261 | 08563 | 93270 | 08564 | 58 |
| 02 | 93270 | 08564 | 93278 | 08566 | 93286 | 08568 | 93294 | 08569 | 93303 | 08571 | 93311 | 08573 | 57 |
| 03 | 93311 | 08573 | 93319 | 08574 | 93327 | 08576 | 93336 | 08577 | 93344 | 08579 | 93352 | 08581 | 56 |
| 04 | 93352 | 08581 | 93360 | 08582 | 93369 | 08584 | 93377 | 08586 | 93385 | 08587 | 93393 | 08589 | 55 |
| 41 | 94863 | 08885 | 94871 | 08886 | 94880 | 08888 | 94888 | 08889 | 94896 | 08891 | 94904 | 08893 | 18 |
| 42 | 94904 | 08893 | 94912 | 08894 | 94920 | 08896 | 94928 | 08898 | 94936 | 08899 | 94944 | 08901 | 17 |
| 43 | 94944 | 08901 | 94952 | 08903 | 94960 | 08904 | 94968 | 08906 | 94977 | 08908 | 94985 | 08909 | 16 |
| 44 | 94985 | 08909 | 94993 | 08911 | 95001 | 08913 | 95009 | 08914 | 95017 | 08916 | 95025 | 08918 | 15 |
| 45 | 95025 | 08918 | 95033 | 08919 | 95041 | 08921 | 95049 | 08923 | 95057 | 08924 | 95065 | 08926 | 14 |
| 46 | 95065 | 08926 | 95073 | 08928 | 95082 | 08929 | 95090 | 08931 | 95098 | 08933 | 95106 | 08934 | 13 |
| 47 | 95106 | 08934 | 95114 | 08936 | 95122 | 08938 | 95130 | 08939 | 95138 | 08941 | 95146 | 08943 | 12 |
| 48 | 95146 | 08943 | 95154 | 08944 | 95162 | 08946 | 95170 | 08948 | 95178 | 08949 | 95186 | 08951 | 11 |
| 49 | 95186 | 08951 | 95194 | 08953 | 95202 | 08954 | 95211 | 08956 | 95219 | 08957 | 95227 | 08959 | 10 |
| 50 | 95227 | 08959 | 95235 | 08961 | 95243 | 08962 | 95251 | 08964 | 95259 | 08966 | 95267 | 08967 | 09 |

**Fig.14.2** Extracts from *Norie's Tables*: Haversine and ABC tables.

## 49° / 229°  LOGS. OF TRIG. FUNCTIONS

| ' | Sine | Parts | Cosec. | Tan. | Parts | Cotan. | Secant | Parts | Cosine | |
|---|------|-------|--------|------|-------|--------|--------|-------|--------|---|
| 00·0 | 1.(9) 87778 | ' | 0.(10) 12222 | 0.(10) 06084 | ' | 1.(9) 93916 | 0.(10) 18306 | ' | 1.(9) 81694 | 60' |
| 01·0 | 87789 | | 12211 | 06109 | | 93891 | 18320 | | 81680 | |
| 02·0 | 87800 | ·1  1 | 12200 | 06135 | ·1  3 | 93865 | 18335 | ·1  1 | 81665 | |
| 03·0 | 87811 | | 12189 | 06160 | | 93840 | 18349 | | 81651 | |
| 04·0 | 87822 | | 12178 | 06186 | | 93814 | 18364 | | 81636 | |
| 05·0 | 87833 | ·2  2 | 12167 | 06211 | ·2  5 | 93789 | 18379 | ·2  3 | 81622 | 55' |
| 06·0 | 87844 | | 12156 | 06237 | | 93763 | 18393 | | 81607 | |
| 07·0 | 87855 | | 12145 | 06262 | | 93738 | 18408 | | 81592 | |
| 08·0 | 87866 | ·3  3 | 12134 | 06288 | ·3  8 | 93712 | 18422 | ·3  4 | 81578 | |
| 09·0 | 87877 | | 12123 | 06313 | | 93687 | 18437 | | 81563 | |
| 10·0 | 87888 | | 12113 | 06339 | | 93661 | 18452 | | 81549 | 50' |
| 11·0 | 87898 | ·4  4 | 12102 | 06365 | ·4  10 | 93636 | 18466 | ·4  6 | 81534 | |
| 12·0 | 87909 | | 12091 | 06390 | | 93610 | 18481 | | 81519 | |
| 13·0 | 87920 | | 12080 | 06416 | | 93584 | 18495 | | 81505 | |
| 14·0 | 87931 | | 12069 | 06441 | | 93559 | 18510 | | 81490 | |
| 15·0 | 87942 | ·5  5 | 12058 | 06467 | ·5  13 | 93533 | 18525 | ·5  7 | 81475 | 45' |
| 16·0 | 87953 | | 12047 | 06492 | | 93508 | 18539 | | 81461 | |
| 17·0 | 87964 | | 12036 | 06518 | | 93482 | 18554 | | 81446 | |
| 18·0 | 87975 | ·6  7 | 12025 | 06543 | ·6  15 | 93457 | 18569 | ·6  9 | 81431 | |
| 19·0 | 87986 | | 12015 | 06569 | | 93431 | 18583 | | 81417 | |
| 20·0 | 87996 | ·7  8 | 12004 | 06594 | | 93406 | 18598 | | 81402 | 40' |
| 21·0 | 88007 | | 11993 | 06620 | ·7  18 | 93380 | 18613 | ·7  10 | 81387 | |

## 21° / 201°  LOGS. OF TRIG. FUNCTIONS

| ' | Sine | Parts | Cosec. | Tan. | Parts | Cotan. | Secant | Parts | Cosine | |
|---|------|-------|--------|------|-------|--------|--------|-------|--------|---|
| 00·0 | 1.(9) 55433 | ' | 0.(10) 44567 | 1.(9) 58418 | ' | 0.(10) 41582 | 0.(10) 02985 | ' | 1.(9) 97015 | 60' |
| 01·0 | 55466 | | 44534 | 58456 | | 41545 | 02990 | | 97010 | |
| 02·0 | 55499 | ·1  3 | 44501 | 58493 | ·1  4 | 41507 | 02995 | ·1  0 | 97006 | |
| 03·0 | 55532 | | 44469 | 58531 | | 41469 | 02999 | | 97001 | |
| 04·0 | 55564 | | 44436 | 58569 | | 41431 | 03004 | | 96996 | |
| 05·0 | 55597 | ·2  7 | 44403 | 58606 | ·2  7 | 41394 | 03009 | ·2  1 | 96991 | 55' |
| 06·0 | 55630 | | 44370 | 58644 | | 41356 | 03014 | | 96986 | |
| 07·0 | 55663 | | 44337 | 58682 | | 41319 | 03019 | | 96981 | |
| 08·0 | 55695 | ·3  10 | 44305 | 58719 | ·3  11 | 41281 | 03024 | ·3  1 | 96976 | |
| 09·0 | 55728 | | 44272 | 58757 | | 41243 | 03029 | | 96971 | |
| 10·0 | 55761 | | 44239 | 58794 | | 41206 | 03034 | | 96967 | 50' |
| 11·0 | 55793 | ·4  13 | 44207 | 58832 | ·4  15 | 41168 | 03038 | ·4  2 | 96962 | |
| 12·0 | 55826 | | 44174 | 58869 | | 41131 | 03043 | | 96957 | |
| 13·0 | 55859 | | 44141 | 58907 | | 41093 | 03048 | | 96952 | |
| 14·0 | 55891 | | 44109 | 58944 | | 41056 | 03053 | | 96947 | |
| 15·0 | 55923 | ·5  16 | 44077 | 58981 | ·5  19 | 41019 | 03058 | ·5  2 | 96942 | 45' |
| 16·0 | 55956 | | 44044 | 59019 | | 40981 | 03063 | | 96937 | |
| 17·0 | 55988 | | 44012 | 59056 | | 40944 | 03068 | | 96932 | |
| 18·0 | 56021 | ·6  20 | 43979 | 59094 | ·6  22 | 40907 | 03073 | ·6  3 | 96927 | |
| 19·0 | 56053 | | 43947 | 59131 | | 40869 | 03078 | | 96922 | |
| 20·0 | 56086 | | 43915 | 59168 | | 40832 | 03083 | | 96917 | 40' |
| 21·0 | 56118 | ·7  23 | 43882 | 59205 | ·7  26 | 40795 | 03088 | ·7  3 | 96912 | |

Fig. 14.2 continued.

| 26° | HAVERSINES | | | | | | | | | | |
|---|---|---|---|---|---|---|---|---|---|---|---|
| → | .0 | | .2 | | .4 | | .6 | | .8 | | |
| | Log. | Nat. | Log. | Nat. | Log. | Nat. | Log. | Nat. | Log. | Nat. | Log. | Nat. |
| ' | $\overline{2}$.or(8.) | 0. | $\overline{2}$.or(8.) | 0. | $\overline{2}$.or(8.) | 0. | $\overline{2}$.or(8.) | 0. | $\overline{2}$.or(8.) | 0. | $\overline{2}$.or(8.) | 0. | ' |
| 00 | 70418 | 05060 | 70429 | 05062 | 70440 | 05063 | 70450 | 05064 | 70461 | 05065 | 70472 | 05067 | 59 |
| 01 | 70472 | 05067 | 70483 | 05068 | 70494 | 05069 | 70505 | 05071 | 70516 | 05072 | 70527 | 05073 | 58 |
| 02 | 70527 | 05073 | 70538 | 05074 | 70549 | 05076 | 70560 | 05077 | 70571 | 05078 | 70582 | 05079 | 57 |
| 03 | 70582 | 05079 | 70593 | 05081 | 70603 | 05082 | 70614 | 05083 | 70625 | 05085 | 70636 | 05086 | 56 |
| 04 | 70636 | 05086 | 70647 | 05087 | 70658 | 05088 | 70669 | 05090 | 70680 | 05091 | 70691 | 05092 | 55 |
| 53 | 73268 | 05404 | 73278 | 05405 | 73289 | 05406 | 73300 | 05407 | 73310 | 05409 | 73321 | 05410 | 06 |
| 54 | 73321 | 05410 | 73331 | 05411 | 73342 | 05413 | 73352 | 05414 | 73363 | 05415 | 73374 | 05417 | 05 |
| 55 | 73374 | 05417 | 73384 | 05418 | 73395 | 05419 | 73405 | 05421 | 73416 | 05422 | 73426 | 05423 | 04 |
| 56 | 73426 | 05423 | 73437 | 05425 | 73447 | 05426 | 73458 | 05427 | 73468 | 05429 | 73479 | 05430 | 03 |
| 57 | 73479 | 05430 | 73490 | 05431 | 73500 | 05433 | 73511 | 05434 | 73521 | 05435 | 73532 | 05436 | 02 |
| 58 | 73532 | 05436 | 73542 | 05438 | 73553 | 05439 | 73563 | 05440 | 73574 | 05442 | 73584 | 05443 | 01 |
| 59 | 73584 | 05443 | 73595 | 05444 | 73605 | 05446 | 73616 | 05447 | 73626 | 05448 | 73637 | 05450 | 00 |
| | | | .8 | | .6 | | .4 | | .2 | | .0 | ← |
| PARTS for 0'.1: | LOGS 5 | | | | | NATURALS 1. | | | | | 333° |

Fig. 14.2 continued above and below.

| 28° | HAVERSINES | | | | | | | | | | |
|---|---|---|---|---|---|---|---|---|---|---|---|
| → | .0 | | .2 | | .4 | | 6 | | .8 | | |
| | Log. | Nat. | Log. | Nat. | Log. | Nat | Log. | Nat. | Log. | Nat. | Log. | Nat. |
| ' | $\overline{2}$.or(8.) | 0 | $\overline{2}$.or(8.) | 0. | $\overline{2}$.or(8.) | 0. | $\overline{2}$.or(8.) | 0. | $\overline{2}$.or(8.) | 0. | $\overline{2}$.or(8.) | 0. | ' |
| 00 | 76735 | 05853 | 76745 | 05854 | 76755 | 05855 | 76765 | 05857 | 76775 | 05858 | 76786 | 05859 | 59 |
| 01 | 76786 | 05859 | 76796 | 05861 | 76806 | 05862 | 76816 | 05864 | 76826 | 05865 | 76834 | 05866 | 58 |
| 02 | 76836 | 05866 | 76847 | 05868 | 76857 | 05869 | 76867 | 05870 | 76877 | 05872 | 76887 | 05873 | 57 |
| 03 | 76887 | 05873 | 76897 | 05874 | 76907 | 05876 | 76917 | 05877 | 76927 | 05879 | 76937 | 05880 | 58 |
| 04 | 76937 | 05880 | 76948 | 05881 | 76958 | 05883 | 76968 | 05884 | 76978 | 05885 | 76988 | 05887 | 55 |
| 05 | 76988 | 05887 | 76998 | 05888 | 77008 | 05890 | 77018 | 05891 | 77028 | 05892 | 77038 | 05894 | 54 |
| 06 | 77038 | 05894 | 77049 | 05895 | 77059 | 05896 | 77069 | 05898 | 77079 | 05899 | 77089 | 05901 | 53 |

## 39° HAVERSINES

| ′ | .0 Log 1̄.or(9.) | .0 Nat 0. | .2 Log 1̄.or(9.) | .2 Nat 0. | .4 Log 1̄.or(9.) | .4 Nat 0. | .6 Log 1̄.or(9.) | .6 Nat 0. | .8 Log 1̄.or(9.) | .8 Nat 0. | Log 1̄.or(9.) | Nat 0. | ′ |
|---|---|---|---|---|---|---|---|---|---|---|---|---|---|
| 00 | 04699 | 11143 | 04706 | 11145 | 04713 | 11146 | 04720 | 11148 | 04728 | 11150 | 04735 | 11152 | 59 |
| 01 | 04735 | 11152 | 04742 | 11154 | 04749 | 11156 | 04756 | 11157 | 04763 | 11159 | 04770 | 11161 | 58 |
| 02 | 04770 | 11161 | 04778 | 11163 | 04785 | 11165 | 04792 | 11167 | 04799 | 11168 | 04806 | 11170 | 57 |
| 03 | 04806 | 11170 | 04813 | 11172 | 04820 | 11174 | 04827 | 11176 | 04834 | 11178 | 04842 | 11179 | 56 |
| 04 | 04842 | 11179 | 04849 | 11181 | 04856 | 11183 | 04863 | 11185 | 04870 | 11187 | 04877 | 11189 | 55 |
| 05 | 04877 | 11189 | 04884 | 11190 | 04891 | 11192 | 04899 | 11194 | 04906 | 11196 | 04913 | 11198 | 54 |
| 06 | 04913 | 11198 | 04920 | 11200 | 04927 | 11201 | 04934 | 11203 | 04941 | 11205 | 04948 | 11207 | 53 |
| 07 | 04948 | 11207 | 04956 | 11209 | 04963 | 11211 | 04970 | 11212 | 04977 | 11214 | 04984 | 11216 | 52 |
| 08 | 04984 | 11216 | 04991 | 11218 | 04998 | 11220 | 05005 | 11222 | 05012 | 11223 | 05019 | 11225 | 51 |
| 09 | 05019 | 11225 | 05027 | 11227 | 05034 | 11229 | 05041 | 11231 | 05048 | 11233 | 05055 | 11234 | 50 |
| 10 | 05055 | 11234 | 05062 | 11236 | 05069 | 11238 | 05076 | 11240 | 05083 | 11242 | 05090 | 11244 | 49 |
| 11 | 05090 | 11244 | 05098 | 11245 | 05105 | 11247 | 05112 | 11249 | 05119 | 11251 | 05126 | 11253 | 48 |
| 12 | 05126 | 11253 | 05133 | 11255 | 05140 | 11256 | 05147 | 11258 | 05154 | 11260 | 05161 | 11262 | 47 |
| 13 | 05161 | 11262 | 05168 | 11264 | 05176 | 11266 | 05183 | 11267 | 05190 | 11269 | 05197 | 11271 | 46 |
| 14 | 05197 | 11271 | 05204 | 11273 | 05211 | 11275 | 05218 | 11277 | 05225 | 11279 | 05232 | 11280 | 45 |
| 15 | 05232 | 11280 | 05239 | 11282 | 05247 | 11284 | 05254 | 11286 | 05261 | 11288 | 05268 | 11290 | 44 |
| 16 | 05268 | 11290 | 05275 | 11291 | 05282 | 11293 | 05289 | 11295 | 05296 | 11297 | 05303 | 11299 | 43 |
| 17 | 05303 | 11299 | 05310 | 11301 | 05317 | 11302 | 05324 | 11304 | 05332 | 11306 | 05339 | 11308 | 42 |

Fig. 14.2 continued above and below.

## TABLE A HOUR ANGLE

| Lat ° | 30° 330° | 31° 329° | 32° 328° | 33° 327° | 34° 326° | 35° 325° | 36° 324° | 37° 323° | 38° 322° | 39° 321° | 40° 320° | 41° 319° | 42° 318° | 43° 317° | 44° 316° | 45° 315° | Lat ° |
|---|---|---|---|---|---|---|---|---|---|---|---|---|---|---|---|---|---|
| 0 | .00 | .00 | .00 | .00 | .00 | .00 | .00 | .00 | .00 | .00 | .00 | .00 | .00 | .00 | .00 | .00 | 0 |
| 1 | .03 | .03 | .03 | .03 | .03 | .02 | .02 | .02 | .02 | .02 | .02 | .02 | .02 | .02 | .02 | .02 | 1 |
| 2 | .06 | .06 | .06 | .05 | .05 | .05 | .05 | .05 | .04 | .04 | .04 | .04 | .04 | .04 | .04 | .04 | 2 |
| 3 | .09 | .09 | .08 | .08 | .08 | .07 | .07 | .07 | .07 | .06 | .06 | .06 | .06 | .06 | .05 | .05 | 3 |
| 4 | .12 | .12 | .11 | .11 | .10 | .10 | .10 | .09 | .09 | .08 | .08 | .08 | .08 | .07 | .07 | .07 | 4 |
| 5 | .15 | .15 | .14 | .13 | .13 | .12 | .12 | .12 | .11 | .11 | .10 | .10 | .10 | .09 | .09 | .09 | 5 |
| 6 | .18 | .17 | .17 | .16 | .16 | .15 | .14 | .14 | .13 | .13 | .13 | .12 | .12 | .11 | .11 | .11 | 6 |
| 46 | 1·79 | 1·72 | 1·66 | 1·59 | 1·54 | 1·48 | 1·43 | 1·37 | 1·33 | 1·28 | 1·23 | 1·19 | 1·15 | 1·11 | 1·07 | 1·04 | 46 |
| 47 | 1·86 | 1·78 | 1·72 | 1·65 | 1·59 | 1·53 | 1·48 | 1·42 | 1·37 | 1·32 | 1·28 | 1·23 | 1·19 | 1·15 | 1·11 | 1·07 | 47 |
| 48 | 1·92 | 1·85 | 1·78 | 1·71 | 1·65 | 1·59 | 1·53 | 1·47 | 1·42 | 1·37 | 1·32 | 1·28 | 1·23 | 1·19 | 1·15 | 1·11 | 48 |
| 49 | 1·99 | 1·91 | 1·84 | 1·77 | 1·71 | 1·64 | 1·58 | 1·53 | 1·47 | 1·42 | 1·37 | 1·32 | 1·28 | 1·23 | 1·19 | 1·15 | 49 |
| 50 | 2·06 | 1·98 | 1·91 | 1·84 | 1·77 | 1·70 | 1·64 | 1·58 | 1·53 | 1·47 | 1·42 | 1·37 | 1·32 | 1·28 | 1·23 | 1·19 | 50 |
| 51 | 2·14 | 2·06 | 1·98 | 1·90 | 1·83 | 1·76 | 1·70 | 1·64 | 1·58 | 1·52 | 1·47 | 1·42 | 1·37 | 1·32 | 1·28 | 1·23 | 51 |
| 52 | 2·22 | 2·13 | 2·05 | 1·97 | 1·90 | 1·83 | 1·76 | 1·70 | 1·64 | 1·58 | 1·52 | 1·47 | 1·42 | 1·37 | 1·33 | 1·28 | 52 |
| 53 | 2·30 | 2·21 | 2·12 | 2·04 | 1·97 | 1·90 | 1·83 | 1·76 | 1·70 | 1·64 | 1·58 | 1·52 | 1·47 | 1·42 | 1·37 | 1·33 | 53 |
| 54 | 2·38 | 2·29 | 2·20 | 2·12 | 2·04 | 1·97 | 1·89 | 1·83 | 1·76 | 1·70 | 1·64 | 1·58 | 1·53 | 1·48 | 1·43 | 1·38 | 54 |
| 55 | 2·47 | 2·38 | 2·29 | 2·20 | 2·12 | 2·04 | 1·97 | 1·90 | 1·83 | 1·76 | 1·70 | 1·64 | 1·59 | 1·53 | 1·48 | 1·43 | 55 |

## TABLE B HOUR ANGLE

| Dec ° | 30° | 31° | 32° | 33° | 34° | 35° | 36° | 37° | 38° | 39° | 40° | 41° | 42° | 43° | 44° | 45° | Dec ° |
|---|---|---|---|---|---|---|---|---|---|---|---|---|---|---|---|---|---|
| | 330° | 329° | 328° | 327° | 326° | 325° | 324° | 323° | 322° | 321° | 320° | 319° | 318° | 317° | 316° | 315° | |
| 0 | ·00 | ·00 | ·00 | ·00 | ·00 | ·00 | ·00 | ·00 | ·00 | ·00 | ·00 | ·00 | ·00 | ·00 | ·00 | ·00 | 0 |
| 1 | ·03 | ·03 | ·03 | ·03 | ·03 | ·03 | ·03 | ·03 | ·03 | ·03 | ·03 | ·03 | ·03 | ·03 | ·03 | ·02 | 1 |
| 2 | ·07 | ·07 | ·07 | ·06 | ·06 | ·06 | ·06 | ·06 | ·06 | ·06 | ·05 | ·05 | ·05 | ·05 | ·05 | ·05 | 2 |
| 3 | ·10 | ·10 | ·10 | ·10 | ·09 | ·09 | ·09 | ·09 | ·09 | ·08 | ·08 | ·08 | ·08 | ·08 | ·08 | ·07 | 3 |
| 4 | ·14 | ·14 | ·13 | ·13 | ·13 | ·12 | ·12 | ·12 | ·11 | ·11 | ·11 | ·11 | ·10 | ·10 | ·10 | ·10 | 4 |
| 5 | ·17 | ·17 | ·17 | ·16 | ·16 | ·15 | ·15 | ·15 | ·14 | ·14 | ·14 | ·13 | ·13 | ·13 | ·13 | ·12 | 5 |
| 6 | ·21 | ·20 | ·20 | ·19 | ·19 | ·18 | ·18 | ·17 | ·17 | ·17 | ·16 | ·16 | ·16 | ·15 | ·15 | ·15 | 6 |
| 7 | ·25 | ·24 | ·23 | ·23 | ·22 | ·21 | ·21 | ·20 | ·20 | ·20 | ·19 | ·19 | ·18 | ·18 | ·18 | ·17 | 7 |
| 8 | ·28 | ·27 | ·27 | ·26 | ·25 | ·25 | ·24 | ·23 | ·23 | ·22 | ·22 | ·21 | ·21 | ·21 | ·20 | ·20 | 8 |
| 9 | ·32 | ·31 | ·30 | ·29 | ·28 | ·28 | ·27 | ·26 | ·26 | ·25 | ·25 | ·24 | ·24 | ·23 | ·23 | ·22 | 9 |
| 10 | ·35 | ·34 | ·33 | ·32 | ·32 | ·31 | ·30 | ·29 | ·29 | ·28 | ·27 | ·27 | ·26 | ·26 | ·25 | ·25 | 10 |
| 11 | ·39 | ·38 | ·37 | ·36 | ·35 | ·34 | ·33 | ·32 | ·32 | ·31 | ·30 | ·30 | ·29 | ·29 | ·28 | ·27 | 11 |
| 12 | ·43 | ·41 | ·40 | ·39 | ·38 | ·37 | ·36 | ·35 | ·35 | ·34 | ·33 | ·32 | ·32 | ·31 | ·31 | ·30 | 12 |
| 13 | ·46 | ·45 | ·44 | ·42 | ·41 | ·40 | ·39 | ·38 | ·37 | ·37 | ·36 | ·35 | ·35 | ·34 | ·33 | ·33 | 13 |
| 14 | ·50 | ·48 | ·47 | ·46 | ·45 | ·43 | ·42 | ·41 | ·40 | ·40 | ·39 | ·38 | ·37 | ·37 | ·36 | ·35 | 14 |
| 15 | ·54 | ·52 | ·51 | ·49 | ·48 | ·47 | ·46 | ·45 | ·44 | ·43 | ·42 | ·41 | ·40 | ·39 | ·39 | ·38 | 15 |
| 16 | ·57 | ·56 | ·54 | ·53 | ·51 | ·50 | ·49 | ·48 | ·47 | ·46 | ·45 | ·44 | ·43 | ·42 | ·41 | ·41 | 16 |
| 17 | ·61 | ·59 | ·58 | ·56 | ·55 | ·53 | ·52 | ·51 | ·50 | ·49 | ·48 | ·47 | ·46 | ·45 | ·44 | ·43 | 17 |
| 18 | ·65 | ·63 | ·61 | ·60 | ·58 | ·57 | ·55 | ·54 | ·53 | ·52 | ·51 | ·50 | ·49 | ·48 | ·47 | ·46 | 18 |
| 19 | ·69 | ·67 | ·65 | ·63 | ·62 | ·60 | ·59 | ·57 | ·56 | ·55 | ·54 | ·52 | ·51 | ·50 | ·50 | ·49 | 19 |
| 20 | ·73 | ·71 | ·69 | ·67 | ·65 | ·63 | ·62 | ·60 | ·59 | ·58 | ·57 | ·55 | ·54 | ·53 | ·52 | ·51 | 20 |
| 21 | ·77 | ·75 | ·72 | ·70 | ·69 | ·67 | ·65 | ·64 | ·62 | ·61 | ·60 | ·59 | ·57 | ·56 | ·55 | ·54 | 21 |
| 22 | ·81 | ·78 | ·76 | ·74 | ·72 | ·70 | ·69 | ·67 | ·66 | ·64 | ·63 | ·62 | ·60 | ·59 | ·58 | ·57 | 22 |
| 23 | ·85 | ·82 | ·80 | ·78 | ·76 | ·74 | ·72 | ·71 | ·69 | ·67 | ·66 | ·65 | ·63 | ·62 | ·61 | ·60 | 23 |
| 24 | ·89 | ·86 | ·84 | ·82 | ·80 | ·78 | ·76 | ·74 | ·72 | ·71 | ·69 | ·68 | ·67 | ·65 | ·64 | ·63 | 24 |
| 25 | ·93 | ·91 | ·88 | ·86 | ·83 | ·81 | ·79 | ·77 | ·76 | ·74 | ·73 | ·71 | ·70 | ·68 | ·67 | ·66 | 25 |

**Fig. 14.2** continued above and below.

## TABLE C

| A±B= | ·90′ | ·92′ | ·94′ | ·96′ | ·98′ | 1·00 | 1·02′ | 1·04′ | 1·06′ | 1·08′ | 1·10′ | 1·12′ | 1·14′ | 1·16′ | 1·18′ | 1·20′ | =A±B |
|---|---|---|---|---|---|---|---|---|---|---|---|---|---|---|---|---|---|
| | | | | | | | **A & B CORRECTION.** | | | | | | | | | | |
| Lat ° | | | | | | | AZIMUTHS | | | | | | | | | | Lat ° |
| 0 | 48·0 | 47·4 | 46·8 | 46·2 | 45·6 | 45·0 | 44·4 | 43·9 | 43·3 | 42·8 | 42·3 | 41·8 | 41·3 | 40·8 | 40·3 | 39·8 | 0 |
| 5 | 48·1 | 47·5 | 46·9 | 46·3 | 45·7 | 45·1 | 44·5 | 44·0 | 43·4 | 42·9 | 42·4 | 41·9 | 41·4 | 40·9 | 40·4 | 39·9 | 5 |
| 10 | 48·4 | 47·8 | 47·2 | 46·6 | 46·0 | 45·4 | 44·9 | 44·3 | 43·8 | 43·2 | 42·7 | 42·2 | 41·7 | 41·2 | 40·7 | 40·2 | 10 |
| 14 | 48·9 | 48·3 | 47·7 | 47·1 | 46·5 | 45·9 | 45·3 | 44·7 | 44·2 | 43·7 | 43·1 | 42·6 | 42·1 | 41·6 | 41·2 | 40·7 | 14 |
| 18 | 49·4 | 48·8 | 48·2 | 47·6 | 47·0 | 46·4 | 45·9 | 45·3 | 44·8 | 44·2 | 43·7 | 43·2 | 42·7 | 42·2 | 41·7 | 41·2 | 18 |
| 20 | 49·8 | 49·2 | 48·5 | 47·9 | 47·4 | 46·8 | 46·2 | 45·7 | 45·1 | 44·6 | 44·1 | 43·5 | 43·0 | 42·5 | 42·0 | 41·6 | 20 |
| 45 | 57·5 | 57·0 | 56·4 | 55·8 | 55·3 | 54·7 | 54·2 | 53·7 | 53·1 | 52·6 | 52·1 | 51·6 | 51·1 | 50·6 | 50·2 | 49·7 | 45 |
| 46 | 58·0 | 57·4 | 56·9 | 56·3 | 55·8 | 55·2 | 54·7 | 54·2 | 53·6 | 53·1 | 52·6 | 52·1 | 51·6 | 51·1 | 50·7 | 50·2 | 46 |
| 47 | 58·5 | 57·9 | 57·3 | 56·8 | 56·2 | 55·7 | 55·2 | 54·7 | 54·1 | 53·6 | 53·1 | 52·6 | 52·1 | 51·7 | 51·2 | 50·7 | 47 |
| 48 | 58·9 | 58·4 | 57·8 | 57·3 | 56·7 | 56·2 | 55·7 | 55·2 | 54·7 | 54·1 | 53·6 | 53·2 | 52·7 | 52·2 | 51·7 | 51·2 | 48 |
| 49 | 59·4 | 58·9 | 58·3 | 57·8 | 57·3 | 56·7 | 56·2 | 55·7 | 55·2 | 54·7 | 54·2 | 53·7 | 53·2 | 52·7 | 52·3 | 51·8 | 49 |
| 50 | 60·0 | 59·4 | 58·9 | 58·3 | 57·8 | 57·3 | 56·7 | 56·2 | 55·7 | 55·2 | 54·7 | 54·2 | 53·8 | 53·3 | 52·8 | 52·4 | 50 |
| 51 | 60·5 | 59·9 | 59·4 | 58·9 | 58·3 | 57·8 | 57·3 | 56·8 | 56·3 | 55·8 | 55·3 | 54·8 | 54·3 | 53·9 | 53·4 | 52·9 | 51 |
| 52 | 61·0 | 60·5 | 59·9 | 59·4 | 58·9 | 58·4 | 57·9 | 57·4 | 56·9 | 56·4 | 55·9 | 55·4 | 54·9 | 54·5 | 54·0 | 53·5 | 52 |
| 53 | 61·6 | 61·0 | 60·5 | 60·0 | 59·5 | 59·0 | 58·5 | 58·0 | 57·5 | 57·0 | 56·5 | 56·0 | 55·5 | 55·1 | 54·6 | 54·2 | 53 |
| 54 | 62·1 | 61·6 | 61·1 | 60·6 | 60·1 | 59·6 | 59·1 | 58·6 | 58·1 | 57·6 | 57·1 | 56·6 | 56·2 | 55·7 | 55·3 | 54·8 | 54 |

For initial course the ABC tables can be used.

A    1.68S
B    0.69N
C    0.99S  = S57.2W = 237.2°

## NP 401

LHA 35°, LAT 49°N, DEC 21° 18′N

|        | Hc       | d      | Z      | Zn     |
|--------|----------|--------|--------|--------|
|        | 50° 33′.0 | + 48.1 | 122.6° | 237.4° |
| d 40   | + 12′.0  |        |        |        |
| 8.1    | 2′.5     |        |        |        |
| Altitude | 50° 47′.5 |      |        |        |

Zenith Distance = 90°−Altitude = 39° 12′.5 = 2352.5M

## 35°, 325° L.H.A.   LATITUDE SAME NAME AS DECLINATION   N. Lat. { L.H.A. greater than 180° ...... Zn=Z / L.H.A. less than 180° ...... Zn=360°−Z

| Dec. | 45° Hc | d | Z | 46° Hc | d | Z | 47° Hc | d | Z | 48° Hc | d | Z | 49° Hc | d | Z | 50° Hc | d | Z | 51° Hc | d | Z | 52° Hc | d | Z | Dec. |
|---|---|---|---|---|---|---|---|---|---|---|---|---|---|---|---|---|---|---|---|---|---|---|---|---|---|
| 0 | 35 23.8 | +51.9 | 135.3 | 34 41.0 | +52.4 | 135.8 | 33 57.8 | +52.8 | 136.2 | 33 14.3 | +53.2 | 136.7 | 32 30.5 | +53.6 | 137.1 | 31 46.3 | +54.0 | 137.6 | 31 01.9 | +54.3 | 138.0 | 30 17.2 | +54.7 | 138.4 | 0 |
| 1 | 36 15.7 | 51.8 | 134.7 | 35 33.4 | 52.2 | 135.2 | 34 50.6 | 52.7 | 135.7 | 34 07.5 | 53.1 | 136.1 | 33 24.1 | 53.5 | 136.6 | 32 40.3 | 53.9 | 137.1 | 31 56.2 | 54.3 | 137.5 | 31 11.9 | 54.6 | 137.9 | 1 |
| 2 | 37 07.5 | 51.5 | 134.0 | 36 25.6 | 52.0 | 134.6 | 35 43.3 | 52.5 | 135.1 | 35 00.6 | 52.9 | 135.6 | 34 17.6 | 53.3 | 136.1 | 33 34.2 | 53.7 | 136.5 | 32 50.5 | 54.1 | 137.0 | 32 06.5 | 54.4 | 137.4 | 2 |
| 3 | 37 59.0 | 51.4 | 133.4 | 37 17.6 | 51.8 | 133.9 | 36 35.8 | 52.3 | 134.5 | 35 53.5 | 52.8 | 135.0 | 35 10.9 | 53.2 | 135.5 | 34 27.9 | 53.6 | 136.0 | 33 44.6 | 54.0 | 136.5 | 33 00.9 | 54.4 | 136.9 | 3 |
| 4 | 38 50.4 | 51.1 | 132.7 | 38 09.4 | 51.7 | 133.3 | 37 28.1 | 52.1 | 133.9 | 36 46.3 | 52.6 | 134.4 | 36 04.1 | 53.0 | 134.9 | 35 21.5 | 53.5 | 135.4 | 34 38.6 | 53.8 | 135.9 | 33 55.3 | 54.2 | 136.4 | 4 |
| 5 | 39 41.5 | +50.8 | 132.1 | 39 01.1 | +51.4 | 132.7 | 38 20.2 | +51.9 | 133.2 | 37 38.9 | +52.3 | 133.8 | 36 57.1 | +52.9 | 134.4 | 36 15.0 | +53.2 | 134.9 | 35 32.4 | +53.7 | 135.4 | 34 49.5 | +54.1 | 135.9 | 5 |
| 6 | 40 32.3 | 50.7 | 131.4 | 39 52.5 | 51.1 | 132.0 | 39 12.1 | 51.7 | 132.6 | 38 31.2 | 52.2 | 133.2 | 37 50.0 | 52.6 | 133.8 | 37 08.2 | 52.3 | 134.3 | 36 26.1 | 53.6 | 134.8 | 35 43.6 | 54.0 | 135.4 | 6 |
| 7 | 41 23.0 | 50.3 | 130.6 | 40 43.6 | 50.9 | 131.3 | 40 03.8 | 51.4 | 131.9 | 39 23.4 | 52.0 | 132.6 | 38 42.6 | 52.5 | 133.1 | 38 01.4 | 52.9 | 133.7 | 37 19.7 | 53.4 | 134.3 | 36 37.6 | 53.8 | 134.8 | 7 |
| 8 | 42 13.3 | 50.1 | 129.9 | 41 34.5 | 50.7 | 130.6 | 40 55.2 | 51.2 | 131.3 | 40 15.4 | 51.7 | 131.9 | 39 35.1 | 52.2 | 132.5 | 38 54.3 | 52.7 | 133.1 | 38 13.1 | 53.2 | 133.7 | 37 31.4 | 53.6 | 134.3 | 8 |
| 9 | 43 03.4 | 49.7 | 129.2 | 42 25.2 | 50.3 | 129.9 | 41 46.4 | 51.0 | 130.6 | 41 07.1 | 51.5 | 131.2 | 40 27.3 | 52.1 | 131.9 | 39 47.0 | 52.6 | 132.5 | 39 06.3 | 53.0 | 133.1 | 38 25.0 | 53.5 | 133.7 | 9 |
| 10 | 43 53.1 | +49.4 | 128.4 | 43 15.5 | +50.1 | 129.1 | 42 37.4 | +50.7 | 129.9 | 41 58.6 | +51.3 | 130.6 | 41 19.4 | +51.8 | 131.2 | 40 39.6 | +52.3 | 131.9 | 39 59.3 | +52.8 | 132.5 | 39 18.5 | +53.3 | 133.1 | 10 |
| 11 | 44 42.5 | 49.1 | 127.6 | 44 05.6 | 49.8 | 128.4 | 43 28.1 | 50.4 | 129.1 | 42 49.9 | 51.0 | 129.8 | 42 11.2 | 51.5 | 130.5 | 41 31.9 | 52.1 | 131.2 | 40 52.1 | 52.6 | 131.9 | 40 11.8 | 53.1 | 132.5 | 11 |
| 12 | 45 31.6 | 48.8 | 126.8 | 44 55.4 | 49.4 | 127.6 | 44 18.5 | 50.0 | 128.4 | 43 40.9 | 50.7 | 129.1 | 43 02.7 | 51.3 | 129.9 | 42 24.0 | 51.9 | 130.6 | 41 44.7 | 52.4 | 131.2 | 41 04.9 | 52.9 | 131.9 | 12 |
| 13 | 46 20.4 | 48.3 | 126.0 | 45 44.8 | 49.1 | 126.8 | 45 08.5 | 49.8 | 127.6 | 44 31.6 | 50.4 | 128.4 | 43 54.0 | 51.1 | 129.1 | 43 15.9 | 51.6 | 129.9 | 42 37.1 | 52.2 | 130.6 | 41 57.8 | 52.7 | 131.3 | 13 |
| 14 | 47 08.7 | 48.0 | 125.1 | 46 33.9 | 48.7 | 126.0 | 45 58.3 | 49.4 | 126.8 | 45 22.0 | 50.1 | 127.6 | 44 45.1 | 50.7 | 128.4 | 44 07.5 | 51.3 | 129.2 | 43 29.3 | 51.9 | 129.9 | 42 50.5 | 52.5 | 130.6 | 14 |
| 15 | 47 56.7 | +47.5 | 124.2 | 47 22.6 | +48.3 | 125.1 | 46 47.7 | +49.1 | 126.0 | 46 12.1 | +49.8 | 126.8 | 45 35.8 | +50.4 | 127.6 | 44 58.8 | +51.1 | 128.4 | 44 21.2 | +51.7 | 129.2 | 43 43.0 | +52.2 | 130.0 | 15 |
| 16 | 48 44.2 | 47.1 | 123.3 | 48 10.9 | 47.9 | 124.2 | 47 36.8 | 48.6 | 125.1 | 47 01.9 | 49.4 | 126.0 | 46 26.2 | 50.1 | 126.9 | 45 49.9 | 50.7 | 127.7 | 45 12.9 | 51.4 | 128.5 | 44 35.2 | 52.0 | 129.3 | 16 |
| 17 | 49 31.3 | 46.6 | 122.3 | 48 58.8 | 47.5 | 123.3 | 48 25.4 | 48.3 | 124.3 | 47 51.3 | 49.0 | 125.2 | 47 16.3 | 49.8 | 126.0 | 46 40.6 | 50.5 | 126.9 | 46 04.3 | 51.0 | 127.8 | 45 27.2 | 51.7 | 128.6 | 17 |
| 18 | 50 17.9 | 46.1 | 121.4 | 49 46.3 | 46.9 | 122.4 | 49 13.7 | 47.8 | 123.4 | 48 40.3 | 48.6 | 124.3 | 48 06.1 | 49.4 | 125.2 | 47 31.1 | 50.1 | 126.1 | 46 55.3 | 50.8 | 127.0 | 46 18.9 | 51.4 | 127.8 | 18 |
| 19 | 51 04.0 | 45.6 | 120.3 | 50 33.2 | 46.5 | 121.4 | 50 01.5 | 47.4 | 122.4 | 49 28.9 | 48.2 | 123.4 | 48 55.5 | 48.9 | 124.4 | 48 21.2 | 49.7 | 125.3 | 47 46.1 | 50.5 | 126.2 | 47 10.3 | 51.1 | 127.1 | 19 |
| 20 | 51 49.6 | +45.0 | 119.3 | 51 19.7 | +46.0 | 120.4 | 50 48.9 | +46.8 | 121.5 | 50 17.1 | +47.8 | 122.5 | 49 44.4 | +48.6 | 123.5 | 49 10.9 | +49.4 | 124.5 | 48 36.6 | +50.1 | 125.4 | 48 01.4 | +50.8 | 126.3 | 20 |
| 21 | 52 34.6 | 44.3 | 118.2 | 52 05.7 | 45.3 | 119.4 | 51 35.7 | 46.4 | 120.5 | 51 04.9 | 47.2 | 121.5 | 50 33.0 | 48.1 | 122.6 | 50 00.3 | 48.9 | 123.6 | 49 26.7 | 49.7 | 124.6 | 48 52.2 | 50.5 | 125.5 | 21 |
| 22 | 53 18.9 | 43.8 | 117.1 | 52 51.0 | 44.8 | 118.3 | 52 22.1 | 45.8 | 119.4 | 51 52.1 | 46.7 | 120.5 | 51 21.1 | 47.7 | 121.6 | 50 49.2 | 48.5 | 122.7 | 50 16.4 | 49.3 | 123.7 | 49 42.7 | 50.0 | 124.7 | 22 |
| 23 | 54 02.7 | 43.0 | 115.9 | 53 35.8 | 44.2 | 117.2 | 53 07.9 | 45.2 | 118.4 | 52 38.8 | 46.2 | 119.5 | 52 08.8 | 47.1 | 120.6 | 51 37.7 | 48.0 | 121.7 | 51 05.7 | 48.9 | 122.8 | 50 32.7 | 49.7 | 123.8 | 23 |
| 24 | 54 45.7 | 42.3 | 114.7 | 54 20.0 | 43.4 | 116.0 | 53 53.1 | 44.5 | 117.3 | 53 25.0 | 45.6 | 118.5 | 52 55.9 | 46.6 | 119.6 | 52 25.7 | 47.6 | 120.8 | 51 54.6 | 48.4 | 121.9 | 51 22.4 | 49.3 | 122.9 | 24 |
| 25 | 55 28.0 | +41.5 | 113.5 | 55 03.4 | +42.8 | 114.8 | 54 37.6 | +43.9 | 116.1 | 54 10.6 | +45.0 | 117.4 | 53 42.5 | +46.0 | 118.6 | 53 13.3 | +47.0 | 119.7 | 52 43.0 | +47.9 | 120.9 | 52 11.7 | +48.8 | 122.0 | 25 |
| 26 | 56 09.5 | 40.7 | 112.2 | 55 46.2 | 41.9 | 113.6 | 55 21.5 | 43.2 | 114.9 | 54 55.6 | 44.3 | 116.2 | 54 28.5 | 45.4 | 117.5 | 54 00.3 | 46.4 | 118.7 | 53 30.9 | 47.4 | 119.9 | 53 00.5 | 48.3 | 121.0 | 26 |
| 27 | 56 50.2 | 39.8 | 110.9 | 56 28.1 | 41.2 | 112.3 | 56 04.7 | 42.4 | 113.7 | 55 39.9 | 43.6 | 115.0 | 55 13.9 | 44.8 | 116.3 | 54 46.7 | 45.8 | 117.6 | 54 18.3 | 46.9 | 118.8 | 53 48.8 | 47.8 | 120.0 | 27 |
| 28 | 57 30.0 | 38.9 | 109.5 | 57 09.3 | 40.2 | 111.0 | 56 47.1 | 41.6 | 112.4 | 56 23.5 | 42.9 | 113.8 | 55 58.7 | 44.0 | 115.2 | 55 32.5 | 45.2 | 116.5 | 55 05.2 | 46.2 | 117.8 | 54 36.6 | 47.3 | 119.0 | 28 |
| 29 | 58 08.9 | 37.9 | 108.1 | 57 49.5 | 39.3 | 109.6 | 57 28.7 | 40.7 | 111.1 | 57 06.4 | 42.0 | 112.5 | 56 42.7 | 43.3 | 113.9 | 56 17.7 | 44.5 | 115.3 | 55 51.4 | 45.7 | 116.6 | 55 23.9 | 46.7 | 117.9 | 29 |

**Fig. 14.3** Extracts from *Sight Reduction Tables for Marine Navigation* (NP401).

## INTERPOLATION TABLE

| Dec. Inc. | Tens 10' | 20' | 30' | 40' | 50' | Decimals | Units 0 1 2 3 4 5 6 7 8 9 | Double Second Diff. and Corr. |
|---|---|---|---|---|---|---|---|---|
| 16.0 | 2.6 | 5.3 | 8.0 | 10.6 | 13.3 | .0 | 0.0 0.3 0.5 0.8 1.1 1.4 1.6 1.9 2.2 2.5 | |
| 16.1 | 2.7 | 5.3 | 8.0 | 10.7 | 13.4 | .1 | 0.0 0.3 0.6 0.9 1.1 1.4 1.7 2.0 2.2 2.5 | 1.0 |
| 16.2 | 2.7 | 5.4 | 8.1 | 10.8 | 13.5 | .2 | 0.1 0.3 0.6 0.9 1.2 1.4 1.7 2.0 2.3 2.5 | 3.0  0.1 |
| 16.3 | 2.7 | 5.4 | 8.1 | 10.9 | 13.6 | .3 | 0.1 0.4 0.6 0.9 1.2 1.5 1.7 2.0 2.3 2.6 | 4.9  0.2 |
| 16.4 | 2.7 | 5.5 | 8.2 | 10.9 | 13.7 | .4 | 0.1 0.4 0.7 0.9 1.2 1.5 1.8 2.0 2.3 2.6 | |
| 16.5 | 2.8 | 5.5 | 8.3 | 11.0 | 13.8 | .5 | 0.1 0.4 0.7 1.0 1.2 1.5 1.8 2.1 2.3 2.6 | 6.9  0.3 |
| 16.6 | 2.8 | 5.5 | 8.3 | 11.1 | 13.8 | .6 | 0.2 0.4 0.7 1.0 1.3 1.5 1.8 2.1 2.4 2.6 | 8.9  0.4 |
| 16.7 | 2.8 | 5.6 | 8.4 | 11.2 | 13.9 | .7 | 0.2 0.5 0.7 1.0 1.3 1.6 1.8 2.1 2.4 2.7 | 10.8  0.5 |
| 16.8 | 2.8 | 5.6 | 8.4 | 11.2 | 14.0 | .8 | 0.2 0.5 0.8 1.0 1.3 1.6 1.9 2.1 2.4 2.7 | 12.8  0.6 |
| 16.9 | 2.9 | 5.7 | 8.5 | 11.3 | 14.1 | .9 | 0.2 0.5 0.8 1.1 1.3 1.6 1.9 2.2 2.4 2.7 | 14.8  0.7 |
| 17.0 | 2.8 | 5.6 | 8.5 | 11.3 | 14.1 | .0 | 0.0 0.3 0.6 0.9 1.2 1.5 1.7 2.0 2.3 2.6 | 16.7  0.8 |
| 17.1 | 2.8 | 5.7 | 8.5 | 11.4 | 14.2 | .1 | 0.0 0.3 0.6 0.9 1.2 1.5 1.8 2.1 2.4 2.7 | 20.7  1.0 |
| 17.2 | 2.8 | 5.7 | 8.6 | 11.4 | 14.3 | .2 | 0.1 0.3 0.6 0.9 1.2 1.5 1.8 2.1 2.4 2.7 | 22.7  1.1 |
| 17.3 | 2.9 | 5.8 | 8.6 | 11.5 | 14.4 | .3 | 0.1 0.4 0.7 1.0 1.3 1.5 1.8 2.1 2.4 2.7 | 24.6  1.2 |
| 17.4 | 2.9 | 5.8 | 8.7 | 11.6 | 14.5 | .4 | 0.1 0.4 0.7 1.0 1.3 1.6 1.9 2.2 2.4 2.7 | 26.6  1.3 |
| 17.5 | 2.9 | 5.8 | 8.8 | 11.7 | 14.6 | .5 | 0.1 0.4 0.7 1.0 1.3 1.6 1.9 2.2 2.5 2.8 | 28.6  1.4 |
| 17.6 | 2.9 | 5.9 | 8.8 | 11.7 | 14.7 | .6 | 0.2 0.5 0.8 1.0 1.3 1.6 1.9 2.2 2.5 2.8 | 30.5  1.5 |
| 17.7 | 3.0 | 5.9 | 8.9 | 11.8 | 14.8 | .7 | 0.2 0.5 0.8 1.1 1.4 1.7 2.0 2.2 2.5 2.8 | 32.5  1.6 |
| 17.8 | 3.0 | 6.0 | 8.9 | 11.9 | 14.9 | .8 | 0.2 0.5 0.8 1.1 1.4 1.7 2.0 2.3 2.6 2.9 | 34.5  1.7 |
| 17.9 | 3.0 | 6.0 | 9.0 | 12.0 | 15.0 | .9 | 0.3 0.6 0.8 1.1 1.4 1.7 2.0 2.3 2.6 2.9 | |
| 18.0 | 3.0 | 6.0 | 9.0 | 12.0 | 15.0 | .0 | 0.0 0.3 0.6 0.9 1.2 1.5 1.8 2.2 2.5 2.8 | |
| 18.1 | 3.0 | 6.0 | 9.0 | 12.0 | 15.1 | .1 | 0.0 0.3 0.6 1.0 1.3 1.6 1.9 2.2 2.5 2.8 | 0.9 |
| 18.2 | 3.0 | 6.0 | 9.1 | 12.1 | 15.1 | .2 | 0.1 0.4 0.7 1.0 1.3 1.6 1.9 2.2 2.5 2.8 | 2.8  0.1 |
| 18.3 | 3.0 | 6.1 | 9.1 | 12.2 | 15.2 | .3 | 0.1 0.4 0.7 1.0 1.3 1.6 1.9 2.3 2.6 2.9 | 4.6  0.2 |
| 18.4 | 3.1 | 6.1 | 9.2 | 12.3 | 15.3 | .4 | 0.1 0.4 0.7 1.0 1.4 1.7 2.0 2.3 2.6 2.9 | 6.5  0.3 |
| 18.5 | 3.1 | 6.2 | 9.3 | 12.3 | 15.4 | .5 | 0.2 0.5 0.8 1.1 1.4 1.7 2.0 2.3 2.6 2.9 | 8.3  0.4 |
| 18.6 | 3.1 | 6.2 | 9.3 | 12.4 | 15.5 | .6 | 0.2 0.5 0.8 1.1 1.4 1.7 2.0 2.3 2.7 3.0 | 10.2  0.5 |
| 18.7 | 3.1 | 6.3 | 9.4 | 12.5 | 15.6 | .7 | 0.2 0.5 0.8 1.1 1.4 1.8 2.1 2.4 2.7 3.0 | 12.0  0.6 |

### AP3270

LHA 35°, LAT 49°N, DEC 21° 18'N

| | Hc | d | Z | Zn |
|---|---|---|---|---|
| | 50° 33' | +48 | 123° | 236° |
| d | +14' | | | |
| Altitude | 50° 47' | | | |

Zenith Distance = 90° − Altitude = 39° 13' = 2353M

Note that for the methods using NP401 and AP3270, the LHA and LAT are rounded to the nearest whole number giving a possible inaccuracy of up to 42M. NP401 does have a method for allowing for minutes of LHA and LAT but it is not straightforward. Note also that a direct course cannot be set from Vancouver to Honolulu.

◄ Fig. 14.3 continued.

## DECLINATION (15°-29°) SAME NAME AS LATITUDE

LAT 49°

N. Lat. { LHA greater than 180° ..... Zn=Z / LHA less than 180° ........ Zn=360−Z }

| LHA | 15° Hc | d | Z | 16° Hc | d | Z | 17° Hc | d | Z | 18° Hc | d | Z | 19° Hc | d | Z | 20° Hc | d | Z | 21° Hc | d | Z | 22° Hc | d | Z |
|---|---|---|---|---|---|---|---|---|---|---|---|---|---|---|---|---|---|---|---|---|---|---|---|---|
| 0 | 56 00 | +60 | 180 | 57 00 | +60 | 180 | 58 00 | +60 | 180 | 59 00 | +60 | 180 | 60 00 | +60 | 180 | 61 00 | +60 | 180 | 62 00 | +60 | 180 | 63 00 | +60 | 180 |
| 1 | 55 59 | 60 | 178 | 56 59 | 60 | 178 | 57 59 | 60 | 178 | 58 59 | 60 | 178 | 59 59 | 60 | 178 | 60 59 | 60 | 178 | 61 59 | 60 | 178 | 62 59 | 60 | 178 |
| 2 | 55 58 | 60 | 177 | 56 58 | 60 | 177 | 57 58 | 60 | 176 | 58 58 | 59 | 176 | 59 57 | 60 | 176 | 60 57 | 60 | 176 | 61 57 | 60 | 176 | 62 57 | 60 | 176 |
| 3 | 55 55 | 60 | 175 | 56 55 | 59 | 175 | 57 54 | 60 | 175 | 58 54 | 60 | 175 | 59 54 | 60 | 174 | 60 54 | 60 | 174 | 61 54 | 60 | 174 | 62 54 | 60 | 174 |
| 4 | 55 51 | 59 | 173 | 56 50 | 60 | 173 | 57 50 | 60 | 173 | 58 50 | 60 | 173 | 59 50 | 59 | 173 | 60 49 | 60 | 172 | 61 49 | 60 | 172 | 62 49 | 60 | 172 |
| 25 | 50 19 | +54 | 140 | 51 13 | +54 | 140 | 52 07 | +53 | 139 | 53 00 | +54 | 138 | 53 54 | +52 | 137 | 54 46 | +53 | 137 | 55 39 | +52 | 136 | 56 31 | +52 | 135 |
| 26 | 49 54 | 54 | 139 | 50 48 | 53 | 138 | 51 41 | 53 | 138 | 52 34 | 53 | 137 | 53 27 | 52 | 136 | 54 19 | 52 | 135 | 55 11 | 52 | 134 | 56 03 | 51 | 133 |
| 27 | 49 28 | 53 | 138 | 50 21 | 53 | 137 | 51 14 | 52 | 136 | 52 06 | 53 | 135 | 52 59 | 52 | 135 | 53 51 | 51 | 134 | 54 42 | 52 | 133 | 55 34 | 50 | 132 |
| 28 | 49 01 | 53 | 136 | 49 54 | 52 | 136 | 50 46 | 52 | 135 | 51 38 | 52 | 134 | 52 30 | 52 | 133 | 53 22 | 51 | 132 | 54 13 | 51 | 131 | 55 04 | 50 | 131 |
| 29 | 48 33 | 53 | 135 | 49 26 | 52 | 134 | 50 18 | 52 | 134 | 51 10 | 51 | 133 | 52 01 | 52 | 132 | 52 53 | 50 | 131 | 53 43 | 51 | 130 | 54 34 | 50 | 129 |
| 30 | 48 05 | +52 | 134 | 48 57 | +52 | 133 | 49 49 | +52 | 132 | 50 41 | +51 | 131 | 51 32 | +51 | 131 | 52 23 | +50 | 130 | 53 13 | +50 | 129 | 54 03 | +49 | 128 |
| 31 | 47 36 | 52 | 133 | 48 28 | 52 | 132 | 49 20 | 51 | 131 | 50 11 | 51 | 130 | 51 02 | 50 | 129 | 51 52 | 50 | 128 | 52 42 | 50 | 128 | 53 32 | 49 | 127 |
| 32 | 47 07 | 51 | 131 | 47 58 | 52 | 131 | 48 50 | 50 | 130 | 49 40 | 51 | 129 | 50 31 | 50 | 128 | 51 21 | 50 | 127 | 52 11 | 49 | 126 | 53 00 | 48 | 125 |
| 33 | 46 37 | 51 | 130 | 47 28 | 51 | 129 | 48 19 | 50 | 128 | 49 09 | 51 | 128 | 50 00 | 49 | 127 | 50 49 | 49 | 126 | 51 38 | 49 | 125 | 52 27 | 49 | 124 |
| 34 | 46 07 | 51 | 129 | 46 58 | 50 | 128 | 47 48 | 50 | 127 | 48 38 | 50 | 126 | 49 28 | 49 | 126 | 50 17 | 49 | 125 | 51 06 | 48 | 124 | 51 54 | 48 | 123 |
| 35 | 45 36 | +50 | 128 | 46 26 | +50 | 127 | 47 16 | +50 | 126 | 48 06 | +50 | 125 | 48 56 | +48 | 124 | 49 44 | +49 | 124 | 50 33 | +48 | 123 | 51 21 | +48 | 122 |
| 36 | 45 04 | 51 | 127 | 45 55 | 49 | 126 | 46 44 | 50 | 125 | 47 34 | 49 | 124 | 48 23 | 48 | 123 | 49 11 | 49 | 122 | 50 00 | 47 | 121 | 50 47 | 48 | 120 |
| 37 | 44 33 | 49 | 125 | 45 22 | 50 | 125 | 46 12 | 49 | 124 | 47 01 | 49 | 123 | 47 50 | 48 | 122 | 48 38 | 48 | 121 | 49 26 | 47 | 120 | 50 13 | 47 | 119 |
| 38 | 44 00 | 50 | 124 | 44 50 | 49 | 123 | 45 39 | 49 | 123 | 46 28 | 48 | 122 | 47 16 | 48 | 121 | 48 04 | 48 | 120 | 48 52 | 47 | 119 | 49 39 | 46 | 118 |
| 39 | 43 27 | 50 | 123 | 44 17 | 49 | 122 | 45 06 | 48 | 122 | 45 54 | 48 | 121 | 46 42 | 48 | 120 | 47 30 | 47 | 119 | 48 17 | 47 | 118 | 49 04 | 46 | 117 |

Fig. 14.4 Extracts from *Sight Reduction Tables for Air Navigation* (AP3270).

**TABLE 5—CORRECTION TO TABULATED ALTITUDE FOR MINUTES OF DECLINATION**

| 40 41 42 | 43 44 45 | 46 47 48 | 49 50 51 | 52 53 54 | 55 56 57 | 58 59 60 | d |
|---|---|---|---|---|---|---|---|
| 0 0 0 | 0 0 0 | 0 0 0 | 0 0 0 | 0 0 0 | 0 0 0 | 0 0 0 | 0 |
| 1 1 1 | 1 1 1 | 1 1 1 | 1 1 1 | 1 1 1 | 1 1 1 | 1 1 1 | 1 |
| 1 1 1 | 1 1 1 | 2 2 2 | 2 2 2 | 2 2 2 | 3 3 3 | 3 3 3 | 2 |
| 2 2 2 | 2 2 2 | 2 2 2 | 2 2 3 | 3 3 3 | 3 3 3 | 3 3 3 | 3 |
| 3 3 3 | 3 3 3 | 3 3 3 | 4 4 4 | 4 4 4 | 4 4 4 | 4 4 4 | 4 |
| 3 3 3 | 3 3 3 | 4 4 4 | 4 4 4 | 5 5 5 | 5 5 5 | 5 5 5 | 5 |
| 4 4 4 | 4 4 4 | 5 5 5 | 5 5 5 | 5 5 5 | 6 6 6 | 6 6 6 | 6 |
| 5 5 5 | 5 5 5 | 5 5 6 | 6 6 6 | 6 6 6 | 6 7 7 | 7 7 7 | 7 |
| 5 5 6 | 6 6 6 | 6 6 6 | 7 7 7 | 7 7 7 | 7 7 8 | 8 8 8 | 8 |
| 6 6 6 | 6 7 7 | 7 7 7 | 7 8 8 | 8 8 8 | 8 9 9 | 9 9 9 | 9 |
| 7 7 7 | 7 7 8 | 8 8 8 | 8 8 8 | 9 9 9 | 9 9 10 | 10 10 10 | 10 |
| 7 8 8 | 8 8 8 | 8 9 9 | 9 9 9 | 10 10 10 | 10 10 10 | 11 11 11 | 11 |
| 8 8 8 | 9 9 9 | 9 9 10 | 10 10 10 | 10 11 11 | 11 11 11 | 12 12 12 | 12 |
| 9 9 9 | 9 10 10 | 10 10 10 | 11 11 11 | 11 11 12 | 12 12 12 | 13 13 13 | 13 |
| 9 10 10 | 10 10 10 | 11 11 11 | 11 11 12 | 12 12 12 | 13 13 13 | 14 14 14 | 14 |
| 10 10 10 | 11 11 11 | 12 12 12 | 12 12 13 | 13 13 14 | 14 14 14 | 15 15 15 | 15 |
| 11 11 11 | 11 12 12 | 12 13 13 | 13 13 14 | 14 14 14 | 15 15 15 | 15 16 16 | 16 |
| 11 12 12 | 12 12 13 | 13 13 14 | 14 14 14 | 15 15 15 | 16 16 16 | 16 17 17 | 17 |
| 12 12 13 | 13 13 14 | 14 14 14 | 15 15 15 | 16 16 16 | 16 17 17 | 17 18 18 | 18 |
| 13 13 13 | 14 14 14 | 15 15 15 | 16 16 16 | 16 17 17 | 17 18 18 | 18 19 19 | 19 |
| 13 14 14 | 14 15 15 | 15 16 16 | 16 17 17 | 17 18 18 | 18 19 19 | 19 20 20 | 20 |
| 14 14 15 | 15 15 16 | 16 16 17 | 17 18 18 | 18 19 19 | 19 20 20 | 20 21 21 | 21 |
| 15 15 15 | 16 16 16 | 17 17 18 | 18 18 19 | 19 19 20 | 20 21 21 | 21 22 22 | 22 |
| 15 16 16 | 16 17 17 | 17 18 18 | 19 19 19 | 20 20 20 | 21 21 22 | 22 23 23 | 23 |
| 16 16 17 | 17 18 18 | 18 19 19 | 20 20 20 | 21 21 21 | 22 22 23 | 23 24 24 | 24 |
| 17 17 18 | 18 18 19 | 19 20 20 | 20 21 21 | 22 22 22 | 23 23 24 | 24 25 25 | 25 |
| 17 18 18 | 19 19 20 | 20 20 21 | 21 22 22 | 23 23 23 | 24 24 25 | 25 26 26 | 26 |

**Fig. 14.4** continued.

## Sailing Directions

The Admiralty publish no less than 72 books of *Sailing Directions* (commonly referred to as 'Pilots'), NP 1 to NP 72, which together cover all navigable seas of the world. When stocking up with charts for a long voyage, it is simplest to consult the Admiralty Catalogue of Charts and Publications which is available for inspection at all appointed chart agents. The Catalogue includes a map of the world on which the borders of the area covered by each of the books of Sailing Directions are marked. Although much of the contents of these 'Pilots' is for commercial vessels, there is much information of practical value to small craft navigation and pilotage particularly in areas not covered by a yachtsman's pilot. The following information is included:

- General description of islands and archipelagos
- Lighthouses, lights and landmarks
- Leading lines, offlying dangers, shoals and rocks
- Tidal streams
- Port facilities, pilot stations, etc
- Meteorological conditions throughout the year

There are an increasing number of long distance passage guides written by yachtsmen for yachtsmen. Some examples are:

*World Cruising Routes* by Jimmy Cornell published by Adlard Coles Nautical
*World Cruising Handbook* by Jimmy Cornell published by Adlard Coles Nautical
*The Atlantic Crossing Guide* by Philip Allen, published by Adlard Coles Nautical

## Charts

The number of charts purchased for a long voyage has to be limited both by consideration of stowage space and of cost. Nevertheless it is imperative that all areas likely to be visited are covered. It is preferable to have medium-scale charts covering all areas rather than the same number of large scale charts covering fewer places. The appropriate 'Pilot' usually contains details for safe pilotage into a port for which a large scale chart is not held.

Typically a voyage may need 50 or more charts. These should be arranged in the sequence in which they are likely to be needed, and divided up into batches of 6 to 12 each. Each batch should be kept flat in a separate folder or 'folio'. It is convenient to keep the working charts in a clear plastic envelope about 32 × 22 inches with the opening along the long side. Each batch should be placed in its folio with all titles (which are printed on one of the lengthwise edges when folded) the same way up. This way one can riffle through the edges to find the chart required, without withdrawing them all. A card should be stuck on to each folio listing the number and title of each chart it contains and its latest date of correction.

The main batch of charts should be purchased from an official chart agent as late as possible before departure to ensure that they have been corrected up-to-date. Older charts should be returned for correction before departure.

## Ocean Passages for the World (NP 136)

This HMSO publication is well worth studying by those planning an extensive trans-ocean voyage.

# 15 Radio and Electronic Aids

There are so many radio and electronic aids to navigation that several books would be required to cover the subject fully. Factors which have to be taken into account in deciding what equipment to carry include: the space and the power available, distances involved and crew carried, and, above all, the depth of one's pocket. It may simplify matters if we divide the subject into the principal uses to which such equipment can be put.

## Communications and distress

**Emergency Position Indicating Radio Beacons (EPIRBs)** The simplest distress communications system is that provided by emergency position indicating radio beacons. They operate on the standard aircraft distress frequencies of 121.5 and 243 MHz and on the Global Maritime Distress and Safety System (GMDSS) on the distress frequency of 406 MHz. They transmit an alarm tone (over several days) to aid the location of the persons in distress. The GMDSS operation is by way of the search and rescue satellite tracking system. The EPIRBs are personalised so that the identity of the vessel or person is included in the alarm signal and the satellite tracking system can pinpoint their location. Great care must be taken to ensure that they are not activated inadvertently.

**VHF radio telephones (VHF R/T)** Short range (up to 40M) communication is available on seagoing small craft by use of the radio telephone operating in the frequency range 156 to 163 MHz. The 55 standard channels (and 16 private channels) can be used for ship-shore link to national telephone networks, for port operations, for inter-ship traffic and for emergency and distress calls.

**HF single sideband radio telephones (HF SSB R/T)** For long range communication (from 40M to perhaps 3000M) a high frequency (1.5 to 30 MHz) single sideband radio telephone is required. A full Radio Operator's Licence is required for transmitting on this equipment. Modern sets can be used for telex and telefax operation which makes them very useful for the receipt of weather bulletins.

All long range radio telephone equipment requires a good antenna and a good earth. The backstay (or triatic stay) fitted with compression insulators normally makes a good antenna. The best earth on a small craft with a non-steel hull is an unpainted copper plate of several square feet on the hull exterior. There are alternative sintered bronze plates which occupy a smaller area.

**Time signals** Probably the most valuable use of radio on long distance passages is for getting time signals. If for any reason exact GMT is 'lost', celestial observations by sextant can only provide

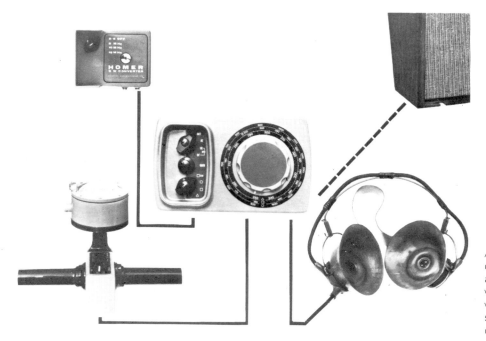

A reliable radio receiver and direction finder. The Brookes and Gatehouse Homer Heron with a short wave converter which is very valuable for time signals at long ranges in the ocean.

the ship's latitude. The determination of longitude depends on an accurate knowledge of GMT: an error of 4 seconds can produce a position error of one mile. Full details of all time signals are included in the *Admiralty List of Radio Signals Volume 5*. Good stations for time signals are BBC Radio 4 on 198 kHz, which normally has a range of more than 1000M, and BBC World Service on frequencies between 1.6 and 30 MHz. The powerful US station WWV transmits continuous time signals on a number of frequencies between 2.5 and 25 MHz.

### Direction finding

Radio direction finding (RDF) is available by a variety of systems. The photograph above shows a Brookes and Gatehouse model. However it

has been to a large extent superseded by electronic position indicating systems such as Decca, Loran and GPS. In more remote parts of the world most harbours have a marine radiobeacon which can be used as a homing aid. Alternatively aero radiobeacons and local radio stations, provided their location is known, can be useful navigational aids.

***Marine radiobeacons*** Along coasts with a high density of shipping there are numerous radiobeacons. Their range is restricted to between 10 and 200 miles to avoid interference with each other. They provide good position-finding when well within their listed range. At distances approaching their listed range, accuracy is unlikely to be better than 3°, though, when used in conjunction with a depth meter, they can be of value particularly in fog, and on coastal and inshore passages. They should not be relied on for making a landfall. Full details of all radiobeacons world-wide are given in the *Admiralty List of Radio Signals (ALRS), Volume 2*. West European and some approach beacons are also in *Macmillan's* and *Reed's Nautical Almanacs*.

**Aero radiobeacons**  Air or aero radiobeacons can also be used for marine navigation. They are listed in the *Admiralty List of Radio Signals Volume 2*. Most aero beacons have a limited range but there are some with a range more than 200M. They are usually sited inshore and their bearing accuracy is unlikely to be better than 5°.

### Position finding systems

In all position finding systems, the first objective is to establish the boat's position as a latitude and longitude. Additional selected positions, known as waypoints, can be entered and the computer will derive direction and distance from the boat's position to any of these waypoints or between any of the waypoints. Course and speed made good can also be displayed.

There are two main position-finding systems used by ships: hyperbolic (Loran, Decca, Omega) and satellite (Global Positioning System).

**Hyperbolic systems**  A hyperbolic system relies on ground transmitters whose accurate positions are known. Two transmitters are used to obtain one position line; and two others to obtain a second position line. The boat's position is the point where the two lines intersect. The two transmitters are synchronised and the times of arrival of the two transmissions are measured. If a boat is equidistant from the two transmitters, both transmissions will arrive together. If a boat is nearer one than the other,

the nearer transmitter's signal will arrive first. A measurement of the difference in time between the arrivals of the two signals will therefore be a measurement of the relative distance of the two transmitters.

There will be many points on the surface of the earth where there will be the same difference in time between the arrival of the two signals. If they were joined by a line, its shape would be a hyperbola. Having located himself on one hyperbola, the navigator must locate himself on another to get an intersection. He achieves this by measuring the time difference between the arrival of signals from two other transmitters. Normally the area is covered by only three transmitters: a main or Master station transmits first and triggers off the other two Slave stations. They transmit after the Master, but since their distance from the Master is known, the delay of these two transmissions is also known and this is allowed for in the receiving equipment on board. Two position lines are thus obtained: one between the Master and Slave A and the other between the Master and Slave B. The hyperbolic position lines can be drawn on a chart, but it is more usual for an onboard computer to work it all out and present the navigator with his position in latitude and longitude.

*Decca*  The Decca system operates in coastal waters around north west Europe (Fig 15.1) and in other local areas around the world. The effective range is 300M but this can diminish during night hours. Because of its limited range it is not suitable for ocean passage making. The accuracy is about 50 metres within 50 miles of the transmitters.

*Loran C*  Loran C has chains covering the North Atlantic, Mediterranean, Norwegian Sea, East Coast of America, North and Central Pacific, South-East Asia and possible extensions to the North Sea and South-East Atlantic. As it uses skywave

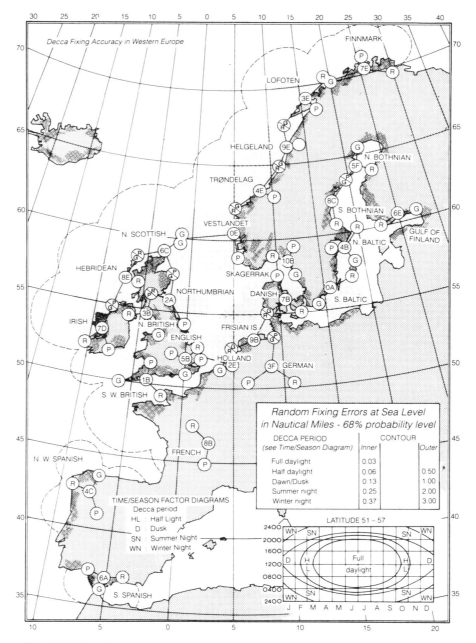

**Fig. 15.1** The Decca system – north west Europe.

transmission as well as groundwave transmission, it has a greater range (1000M) than Decca. At long ranges the accuracy is 200 metres but this decreases to 70 metres at closer distances.

*Omega* Omega uses very low frequencies and very high power and is, as a consequence, a world-wide system. The accuracy is generally 1 mile by day and 2 miles by night; but this can increase to 6 miles in regions such as the South Atlantic. Special charts with an Omega lattice are required.

**Satellite navigation systems** For world-wide position fixing, the use of radio broadcasts from orbiting navigation satellites is by far the most effective. The principal satellite navigation system is the Global Positioning System (GPS).

*Global Positioning System* A network of 24 satellites orbits the earth at a height of 11,000 miles with their orbital plane at 55° to the equator. The satellites transmit continuously to earth on two frequencies in the D band (1 to 2 GHz) and supply users with their position, velocity and time. Time is obtained from three atomic clocks which are so accurate that they will gain or lose only one second in 50,000 years. The satellites have an elaborate control system. There are five ground control monitor stations located round the earth to receive technical telemetered data from the satellites. The master control station sifts all the information it receives and transmits to the satellites their own true positions in space and the satellites in turn transmit their positions to the users.

A small craft will normally have a two-channel

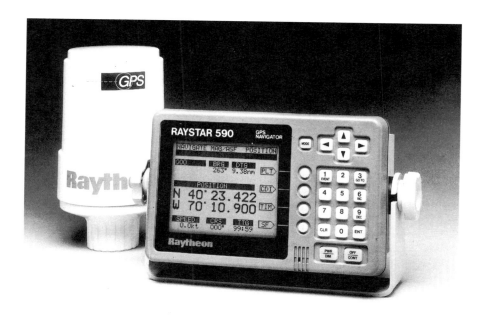

Raytheon Raystar 590 GPS Navigator and antenna.

receiver (see photograph on page 111. To use the receiver, switch it on and enter DR position, course and speed and ship's time. The receiver then searches for available satellites, selects the most suitable, and starts tracking them. From each such satellite it receives the satellite's position, its identity number and accurate time. The receiver then calculates the satellite's range by measuring the time of receipt of the signal and multiplying the time taken for the signal to come from the satellite by the speed of radio waves in air. The receiver thus locates itself on a sphere of radius $R_1$, whose centre is the transmitting satellite. The receiver then measures the range of the second and third satellites to define spheres of radius $R_2$ and $R_3$. The receiver can then work out where the spheres intersect and display this point as a latitude and longitude. More sophisticated receivers have five channels which makes the operation more efficient.

The accuracy of the Global Positioning System is potentially extremely high (less than 16 metres) but for security reasons commercially available sets have an accuracy of about 100 metres.

### Other navigational aids

**Compass** A master magnetic compass directing one or more repeater heads or compass displays has some advantages. The master compass can be located anywhere on the craft, perhaps in the position where it suffers least yaw and pitch movement and away from any ferrous material. More reliable and steadier readings can be expected under rough conditions. The repeater heads can be sited wherever they will be most visible and useful. Some have grid-steering facilities which remove much of the strain of keeping the lubberline on a particular compass reading. Modern electronic compasses automatically compensate for deviation. Electronic or master compasses require a constant

and reliable electrical supply, albeit of only 100 milliamps. If such a compass is the principal steering compass, it is essential that a normal magnetic compass is also carried. An off-course alarm is invaluable if a boat is steering by a wind-vane or autopilot.

**Log** Probably the second most important instrument, after the compass, is the log necessary for recording the distance sailed through the water. The traditional and well-proven method is with the so-called 'patent log' by Walkers and other manufacturers. It comprises a rotator towed on a long line connected to a deck-mounted head or recorder. These are also available with a speed indicator. There are a number of electronic logs which are driven by a small rotating impeller protruding only an inch or two from the hull. They are less susceptible to fouling by weed and to being bitten off by sharks, which can happen to a towed log.

**Depth meters** Most boats have a depth meter or echo sounder. The less expensive ones are usually calibrated only to 120 metres. They are excellent for inshore work, but their value for offshore sailing is somewhat limited. It is useful to be able to take soundings when approaching or over the Continental shelf. For these purposes a depth meter which will register to 200 metres or more can be of great help to the ocean navigator. These are available at not unreasonable cost, but they need to work off the boat's electricity supply.

**Barometer and barograph** Changes in barometric pressure are vital indications of a forthcoming change in the weather pattern. A regular record of barometric pressure should be maintained. An aneroid barometer (the type most usually carried) should be read and recorded in the deck log at four hourly intervals. When in the tropics or other areas where tropical revolving storms are prevalent, the pressure should be recorded at least every two hours. If space and pocket permit, a barograph is preferable as it gives a continuous trace of pressure from which the steepness of the line shows, at a glance, the rate of change.

## Telex and facsimile services

***Navtex*** Navigators of ocean-going craft rely on up-to-date and accurate information. Charts need to be corrected; sailing directions amended; Notices to Mariners consulted; navigation warnings broadcast on coast radio stations noted; and weather forecasts

and gale warnings considered. The International Maritime Organization (IMO) operates a data transmission service known as NAVTEX. It is a system for broadcasting by teleprinter (on a frequency of 518 kHz) navigation and safety messages affecting various sea areas. The service is free, requires neither a licence nor a skilled operator, and can be accessed on a small receiver capable of being fitted to all small craft. The broadcasts can be received by ship's radio-telex installations, but to obtain full benefit from the system a dedicated installation is recommended. The dedicated equipment comprises a small unit containing a receiver, permanently tuned to the broadcast frequency, and a printer using 'cash-roll' paper. The

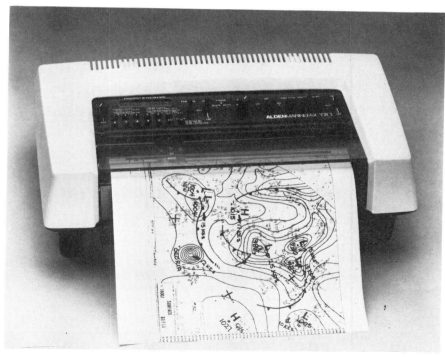

A weatherfax receiver.

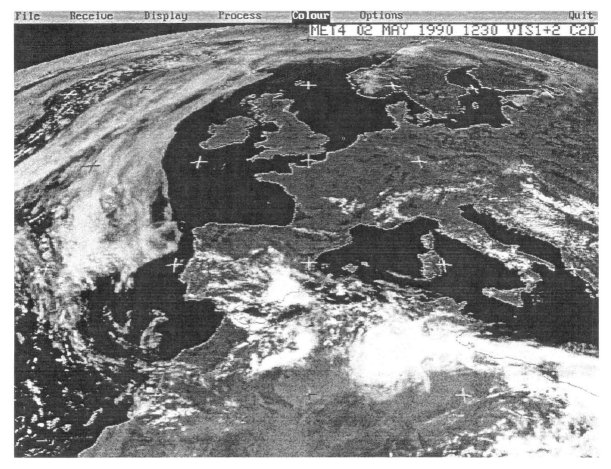

File    Receive    Display    Process    **Colour**    Options                                    Quit
                                      MET4 02 MAY 1990 1230 VIS1+2 C2D

Satellite weather picture.

unit is switched on continuously and may be programmed to receive only selected stations or categories of message.

**Weatherfax**  A facsimile (fax) printer (see photograph on page 113) can be connected to any single sideband (SSB) receiver to obtain weather charts broadcast in accordance with the World Meteorological Organization (WMO) standards (see photograph above). The normal system supplied includes its own radio receiver which can, in emergency, be used as a backup unit for the vessel's main SSB receiver.

**Navigational calculators**
Most celestial navigation problems involve the

Tamaya NC–88 calculator.

solution of a spherical triangle. As an alternative to using tables, several types of calculator are available which, given the known angles or sides of a spherical triangle, will calculate the remaining angles and sides. The requirements for such a calculator are that it must have scientific notation, conversion for degrees and minutes to degrees and decimals of a degree, polar to x-y co-ordinate conversion, and at least two memory registers.

Some calculators have pre-programmed modules, such as the Tamaya NC – 88 (see photograph above) which effectively contain sections of the *Nautical Almanac* and have separate programs for various problems such as finding latitude by meridian altitude. Such calculators are useful for

celestial navigation as no special knowledge of spherical geometry is required and considerable time and effort can be saved.

**Formulas**  The basic formulas for solving a spherical triangle on a scientific calculator are as follows:

**a)**  To find the third side of a spherical triangle (sides a, b, c and opposite angles A, B, C) given two sides and an angle

$$\cos a = \cos b . \cos c + \sin b . \sin c . \cos A$$

**b)**  To find any angle of a spherical triangle given three sides

$$\cos A = \frac{\cos a - \cos b . \cos c}{\sin b . \sin c}$$

Traverse table problems can also be solved on a calculator:

**a)**  To find departure
Departure = D Long × cos Lat

**b)**  To find D Long
$$D \; Long = \frac{Departure}{\cos Lat}$$

**c)**  To find D Lat (after a run)
D Lat = distance × cos course

**d)**  To find departure (after a run)
departure = distance × sin course

# Test Paper

*Use the extracts at the back of the book.*
Plotting can be done on the portion of plotting sheet 5333A provided (Fig 11.1), on squared paper, or on a chart if a suitable one is available.

1 What is the Greenwich Mean Time of the meridian passage of the sun in DR position 48° 20'N 14° 30'W on 10 May?

2 On 19 May in DR position 49° 50'N 4° 20'W a p.m. sight of the sun was taken when the chronometer showed 15h 54m 33s GMT. The sextant altitude of the lower limb was 36° 54'.9, index error + 2'.0, height of eye 2.0 metres. Work out the chosen position, intercept and azimuth ready for plotting.

3 What are the times (GMT) of dawn civil twilight, dusk civil twilight, sunrise and sunset on 29 August in position 52°N 3°E?

4 A boat travelling from England to Boston has passed the Scilly Isles. When should the ship's clock be altered and how should this be written in the deck log? Is it necessary to alter the deck watch?

5 A boat is on passage from Panama to New Zealand. On 7 February she is in a position estimated as about 32°S 179°W. The deck log time column is headed Z + 12. She is expected to cross the international date line shortly. What entries would be put in the deck log and what alterations should be made to the ship's clock and the chronometer?

6 On 19 May in DR position 50° 00'N 5° 45'W an observation of Polaris was taken at dawn twilight when the time by chronometer was 3h 55m. The sextant altitude was 49° 49'.1, index error − 4'.3, height of eye 2.5 metres. What was the latitude?

7 On 30 August in DR position 50° 20'N 2° 50'W a sight was taken of Jupiter at 04h 55m 17s GMT. The sextant altitude was 42° 32'.8, index error + 1'.0, height of eye 2.5 metres. Give the chosen position, intercept and azimuth.

8 a On 21 May in DR position 50° 10'N 6° 00'W it is planned to take star sights at dawn. Using AP3270 Volume 1, choose the three stars best placed in azimuth. List their names, tabulated altitudes and azimuths to assist identification.

b The sextant altitudes of the three stars chosen are given below together with the GMT when they were taken. Find the chosen position, intercept and azimuth of each star:

|          | GMT<br>h  m  s | SA         |
|----------|----------------|------------|
| 1st star | 03 53 44       | 22° 33'.9  |
| 2nd star | 03 54 20       | 48° 17'.4  |
| 3rd star | 03 55 05       | 22° 53'.3  |

Index error − 4'.0, height of eye 2.0 metres.

9 On 31 August in DR position 50° 20'N 3° 10'W, the following stars were observed:

| Star | GMT | SA |
|------|-----|-----|
|      | h  m  s |    |
| Altair | 19 53 12 | 44° 30'.1 |
| Arcturus | 19 53 41 | 33° 16'.9 |

Index error −1'.3, height of eye 2.5m.

Using *AP3270 Volume 3*, find the chosen position, intercept and azimuth of each star.

**10** On 19 May in DR position 50° 20'N 2° 50'W, an observation was taken of the moon's lower limb at 16h 53m 22s GMT, sextant altitude 30° 51'.8, index error −4'.0, height of eye 2.5 metres. Find the chosen position, intercept and azimuth.

**11** On 19 May in DR position 56° 50'N 9° 30'W, the sextant altitude of the moon's upper limb at meridian passage was 33° 06'.0, index error −3'.3, height of eye 2.5 metres. The sight was taken at 19h 54m 00s GMT, bearing south. What was the latitude?

**12** A boat in DR position 50° 15'N 6° 10'W takes dawn twilight sights as follows:

| Star | C long | Intercept | Azimuth |
|------|--------|-----------|---------|
| Mirfak | 5° 36'.5W | 6.1 T | 037° |
| Altair | 5° 45'.5W | 17.0 A | 170° |
| Arcturus | 5° 56'.8W | 2.5 T | 273° |

C Lat 50° N

Find the observed position.

**13** On 19 May in DR position 49° 50'N 4° 20'W a check of the boat's steering compass is made by the sun's azimuth at 07h 53m 15s GMT. The sun's bearing was 099°C, variation 7°W. What was the deviation and the compass error for the boat's heading at the time of the sight?

**14 a** On 19 May in DR position 49° 50'N 4° 20'W an a.m. sight of the sun's lower limb was taken at 07h 53m 15s GMT, giving a sextant altitude of 30° 37'.4, index error −3'.0, height of eye 2.5 metres. The boat then travelled 21 miles on a course of 240°T when the sun's meridian altitude was taken at 12h 16m 00s. The sextant altitude of the lower limb was 59° 59'.6; index error and height of eye as above. Find the observed position at 1216.

**b** From this position the boat then travelled 48 miles on a course of 292°T, when the following sights were taken at dusk twilight:

| Body | GMT | SA |
|------|-----|-----|
|      | h  m  s |    |
| Saturn | 20 52 10 | 25° 21'.2 |
| Moon LL | 20 52 41 | 37° 23'.3 |
| Arcturus | 20 53 05 | 51° 37'.8 |
| Spica | 20 53 50 | 27° 35'.2 |
| Regulus | 20 54 15 | 43° 52'.8 |

Index error and height of eye as above.

Find the observed position. (Assume that *AP3270 Volume 1* is not available.)

**c** The boat travels a further 30 miles on a course of 264°T when the following dawn twilight sights are taken:

| Star | GMT | SA |
|------|-----|-----|
|      | h  m  s |    |
| Polaris | 03 52 00 | 49° 33'.5 |
| Mirfak | 03 52 13 | 21° 10'.5 |
| Altair | 03 52 55 | 48° 37'.2 |
| Arcturus | 03 53 25 | 24° 15'.7 |

Index error and height of eye as above.

What was the observed position?

# Answers to Exercises

## Chapter 4

**4.1**

| | | |
|---|---|---|
| SA LL | 20° 43′.6 | |
| *IE | − 1′.9 | |
| | 20° 41′.7 | |
| *dip | − 2′.8 | |
| AA | 20° 38′.9 | |
| corrn | + 13′.5 | |
| TA | 20° 52′.4 | |

*Index Error and Dip can be applied together: − 4.7

**4.2**

| | |
|---|---|
| SA LL | 19° 57′.2 |
| IE | − 3′.0 |
| | 19° 54′.2 |
| dip | − 2′.8 |
| AA | 19° 51′.4 |
| corrn | + 13′.6 |
| TA | 20° 05′.0 |

**4.3**

| | |
|---|---|
| SA LL | 28° 51′.4 |
| IE | + 2′.0 |
| | 28° 53′.4 |
| dip | − 2′.5 |
| AA | 28° 50′.9 |
| corrn | + 14′.3 |
| TA | 29° 05′.2 |

**4.4**

| | |
|---|---|
| SA UL | 20° 54′.1 |
| IE | − 2′.6 |
| | 20° 51′.5 |
| dip | − 2′.5 |
| AA | 20° 49′.0 |
| corrn | − 18′.3 |
| TA | 20° 30′.7 |

**4.5**

| | |
|---|---|
| SA LL | 48° 31′.8 |
| IE | − 2′.6 |
| | 48° 29′.2 |
| dip | − 2′.8 |
| AA | 48° 26′.4 |
| corrn | + 15′.1 |
| TA | 48° 41′.5 |

## Chapter 5

**5.1**

**a**

| | | | | |
|---|---|---|---|---|
| GHA | 08h | 300° 53′.4 | Dec | N19° 52′.3 |
| Inc 53m | 15s | + 13° 18′.8 | d + 0.5 | + 0.4 |
| | | 314° 12′.2 | | N19° 52′.7 |

**b**

| | | | | |
|---|---|---|---|---|
| GHA | 20h | 119° 54′.8 | Dec | N8° 39′.0 |
| Inc 55m | 40s | + 13° 55′.0 | d − 0.9 | − 0′.8 |
| | | 133° 49′.8 | | N8°38′.2 |

**c**

| | | | | |
|---|---|---|---|---|
| GHA | 19h | 101° 29′.0 | Dec | S11° 59′.9 |
| Inc 52m | 32s | + 13° 08′.0 | d − 0.9 | − 0′.8 |
| | | 114° 37′.0 | | S11° 59′.1 |

**d** 

| GHA | 05h | 251° 27'.5 | Dec | S12° 32'.9 |
|---|---|---|---|---|
| Inc 55m | 25s | + 13° 51'.3 | d − 0.9 | − 0'.8 |
| | | 265° 18'.8 | | S12° 32'.1 |

**e**

| GHA | 15h | 45° 53'.1 | Dec | N19° 56'.0 |
|---|---|---|---|---|
| Inc 54m | 40s | + 13° 40'.0 | d + 0.5 | + 0'.5 |
| | | 59° 33'.1 | | N19° 56'.5 |

**5.2**

**a**
| GHA | 314° 12'.2 |
|---|---|
| C Long W | − 18° 12'.2 |
| LHA | 296° |
| C Lat 50° N | |

**b**
| GHA | 133° 49'.8 |
|---|---|
| C Long E | + 165° 10'.2 |
| LHA | 299° |
| C Lat 50° S | |

**c**
| GHA | 114° 37'.0 |
|---|---|
| C Long W | − 41° 37'.0 |
| LHA | 73° |
| C Lat 50°S | |

**d**
| GHA | 265° 18'.8 |
|---|---|
| C Long E | + 165° 41'.2 |
| | 431° |
| | − 360° |
| LHA | 71° |
| C Lat 50°S | |

**e**
| GHA | 59° 33'.1 |
|---|---|
| | + 360° |
| | 419° 33'.1 |
| C Long W | − 127° 33'.1 |
| LHA | 292° |
| C Lat 50°N | |

**5.3**

**a**

| | Hc | d | Z | Zn |
|---|---|---|---|---|
| | 31° 03' | + 44 | 97° | 097° |
| | + 39' | | | |
| Tab Alt | 31° 42' | | | |

**b**

| | Hc | d | Z | Zn |
|---|---|---|---|---|
| | 11° 39' | − 49 | 118° | 062° |
| | − 31' | | | |
| Tab Alt | 11° 08' | | | |

**c**

| | Hc | d | Z | Zn |
|---|---|---|---|---|
| | 19° 19' | + 45 | 96° | 276° |
| | + 44' | | | |
| Tab Alt | 20° 03' | | | |

**d**

| | Hc | d | Z | Zn |
|---|---|---|---|---|
| | 21° 21' | + 45 | 97° | 277° |
| | + 24' | | | |
| Tab Alt | 21° 45' | | | |

**e**

| | Hc | d | Z | Zn |
|---|---|---|---|---|
| | 28° 30' | + 44 | 94° | 094° |
| | + 41' | | | |
| Tab Alt | 29° 11' | | | |

## Chapter 6

See plots

**6.1**

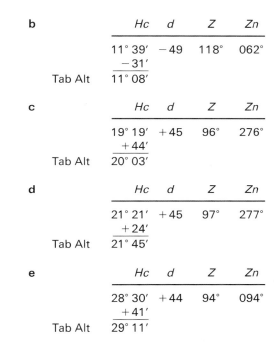

**6.2**

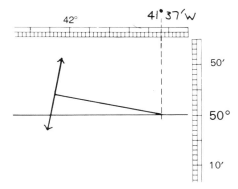

**6.3**

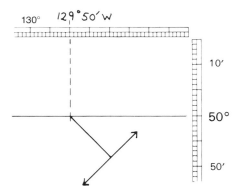

**6.4**

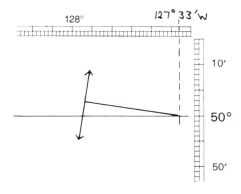

## Chapter 7

|  |  | h | m |  |
|---|---|---|---|---|
| **7.1** | MP sun Feb 16 | 12 | 14 | LMT |
|  | DR long 165°E | −11 | 00 |  |
|  | MP sun Feb 16 | 01 | 14 | GMT |

**7.2** to **7.5**   See Sight Reduction Forms

.2

# SIGHT REDUCTION FORM - SUN MERIDIAN ALTITUDE

Date        May 20

|  |  |  |  |
|---|---|---|---|
| | | DR  Latitude | 49  50.0N |
| Meridian Passage | h    m | on Greenwich meridian | Longitude    127  40.0W |
| Long in time | _____ | | |
| Time of Transit | 20  27  00  GMT | Height of Eye    2.0 | |

| | | |
|---|---|---|
| Dec  N/S | N19  58.6 | |
| d  +0.5 | +0.2 | |
| | N19  58.8 | |

| | | |
|---|---|---|
| Sextant Altitude | 60  11.9 | LL |
| IE    +2.0 | | |
| Dip   -2.5 | -0.5 | |
| Apparent Altitude | 60  11.4 | |
| Alt Corr | +15.4 | |
| True Altitude | 60  26.8 | |
| from 90 | 90 | |
| True Zenith Distance | 29  33.2 | N reverse pole |
| Declination | 19  58.8 | N |
| **Latitude** | 49  32.0 | N |

7.3

---

# SIGHT REDUCTION FORM  -  SUN MERIDIAN ALTITUDE

Date      August 30

|  |  | DR  Latitude | 50  27.0N |
|---|---|---|---|
| Meridian Passage | h    m    on Greenwich meridian | Longitude | 6  00.0W |
| Long in time |  |  |  |
| Time of Transit | 12  25  00  GMT | Height of Eye | 2.5 |

|  | Dec  N/S | N9  07.7 |
|---|---|---|
|  | d  -0.9 | -0.4 |
|  |  | N9  07.3 |

| | | |
|---|---|---|
| Sextant Altitude | 49  00.2 | UL |
| IE    +1.0 | | |
| Dip   -2.8 | -1.8 | |
| Apparent Altitude | 48  58.4 | |
| Alt Corr | -16.6 | |
| True Altitude | 48  41.8 | |
| from 90 | 90 | |
| True Zenith Distance | 41  18.2 | N  reverse pole |
| Declination | 9  07.3 | N |
| **Latitude** | 50  25.5 | N |

7.4

---

# SIGHT REDUCTION FORM  -  POLARIS

Date        May 19        h  m  s

| | | | DR  Latitude | 49  40.0N |
|---|---|---|---|---|
| | | DWT | Longitude | 6  25.0W |
| | | DWE | Height of Eye | 1.5 |
| | 03 54 08 | GMT | | |

| GHA Aries | 03 h | 281 10.1 |
|---|---|---|
| Inc | 54 m  08 s | 13 34.2 |
| | | 294 44.3 |
| DR Long E+/W- | | -6 25.0 |
| LHA Aries | | **288  19.3** |

| | |
|---|---|
| Sextant Altitude | 49  29.3 |
| IE    -2.6 | |
| Dip   -2.2 | -4.8 |
| Apparent Altitude | 49  24.5 |
| Alt Corr | -0.8 |
| True Altitude | 49  23.7 |
| $a_0$ | 1  11.3 |
| $a_1$ | 0.6 |
| $a_2$ | 0.3 |
| | -1 |
| **Latitude** | 49  35.9 |

7.5

# SIGHT REDUCTION FORM - POLARIS

Date     August 31          h  m  s

|  |  |  |  |
|---|---|---|---|
| | | DWT | DR Latitude    29 00.0N |
| | | DWE | Longitude    45 00.0W |
| | 21 53 00 | GMT | Height of Eye    2.5 |

GHA Aries    21 h        294  24.9
  Inc    053 m  00 s      13  17.2

                         307  42.2
DR Long E+/W-            -45  00.0

        LHA Aries       **262  42.1**

| | | |
|---|---|---|
| Sextant Altitude | | 28  18.1 |
| IE    +3.0 | | |
| Dip   -2.8 | | +0.2 |
| Apparent Altitude | | 28  18.3 |
| Alt Corr | | -1.8 |
| True Altitude | | 28  16.5 |
| $a_0$ | | 1  16.5 |
| $a_1$ | | 0.5 |
| $a_2$ | | 0.9 |
| | | -1 |
| **Latitude** | | 28  49.2 |

# Chapter 8

See plots

## 8.1

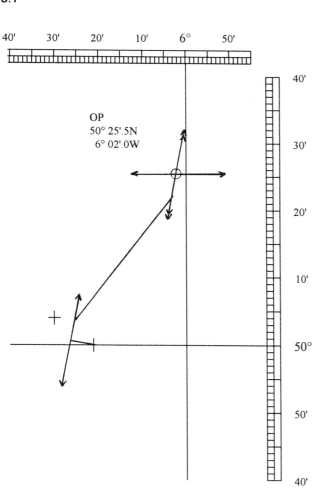

## 8.2

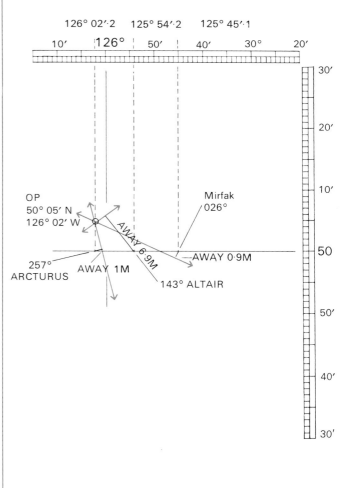

## Chapter 9

**9.1**

|        | m | s  |              |
|--------|---|----|--------------|
| 10th   | 3 | 42 |              |
| 14th   | 3 | 34 |              |
|        |   | 8  | = daily gain 2s |

By 21st it has gained 14s

| m | s    |              |
|---|------|--------------|
| 3 | 34   |              |
|   | −14  |              |
| 3 | 20   | slow on the 21st |

| h  | m   | s  |             |
|----|-----|----|-------------|
| 16 | 43  | 18 |             |
|    | +3  | 20 |             |
| 16 | 46  | 38 | correct GMT |

**9.2**

|       | h  | m  |     |
|-------|----|----|-----|
|       | 12 | 00 | LMT |
| Z+8   | 8  | 00 |     |
|       | 20 | 00 | GMT |

**9.3**

|                  | h  | m  |         |
|------------------|----|----|---------|
| evening twilight | 20 | 26 | LMT 20d |
| long W           | +8 | 32 |         |
|                  | 4  | 58 | GMT 21d |

**9.4**

|                  | h   | m  |         | h  | m  | s  |
|------------------|-----|----|---------|----|----|----|
| morning twilight | 05  | 26 | LMT 15d | 10 | 48 | 20 |
| long E           | −6  | 40 |         |    | −1 | 32 |
|                  | 22  | 46 | GMT 14d | 10 | 46 | 48 |
|                  |     |    | = 22h 46m 48s GMT |  |  |  |

When a boat crosses the date line it is important to keep track of both the date and the zone time.

# Chapter 10

See sight reduction forms

10.1

---

## SIGHT REDUCTION FORM  -  PLANET

| | | | | | Planet: VENUS | |
|---|---|---|---|---|---|---|
| Date | May 20 | h  m  s | | | | |
| | | | DWT | | DR  Latitude | 49  40.0N |
| | | | DWE | | Longitude | 3  40.0W |
| | | 20  53  55 | GMT | | Height of Eye | 2.0 |

| | | | | | | |
|---|---|---|---|---|---|---|
| GHA | 20 h | 74  15.8 | Dec N/S | N25  26.0 | | |
| Inc | 53 m   55 s | 13  28.8 | d  -0.2 | -0.2 | | |
| v | -0.6 | -0.5 | | | | |
| | | 87  44.1 | | N25  25.8 | | |
| CP Long  E+/W- | | -3  44.1 | | | | |
| LHA | | 84 | | | | |

CP Lat  N/S          50 N

| | | | | Sextant Altitude | 23  02.5 |
|---|---|---|---|---|---|
| Hc | 22  37 | Z  78 | | IE    -2.6 | |
| d  +44 | +19 | | | Dip  -2.5 | -5.1 |
| Tab Alt | 22  56 | | | Apparent Altitude | 22  57.4 |
| | | | | Alt Corr | -2.3 |
| | | | | add. corr | +0.1 |
| | | | | True Altitude | 22  55.2 |
| | | | | Tab Alt | 22  56.0 |

| | | | |
|---|---|---|---|
| Azimuth Zn  282 | | Intercept | 0.8  A |

True Altitude greater than Tab: TOWARDS.
True Altitude less than Tab: AWAY.

10.2

## SIGHT REDUCTION FORM - PLANET

| Date | Feb 15 | h m s | | | Planet: MARS | |
|---|---|---|---|---|---|---|

| | | | DWT | | DR Latitude | 49 50.0N |
|---|---|---|---|---|---|---|
| | | | DWE | | Longitude | 130 00.0W |
| | | 17 53 15 | GMT | | Height of Eye | 2.5 |

| GHA | | 17 h | 110 03.4 | Dec N/S | S22 54.0 |
|---|---|---|---|---|---|
| Inc | 53 m | 15 s | 13 18.8 | d  -0.2 | -0.2 |
| v | +0.5 | | 0.4 | | |
| | | | 123 22.6 | | S22 53.8 |
| CP Long  E+/W- | | | -130 22.6 | | |
| | LHA | | 353 | | |

CP Lat N/S        50 N

| | | | | | Sextant Altitude | 17 12.5 |
|---|---|---|---|---|---|---|
| | Hc | | 17 44 | Z 173 | IE  -2.1 | |
| | d  -60 | | -54 | | Dip  -2.8 | -4.9 |
| | Tab Alt | | 16 50 | | Apparent Altitude | 17 07.6 |
| | | | | | Alt Corr | -3.1 |
| | | | | | add. corr | +0.1 |
| | | | | | True Altitude | 17 04.6 |
| | | | | | Tab Alt | 16 50.0 |
| **Azimuth Zn** 173 | | | | | **Intercept** | 14.6  T |

True Altitude greater than Tab: TOWARDS.
True Altitude less than Tab: AWAY.

10.3

SIGHT REDUCTION FORM  -  STAR 2   (AP 3270 Volume 1)

| | | h  m | | | |
|---|---|---|---|---|---|
| Date | May 19 | | | DR Latitude | 49 40.0N |
| *Plan* | Twilight | 03 28 | LMT | Longitude | 6 25.0W |
| | DR Long | 26 | | Height of Eye | 2.0 |
| | | 03 54 | GMT  19  GD | | |

| | | | |
|---|---|---|---|
| GHA Aries  03 h | 281 10.1 | | |
| Inc  54 m   00 s | 13 32.2 | | |
| | 294 42.3 | | |
| DR Long  W/E | -6 25.0 | | |
| LHA Aries | 288 | | |

| Selected Stars | Hc | Zn | |
|---|---|---|---|
| Mirfak | 21 10 | 036 | x |
| Alpheratz | 31 52 | 082 | |
| ALTAIR | 48 04 | 166 | x |
| Rasalhague | 47 31 | 217 | |
| ARCTURUS | 24 38 | 271 | x |
| Alkaid | 40 09 | 303 | |
| Kochab | 54 07 | 335 | |

*Sights taken*

| STAR | ALTAIR | | Mirfak | | ARCTURUS |
|---|---|---|---|---|---|
| GMT | 03 54  42 | | 03 55  10 | | 03 55  50 |
| GHA ARIES | 281 10.1 | | 281 10.1 | | 281 10.1 |
| Inc  54 m  42 s | 13 42.7 | 55m   10 s | 13 49.8 | 55 m   50 s | 13 59.8 |
| | 294 52.8 | | 294 59.9 | | 295 09.9 |
| CP Long E+/W - | -6 52.8 | | -5 59.9 | | -6 09.9 |
| LHA ARIES | 288 | | 289 | | 289 |
| CP Lat  N/S | 50 N | | 50 N | | 50 N |
| Tab Alt (Hc) | 48 04 | | 21 32 | | 23 59 |
| Azimuth (Zn) | 166 | | 036 | | 272 |
| Sextant Altitude | 48 35.9 | | 21 04.9 | | 24 18.8 |
| IE      -2.6 | | | | | |
| Dip    -2.5 | -5.1 | | -5.1 | | -5.1 |
| Apparent Altitude | 48 30.8 | | 20 59.8 | | 24 13.7 |
| Alt Corr | -0.9 | | -2.5 | | -2.1 |
| True Altitude | 48 29.9 | | 20 57.3 | | 24 11.6 |
| Tab Alt | 48 04.4 | | 21 32.0 | | 23 59.0 |
| Intercept | 25.9 T | | 34.7 A | | 12.6 T |

True Altitude greater than Tab:  TOWARDS
True Altitude less than Tab:  AWAY

10.4

---

## SIGHT REDUCTION FORM - MOON

Date    August 31        h  m  s

|  |  |  |  |
|---|---|---|---|
| | DWT | DR Latitude | 49 45.0S |
| | DWE | Longitude | 165 00.0E |
| 20 54 50 | GMT | Height of Eye | 2.5 |

| GHA | 20 h | 189 07.4 | Dec N/S | N20 32.6 |
|---|---|---|---|---|
| Inc | 54 m 50 s | 13 05.0 | d  -2.6 | -2.4 |
| v | +7.6 | 6.9 | | |
| | | 202 19.3 | | N20 30.2 |
| CP Long E+/W- | | +164 40.7 | | |
| LHA | | 7 | | |

CP Lat N/S        50 S

| | | Sextant Altitude | 18 28.7  LL |
|---|---|---|---|
| Hc | 19 44    Z 173 | IE   -1.9 | |
| d  -60 | -30 | Dip  -2.8 | -4.7 |
| Tab Alt | 19 14 | Apparent Altitude | 18 24.0 |
| | | Alt Corr | 62.5 |
| | | HP   57.8 | 5.1 |
| | | If UL, -30' | |
| | | True Altitude | 19 31.6 |
| | | Tab Alt | 19 14.0 |
| Azimuth Zn   353 | | Intercept | 17.6  T |

True Altitude greater than Tab: TOWARDS.
True Altitude less than Tab: AWAY.

10.5

---

# SIGHT REDUCTION FORM - MOON MERIDIAN ALTITUDE

Date      Feb 16

| | d | h | m |
|---|---|---|---|
| Mer Pass | 16 | 14 | 51 |
| | 17 | 16 | 37 |
| Daily difference | | | 46 |

Corr $= \dfrac{45}{360}$ X  46 $=$  6

DR  Latitude      56  00.0S

Longitude      44  30.0W

Height of Eye      2.5

| | h | m |
|---|---|---|
| | 15 | 51 |
| | +6 | |
| Meridian Passage | 15 | 57 |
| Long in time | +2 | 58 |
| Time of Transit | 18 | 55 |

on Greenwich meridian

GMT

Dec  N/S      N13  37.9
d  +9.0      +8.3

N13  46.2

| | | |
|---|---|---|
| Sextant Altitude | 18 49.5 | LL |
| IE    -1.9 | | |
| Dip  -2.8 | -4.7 | |
| Apparent Altitude | 18 44.8 | |
| Alt Corr | 62.4 | |
| HP    55.0 | 1.7 | |
| If UL, -30 | | |
| True Altitude | 19 48.9 | |
| from 90 | 90 | |
| True Zenith Distance | 70 11.1 | S  reverse pole |
| Declination | 13 46.2 | N |
| **Latitude** | 56 24.9 | S |

## Chapter 11

**11.1 a**

| Co | | Dist | D Lat<br>N | Dep<br>E | |
|---|---|---|---|---|---|
| 040° | | 25M | 19.2 | 16.1 = 21'.0 D Long | |
| DR Lat | 39° 50'.0N | | Long | 3° 25'.0E | |
| D Lat | +19'.2N | | D Long | +21'.0E | |
| New DR | 40° 09'.2N | | | 3° 46'.0E | |

**b**

| Co | | Dist | D Lat<br>S | Dep<br>E | |
|---|---|---|---|---|---|
| 140° | 24M | | 18.4 | 15.4 = 20'.1 D Long | |
| DR Lat | 40° 10'.0N | | Long | 6° 24'.0W | |
| D Lat | −18'.4S | | D Long | −20'.1E | |
| New DR | 39° 51'.6N | | | 6° 03'.9W | |

**c**

| Co | | Dist | D Lat<br>S | Dep<br>W | |
|---|---|---|---|---|---|
| 230° | | 21M | 13.5 | 16.1 = 21'.0 D Long | |
| DR Lat | 40° 15'.0S | | Long | 12° 30'.0E | |
| D Lat | +13'.5S | | D Long | −21'.0W | |
| New DR | 40° 28'.5S | | | 12° 09'.0E | |

**d**

| Co | | Dist | D Lat<br>S | Dep<br>E | |
|---|---|---|---|---|---|
| 130° | | 30M | 19.3 | 23.0 = 35'.9 D Long | |
| DR Lat | 50° 10'.0S | | Long | 18° 20'.0W | |
| D Lat | +19'.3S | | D Long | −35'.9E | |
| New DR | 50° 29'.3S | | | 17° 44'.1W | |

**e**

| Co | | Dist | D Lat<br>N | Dep<br>W | |
|---|---|---|---|---|---|
| 310° | | 67M | 43.1 | 51.3 = 79'.9 D Long | |
| DR Lat | 49° 45'.0N | | Long | 175° 25'.0E | |
| D Lat | 43'.1N | | D Long | −1° 19'.9W | |
| New DR | 50° 28'.1N | | | 174° 05'.1E | |

**1.2** to **11.4** See plots.

**1.2**

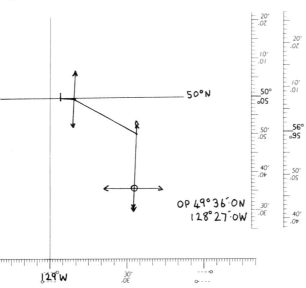

**1.3**

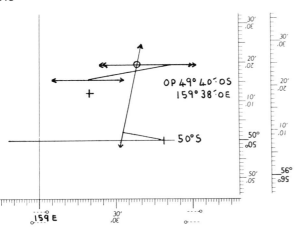

**11.4**

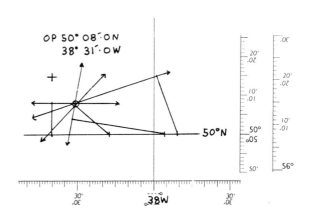

## Chapter 12

**12.1**

<table>
<tr><td></td><td></td><td></td><td>h</td><td>m</td><td></td></tr>
<tr><td>Sunrise</td><td>LMT</td><td></td><td>06</td><td>27</td><td></td></tr>
<tr><td></td><td>Long 48°W</td><td></td><td>+3</td><td>12</td><td></td></tr>
<tr><td></td><td>GMT</td><td></td><td>09</td><td>39</td><td>GD 17</td></tr>
</table>

Dec S12° 08'.2
Amplitude E12.8°S or 103°T
Compass Error 114°–103° = 11°W
Deviation 6°E

12.3

| | | | h | m | |
|---|---|---|---|---|---|
| Sunrise | LMT | | 06 | 38 | |
| | Long 165°E | | 11 | 00 | |
| | GMT | | 19 | 38 | GD 29 |

Dec  N9° 22'.2
Amplitude  E14.4°N or 076°T
Compass Error  076°–050° = 26°E
Deviation  7°E

## Test Paper

1

| | | h | m | |
|---|---|---|---|---|
| Mer Pass | | 11 | 56 | LMT 20d |
| long W | | | 58 | |
| Mer pass | | 12 | 54 | GMT 20d at DR |

2  See sight reduction form.

---

## SIGHT REDUCTION FORM - SUN

| Date | May 19 | h  m  s | | | |
|---|---|---|---|---|---|
| | | | DWT | DR Latitude | 49  50.0N |
| | | | DWE | Longitude | 4  20.0W |
| | | 15  54  33 | GMT | Height of Eye | 2.0 |

| | | | | | Dec N/S | N19  43.2 | |
|---|---|---|---|---|---|---|---|
| GHA | | 15 h | 45  53.9 | | | | |
| Inc | 54 m | 33 s | 13  38.3 | | d  +0.5 | +0.5 | |
| | | | 59  32.2 | | | N19  43.7 | |
| **CP Long E+/W-** | | | -4  32.2 | | | | |
| LHA | | | 55 | | | | |

| | | | | | Sextant Altitude | 36  54.9  LL |
|---|---|---|---|---|---|---|
| **CP Lat N/S** | | 50 N | | | IE    +2.0 | |
| | | | | | Dip   -2.5 | -0.5 |
| | Hc | | 36  44 | Z 105 | Apparent Altitude | 36  54.4 |
| | d +45 | | +33 | | Alt Corr | +14.7 |
| | Tab Alt | | 37  17 | | True Altitude | 37  09.1 |
| | | | | | Tab Alt | 37  17.0 |
| | | | | | **Intercept** | 7.9  A |
| **Azimuth Zn** | 255 | | | | | |

True Altitude greater than Tab: TOWARDS.
True Altitude less than Tab: AWAY.

**3**

| | Civil Twilight | Sunrise | Sunset | Civil Twilight |
|---|---|---|---|---|
| | h  m | h  m | h  m | h  m |
| LMT | 04 31 | 05 07 | 18 53 | 19 29 |
| Long E | −12 | −12 | −12 | −12 |
| GMT at DR | 04 19 | 04 55 | 18 41 | 19 17 |

**4**  As the DR position reaches about 7° 30′W, 22° 30′W, 37° 30′W and each successive 15° further west, the ship's clock should be put *back* one hour. A line should be drawn across the page in the deck log and the new zone number entered. Between 7° 30′W and 22° 30′W this should be Z + 1, the number being increased as each zone is entered. The chronometer or deckwatch, both of which show GMT, should not be altered.

**5**  At midnight on the night the boat crosses the 180° meridian, a line is drawn across the page in the deck log under the last entry. Z + 12 is altered to Z − 12 and the date *advanced* by two days. The ship's clock and the chronometer are not altered:

$$
\begin{array}{ll}
 & Z + 12 \\
\text{5 Aug} & \underline{\text{23h 30m}} \\
 & Z - 12 \\
\text{7 Aug} & \text{00h 15m}
\end{array}
$$

**6**   See sight reduction form.

---

## SIGHT REDUCTION FORM - POLARIS

| Date | May 19 | h m s | | |
|------|--------|-------|---|---|
| | | | DWT | DR Latitude 50 00.0N |
| | | | DWE | Longitude 5 45.0W |
| | | 03 55 00 | GMT | Height of Eye 2.5 |

| GHA Aries | 03 h | 281 10.1 |
|-----------|------|----------|
| Inc | 55 m 00 s | 13 47.3 |
| | | 294 57.4 |
| DR Long E+/W- | | -5 45.0 |
| **LHA Aries** | | **289 12.4** |

| Sextant Altitude | 49 49.1 |
|------------------|---------|
| IE   -4.3 | |
| Dip   -2.8 | -7.1 |
| Apparent Altitude | 49 42.0 |
| Alt Corr | -0.8 |
| True Altitude | 49 41.2 |
| $a_0$ | 1 10.6 |
| $a_1$ | 0.6 |
| $a_2$ | 0.3 |
| | -1 |
| **Latitude** | 49 52.7 |

7  See sight reduction form.

# SIGHT REDUCTION FORM - PLANET

Planet: JUPITER

| Date | August 30 | h m s | | | | |
|------|-----------|-------|---|---|---|---|

| | | | DWT | | DR  Latitude | 50  20.0N |
|---|---|---|---|---|---|---|
| | | | DWE | | Longitude | 2  50.0W |
| | | 04 55 17 | GMT | | Height of Eye | 2.5 |

| GHA | | 04 h | 14  38.9 | Dec N/S | N8  00.5 |
|-----|---|------|----------|---------|----------|
| Inc | 55 m | 17 s | 13  49.3 | d  -0.1 | -0.1 |
| v | 2.6 | | 2.4 | | |
| | | | | | N8  00.4 |
| | | | 28  30.6 | | |
| CP Long  E+/W- | | | -2  30.6 | | |
| LHA | | | 26 | | |

CP Lat  N/S        50 N

| | | | | | Sextant Altitude | 42  32.8 |
|---|---|---|---|---|------------------|----------|
| | Hc | | 42  45 | Z  144 | IE  +1.0 | |
| | d  +55 | | 00 | | Dip  -2.8 | -1.8 |
| | Tab Alt | | 42  45 | | Apparent Altitude | 42  31.0 |
| | | | | | Alt Corr | -1.1 |
| | | | | | add. corr | |
| | | | | | True Altitude | 42  29.9 |
| | | | | | Tab Alt | 42  45.0 |
| **Azimuth Zn** 216 | | | | | **Intercept** | 15.1  A |

True Altitude greater than Tab: TOWARDS.
True Altitude less than Tab: AWAY.

**8**  See sight reduction form.

## SIGHT REDUCTION FORM - STAR 2  (AP 3270 Volume 1)

| Date | May 21 | | |
|---|---|---|---|
| | | h  m | |
| *Plan* | Twilight | 03  28  LMT | |
| | DR Long | +24 | |
| | | 03  52  GMT  21  GD | |

| | | |
|---|---|---|
| GHA Aries  03 h | 283  08.3 | |
| Inc  52 m  00 s | 13  02.1 | |
| | 296  10.4 | |
| DR Long  W/E | 6  00.0 | |
| LHA Aries | 290 | |

| | | |
|---|---|---|
| DR  Latitude | 50  10.0 | |
| Longitude | 6  00.0 | |
| Height of Eye | 2.0 | |

| Selected Stars | Hc | Zn |
|---|---|---|
| Mirfak | 21  55 | 037  x |
| ALTAIR | 48  21 | 169  x |
| ARCTURUS | 23  21 | 273  x |

*Sights taken*

| | Altair | Arcturus | Mirfak |
|---|---|---|---|
| STAR | Altair | Arcturus | Mirfak |
| GMT | 03  55  05 | 03  53  44 | 03  54  20 |
| GHA ARIES | 283  08.3 | 283  08.3 | 283  08.3 |
| Inc  53 m  44 s | 13  28.2 | 54m  20 s  13  37.2 | 55 m  05 s  13  48.5 |
| | 296  36.5 | 296  45.5 | 296  56.8 |
| CP Long E+/W- | -5  36.5 | -5  45.5 | -5  56.8 |
| LHA ARIES | 291 | 291 | 291 |
| CP Lat  N/S | 50 N | 50 N | 50 N |
| Tab Alt (Hc) | 22  19 | 48  28 | 22  42 |
| Azimuth (Zn) | 037 | 170 | 273 |
| Sextant Altitude | 22  33.9 | 48  17.4 | 22  53.3 |
| IE  -4.0 | | | |
| Dip  -2.5 | -6.5 | -6.5 | -6.5 |
| Apparent Altitude | 22  27.4 | 48  10.9 | 22  46.8 |
| Alt Corr | -2.3 | -0.9 | -2.3 |
| True Altitude | 22  25.1 | 48  10.0 | 22  44.5 |
| Tab Alt | 22  19.0 | 48  28.0 | 22  42.0 |
| Intercept | 18.0 T | 2.5 A | 6.1 T |

True Altitude greater than Tab:  TOWARDS
True Altitude less than Tab:  AWAY

**9**   See sight reduction forms.

---

## SIGHT REDUCTION FORM  -  STAR 1   (AP 3270 Volumes 2 or 3)

| | | | Star: | Altair |
|---|---|---|---|---|
| Date   August 31 | h  m  s | | | |
| | | DWT | DR  Latitude | 50  20.0N |
| | | DWE | Longitude | 3  10.0W |
| | 19  53  12 | GMT | Height of Eye | 2.5 |

| | | | Dec N/S | N8  48.5 |
|---|---|---|---|---|
| SHA Star | 62  35.6 | | | |
| GHA Aries   19 h | 264  19.9 | | d | |
| Inc   53 m  12 s | 13  20.2 | | | N8  48.5 |
| | 340  15.7 | | | |
| **CP Long E+/W-** | -3  15.7 | | | |
| LHA Star | 337 | | | |

Sextant Altitude    44  30.1
    IE    -1.3
    Dip   -2.8                     -4.1

**CP Lat  N/S**    50 N

| | | | |
|---|---|---|---|
| Hc | 43  50 | Z 148 | |
| d  +56 | +46 | | |
| Tab Alt | 44  36 | | |

Apparent Altitude    44  26.0
Alt Corr                  -1.0

True Altitude         44  25.0
Tab Alt                 44  36.0

**Intercept**              11.0  A

**Azimuth Zn**    148

True Altitude greater than Tab: TOWARDS.
True Altitude less than Tab: AWAY.

**9**   continued.

## SIGHT REDUCTION FORM  -  STAR 1   (AP 3270 Volumes 2 or 3)

| | | | | | |
|---|---|---|---|---|---|
| Date | August 31 | h  m  s | | Star: | Arcturus |
| | | | DWT | DR  Latitude | 50  20.0N |
| | | | DWE | Longitude | 3  10.0W |
| | | 19 53 41 | GMT | Height of Eye | 2.5 |

| | | | | | |
|---|---|---|---|---|---|
| SHA Star | | 146  21.7 | Dec  N/S | N19  18.7 | |
| GHA Aries | 19 h | 264  19.9 | d | | |
| Inc   53 m   41 s | | 13  27.5 | | | |
| | | 64  09.1 | | N19  18.7 | |
| **CP Long E+/W-** | | -3  09.1 | | | |
| LHA Star | | 61 | | | |

| | | | | |
|---|---|---|---|---|
| **CP Lat  N/S** | 50 N | | Sextant Altitude | 33  16.9 |
| | | | IE     -1.3 | |
| | | | Dip    -2.8 | -4.1 |
| Hc | 32  58 | Z 100 | Apparent Altitude | 33  12.8 |
| d  +44 | +14 | | Alt Corr | -1.5 |
| Tab Alt | 33  12 | | True Altitude | 33  11.3 |
| | | | Tab Alt | 33  12.0 |
| **Azimuth Zn**   260 | | | **Intercept** | 0.7  A |

True Altitude greater than Tab: TOWARDS.
True Altitude less than Tab: AWAY.

**10**  See sight reduction form.

---

## SIGHT REDUCTION FORM - MOON

| Date | May 19 | h m s | | | |
|---|---|---|---|---|---|
| | | | DWT | DR Latitude | 50 20.0N |
| | | | DWE | Longitude | 2 50.0W |
| | | 16 53 22 | GMT | Height of Eye | 2.5 |

| GHA | 16 h | 313 01.8 | Dec N/S | N1 23.4 |
|---|---|---|---|---|
| Inc | 53 m  22 s | 12 44.0 | d  -12.9 | -11.5 |
| v | +10.2 | +9.1 | | |
| | | 325 54.9 | | N1 11.9 |
| CP Long E+/W- | | -2 54.9 | | |
| LHA | | 323 | | |

CP Lat  N/S          50 N

| | Hc | 31 47 | Z 135 |
|---|---|---|---|
| | d  +53 | +11 | |
| | Tab Alt | 31 58 | |

| Sextant Altitude | 30 51.8  LL |
|---|---|
| IE  -4.0 | |
| Dip  -2.8 | -6.8 |
| Apparent Altitude | 30 45.0 |
| Alt Corr | 58.6 |
| HP  59.5 | 7.0 |
| If UL, -30' | |
| True Altitude | 31 50.6 |
| Tab Alt | 31 58.0 |
| **Intercept** | 7.4  A |

**Azimuth Zn**    135

True Altitude greater than Tab: TOWARDS.
True Altitude less than Tab: AWAY.

**11**   See sight reduction form.

---

## SIGHT REDUCTION FORM  -  MOON MERIDIAN ALTITUDE

Date       May 19

| | d | h | m |
|---|---|---|---|
| Mer Pass | 19 | 19 | 15 |
| | 20 | 20 | 06 |

Daily difference                    51

$$\text{Corr} = \frac{9.5}{360} \times 51 = 1.3$$

| | h | m |
|---|---|---|
| | 19 | 15 |
| | | +01 |
| Meridian Passage | 19 | 16   on Greenwich meridian |
| Long in time | | +38 |
| Time of Transit | 19 | 54   GMT |

DR  Latitude          56  50.0N

Longitude           9  30.0W

Height of Eye               2.5

| Dec  N/S | NO  44.5 |
|---|---|
| d  -13.0 | -11.8 |
| | NO  32.7 |

| Sextant Altitude | 33  06.0  UL |
|---|---|
| IE      -3.3 | |
| Dip    -2.8 | -6.1 |
| Apparent Altitude | 32  59.9 |
| Alt Corr | 57.5 |
| HP      59.5 | 4.6 |
| If UL, -30 | -30.0 |
| True Altitude | 33  32.0 |
| from 90 | 90 |
| True Zenith Distance | 56  28.0   N   reverse pole |
| Declination | 0  32.7   N |
| **Latitude** | 57  00.7   N |

**12**  See plot TA1 below.

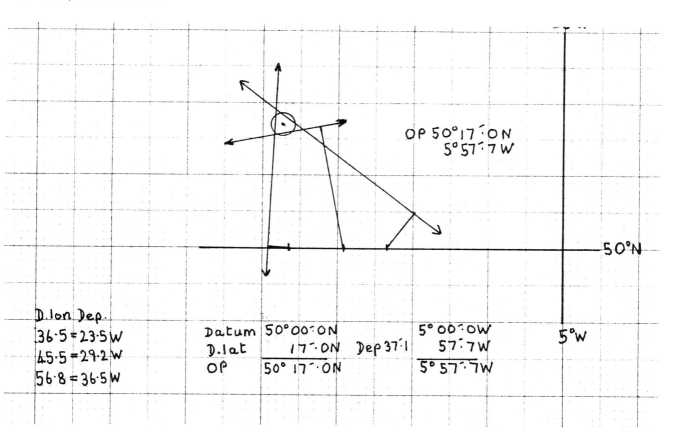

D.lon Dep.
36·5 = 23·5 W
45·5 = 29·2 W
56·8 = 36·5 W

| | | | |
|---|---|---|---|
| Datum | 50°00′·0N | | 5°00′·0W |
| D.lat | 17′·0N | Dep 37·1 | 57′·7W |
| OP | 50°17′·0N | | 5°57′·7W |

OP 50°17′·0N
5°57′·7W

50°N
5°W

**13**

| | | | |
|---|---|---|---|
| GHA 07h | 285° 54′.1 | Dec | N19° 38′.9 |
| Inc 53m 15s | 13° 18′.8 | d + 0.5 | + 0′.4 |
| | 299° 12′.9 | | N19° 39′.3 |
| DR Long W | 4° 20′.0 | | |
| LHA | 294° 52′.9 | (Use 295°) | |

C Lat 50°N
Dec 19° 39′

Z = Zn = 096° T

| | |
|---|---|
| True bearing of sun | 096°T |
| Compass bearing | 099°C |
| Compass Error | 3°W |
| Variation | 7°W |
| | |
| Deviation | 4°E |

**14**   See sight reduction forms and plots TA2 to TA4 (page 153)      **14a(i)**

---

## SIGHT REDUCTION FORM  -  SUN

| | | | | | | | |
|---|---|---|---|---|---|---|---|
| Date | May 19 | h  m  s | | | DR  Latitude | | 49  50.0N |
| | | | DWT | | Longitude | | 4  20.0W |
| | | | DWE | | Height of Eye | | 2.5 |
| | | 07  53  15 | GMT | | | | |

| | | | | | | |
|---|---|---|---|---|---|---|
| GHA | 07 h | 285  54.1 | Dec N/S | N19  38.9 | | |
| Inc | 53 m  15 s | 13  18.8 | d  +0.5 | +0.4 | | |
| | | 299  12.9 | | N19  39.3 | | |
| CP Long E+/W- | | -4  12.9 | | | | |
| LHA | | 295 | | | | |

| | |
|---|---|
| CP Lat  N/S | 50 N |

| | | |
|---|---|---|
| Hc | 30  25 | Z  96 |
| d +44 | +29 | |
| Tab Alt | 30  54 | |

Azimuth Zn   096

| | |
|---|---|
| Sextant Altitude | 30  37.4  LL |
| IE    -3.0 | |
| Dip   -2.8 | -5.8 |
| Apparent Altitude | 30  31.6 |
| Alt Corr | +14.4 |
| True Altitude | 30  46.0 |
| Tab Alt | 30  54.0 |
| **Intercept** | 8.0  A |

True Altitude greater than Tab: TOWARDS.
True Altitude less than Tab: AWAY.

14a(ii)

# SIGHT REDUCTION FORM - SUN MERIDIAN ALTITUDE

Date        May 19

|  |  | h  m |  |  | DR Latitude | 49  37.0N |
|--|--|------|--|--|-------------|-----------|
| Meridian Passage |  | 11  56 | on Greenwich meridian | | Longitude | 4  55.0W |
| Long in time |  | +20 |  |  |  |  |
| Time of Transit |  | 12  16 | GMT |  | Height of Eye | 2.5 |

| Dec  N/S |  | N19  41.6 |
|----------|--|-----------|
| d ˙ +0.5 |  | +0.1 |
|  |  | N19  41.7 |

|  | Sextant Altitude | 59  59.6 | LL |
|--|------------------|----------|----|
|  | IE    -3.0 |  |  |
|  | Dip   -2.8 | -5.8 |  |
|  | Apparent Altitude | 59  53.8 |  |
|  | Alt Corr | +15.4 |  |
|  | True Altitude | 60  09.2 |  |
|  | from 90 | 90 |  |
|  | True Zenith Distance | 29  50.8 | N reverse pole |
|  | Declination | 19  41.7 | N |
|  | **Latitude** | 49  32.5 | N |

**14b(i)**

# SIGHT REDUCTION FORM  -  PLANET

Planet: SATURN

| | | | | | | | |
|---|---|---|---|---|---|---|---|
| Date | May 19 | h  m  s | | | | Planet: SATURN | |
| | | | DWT | | DR Latitude | 49 50.5N | |
| | | | DWE | | Longitude | 6 05.0W | |
| | | 20 52 10 | GMT | | Height of Eye | 2.5 | |

| | | | |
|---|---|---|---|
| GHA | 20 h | 69 53.2 | Dec N/S |
| Inc | 52 m  10 s | 13 02.5 | d 0.0 |
| v | +2.2 | +1.9 | |
| | | 82 57.6 | |
| CP Long E+/W- | | -5 57.6 | |
| LHA | | 77 | |

Dec N/S
N22 23.9
0
N22 23.9

CP Lat N/S    50 N

| | | |
|---|---|---|
| Hc | 24 54 | Z 85 |
| d  +43 | +17 | |
| Tab Alt | 25 11 | |

| | |
|---|---|
| Sextant Altitude | 25 21.2 |
| IE   -3.0 | |
| Dip  -2.8 | -5.8 |
| Apparent Altitude | 25 15.4 |
| Alt Corr | -2.0 |
| add. corr | 0 |
| True Altitude | 25 13.4 |
| Tab Alt | 25 11.0 |
| **Intercept** | 2.4 T |

**Azimuth Zn** 275

True Altitude greater than Tab: TOWARDS.
True Altitude less than Tab: AWAY.

**14b(ii)**

---

# SIGHT REDUCTION FORM - MOON

Date     May 19     h   m   s

|  |  |  |  |
|---|---|---|---|
| | DWT | | DR   Latitude     49   50.5N |
| | DWE | | Longitude     6   05.0W |
| 20   52   41 | GMT | | Height of Eye     2.5 |

| | | | | |
|---|---|---|---|---|
| GHA | 20 h | 10   58.7 | Dec   N/S | N0   31.5 |
| Inc | 52 m   41 s | 12   34.2 | d   -12.9 | -11.3 |
| v | +10.3 | +9.0 | | |
| | | 23   41.9 | | N0   20.2 |
| **CP Long E+/W-** | | -5   41.9 | | |
| LHA | | 18 | | |

**CP Lat N/S**     50 N

| | | | |
|---|---|---|---|
| | | | Sextant Altitude     37   23.3   LL |
| Hc | 37   41 | Z   157 | IE   -3.0 |
| d   +58 | +19 | | Dip   -2.8      -5.8 |
| Tab Alt | 38   00 | | |
| | | | Apparent Altitude     37   17.5 |
| | | | Alt Corr     +55.2 |
| | | | HP    59.5     +6.9 |
| | | | If UL; -30' |
| | | | True Altitude     38   19.6 |
| | | | Tab Alt     38   00.0 |
| **Azimuth Zn**   203 | | | **Intercept**     19.6   T |

True Altitude greater than Tab: TOWARDS.
True Altitude less than Tab: AWAY.

14b(iii)

---

## SIGHT REDUCTION FORM - STAR 1 (AP 3270 Volumes 2 or 3)

| | | | | | |
|---|---|---|---|---|---|
| Date | May 19 | h  m  s | | Star: | Arcturus |
| | | | DWT | DR  Latitude | 49  50.5N |
| | | | DWE | Longitude | 6  05.0W |
| | | 20  53  05 | GMT | Height of Eye | 2.5 |

| | | | | Dec N/S | N19 18.5 |
|---|---|---|---|---|---|
| SHA Star | | 146  21.5 | | | |
| GHA Aries | 20 h | 176  52.0 | | | |
| Inc  53 m  05 s | | 13  18.4 | | | |
| | | 336  31.9 | | | |
| **CP Long E+/W -** | | -6  31.9 | | | |
| LHA Star | | 330 | | | |

| | | | | Sextant Altitude | 51  37.8 |
|---|---|---|---|---|---|
| **CP Lat  N/S** | 50 N | | | IE    -3.0 | |
| | | | | Dip   -2.8 | -5.8 |
| | | | | Apparent Altitude | 51  32.0 |
| Hc | 50  52 | Z 132 | | Alt Corr | -0.8 |
| d  +52 | +16 | | | True Altitude | 51  31.2 |
| Tab Alt | 51  08 | | | Tab Alt | 51  08.0 |
| | | | | Intercept | 23.2  T |
| **Azimuth Zn**   132 | | | | | |

True Altitude greater than Tab: TOWARDS.
True Altitude less than Tab: AWAY.

14b(iv)

## SIGHT REDUCTION FORM - STAR 1 (AP 3270 Volumes 2 or 3)

Date        May 19        h  m  s                    Star:        Spica

                          DWT                        DR  Latitude        49 50.5N

                          DWE                            Longitude       6 05.0W

              20 53 50    GMT                         Height of Eye       2.5

| | | | | | |
|---|---|---|---|---|---|
| SHA Star | | 159 01.1 | Dec N/S | S11 02.2 | |
| GHA Aries | 20 h | 176 52.0 | | | |
| Inc   53 m | 50 s | 13 29.7 | | | |
| | | 349 22.8 | | | |
| CP Long E+/W- | | -6 22.8 | | | |
| LHA Star | | 343 | | | |

CP Lat N/S        50 N

| | | | |
|---|---|---|---|
| | | | Sextant Altitude | 27 35.2 |

Sextant Altitude        27 35.2
   IE    -3.0
   Dip   -2.8                           -5.8

Hc           27 13    Z 161       Apparent Altitude    27 29.4
 d  -59        -2                 Alt Corr             -1.9
Tab Alt      27 11

True Altitude        27 27.5
Tab Alt              27 11.0

Azimuth Zn    161                 **Intercept**            16.5  T

True Altitude greater than Tab: TOWARDS.
True Altitude less than Tab: AWAY.

14b(v)

## SIGHT REDUCTION FORM - STAR 1 (AP 3270 Volumes 2 or 3)

| | | | | Star: | Regulus |
|---|---|---|---|---|---|
| Date | May 19 | h m s | | | |
| | | | DWT | DR Latitude | 49 50.5N |
| | | | DWE | Longitude | 6 05.0W |
| | | 20 54 15 | GMT | Height of Eye | 2.5 |

| | | | Dec N/S | N12 05.2 |
|---|---|---|---|---|
| SHA Star | 208 13.9 | | | |
| GHA Aries 20 h | 176 52.0 | | | |
| Inc 54 m 15 s | 13 36.0 | | | |
| | 38 41.9 | | | |
| **CP Long E+/W-** | -5 41.9 | | | |
| LHA Star | 33 | | | |

**CP Lat N/S**  50 N

| | | | Sextant Altitude | 43 52.8 |
|---|---|---|---|---|
| | | | IE -3.0 | |
| | | | Dip -2.8 | -5.8 |
| Hc | 43 22 | Z 133 | Apparent Altitude | 43 47.0 |
| d +52 | +4 | | Alt Corr | -1.0 |
| Tab Alt | 43 26 | | True Altitude | 43 46.0 |
| | | | Tab Alt | 43 26.0 |
| | | | **Intercept** | 20.0 T |

**Azimuth Zn**  227

True Altitude greater than Tab: TOWARDS.
True Altitude less than Tab: AWAY.

14c(i)

---

## SIGHT REDUCTION FORM  -  POLARIS

| Date | May 20 | h  m  s | | DR  Latitude | 49  42.9N |
|---|---|---|---|---|---|
| | | | DWT | | |
| | | | DWE | Longitude | 6  50.0W |
| | | 03  52  00 | GMT | Height of Eye | 2.5 |

| | | | |
|---|---|---|---|
| GHA Aries | 03 h | 282  09.2 | |
| Inc | 52 m   00 s | 13  02.1 | |
| | | 295  11.3 | |
| DR Long E+/W- | | -6  50.0 | |
| LHA Aries | | **288  21.3** | |

| Sextant Altitude | 49  33.5 |
|---|---|
| IE    -3.0 | |
| Dip   -2.8 | -5.8 |
| Apparent Altitude | 49  27.7 |
| Alt Corr | -0.8 |
| True Altitude | 49  26.9 |
| $a_0$ | 1  11.3 |
| $a_1$ | 0.6 |
| $a_2$ | 0.3 |
| | -1 |
| **Latitude** | 49  39.1 |

**14c(ii)**

## SIGHT REDUCTION FORM - STAR 2     (AP 3270 Volume 1)

| | | | |
|---|---|---|---|
| Date | May 20 | | |
| *Plan* | Twilight | LMT | |
| | DR Long _____ | | |
| | | GMT   GD | |

DR Latitude     49 42.9N
Longitude     6 50.0W
Height of Eye     2.5

GHA Aries    h
Inc    m    s _____

Selected Stars    Hc    Zn

DR Long   W/E _____
LHA Aries

---

### *Sights taken*

| STAR | Mirfak | | Altair | | Arcturus |
|---|---|---|---|---|---|
| GMT | 03 52 13 | | 03 52 55 | | 03 53 25 |
| GHA ARIES | 282 09.2 | | 282 09.2 | | 282 09.2 |
| Inc 52 m 13 s | 13 05.4 | 52m 55s | 13 15.9 | 53 m 25 s | 13 23.4 |
| | 295 14.6 | | 295 25.1 | | 295 32.6 |
| CP Long E+/W- | -7 14.6 | | -6 25.1 | | -6 32.6 |
| LHA ARIES | 288 | | 289 | | 289 |
| CP Lat N/S | 50 N | | 50 N | | 50 N |
| Tab Alt (Hc) | 21 10 | | 48 13 | | 23 59 |
| Azimuth (Zn) | 036 | | 168 | | 272 |
| Sextant Altitude | 21 10.5 | | 48 37.2 | | 24 15.7 |
| IE -3.0 | | | | | |
| Dip -2.8 | -5.8 | | -5.8 | | -5.8 |
| Apparent Altitude | 21 04.7 | | 48 31.4 | | 24 09.9 |
| Alt Corr | -2.5 | | -0.9 | | -2.2 |
| True Altitude | 21 02.2 | | 48 30.5 | | 24 07.7 |
| Tab Alt | 21 10.0 | | 48 13.0 | | 23 59.0 |
| Intercept | 7.8 A | | 17.5 T | | 8.7 T |

True Altitude greater than Tab: TOWARDS
True Altitude less than Tab: AWAY

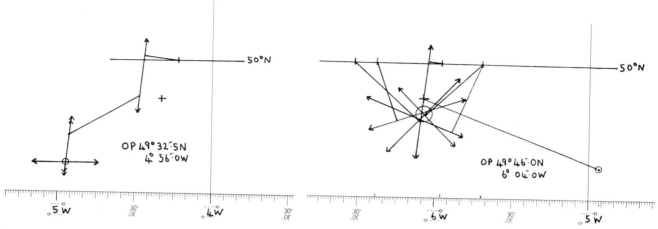

50°N

OP 49° 32.5N
4° 56.0W

.5 W
30'
.0E
.4 W
30'
.0E

Plot TA2.

50°N

OP 49° 46.0N
6° 04.0W

30'
.0E
.6 W
30'
.0E
.5 W

Plot TA3.

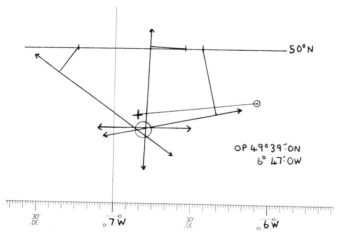

50°N

OP 49° 39.0N
6° 47.0W

30'
.0E
.7 W
30'
.0E
.6 W

Plot TA4.

# Appendix 1
# Sight Reduction Tables for Marine Navigation NP 401

These involve about the same amount of work as for *AP 3270, Volumes 2 and 3*.

> Latitude 50°N
> Declination S4° 27'.5
> LHA 306°

*NP 401* is entered with chosen latitude 50°N, LHA 306° and declination 4° (Fig A1.1). The table labelled *CONTRARY* is used as latitude (N) and declination (S) are contrary. Hc at the top of the columns is altitude, d is altitude difference (used to find the correction to apply to Hc for extra minutes of declination) and Z is azimuth angle. The rules for converting Z to Zn (azimuth) are at the top or bottom of the page (see the full extract in Appendix 6).

The tabulations for latitude 50° N, LHA 306° and declination 4° are:

| Hc | d | Z |
|----|----|----|
| 18° 52'.4 − | − 50'.2 | 121.5 |

(The minus or plus sign for d is shown once every five tabulations.) The Interpolation Table (found inside both covers) is entered down the left hand side with the declination increment (27'.5) and along the top with altitude difference (d) (−50'.2). The first part of the table is for tens and the second part for units and decimals (Fig A1.2).

The correction found is applied to Hc:

|  | Hc |
|----|----|
|  | 18° 52'.4 − |
| corrn for 50'.0 | 22'.9 |
| corrn for 0'.2 | 00'.1 |
| altitude | 18° 29'.4 |

**LATITUDE CONTRARY NAME TO DECLINATION          L.H.A. 54°, 306°**

| 47° | | | 48° | | | 49° | | | 50° | | | 51° | | | 52° | | | |
|------|------|------|------|------|------|------|------|------|------|------|------|------|------|------|------|------|------|------|
| Hc | d | Z | Hc | d | Z | Hc | d | Z | Hc | d | Z | Hc | d | Z | Hc | d | Z | Dec. |
| 23 37.9 | −47.9 | 118.0 | 23 09.6 | −48.6 | 118.4 | 22 40.9 | −49.1 | 118.7 | 22 11.9 | −49.7 | 119.1 | 21 42.6 | −50.3 | 119.5 | 21 12.9 | −50.7 | 119.8 | 0 |
| 22 50.0 | 48.2 | 118.6 | 22 21.0 | 48.7 | 119.0 | 21 51.8 | 49.3 | 119.4 | 21 22.2 | 49.8 | 119.7 | 20 52.3 | 50.3 | 120.0 | 20 22.2 | 50.9 | 120.4 | 1 |
| 22 01.8 | 48.3 | 119.3 | 21 32.3 | 48.8 | 119.6 | 21 02.5 | 49.4 | 120.0 | 20 32.4 | 50.0 | 120.3 | 20 02.0 | 50.5 | 120.6 | 19 31.3 | 51.0 | 120.9 | 2 |
| 21 13.5 | 48.3 | 119.9 | 20 43.5 | 49.0 | 120.3 | 20 13.1 | 49.6 | 120.6 | 19 42.4 | 50.0 | 120.9 | 19 11.5 | 50.6 | 121.2 | 18 40.3 | 51.1 | 121.5 | 3 |
| 20 25.1 | 48.6 | 120.6 | 19 54.5 | 49.2 | 120.9 | 19 23.5 | 49.6 | 121.2 | 18 52.4 | 50.2 | 121.5 | 18 20.9 | 50.7 | 121.8 | 17 49.2 | 51.2 | 122.0 | 4 |
| 19 36.5 | −48.6 | 121.2 | 19 05.3 | −49.2 | 121.5 | 18 33.9 | −49.8 | 121.8 | 18 02.2 | −50.3 | 122.0 | 17 30.2 | −50.8 | 122.3 | 16 58.0 | −51.2 | 122.6 | 5 |
| 18 47.9 | 48.8 | 121.8 | 18 16.1 | 49.3 | 122.1 | 17 44.1 | 49.9 | 122.4 | 17 11.9 | 50.4 | 122.6 | 16 39.4 | 50.8 | 122.9 | 16 06.8 | 51.4 | 123.1 | 6 |
| 17 59.0 | 48.9 | 122.4 | 17 26.8 | 49.5 | 122.7 | 16 54.2 | 49.9 | 122.9 | 16 21.5 | 50.5 | 123.2 | 15 48.6 | 51.0 | 123.4 | 15 15.4 | 51.4 | 123.7 | 7 |
| 17 10.1 | 49.0 | 123.0 | 16 37.3 | 49.6 | 123.3 | 16 04.3 | 50.1 | 123.5 | 15 31.0 | 50.5 | 123.8 | 14 57.6 | 51.0 | 124.0 | 14 24.0 | 51.5 | 124.2 | 8 |
| 16 21.1 | 49.2 | 123.6 | 15 47.7 | 49.6 | 123.9 | 15 14.2 | 50.1 | 124.1 | 14 40.5 | 50.6 | 124.3 | 14 06.6 | 51.1 | 124.5 | 13 32.5 | 51.6 | 124.7 | 9 |

**Fig. A1.1** Extract from *NP401*.

## INTERPOLATION TABLE

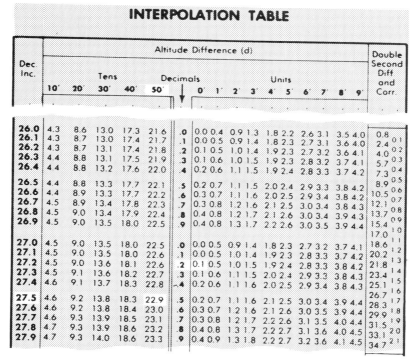

| Dec. Inc. | Altitude Difference (d) | | | | | | | | | | | | | | | Double Second Diff and Corr. |
|---|---|---|---|---|---|---|---|---|---|---|---|---|---|---|---|---|
| | Tens | | | | | Decimals | 0' | 1' | 2' | 3' | 4' | 5' | 6' | 7' | 8' 9' | |
| | 10' | 20' | 30' | 40' | 50' | ↓ | | | | | Units | | | | | |
| 26.0 | 4.3 | 8.6 | 13.0 | 17.3 | 21.6 | .0 | 0.0 0.4 | 0.9 1.3 | 1.8 2.2 | 2.6 3.1 | 3.5 4.0 | | | | | 0.8 |
| 26.1 | 4.3 | 8.7 | 13.0 | 17.4 | 21.7 | .1 | 0.0 0.5 | 0.9 1.4 | 1.8 2.3 | 2.7 3.1 | 3.6 4.0 | | | | | 2.4 0.1 |
| 26.2 | 4.3 | 8.7 | 13.1 | 17.4 | 21.8 | .2 | 0.1 0.5 | 1.0 1.4 | 1.9 2.3 | 2.7 3.2 | 3.6 4.1 | | | | | 4.0 0.2 |
| 26.3 | 4.4 | 8.8 | 13.1 | 17.5 | 21.9 | .3 | 0.1 0.6 | 1.0 1.5 | 1.9 2.3 | 2.8 3.2 | 3.7 4.1 | | | | | 5.7 0.3 |
| 26.4 | 4.4 | 8.8 | 13.2 | 17.6 | 22.0 | .4 | 0.2 0.6 | 1.1 1.5 | 1.9 2.4 | 2.8 3.3 | 3.7 4.2 | | | | | 7.3 0.4 |
| 26.5 | 4.4 | 8.8 | 13.3 | 17.7 | 22.1 | .5 | 0.2 0.7 | 1.1 1.5 | 2.0 2.4 | 2.9 3.3 | 3.8 4.2 | | | | | 8.9 0.5 |
| 26.6 | 4.4 | 8.9 | 13.3 | 17.7 | 22.2 | .6 | 0.3 0.7 | 1.1 1.6 | 2.0 2.5 | 2.9 3.4 | 3.8 4.2 | | | | | 10.5 0.6 |
| 26.7 | 4.5 | 8.9 | 13.4 | 17.8 | 22.3 | .7 | 0.3 0.8 | 1.2 1.6 | 2.1 2.5 | 3.0 3.4 | 3.8 4.3 | | | | | 12.1 0.7 |
| 26.8 | 4.5 | 9.0 | 13.4 | 17.9 | 22.4 | .8 | 0.4 0.8 | 1.2 1.7 | 2.1 2.6 | 3.0 3.4 | 3.9 4.3 | | | | | 13.7 0.8 |
| 26.9 | 4.5 | 9.0 | 13.5 | 18.0 | 22.5 | .9 | 0.4 0.8 | 1.3 1.7 | 2.2 2.6 | 3.0 3.5 | 3.9 4.4 | | | | | 15.4 0.9 |
| | | | | | | | | | | | | | | | | 17.0 1.0 |
| 27.0 | 4.5 | 9.0 | 13.5 | 18.0 | 22.5 | .0 | 0.0 0.5 | 0.9 1.4 | 1.8 2.3 | 2.7 3.2 | 3.7 4.1 | | | | | 18.6 1.1 |
| 27.1 | 4.5 | 9.0 | 13.5 | 18.0 | 22.6 | .1 | 0.0 0.5 | 1.0 1.4 | 1.9 2.3 | 2.8 3.3 | 3.7 4.2 | | | | | 20.2 1.2 |
| 27.2 | 4.5 | 9.0 | 13.6 | 18.1 | 22.6 | .2 | 0.1 0.5 | 1.0 1.5 | 1.9 2.4 | 2.8 3.3 | 3.8 4.2 | | | | | 21.8 1.3 |
| 27.3 | 4.5 | 9.1 | 13.6 | 18.2 | 22.7 | .3 | 0.1 0.6 | 1.1 1.5 | 2.0 2.4 | 2.9 3.3 | 3.8 4.3 | | | | | 23.4 1.4 |
| 27.4 | 4.6 | 9.1 | 13.7 | 18.3 | 22.8 | .4 | 0.2 0.6 | 1.1 1.6 | 2.0 2.5 | 2.9 3.4 | 3.8 4.3 | | | | | 25.1 1.5 |
| 27.5 | 4.6 | 9.2 | 13.8 | 18.3 | 22.9 | .5 | 0.2 0.7 | 1.1 1.6 | 2.1 2.5 | 3.0 3.4 | 3.9 4.4 | | | | | 26.7 1.6 |
| 27.6 | 4.6 | 9.2 | 13.8 | 18.4 | 23.0 | .6 | 0.3 0.7 | 1.2 1.6 | 2.1 2.6 | 3.0 3.5 | 3.9 4.4 | | | | | 28.3 1.7 |
| 27.7 | 4.6 | 9.3 | 13.9 | 18.5 | 23.1 | .7 | 0.3 0.8 | 1.2 1.7 | 2.2 2.6 | 3.1 3.5 | 4.0 4.4 | | | | | 29.9 1.8 |
| 27.8 | 4.7 | 9.3 | 13.9 | 18.6 | 23.2 | .8 | 0.4 0.8 | 1.3 1.7 | 2.2 2.7 | 3.1 3.6 | 4.0 4.5 | | | | | 31.5 1.9 |
| 27.9 | 4.7 | 9.3 | 14.0 | 18.6 | 23.3 | .9 | 0.4 0.9 | 1.3 1.8 | 2.2 2.7 | 3.2 3.6 | 4.1 4.5 | | | | | 33.1 2.0 |
| | | | | | | | | | | | | | | | | 34.7 2.1 |

**Fig. A1.2** Extract from *NP401*.

Z (azimuth angle) can be interpolated mentally between declinations 4° and 5° and then converted to Zn (azimuth). The azimuth, after interpolation, is 121°.7 T. Further calculations may be done if extra precision is desired but this increases the figure work involved which can always lead to error and is not necessary for normal use (unless d is printed in italic type and accompanied by a dot).

# Appendix 2
# PZX Triangle

The tabulated altitude of a heavenly body, as observed from a position of known latitude and longitude, can be found by calculation instead of by sight reduction tables. Calculation requires the solution of a spherical triangle, commonly referred to as a PZX triangle, where P is the pole, Z the chosen position and X the geographical position of the observed body (Fig A2.1).

In spherical trigonometry the sides of a spherical triangle are measured as an arc (in degrees and minutes) as subtended at the centre of the sphere. The arc ZX is the angular distance, measured at the centre of the earth, between Z and X. It is part of a great circle and is the zenith distance of the heavenly body (X) from the observer's position (Z). The complement of zenith distance is altitude.

If the angle ZX can be found, the calculated altitude at Z can be determined. This can then be compared with the true altitude of the body and the intercept deduced.

If two sides of a spherical triangle and the included angle are known, the third side and the other two angles can be deduced.

Refer to Fig A2.1. The following is known:

- The latitude of the chosen position subtracted from 90° will give the co-latitude which is side PZ.
- The declination of the body subtracted from 90° will give the polar distance (or co-declination)

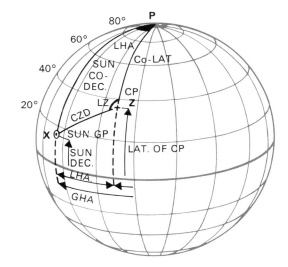

**Fig. A2.1**  PZX triangle.

which is side PX.
- The LHA of the body is angle P at the pole.

The formula for finding the calculated zenith distance, which is side ZX, is:

Hav ZX = (Hav P × sin PZ × sin PX) + Hav (PZ ∼ PX)

We can substitute:

Hav CZD = (Hav LHA × cos lat × cos dec) + Hav (lat ∼ dec)

As logs are being used, multiplication is not required, and the formula can be written out as follows:

|  |  |
|---|---|
| log Hav LHA | _ _ _ _ _ _ _ _ |
| + log cos lat | _ _ _ _ _ _ _ _ |
| + log cos dec | _____ |
| = log Hav | _ _ _ _ _ _ _ _ |
| = nat Hav | _ _ _ _ _ _ _ _ |
| + nat Hav (lat ~ dec) | _____ |
| = nat Hav | _ _ _ _ _ _ _ _ |
| = CZD | _ _ _ _ _ _ _ _ |
| From 90° | 90° 0'.0 |
|  | _____ |

Calculated altitude

(Lat ~ dec, *same* names *subtract* the smaller from the larger, *contrary* names *combine*.)

A bearing of the geographical position of the body from the chosen position is also needed. This is the angle PZX and is the azimuth angle (Z) found when using AP3270 Volume 1. This too can be calculated, but it is easily found by using the ABC tables as explained in Appendix 3.

# Appendix 3
# Marcq St Hilaire Haversine Method

This method is of value:

- If no sight reduction tables are available, or those available do not cover the boat's latitude or the heavenly body's declination;
- If it is desired to purchase or carry the minimum number of books. Only a *Nautical Almanac* and a copy of *Norie's Tables* is needed.

The method requires:

- The Local Hour Angle (LHA) of the body.
- The Latitude (Lat) by DR.
- The Declination (Dec) of the body.

*Example A3a*
Calculated Altitude

| | | | |
|---|---|---|---|
| GHA | 46° 08′ | | |
| Inc | 8° 02′ | | |
| | 54° 22′ | | |
| DR Long W | −10° 22′ | | |
| LHA | 44° 00′ | log Hav | 9.14715 |
| DR Lat N | 50° | log Cos | 9.80807 |
| Dec S | 16° 57′ | log Cos | 9.98071 |
| | | log Hav | 8.93593 |
| | | = nat Hav | 0.08628 |
| Lat ~ Dec | 66° 57′ | nat Hav | 0.30423 |
| Calc ZD | 77° 21′.1 | nat Hav | 0.39051 |

Calculated altitude = 90° − Calc ZD = 12° 38′.9

Sequence of work:
Use the extracts from *Norie's Tables* provided.

1 Work out the Lat ~ Dec (same names subtract, contrary names add): N 50° + S 16° 57′ = 66° 57′.

2 With the LHA of 44° 00′ using the Haversine tables, find the page with 44° in the top left hand corner (Fig A3.1). As there are no minutes the figure to extract will be the first entry which is in bold type .**14715**. At the top of the column there is a 9 which should be written in front of the figure just found: **9.14715**. This is the log Haversine.

3 With the Lat of 50° and the Dec of 16° 57′, use the table of Logs of Trig Functions to find the log cosine for latitude and declination. The pages marked 50° and 16° are required. The cosine column is to the right on the page. The cosine for latitude 50° is 9.80807, and for declination 16° 57′ is **9.98071** (Figs A3.2, A3.3).

4 Add the log Haversine and the log cosines to obtain the log Haversine **28.93593**. Discard any tens as the method only used units: **8.93593**.

5 Find **8.93593** (or the figure nearest to it **8.93591**) in the Haversine tables. This will be in bold type with a fainter figure alongside, 0.08628. This is a natural Haversine and is required for the next stage (Fig A3.4).

6 With Lat ~ Dec of 66° 57′, find the natural

Haversine: 0.30423 (Fig A3.5).

7 Add together the two natural Haversines to give natural Haversine 0.39051.

8 Find 0.39051 in the Haversine tables. Read off the degrees at the top of the page: 77°. From the left-hand column read off the minutes (21') and the decimals of a minute along the top row (0.1'). The figure found ( 77° 21'.1) is the calculated zenith distance (Fig A3.6).

9 Take the calculated zenith distance from 90° to find the calculated altitude: 12° 38'.9.

*Example A3b*
*To find the azimuth, the ABC tables in Norie's are used.*

The same co-ordinates used to find calculated altitude are required: Local Hour Angle, Latitude and Declination.

1 Enter table A with LHA (44°) along the top and latitude (50°) down the side. The resultant figure

1.23 is labelled S which is opposite to latitude because the hour angle was *not* between 90° and 270° (Fig A3.7).

2 Enter table B with LHA (44°) along the top and declination (use 17°) down the side. The resultant figure 0.44 is labelled S the same as declination (Fig A3.8).

3 As both A and B are labelled S they are added together to find C which is S1.67.

4 Enter table C with C (1.67) and latitude (50°) to find the azimuth 42.8° (use 43°), which is labelled S 43°W because C correction was S and W as LHA is less than 180°. S 43°W is a quadrantal azimuth and must be converted to a three figure azimuth before plotting: 180° + 43° = 223°T (Fig A3.9).

Intercepts can be plotted from the DR position without conversion to chosen position. Fig A3.10 shows an observed position plotted from a DR position.

## Extracts from Norie's Tables

| 44° | HAVERSINES | | | | | | | | | | | |
|---|---|---|---|---|---|---|---|---|---|---|---|---|
| → | .0 | | .2 | | .4 | | .6 | | .8 | | | |
| | Log. | Nat. | Log. | Nat. | Log. | Nat. | Log. | Nat. | Log. | Nat. | Log. | Nat. |
| ' | 1.or(9.) | 0. | 1.or(9.) | 0. | 1.or(9.) | 0. | 1.or(9.) | 0. | 1.or(9.) | 0. | 1.or(9.) | 0. | ' |
| 00 | 14715 | 14033 | 14721 | 14035 | 14728 | 14037 | 14734 | 14039 | 14740 | 14041 | 14746 | 14043 | 59 |
| 01 | 14746 | 14043 | 14753 | 14045 | 14759 | 14047 | 14765 | 14049 | 14771 | 14051 | 14778 | 14053 | 58 |
| 02 | 14778 | 14053 | 14784 | 14055 | 14790 | 14057 | 14796 | 14059 | 14803 | 14061 | 14809 | 14063 | 57 |
| 03 | 14809 | 14063 | 14815 | 14065 | 14821 | 14067 | 14828 | 14069 | 14834 | 14071 | 14840 | 14073 | 56 |
| 04 | 14840 | 14073 | 14846 | 14075 | 14852 | 14077 | 14859 | 14080 | 14865 | 14082 | 14871 | 14084 | 55 |
| 05 | 14871 | 14084 | 14877 | 14086 | 14884 | 14088 | 14890 | 14090 | 14896 | 14092 | 14902 | 14094 | 54 |
| 06 | 14902 | 14094 | 14909 | 14096 | 14915 | 14098 | 14921 | 14100 | 14927 | 14102 | 14934 | 14104 | 53 |
| 07 | 14934 | 14104 | 14940 | 14106 | 14946 | 14108 | 14952 | 14110 | 14959 | 14112 | 14965 | 14114 | 52 |
| 08 | 14965 | 14114 | 14971 | 14116 | 14977 | 14118 | 14984 | 14120 | 14990 | 14122 | 14996 | 14124 | 51 |
| 09 | 14996 | 14124 | 15002 | 14126 | 15008 | 14128 | 15015 | 14130 | 15021 | 14132 | 15027 | 14134 | 50 |
| 10 | 15027 | 14134 | 15033 | 14136 | 15040 | 14138 | 15046 | 14140 | 15052 | 14142 | 15058 | 14144 | 49 |

Fig. A3.1

| 50° | | | | | LOGS. OF TRIG. FUNCTIONS | | | | | | | |
|---|---|---|---|---|---|---|---|---|---|---|---|---|
| 230° | | | | | | | | | | | | |
| ´ | Sine | *Parts* | Cosec. | Tan. | *Parts* | Cotan. | Secant | *Parts* | Cosine | | | |
| 00·0 | 1̄.(9) 88425 | ´ | 0.(10) 11575 | 0.(10) 07619 | ´ | 1̄.(9) 92381 | 0.(10) 19193 | ´ | 1̄.(9) 80807 | 60´ |
| 01·0 | 88436 | | 11564 | 07644 | | 92356 | 19208 | | 80792 | |
| 02·0 | 88447 | ·1    1 | 11553 | 07670 | ·1    3 | 92330 | 19223 | ·1    2 | 80777 | |
| 03·0 | 88457 | | 11543 | 07696 | | 92304 | 19239 | | 80762 | |
| 04·0 | 88468 | | 11532 | 07721 | | 92279 | 19254 | | 80747 | |
| 05·0 | 88478 | ·2    2 | 11522 | 07747 | ·2    5 | 92253 | 19269 | ·2    3 | 80731 | 55´ |
| 06·0 | 88489 | | 11511 | 07773 | | 92227 | 19284 | | 80716 | |
| 07·0 | 88499 | | 11501 | 07798 | | 92202 | 19299 | | 80701 | |
| 08·0 | 88510 | ·3    3 | 11490 | 07824 | ·3    8 | 92176 | 19314 | ·3    5 | 80686 | |
| 09·0 | 88521 | | 11479 | 07850 | | 92150 | 19329 | | 80671 | |
| 10·0 | 88531 | | 11469 | 07875 | | 92125 | 19344 | | 80656 | 50´ |

Fig. A3.2

| 16° | | | | | LOGS. OF TRIG. FUNCTIONS | | | | | | | |
|---|---|---|---|---|---|---|---|---|---|---|---|---|
| 196° | | | | | | | | | | | | |
| ´ | Sine | *Parts* | Cosec. | Tan. | *Parts* | Cotan. | Secant | *Parts* | Cosine | | | |
| 00·0 | 1̄.(9) 44034 | | 0.(10) 55966 | 1̄.(9) 45750 | | 0.(10) 54250 | 0.(10) 01716 | ´ | 1̄.(9) 98284 | 60´ |
| 01·0 | 44078 | | 55922 | 45797 | | 54203 | 01720 | | 98281 | |
| 02·0 | 44122 | 1    4 | 55878 | 45845 | ·1    5 | 54155 | 01723 | ·1    0 | 98277 | |
| 03·0 | 44166 | | 55834 | 45893 | | 54108 | 01727 | | 98273 | |
| 04·0 | 44210 | ·2    9 | 55790 | 45940 | ·2    9 | 54060 | 01730 | ·2    1 | 98270 | |
| 05·0 | 44254 | | 55747 | 45988 | | 54013 | 01734 | | 98266 | 55´ |
| 06·0 | 44297 | ·3    13 | 55703 | 46035 | ·3    14 | 53965 | 01738 | ·3    1 | 98262 | |
| 07·0 | 44341 | | 55659 | 46082 | | 53918 | 01741 | | 98259 | |
| 08·0 | 44385 | ·4    17 | 55615 | 46130 | ·4    19 | 53870 | 01745 | ·4    1 | 98255 | |
| 09·0 | 44428 | | 55572 | 46177 | | 53823 | 01749 | | 98251 | |
| 10·0 | 44472 | ·5    22 | 55528 | 46224 | ·5    24 | 53776 | 01752 | ·5    2 | 98248 | 50´ |
| 54·0 | 46345 | | 53655 | 48262 | | 51738 | 01917 | | 98083 | |
| 55·0 | 46386 | ·8    33 | 53614 | 48308 | 8    36 | 51693 | 01921 | ·8    3 | 98079 | 5´ |
| 56·0 | 46428 | | 53572 | 48353 | | 51647 | 01925 | | 98075 | |
| 57·0 | 46469 | ·9    38 | 53531 | 48398 | ·9    41 | 51602 | 01929 | ·9    3 | 98071 | |
| 58·0 | 46511 | | 53489 | 48444 | | 51557 | 01933 | | 98067 | |
| 59·0 | 46552 | | 53448 | 48489 | | 51511 | 01937 | | 98064 | |
| 60·0 | 46594 | | 53407 | 48534 | | 51466 | 01940 | | 98060 | 0´ |
| | | | | | | | | | 163° | |
| | | | | | | | | | 343° | |

Fig. A3.3

## 34° HAVERSINES

| ' | .0 Log. 2.or(8.) | .0 Nat. 0. | .2 Log. 2.or(8.) | .2 Nat. 0. | .4 Log. 2.or(8.) | .4 Nat. 0. | .6 Log. 2.or(8.) | .6 Nat. 0. | .8 Log. 2.or(8.) | .8 Nat. 0. | Log. 2.or(8.) | Nat. 0. | ' |
|----|------|------|------|------|------|------|------|------|------|------|------|------|----|
| 00 | 93187 | 08548 | 93195 | 08550 | 93204 | 08551 | 93212 | 08553 | 93220 | 08555 | 93228 | 08556 | 59 |
| 01 | 93228 | 08556 | 93237 | 08558 | 93245 | 08560 | 93253 | 08561 | 93261 | 08563 | 93270 | 08564 | 58 |
| 02 | 93270 | 08564 | 93278 | 08566 | 93286 | 08568 | 93294 | 08569 | 93303 | 08571 | 93311 | 08573 | 57 |
| 03 | 93311 | 08573 | 93319 | 08574 | 93327 | 08576 | 93336 | 08577 | 93344 | 08579 | 93352 | 08581 | 56 |
| 04 | 93352 | 08581 | 93360 | 08582 | 93369 | 08584 | 93377 | 08586 | 93385 | 08587 | 93393 | 08589 | 55 |
| 05 | 93393 | 08589 | 93402 | 08590 | 93410 | 08592 | 93418 | 08594 | 93426 | 08595 | 93435 | 08597 | 54 |
| 06 | 93435 | 08597 | 93443 | 08599 | 93451 | 08600 | 93459 | 08602 | 93468 | 08604 | 93476 | 08605 | 53 |
| 07 | 93476 | 08605 | 93484 | 08607 | 93492 | 08608 | 93501 | 08610 | 93509 | 08612 | 93517 | 08613 | 52 |
| 08 | 93517 | 08613 | 93525 | 08615 | 93533 | 08617 | 93542 | 08618 | 93550 | 08620 | 93558 | 08621 | 51 |
| 09 | 93558 | 08621 | 93566 | 08623 | 93574 | 08625 | 93583 | 08626 | 93591 | 08628 | 93599 | 08630 | 50 |
| 10 | 93599 | 08630 | 93607 | 08631 | 93616 | 08633 | 93624 | 08635 | 93632 | 08636 | 93640 | 08638 | 49 |
| 11 | 93640 | 08638 | 93649 | 08639 | 93657 | 08641 | 93665 | 08643 | 93673 | 08644 | 93681 | 08646 | 48 |
| 12 | 93681 | 08646 | 93690 | 08648 | 93698 | 08649 | 93706 | 08651 | 93714 | 08653 | 93722 | 08654 | 47 |
| 13 | 93722 | 08654 | 93731 | 08656 | 93739 | 08657 | 93747 | 08659 | 93755 | 08661 | 93763 | 08662 | 46 |
| 14 | 93763 | 08662 | 93772 | 08664 | 93780 | 08666 | 93788 | 08667 | 93796 | 08669 | 93804 | 08671 | 45 |
| 15 | 93804 | 08671 | 93813 | 08672 | 93821 | 08674 | 93829 | 08675 | 93837 | 08677 | 93845 | 08679 | 44 |

Fig. A3.4

## 66° HAVERSINES

| ' | .0 Log. 1.or(9.) | .0 Nat. 0. | .2 Log. 1.or(9.) | .2 Nat. 0. | .4 Log. 1.or(9.) | .4 Nat. 0. | .6 Log. 1.or(9.) | .6 Nat. 0. | .8 Log. 1.or(9.) | .8 Nat. 0. | Log. 1.or(9.) | Nat. 0. | ' |
|----|------|------|------|------|------|------|------|------|------|------|------|------|----|
| 00 | 47222 | 29663 | 47226 | 29666 | 47230 | 29668 | 47233 | 29671 | 47237 | 29674 | 47241 | 29676 | 59 |
| 01 | 47241 | 29676 | 47245 | 29679 | 47249 | 29682 | 47253 | 29684 | 47257 | 29687 | 47261 | 29690 | 58 |
| 02 | 47261 | 29690 | 47264 | 29692 | 47268 | 29695 | 47272 | 29698 | 47276 | 29700 | 47280 | 29703 | 57 |
| 03 | 47280 | 29703 | 47284 | 29706 | 47288 | 29708 | 47292 | 29711 | 47296 | 29714 | 47300 | 29716 | 56 |
| 04 | 47300 | 29716 | 47303 | 29719 | 47307 | 29722 | 47311 | 29724 | 47315 | 29727 | 47319 | 29730 | 55 |
| 05 | 47319 | 29730 | 47323 | 29732 | 47327 | 29735 | 47331 | 29738 | 47335 | 29740 | 47338 | 29743 | 54 |
| 06 | 47338 | 29743 | 47342 | 29746 | 47346 | 29748 | 47350 | 29751 | 47354 | 29754 | 47358 | 29756 | 53 |
| 07 | 47358 | 29756 | 47362 | 29759 | 47366 | 29762 | 47369 | 29764 | 47373 | 29767 | 47377 | 29770 | 52 |
| 52 | 48225 | 30356 | 48229 | 30359 | 48233 | 30362 | 48237 | 30364 | 48240 | 30367 | 48244 | 30370 | 07 |
| 53 | 48244 | 30370 | 48248 | 30372 | 48252 | 30375 | 48256 | 30378 | 48259 | 30380 | 48263 | 30383 | 06 |
| 54 | 48263 | 30383 | 48267 | 30386 | 48271 | 30388 | 48275 | 30391 | 48279 | 30394 | 48282 | 30397 | 05 |
| 55 | 48282 | 30397 | 48286 | 30399 | 48290 | 30402 | 48294 | 30405 | 48298 | 30407 | 48302 | 30410 | 04 |
| 56 | 48302 | 30410 | 48305 | 30413 | 48309 | 30415 | 48313 | 30418 | 48317 | 30421 | 48321 | 30423 | 03 |
| 57 | 48321 | 30423 | 48324 | 30426 | 48328 | 30429 | 48332 | 30431 | 48336 | 30434 | 48340 | 30437 | 02 |
| 58 | 48340 | 30437 | 48344 | 30439 | 48347 | 30442 | 48351 | 30445 | 48355 | 30447 | 48359 | 30450 | 01 |
| 59 | 48359 | 30450 | 48363 | 30453 | 48366 | 30455 | 48370 | 30458 | 48374 | 30461 | 48378 | 30463 | 00 |

| | .8 | .6 | .4 | .2 | 0 ← |

| PARTS for 0'.1: | LOGS 2 | NATURALS 1 | **293°** |

Fig. A3.5

## 77° HAVERSINES

| | .0 | | .2 | | .4 | | .6 | | .8 | | | |
|---|---|---|---|---|---|---|---|---|---|---|---|---|
| ′ | Log. | Nat. | Log. | Nat. | Log. | Nat. | Log. | Nat. | Log. | Nat. | Log. | Nat. | ′ |
| | 1̄.or(9.) | 0. | 1̄.or(9.) | 0. | 1̄.or(9.) | 0. | 1̄.or(9.) | 0. | 1̄.or(9.) | 0. | 1̄.or(9.) | 0. | |
| 00 | 58830 | 38752 | 58833 | 38755 | 58836 | 38758 | 58839 | 38761 | 58843 | 38764 | 58846 | 38767 | 59 |
| 01 | 58846 | 38767 | 58849 | 38769 | 58852 | 38772 | 58855 | 38775 | 58858 | 38778 | 58862 | 38781 | 58 |
| 02 | 58862 | 38781 | 58865 | 38784 | 58868 | 38786 | 58871 | 38789 | 58874 | 38792 | 58878 | 38795 | 57 |
| 03 | 58878 | 38795 | 58881 | 38798 | 58884 | 38801 | 58887 | 38803 | 58890 | 38806 | 58893 | 38809 | 56 |
| 04 | 58893 | 38809 | 58897 | 38812 | 58900 | 38815 | 58903 | 38818 | 58906 | 38820 | 58909 | 38823 | 55 |
| 05 | 58909 | 38823 | 58912 | 38826 | 58916 | 38829 | 58919 | 38832 | 58922 | 38835 | 58925 | 38837 | 54 |
| 06 | 58925 | 38837 | 58928 | 38840 | 58932 | 38843 | 58935 | 38846 | 58938 | 38849 | 58941 | 38852 | 53 |
| 07 | 58941 | 38852 | 58944 | 38854 | 58947 | 38857 | 58950 | 38860 | 58954 | 38863 | 58957 | 38866 | 52 |
| 08 | 58957 | 38866 | 58960 | 38869 | 58963 | 38872 | 58966 | 38874 | 58969 | 38877 | 58973 | 38880 | 51 |
| 09 | 58973 | 38880 | 58976 | 38883 | 58979 | 38886 | 58982 | 38889 | 58985 | 38891 | 58988 | 38894 | 50 |
| 10 | 58988 | 38894 | 58992 | 38897 | 58995 | 38900 | 58998 | 38903 | 59001 | 38906 | 59004 | 38908 | 49 |
| 11 | 59004 | 38908 | 59008 | 38911 | 59011 | 38914 | 59014 | 38917 | 59017 | 38920 | 59020 | 38923 | 48 |
| 12 | 59020 | 38923 | 59023 | 38925 | 59027 | 38928 | 59030 | 38931 | 59033 | 38934 | 59036 | 38937 | 47 |
| 13 | 59036 | 38937 | 59039 | 38940 | 59042 | 38942 | 59045 | 38945 | 59049 | 38948 | 59052 | 38951 | 46 |
| 14 | 59052 | 38951 | 59055 | 38954 | 59058 | 38957 | 59061 | 38959 | 59064 | 38962 | 59068 | 38965 | 45 |
| 15 | 59068 | 38965 | 59071 | 38968 | 59074 | 38971 | 59077 | 38974 | 59080 | 38976 | 59083 | 38979 | 44 |
| 16 | 59083 | 38979 | 59087 | 38982 | 59090 | 38985 | 59093 | 38988 | 59096 | 38991 | 59099 | 38994 | 43 |
| 17 | 59099 | 38994 | 59102 | 38996 | 59106 | 38999 | 59109 | 39002 | 59112 | 39005 | 59115 | 39008 | 42 |
| 18 | 59115 | 39008 | 59118 | 39011 | 59121 | 39013 | 59124 | 39016 | 59128 | 39019 | 59131 | 39022 | 41 |
| 19 | 59131 | 39022 | 59134 | 39025 | 59137 | 39028 | 59140 | 39030 | 59143 | 39033 | 59147 | 39036 | 40 |
| 20 | 59147 | 39036 | 59150 | 39039 | 59153 | 39042 | 59156 | 39045 | 59159 | 39047 | 59162 | 39050 | 39 |
| 21 | 59162 | 39050 | 59166 | 39053 | 59169 | 39056 | 59172 | 39059 | 59175 | 39062 | 59178 | 39064 | 38 |
| 22 | 59178 | 39064 | 59181 | 39067 | 59185 | 39070 | 59188 | 39073 | 59191 | 39076 | 59194 | 39079 | 37 |
| 23 | 59194 | 39079 | 59197 | 39081 | 59200 | 39084 | 59203 | 39087 | 59207 | 39090 | 59210 | 39093 | 36 |
| 24 | 59210 | 39093 | 59213 | 39096 | 59216 | 39099 | 59219 | 39101 | 59222 | 39104 | 59225 | 39107 | 35 |
| 25 | 59225 | 39107 | 59229 | 39110 | 59232 | 39113 | 59235 | 39116 | 59238 | 39118 | 59241 | 39121 | 34 |

Fig. A3.6

## TABLE A HOUR ANGLE

| Lat ° | 30° | 31° | 32° | 33° | 34° | 35° | 36° | 37° | 38° | 39° | 40° | 41° | 42° | 43° | 44° | 45° | Lat ° |
|---|---|---|---|---|---|---|---|---|---|---|---|---|---|---|---|---|---|
| | 330° | 329° | 328° | 327° | 326° | 325° | 324° | 323° | 322° | 321° | 320° | 319° | 318° | 317° | 316° | 315° | |
| 0 | ·00 | ·00 | ·00 | ·00 | ·00 | ·00 | ·00 | ·00 | ·00 | ·00 | ·00 | ·00 | ·00 | ·00 | ·00 | ·00 | 0 |
| 1 | ·03 | ·03 | ·03 | ·03 | ·03 | ·02 | ·02 | ·02 | ·02 | ·02 | ·02 | ·02 | ·02 | ·02 | ·02 | ·02 | 1 |
| 2 | ·06 | ·06 | ·06 | ·05 | ·05 | ·05 | ·05 | ·05 | ·04 | ·04 | ·04 | ·04 | ·04 | ·04 | ·04 | ·04 | 2 |
| 3 | ·09 | ·09 | ·08 | ·08 | ·08 | ·07 | ·07 | ·07 | ·07 | ·06 | ·06 | ·06 | ·06 | ·06 | ·05 | ·05 | 3 |
| 4 | ·12 | ·12 | ·11 | ·11 | ·10 | ·10 | ·10 | ·09 | ·09 | ·09 | ·08 | ·08 | ·08 | ·07 | ·07 | ·07 | 4 |
| 5 | ·15 | ·15 | ·14 | ·13 | ·13 | ·12 | ·12 | ·12 | ·11 | ·11 | ·10 | ·10 | ·10 | ·09 | ·09 | ·09 | 5 |
| 6 | ·18 | ·17 | ·17 | ·16 | ·16 | ·15 | ·14 | ·14 | ·13 | ·13 | ·13 | ·12 | ·12 | ·11 | ·11 | ·11 | 6 |
| 49 | 1·99 | 1·91 | 1·84 | 1·77 | 1·71 | 1·64 | 1·58 | 1·53 | 1·47 | 1·42 | 1·37 | 1·32 | 1·28 | 1·23 | 1·19 | 1·15 | 49 |
| 50 | 2·06 | 1·98 | 1·91 | 1·84 | 1·77 | 1·70 | 1·64 | 1·58 | 1·53 | 1·47 | 1·42 | 1·37 | 1·32 | 1·28 | 1·23 | 1·19 | 50 |
| 51 | 2·14 | 2·06 | 1·98 | 1·90 | 1·83 | 1·76 | 1·70 | 1·64 | 1·58 | 1·52 | 1·47 | 1·42 | 1·37 | 1·32 | 1·28 | 1·23 | 51 |
| 52 | 2·22 | 2·13 | 2·05 | 1·97 | 1·90 | 1·83 | 1·76 | 1·70 | 1·64 | 1·58 | 1·52 | 1·47 | 1·42 | 1·37 | 1·33 | 1·28 | 52 |
| 53 | 2·30 | 2·21 | 2·12 | 2·04 | 1·97 | 1·90 | 1·83 | 1·76 | 1·70 | 1·64 | 1·58 | 1·52 | 1·47 | 1·42 | 1·37 | 1·33 | 53 |
| 54 | 2·38 | 2·29 | 2·20 | 2·12 | 2·04 | 1·97 | 1·89 | 1·83 | 1·76 | 1·70 | 1·64 | 1·58 | 1·53 | 1·48 | 1·43 | 1·38 | 54 |
| 55 | 2·47 | 2·38 | 2·29 | 2·20 | 2·12 | 2·04 | 1·97 | 1·90 | 1·83 | 1·76 | 1·70 | 1·64 | 1·59 | 1·53 | 1·48 | 1·43 | 55 |
| 56 | 2·57 | 2·47 | 2·37 | 2·28 | 2·20 | 2·12 | 2·04 | 1·97 | 1·90 | 1·83 | 1·77 | 1·71 | 1·65 | 1·59 | 1·54 | 1·48 | 56 |
| 57 | 2·67 | 2·56 | 2·46 | 2·37 | 2·28 | 2·20 | 2·12 | 2·04 | 1·97 | 1·90 | 1·84 | 1·77 | 1·71 | 1·65 | 1·59 | 1·54 | 57 |
| 58 | 2·77 | 2·66 | 2·56 | 2·46 | 2·37 | 2·29 | 2·20 | 2·12 | 2·05 | 1·98 | 1·91 | 1·84 | 1·78 | 1·72 | 1·66 | 1·60 | 58 |
| 59 | 2·88 | 2·77 | 2·66 | 2·56 | 2·47 | 2·38 | 2·29 | 2·21 | 2·13 | 2·06 | 1·98 | 1·91 | 1·85 | 1·78 | 1·72 | 1·66 | 59 |
| 60 | 3·00 | 2·88 | 2·77 | 2·67 | 2·57 | 2·47 | 2·38 | 2·30 | 2·22 | 2·14 | 2·06 | 1·99 | 1·92 | 1·86 | 1·79 | 1·73 | 60 |
| Lat | 150° | 149° | 148° | 147° | 146° | 145° | 144° | 143° | 142° | 141° | 140° | 139° | 138° | 137° | 136° | 135° | Lat |
| | 210° | 211° | 212° | 213° | 214° | 215° | 216° | 217° | 218° | 219° | 220° | 221° | 222° | 223° | 224° | 225° | |

### HOUR ANGLE

A - Named opposite to Latitude, **except** when **Hour Angle** is between 90° and 270°

Fig. A3.7

## TABLE B  HOUR ANGLE

| Dec.° | 30° 330° | 31° 329° | 32° 328° | 33° 327° | 34° 326° | 35° 325° | 36° 324° | 37° 323° | 38° 322° | 39° 321° | 40° 320° | 41° 319° | 42° 318° | 43° 317° | 44° 316° | 45° 315° | Dec.° |
|---|---|---|---|---|---|---|---|---|---|---|---|---|---|---|---|---|---|
| 0 | ·00 | ·00 | ·00 | ·00 | ·00 | ·00 | ·00 | ·00 | ·00 | ·00 | ·00 | ·00 | ·00 | ·00 | ·00 | ·00 | 0 |
| 1 | ·03 | ·03 | ·03 | ·03 | ·03 | ·03 | ·03 | ·03 | ·03 | ·03 | ·03 | ·03 | ·03 | ·03 | ·03 | ·02 | 1 |
| 2 | ·07 | ·07 | ·07 | ·06 | ·06 | ·06 | ·06 | ·06 | ·06 | ·06 | ·05 | ·05 | ·05 | ·05 | ·05 | ·05 | 2 |
| 3 | ·10 | ·10 | ·10 | ·10 | ·09 | ·09 | ·09 | ·09 | ·09 | ·08 | ·08 | ·08 | ·08 | ·08 | ·08 | ·07 | 3 |
| 4 | ·14 | ·14 | ·13 | ·13 | ·13 | ·12 | ·12 | ·12 | ·11 | ·11 | ·11 | ·11 | ·10 | ·10 | ·10 | ·10 | 4 |
| 5 | ·17 | ·17 | ·17 | ·16 | ·16 | ·15 | ·15 | ·15 | ·14 | ·14 | ·14 | ·13 | ·13 | ·13 | ·13 | ·12 | 5 |
| 6 | ·21 | ·20 | ·20 | ·19 | ·19 | ·18 | ·18 | ·17 | ·17 | ·17 | ·16 | ·16 | ·16 | ·15 | ·15 | ·15 | 6 |
| 7 | ·25 | ·24 | ·23 | ·23 | ·22 | ·21 | ·21 | ·20 | ·20 | ·20 | ·19 | ·19 | ·18 | ·18 | ·18 | ·17 | 7 |
| 8 | ·28 | ·27 | ·27 | ·26 | ·25 | ·25 | ·24 | ·23 | ·23 | ·22 | ·22 | ·21 | ·21 | ·21 | ·20 | ·20 | 8 |
| 9 | ·32 | ·31 | ·30 | ·29 | ·28 | ·28 | ·27 | ·26 | ·26 | ·25 | ·25 | ·24 | ·24 | ·23 | ·23 | ·22 | 9 |
| 10 | ·35 | ·34 | ·33 | 32 | ·32 | ·31 | ·30 | ·29 | ·29 | ·28 | ·27 | ·27 | ·26 | ·26 | ·25 | ·25 | 10 |
| 11 | ·39 | ·38 | ·37 | ·36 | ·35 | ·34 | ·33 | ·32 | ·32 | ·31 | ·30 | ·30 | ·29 | ·29 | ·28 | ·27 | 11 |
| 12 | ·43 | ·41 | ·40 | ·39 | ·38 | ·37 | ·36 | ·35 | ·35 | ·34 | ·33 | ·32 | ·32 | ·31 | ·31 | ·30 | 12 |
| 13 | ·46 | ·45 | ·44 | ·42 | ·41 | ·40 | ·39 | ·38 | ·37 | ·37 | ·36 | ·35 | ·35 | ·34 | ·33 | ·33 | 13 |
| 14 | ·50 | ·48 | ·47 | ·46 | ·45 | ·43 | ·42 | ·41 | ·40 | ·40 | ·39 | ·38 | ·37 | ·37 | ·36 | ·35 | 14 |
| 15 | ·54 | ·52 | ·51 | ·49 | ·48 | ·47 | ·46 | ·45 | ·44 | ·43 | ·42 | ·41 | ·40 | ·39 | ·39 | ·38 | 15 |
| 16 | ·57 | ·56 | ·54 | ·53 | ·51 | ·50 | ·49 | ·48 | ·47 | ·46 | ·45 | ·44 | ·43 | ·42 | ·41 | ·41 | 16 |
| 17 | ·61 | ·59 | ·58 | ·56 | ·55 | ·53 | ·52 | ·51 | ·50 | ·49 | ·48 | ·47 | ·46 | ·45 | ·44 | ·43 | 17 |
| 18 | ·65 | ·63 | ·61 | ·60 | ·58 | ·57 | ·55 | ·54 | ·53 | ·52 | ·51 | ·50 | ·49 | ·48 | ·47 | ·46 | 18 |
| 19 | ·69 | ·67 | ·65 | ·63 | ·62 | ·60 | ·59 | ·57 | ·56 | ·55 | ·54 | ·52 | ·51 | ·50 | ·50 | ·49 | 19 |
| 20 | ·73 | ·71 | ·69 | ·67 | ·65 | ·63 | ·62 | ·60 | ·59 | ·58 | ·57 | ·55 | ·54 | ·53 | ·52 | ·51 | 20 |

B - Always named the **same** as Declination

Fig. A3.8

## TABLE C

### A & B CORRECTION.

| A±B= | 1·20' | 1·24' | 1·28' | 1·32' | 1·36' | 1·40' | 1·44' | 1·48' | 1·52' | 1·56' | 1·60' | 1·64' | 1·68' | 1·72' | 1·76' | 1·80'=A±B |
|---|---|---|---|---|---|---|---|---|---|---|---|---|---|---|---|---|
| **Lat.** | | | | | | | **AZIMUTHS** | | | | | | | | | **Lat.** |
| 0 | 39·8 | 38·9 | 38·0 | 37·1 | 36·3 | 35·5 | 34·8 | 34·0 | 33·3 | 32·7 | 32·0 | 31·4 | 30·8 | 30·2 | 29·6 | 29·1 · 0 |
| 5 | 39·9 | 39·0 | 38·1 | 37·3 | 36·4 | 35·6 | 34·9 | 34·1 | 33·4 | 32·8 | 32·1 | 31·5 | 30·9 | 30·3 | 29·7 | 29·2 · 5 |
| 10 | 40·2 | 39·3 | 38·4 | 37·6 | 36·8 | 36·0 | 35·2 | 34·5 | 33·8 | 33·1 | 32·4 | 31·8 | 31·2 | 30·6 | 30·0 | 29·4 · 10 |
| 14 | 40·7 | 39·7 | 38·8 | 38·0 | 37·2 | 36·4 | 35·6 | 34·9 | 34·2 | 33·5 | 32·8 | 32·1 | 31·5 | 30·9 | 30·4 | 29·8 · 14 |
| 18 | 41·2 | 40·3 | 39·4 | 38·5 | 37·7 | 36·9 | 36·1 | 35·4 | 34·7 | 34·0 | 33·3 | 32·7 | 32·0 | 31·4 | 30·9 | 30·3 · 18 |
| 48 | 51·2 | 50·3 | 49·4 | 48·5 | 47·7 | 46·9 | 46·1 | 45·3 | 44·5 | 43·8 | 43·0 | 42·3 | 41·7 | 41·0 | 40·3 | 39·7 · 48 |
| 49 | 51·8 | 50·9 | 50·0 | 49·1 | 48·3 | 47·4 | 46·6 | 45·8 | 45·1 | 44·3 | 43·6 | 42·9 | 42·2 | 41·5 | 40·9 | 40·3 · 49 |
| 50 | 52·4 | 51·5 | 50·6 | 49·7 | 48·8 | 48·0 | 47·2 | 46·4 | 45·7 | 44·9 | 44·2 | 43·5 | 42·8 | 42·1 | 41·5 | 40·8 · 50 |
| 51 | 52·9 | 52·0 | 51·2 | 50·3 | 49·4 | 48·6 | 47·8 | 47·0 | 46·3 | 45·5 | 44·8 | 44·1 | 43·4 | 42·7 | 42·1 | 41·4 · 51 |
| 52 | 53·5 | 52·6 | 51·8 | 50·9 | 50·1 | 49·2 | 48·4 | 47·7 | 46·9 | 46·2 | 45·4 | 44·7 | 44·0 | 43·4 | 42·7 | 42·1 · 52 |
| 53 | 54·2 | 53·3 | 52·4 | 51·5 | 50·7 | 49·9 | 49·1 | 48·3 | 47·5 | 46·8 | 46·1 | 45·4 | 44·7 | 44·0 | 43·4 | 42·7 · 53 |
| 54 | 54·8 | 53·9 | 53·0 | 52·2 | 51·4 | 50·6 | 49·8 | 49·0 | 48·2 | 47·5 | 46·8 | 46·1 | 45·4 | 44·7 | 44·0 | 43·4 · 54 |
| 55 | 55·5 | 54·6 | 53·7 | 52·9 | 52·0 | 51·2 | 50·5 | 49·7 | 48·9 | 48·2 | 47·5 | 46·8 | 46·1 | 45·4 | 44·7 | 44·1 · 55 |
| 56 | 56·1 | 55·3 | 54·4 | 53·6 | 52·7 | 51·9 | 51·2 | 50·4 | 49·6 | 48·9 | 48·2 | 47·5 | 46·8 | 46·1 | 45·5 | 44·8 · 56 |
| 57 | 56·8 | 56·0 | 55·1 | 54·3 | 53·5 | 52·7 | 51·9 | 51·1 | 50·4 | 49·7 | 48·9 | 48·2 | 47·5 | 46·9 | 46·2 | 45·6 · 57 |
| 58 | 57·5 | 56·7 | 55·9 | 55·0 | 54·2 | 53·4 | 52·7 | 51·9 | 51·1 | 50·4 | 49·7 | 49·0 | 48·3 | 47·7 | 47·0 | 46·4 · 58 |
| 59 | 58·3 | 57·4 | 56·6 | 55·8 | 55·0 | 54·2 | 53·4 | 52·7 | 51·9 | 51·2 | 50·5 | 49·8 | 49·1 | 48·5 | 47·8 | 47·2 · 59 |
| 60 | 59·0 | 58·2 | 57·4 | 56·6 | 55·8 | 55·0 | 54·2 | 53·5 | 52·8 | 52·0 | 51·3 | 50·6 | 50·0 | 49·3 | 48·7 | 48·0 · 60 |
| 61 | 59·8 | 59·0 | 58·2 | 57·4 | 56·6 | 55·8 | 55·1 | 54·3 | 53·6 | 52·9 | 52·2 | 51·5 | 50·8 | 50·2 | 49·5 | 48·9 · 61 |
| 62 | 60·6 | 59·8 | 59·0 | 58·2 | 57·4 | 56·7 | 55·9 | 55·2 | 54·5 | 53·8 | 53·1 | 52·4 | 51·7 | 51·1 | 50·4 | 49·8 · 62 |
| 63 | 61·4 | 60·6 | 59·8 | 59·1 | 58·3 | 57·6 | 56·8 | 56·1 | 55·4 | 54·7 | 54·0 | 53·3 | 52·7 | 52·0 | 51·4 | 50·7 · 63 |
| 64 | 62·3 | 61·5 | 60·7 | 59·9 | 59·2 | 58·5 | 57·7 | 57·0 | 56·3 | 55·6 | 55·0 | 54·3 | 53·6 | 53·0 | 52·4 | 51·7 · 64 |
| 65 | 63·1 | 62·3 | 61·6 | 60·8 | 60·1 | 59·4 | 58·7 | 58·0 | 57·3 | 56·6 | 55·9 | 55·3 | 54·6 | 54·0 | 53·4 | 52·7 · 65 |
| 66 | 64·0 | 63·2 | 62·5 | 61·8 | 61·1 | 60·3 | 59·6 | 59·0 | 58·3 | 57·6 | 56·9 | 56·3 | 55·7 | 55·0 | 54·4 | 53·8 · 66 |
| 67 | 64·9 | 64·1 | 63·4 | 62·7 | 62·0 | 61·3 | 60·6 | 60·0 | 59·3 | 58·6 | 58·0 | 57·3 | 56·7 | 56·1 | 55·5 | 54·9 · 67 |
| 68 | 65·8 | 65·1 | 64·4 | 63·7 | 63·0 | 62·3 | 61·7 | 61·0 | 60·3 | 59·7 | 59·1 | 58·4 | 57·8 | 57·2 | 56·6 | 56·0 · 68 |

A±B=1·20' 1·24' | 1·28' 1·32' | 1·36' 1·40' | 1·44' 1·48' | 1·52' 1·56' | 1·60' 1·64' | 1·68' 1·72' | 1·76' 1·80'=A±B

A & B **S**ame Names take **S**um. (add) } RULE TO FIND { A & B **D**ifferent names take **D**ifference (Sub.)
C CORRECTION

C CORRECTION. (A ± B) is named the same as the greater of these quantities.

**AZIMUTH** takes combined names of C Correction and Hour Angle

Fig. A3.9

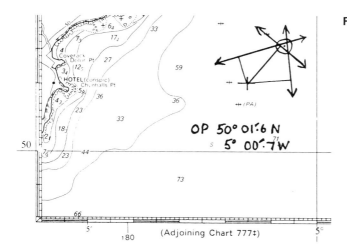

OP 50° 01'.6 N
5° 00'.7 W

(Adjoining Chart 777‡)

**Fig. A3.10** Plotting from a DR position
DR position 50° 01'.0N
5° 01'.5W

| Star | Intercept | Azimuth |
|------|-----------|---------|
| 1 | 0.7T | 040°T |
| 2 | 0.6T | 085°T |
| 3 | 0.4A | 163°T |
| OP | 50° 01'.5N | |
| | 5° 00'.7W | |

# Appendix 4
# Sight Reduction Forms

Fig. A4.1

---

## SIGHT REDUCTION FORM - SUN

Date        h  m  s

                    DWT               DR  Latitude

                    DWE                   Longitude

                    GMT               Height of Eye

GHA         h            Dec  N/S
Inc     m     s               d

**CP Long E+/W-**

        LHA

**CP Lat  N/S**

                                          Sextant Altitude
                                            IE
                                            Dip

        Hc                  Z              Apparent Altitude
        d                                   Alt Corr
      Tab Alt                              True Altitude
                                            Tab Alt

**Azimuth Zn**                                     **Intercept**

                                           True Altitude greater than Tab: TOWARDS.
                                         True Altitude less than Tab: AWAY.

Fig. A4.2

# SIGHT REDUCTION FORM  -  SUN MERIDIAN ALTITUDE

Date

DR  Latitude

h    m

Meridian Passage                    on Greenwich meridian              Longitude
Long in time
_____

Time of Transit                    GMT

Height of Eye

Dec  N/S
d
_____

Sextant Altitude
IE
Dip
_____

Apparent Altitude
Alt Corr
_____

True Altitude
from 90                          90
_____

True Zenith Distance                                              reverse pole
Declination
_____

**Latitude**

Fig. A4.3

# SIGHT REDUCTION FORM  -  POLARIS

Date          h  m  s

                  DWT                   DR  Latitude

                  DWE                      Longitude

                  GMT                   Height of Eye

GHA Aries     h

  Inc        m      s

DR Long E+/W-

      LHA Aries

                                     Sextant Altitude

                                         IE

                                         Dip

                                     Apparent Altitude

                                         Alt Corr

                                     True Altitude

                                           $a_0$

                                           $a_1$

                                           $a_2$

                                             -1

                                   **Latitude**

Fig. A4.4

# SIGHT REDUCTION FORM  -  PLANET

Date                           h  m  s                    Planet:

                                        DWT                    DR  Latitude

                                        DWE                           Longitude

                                        GMT                    Height of Eye

GHA                  h                   Dec  N/S
   Inc        m      s                      d
   v                   _____          _____

CP Long  E+/W-       _____

        LHA

CP Lat  N/S

            Hc                      Z          Sextant Altitude
            d                                  IE
            Tab Alt    _____             Dip            _____

                                               Apparent Altitude
                                               Alt Corr
                                                  add. corr

                                               True Altitude    _____
                                               Tab Alt

**Azimuth Zn**                                 **Intercept**

                                               True Altitude greater than Tab: TOWARDS.
                                               True Altitude less than Tab: AWAY.

Fig. A4.5

# SIGHT REDUCTION FORM - STAR 1   (AP 3270 Volumes 2 or 3)

Date                              h  m  s

DWT                           DR  Latitude

DWE                                 Longitude

GMT                                 Height of Eye

SHA Star                                    Dec  N/S
GHA Aries        h                               d
  Inc      m      s _____

**CP Long   W/E** _____
  LHA Star

**CP Lat   N/S**
                                            Sextant Altitude
                                                IE
                                                Dip
                                                        _____
        Hc                    Z              Apparent Altitude
        d                                    Alt Corr
      Tab Alt      _____                            _____

                                            True Altitude
                                            Tab Alt
                                                     _____

                                            **Intercept**

**Azimuth Zn**
                                            True Altitude greater than Tab: TOWARDS.
                                            True Altitude less than Tab: AWAY.

Fig. A4.6

## SIGHT REDUCTION FORM - STAR 2   (AP 3270 Volume 1)

Date                          h  m
_Plan_      Twilight          LMT                    DR  Latitude
            DR Long  _____                             Longitude
                              GMT     GD               Height of Eye

     GHA Aries    h
     Inc    m     s _____            Selected Stars      Hc      Zn

     DR Long  W/E _____
     LHA Aries

..................................................................................................................

     _Sights taken_

          STAR

          GMT

     GHA ARIES
        Inc    m    s _____      m    s _____      m    s _____

**CP Long E+/W-**    _____           _____           _____
     LHA ARIES
**CP Lat  N/S**

     Tab Alt (Hc)
**Azimuth (Zn)**


Sextant Altitude
     IE
     Dip        _____           _____           _____
Apparent Altitude
     Alt Corr   _____           _____           _____
True Altitude
     Tab Alt    _____           _____           _____
**Intercept**

                        True Altitude greater than Tab:  TOWARDS
                        True Altitude less than Tab:  AWAY

Fig. A4.7

# SIGHT REDUCTION FORM  -  MOON

Date                          h  m  s

DWT                                         DR  Latitude

DWE                                              Longitude

_____

GMT                                          Height of Eye

GHA                    h                   Dec N/S

Inc          m        s                        d

v                          _____            _____

**CP Long E+/W-**            _____

LHA

**CP Lat  N/S**

Hc                        Z              Sextant Altitude

d                                              IE

_____              Dip

Tab Alt                                                    _____

Apparent Altitude

Alt Corr

HP

If UL, -30'                        _____

True Altitude

Tab Alt

_____

**Azimuth Zn**                              **Intercept**

True ALtitude greater than Tab: TOWARDS.
True Altitude less than Tab: AWAY.

# Appendix 5
## *Nautical Almanac* Extracts

# A2 ALTITUDE CORRECTION TABLES 10°–90°—SUN, STARS, PLANETS

## OCT.—MAR. SUN APR.—SEPT.

| App. Alt. | Lower Limb | Upper Limb | App. Alt. | Lower Limb | Upper Limb |
|---|---|---|---|---|---|
| 9 34 | +10.8 | −21.5 | 9 39 | +10.6 | −21.2 |
| 9 45 | +10.9 | −21.4 | 9 51 | +10.7 | −21.1 |
| 9 56 | +11.0 | −21.3 | 10 03 | +10.8 | −21.0 |
| 10 08 | +11.1 | −21.2 | 10 15 | +10.9 | −20.9 |
| 10 21 | +11.2 | −21.1 | 10 27 | +11.0 | −20.8 |
| 10 34 | +11.3 | −21.0 | 10 40 | +11.1 | −20.7 |
| 10 47 | +11.4 | −20.9 | 10 54 | +11.2 | −20.6 |
| 11 01 | +11.5 | −20.8 | 11 08 | +11.3 | −20.5 |
| 11 15 | +11.6 | −20.7 | 11 23 | +11.4 | −20.4 |
| 11 30 | +11.7 | −20.6 | 11 38 | +11.5 | −20.3 |
| 11 46 | +11.8 | −20.5 | 11 54 | +11.6 | −20.2 |
| 12 02 | +11.9 | −20.4 | 12 10 | +11.7 | −20.1 |
| 12 19 | +12.0 | −20.3 | 12 28 | +11.8 | −20.0 |
| 12 37 | +12.1 | −20.2 | 12 46 | +11.9 | −19.9 |
| 12 55 | +12.2 | −20.1 | 13 05 | +12.0 | −19.8 |
| 13 14 | +12.3 | −20.0 | 13 24 | +12.1 | −19.7 |
| 13 35 | +12.4 | −19.9 | 13 45 | +12.2 | −19.6 |
| 13 56 | +12.5 | −19.8 | 14 07 | +12.3 | −19.5 |
| 14 18 | +12.6 | −19.7 | 14 30 | +12.4 | −19.4 |
| 14 42 | +12.7 | −19.6 | 14 54 | +12.5 | −19.3 |
| 15 06 | +12.8 | −19.5 | 15 19 | +12.6 | −19.2 |
| 15 32 | +12.9 | −19.4 | 15 46 | +12.7 | −19.1 |
| 15 59 | +13.0 | −19.3 | 16 14 | +12.8 | −19.0 |
| 16 28 | +13.1 | −19.2 | 16 44 | +12.9 | −18.9 |
| 16 59 | +13.2 | −19.1 | 17 15 | +13.0 | −18.8 |
| 17 32 | +13.3 | −19.0 | 17 48 | +13.1 | −18.7 |
| 18 06 | +13.4 | −18.9 | 18 24 | +13.2 | −18.6 |
| 18 42 | +13.5 | −18.8 | 19 01 | +13.3 | −18.5 |
| 19 21 | +13.6 | −18.7 | 19 42 | +13.4 | −18.4 |
| 20 03 | +13.7 | −18.6 | 20 25 | +13.5 | −18.3 |
| 20 48 | +13.8 | −18.5 | 21 11 | +13.6 | −18.2 |
| 21 35 | +13.9 | −18.4 | 22 00 | +13.7 | −18.1 |
| 22 26 | +14.0 | −18.3 | 22 54 | +13.8 | −18.0 |
| 23 22 | +14.1 | −18.2 | 23 51 | +13.9 | −17.9 |
| 24 21 | +14.2 | −18.1 | 24 53 | +14.0 | −17.8 |
| 25 26 | +14.3 | −18.0 | 26 00 | +14.1 | −17.7 |
| 26 36 | +14.4 | −17.9 | 27 13 | +14.2 | −17.6 |
| 27 52 | +14.5 | −17.8 | 28 33 | +14.3 | −17.5 |
| 29 15 | +14.6 | −17.7 | 30 00 | +14.4 | −17.4 |
| 30 46 | +14.7 | −17.6 | 31 35 | +14.5 | −17.3 |
| 32 26 | +14.8 | −17.5 | 33 20 | +14.6 | −17.2 |
| 34 17 | +14.9 | −17.4 | 35 17 | +14.7 | −17.1 |
| 36 20 | +15.0 | −17.3 | 37 26 | +14.8 | −17.0 |
| 38 36 | +15.1 | −17.2 | 39 50 | +14.9 | −16.9 |
| 41 08 | +15.2 | −17.1 | 42 31 | +15.0 | −16.8 |
| 43 59 | +15.3 | −17.0 | 45 31 | +15.1 | −16.7 |
| 47 10 | +15.4 | −16.9 | 48 55 | +15.2 | −16.6 |
| 50 46 | +15.5 | −16.8 | 52 44 | +15.3 | −16.5 |
| 54 49 | +15.6 | −16.7 | 57 02 | +15.4 | −16.4 |
| 59 23 | +15.7 | −16.6 | 61 51 | +15.5 | −16.3 |
| 64 30 | +15.8 | −16.5 | 67 17 | +15.6 | −16.2 |
| 70 12 | +15.9 | −16.4 | 73 16 | +15.7 | −16.1 |
| 76 26 | +16.0 | −16.3 | 79 43 | +15.8 | −16.0 |
| 83 05 | +16.1 | −16.2 | 86 32 | +15.9 | −15.9 |
| 90 00 | | | 90 00 | | |

## STARS AND PLANETS

| App. Alt. | Corrn |
|---|---|
| 9 56 | −5.3 |
| 10 08 | −5.2 |
| 10 20 | −5.1 |
| 10 33 | −5.0 |
| 10 46 | −4.9 |
| 11 00 | −4.8 |
| 11 14 | −4.7 |
| 11 29 | −4.6 |
| 11 45 | −4.5 |
| 12 01 | −4.4 |
| 12 18 | −4.3 |
| 12 35 | −4.2 |
| 12 54 | −4.1 |
| 13 13 | −4.0 |
| 13 33 | −3.9 |
| 13 54 | −3.8 |
| 14 16 | −3.7 |
| 14 40 | −3.6 |
| 15 04 | −3.5 |
| 15 30 | −3.4 |
| 15 57 | −3.3 |
| 16 26 | −3.2 |
| 16 56 | −3.1 |
| 17 28 | −3.0 |
| 18 02 | −2.9 |
| 18 38 | −2.8 |
| 19 17 | −2.7 |
| 19 58 | −2.6 |
| 20 42 | −2.5 |
| 21 28 | −2.4 |
| 22 19 | −2.3 |
| 23 13 | −2.2 |
| 24 11 | −2.1 |
| 25 14 | −2.0 |
| 26 22 | −1.9 |
| 27 36 | −1.8 |
| 28 56 | −1.7 |
| 30 24 | −1.6 |
| 32 00 | −1.5 |
| 33 45 | −1.4 |
| 35 40 | −1.3 |
| 37 48 | −1.2 |
| 40 08 | −1.1 |
| 42 44 | −1.0 |
| 45 36 | −0.9 |
| 48 47 | −0.8 |
| 52 18 | −0.7 |
| 56 11 | −0.6 |
| 60 28 | −0.5 |
| 65 08 | −0.4 |
| 70 11 | −0.3 |
| 75 34 | −0.2 |
| 81 13 | −0.1 |
| 87 03 | 0.0 |
| 90 00 | |

### App. Alt. Additional Corrn

**VENUS**

Jan. 1 – June 7
0 +0.1 / 42

June 8 – July 21
0 +0.3 / 46

July 22 – Aug. 6
0 +0.4 / 11 +0.5 / 41

Aug. 7 – Aug. 15
0 +0.5 / 6 +0.6 / 20 +0.7 / 31

Aug. 16 – Sept. 10
0 +0.6 / 4 +0.7 / 12 +0.8 / 22

Sept. 11 – Sept. 19
0 +0.5 / 6 +0.6 / 20 +0.7 / 31

Sept. 20 – Oct. 5
0 +0.4 / 11 +0.5 / 41

Oct. 6 – Nov. 22
0 +0.3 / 46

Nov. 23 – Dec. 31
0 +0.1 / 42

**MARS**

Jan. 1 – Sept. 8
0 +0.1 / 60

Sept. 9 – Nov. 22
0 +0.2 / 41 +0.1 / 75

Nov. 23 – Dec. 31
0 +0.3 / 34 +0.2 / 60 +0.1 / 80

## DIP

| Ht. of Eye | Corrn | Ht. of Eye | Ht. of Eye | Corrn |
|---|---|---|---|---|
| m | | ft. | m | |
| 2.4 | −2.8 | 8.0 | 1.0 | −1.8 |
| 2.6 | −2.9 | 8.6 | 1.5 | −2.2 |
| 2.8 | −3.0 | 9.2 | 2.0 | −2.5 |
| 3.0 | | 9.8 | 2.5 | −2.8 |
| 3.2 | −3.1 | 10.5 | 3.0 | −3.0 |
| 3.4 | −3.2 | 11.2 | See table | |
| 3.6 | −3.3 | 11.9 | ← | |
| 3.8 | −3.4 | 12.6 | m | |
| 4.0 | −3.5 | 13.3 | 20 | −7.9 |
| 4.3 | −3.6 | 14.1 | 22 | −8.3 |
| 4.5 | −3.7 | 14.9 | 24 | −8.6 |
| 4.7 | −3.8 | 15.7 | 26 | −9.0 |
| 5.0 | −3.9 | 16.5 | 28 | −9.3 |
| 5.2 | −4.0 | 17.4 | | |
| 5.5 | −4.1 | 18.3 | 30 | −9.6 |
| 5.8 | −4.2 | 19.1 | 32 | −10.0 |
| 6.1 | −4.3 | 20.1 | 34 | −10.3 |
| 6.3 | −4.4 | 21.0 | 36 | −10.6 |
| 6.6 | −4.5 | 22.0 | 38 | −10.8 |
| 6.9 | −4.6 | 22.9 | | |
| 7.2 | −4.7 | 23.9 | 40 | −11.1 |
| 7.5 | −4.8 | 24.9 | 42 | −11.4 |
| 7.9 | −4.9 | 26.0 | 44 | −11.7 |
| 8.2 | −5.0 | 27.1 | 46 | −11.9 |
| 8.5 | −5.1 | 28.1 | 48 | −12.2 |
| 8.8 | −5.2 | 29.2 | | |
| 9.2 | −5.3 | 30.4 | ft. | |
| 9.5 | −5.4 | 31.5 | 2 | −1.4 |
| 9.9 | −5.5 | 32.7 | 4 | −1.9 |
| 10.3 | −5.6 | 33.9 | 6 | −2.4 |
| 10.6 | −5.7 | 35.1 | 8 | −2.7 |
| 11.0 | −5.8 | 36.3 | 10 | −3.1 |
| 11.4 | −5.9 | 37.6 | See table | |
| 11.8 | −6.0 | 38.9 | ← | |
| 12.2 | −6.1 | 40.1 | ft. | |
| 12.6 | −6.2 | 41.5 | 70 | −8.1 |
| 13.0 | −6.3 | 42.8 | 75 | −8.4 |
| 13.4 | −6.4 | 44.2 | 80 | −8.7 |
| 13.8 | −6.5 | 45.5 | 85 | −8.9 |
| 14.2 | −6.6 | 46.9 | 90 | −9.2 |
| 14.7 | −6.7 | 48.4 | 95 | −9.5 |
| 15.1 | −6.8 | 49.8 | | |
| 15.5 | −6.9 | 51.3 | 100 | −9.7 |
| 16.0 | −7.0 | 52.8 | 105 | −9.9 |
| 16.5 | −7.1 | 54.3 | 110 | −10.2 |
| 16.9 | −7.2 | 55.8 | 115 | −10.4 |
| 17.4 | −7.3 | 57.4 | 120 | −10.6 |
| 17.9 | −7.4 | 58.9 | 125 | −10.8 |
| 18.4 | −7.5 | 60.5 | | |
| 18.8 | −7.6 | 61.9 | 130 | −11.1 |
| 19.3 | −7.7 | 63.8 | 135 | −11.3 |
| 19.8 | −7.8 | 65.4 | 140 | −11.5 |
| 20.4 | −7.9 | 67.1 | 145 | −11.7 |
| 20.9 | −8.0 | 68.8 | 150 | −11.9 |
| 21.4 | −8.1 | 70.5 | 155 | −12.1 |

App. Alt. = Apparent altitude = Sextant altitude corrected for index error and dip.
For daylight observations of Venus, see page 260.

A5.1

40             FEBRUARY 15, 16, 17 (SAT., SUN., MON.)

| G.M.T. | ARIES G.H.A. | VENUS −3.4 G.H.A. | Dec. | MARS +1.5 G.H.A. | Dec. | JUPITER −1.6 G.H.A. | Dec. | SATURN 0.0 G.H.A. | Dec. | STARS Name | S.H.A. | Dec. |
|---|---|---|---|---|---|---|---|---|---|---|---|---|
| 15 00 | 144 22.8 | 153 25.9 S 5 19.6 | | 214 55.7 S22 57.8 | | 150 52.2 S 3 59.3 | | 40 41.6 N22 32.0 | | Acamar | 315 40.2 S40 24.5 | |
| 01 | 159 25.3 | 168 25.5 | 18.3 | 229 56.1 | 57.6 | 165 54.1 | 59.0 | 55 44.2 | 32.0 | Achernar | 335 48.3 S57 22.0 | |
| 02 | 174 27.7 | 183 25.1 | 17.0 | 244 56.6 | 57.4 | 180 56.1 | 58.8 | 70 46.8 | 32.0 | Acrux | 173 41.0 S62 57.7 | |
| 03 | 189 30.2 | 198 24.8 ·· | 15.8 | 259 57.0 ·· | 57.1 | 195 58.0 ·· | 58.6 | 85 49.4 ·· | 32.0 | Adhara | 255 34.8 S28 56.5 | |
| 04 | 204 32.7 | 213 24.4 | 14.5 | 274 57.5 | 56.9 | 211 00.0 | 58.4 | 100 52.0 | 32.1 | Aldebaran | 291 22.3 N16 27.6 | |
| 05 | 219 35.1 | 228 24.0 | 13.2 | 289 57.9 | 56.7 | 226 01.9 | 58.1 | 115 54.6 | 32.1 | | | |
| 06 | 234 37.6 | 243 23.6 S 5 11.9 | | 304 58.4 S22 56.5 | | 241 03.8 S 3 57.9 | | 130 57.1 N22 32.1 | | Alioth | 166 45.4 N56 05.3 | |
| 07 | 249 40.0 | 258 23.3 | 10.7 | 319 58.9 | 56.3 | 256 05.8 | 57.7 | 145 59.7 | 32.1 | Alkaid | 153 21.2 N49 25.9 | |
| S 08 | 264 42.5 | 273 22.9 | 09.4 | 334 59.3 | 56.0 | 271 07.7 | 57.4 | 161 02.3 | 32.1 | Al Na'ir | 28 20.1 S47 04.9 | |
| A 09 | 279 45.0 | 288 22.5 ·· | 08.1 | 349 59.8 ·· | 55.8 | 286 09.6 ·· | 57.2 | 176 04.9 ·· | 32.1 | Alnilam | 276 15.3 S 1 13.2 | |
| T 10 | 294 47.4 | 303 22.1 | 06.8 | 5 00.2 | 55.6 | 301 11.6 | 57.0 | 191 07.5 | 32.2 | Alphard | 218 24.0 S 8 33.2 | |
| U 11 | 309 49.9 | 318 21.8 | 05.6 | 20 00.7 | 55.4 | 316 13.5 | 56.8 | 206 10.1 | 32.2 | | | |
| R 12 | 324 52.4 | 333 21.4 S 5 04.3 | | 35 01.1 S22 55.2 | | 331 15.4 S 3 56.5 | | 221 12.7 N22 32.2 | | Alphecca | 126 35.3 N26 47.6 | |
| D 13 | 339 54.8 | 348 21.0 | 03.0 | 50 01.6 | 54.9 | 346 17.4 | 56.3 | 236 15.3 | 32.2 | Alpheratz | 358 13.5 N28 57.3 | |
| A 14 | 354 57.3 | 3 20.7 | 01.7 | 65 02.1 | 54.7 | 1 19.3 | 56.1 | 251 17.9 | 32.2 | Altair | 62 36.5 N 8 48.1 | |
| Y 15 | 9 59.8 | 18 20.3 | 5 00.5 | 80 02.5 ·· | 54.5 | 16 21.3 ·· | 55.9 | 266 20.5 ·· | 32.2 | Ankaa | 353 44.3 S42 26.6 | |
| 16 | 25 02.2 | 33 19.9 | 4 59.2 | 95 03.0 | 54.3 | 31 23.2 | 55.6 | 281 23.1 | 32.3 | Antares | 113 01.6 S26 22.6 | |
| 17 | 40 04.7 | 48 19.5 | 57.9 | 110 03.4 | 54.0 | 46 25.1 | 55.4 | 296 25.7 | 32.3 | | | |
| 18 | 55 07.2 | 63 19.2 S 4 56.6 | | 125 03.9 S22 53.8 | | 61 27.1 S 3 55.1 | | 311 28.3 N22 32.3 | | Arcturus | 146 21.8 N19 18.4 | |
| 19 | 70 09.6 | 78 18.8 | 55.3 | 140 04.4 | 53.6 | 76 29.0 | 54.9 | 326 30.8 | 32.3 | Atria | 108 29.4 S68 58.8 | |
| 20 | 85 12.1 | 93 18.4 | 54.1 | 155 04.8 | 53.4 | 91 30.9 | 54.7 | 341 33.4 | 32.3 | Avior | 234 29.2 S59 26.0 | |
| 21 | 100 14.5 | 108 18.1 ·· | 52.8 | 170 05.3 ·· | 53.1 | 106 32.9 ·· | 54.5 | 356 36.0 ·· | 32.3 | Bellatrix | 279 02.7 N 6 19.6 | |
| 22 | 115 17.0 | 123 17.7 | 51.5 | 185 05.7 | 52.9 | 121 34.8 | 54.2 | 11 38.6 | 32.4 | Betelgeuse | 271 32.2 N 7 24.1 | |
| 23 | 130 19.5 | 138 17.3 | 50.2 | 200 06.2 | 52.7 | 136 36.7 | 54.0 | 26 41.2 | 32.4 | | | |
| 16 00 | 145 21.9 | 153 17.0 S 4 49.0 | | 215 06.6 S22 52.5 | | 151 38.7 S 3 53.8 | | 41 43.8 N22 32.4 | | Canopus | 264 08.5 S52 41.2 | |
| 01 | 160 24.4 | 168 16.6 | 47.7 | 230 07.1 | 52.2 | 166 40.6 | 53.5 | 56 46.4 | 32.4 | Capella | 281 16.7 N45 58.6 | |
| 02 | 175 26.9 | 183 16.2 | 46.4 | 245 07.6 | 52.0 | 181 42.5 | 53.3 | 71 49.0 | 32.4 | Deneb | 49 51.5 N45 11.4 | |
| 03 | 190 29.3 | 198 15.9 ·· | 45.1 | 260 08.0 ·· | 51.8 | 196 44.5 ·· | 53.1 | 86 51.6 ·· | 32.4 | Denebola | 183 02.6 N14 42.4 | |
| 04 | 205 31.8 | 213 15.5 | 43.8 | 275 08.5 | 51.6 | 211 46.4 | 52.9 | 101 54.2 | 32.5 | Diphda | 349 24.9 S18 07.5 | |
| 05 | 220 34.3 | 228 15.1 | 42.6 | 290 08.9 | 51.3 | 226 48.3 | 52.6 | 116 56.7 | 32.5 | | | |
| 06 | 235 36.7 | 243 14.8 S 4 41.3 | | 305 09.4 S22 51.1 | | 241 50.3 S 3 52.4 | | 131 59.3 N22 32.5 | | Dubhe | 194 26.1 N61 52.9 | |
| 07 | 250 39.2 | 258 14.4 | 40.0 | 320 09.9 | 50.9 | 256 52.2 | 52.2 | 147 01.9 | 32.5 | Elnath | 278 48.8 N28 35.3 | |
| 08 | 265 41.6 | 273 14.0 | 38.7 | 335 10.3 | 50.6 | 271 54.1 | 51.9 | 162 04.5 | 32.5 | Eltanin | 90 59.8 N51 29.3 | |
| S 09 | 280 44.1 | 288 13.6 ·· | 37.4 | 350 10.8 ·· | 50.4 | 286 56.1 ·· | 51.7 | 177 07.1 ·· | 32.5 | Enif | 34 15.6 N 9 45.6 | |
| U 10 | 295 46.6 | 303 13.3 | 36.2 | 5 11.2 | 50.2 | 301 58.0 | 51.5 | 192 09.7 | 32.6 | Fomalhaut | 15 55.9 S29 45.3 | |
| N 11 | 310 49.0 | 318 12.9 | 34.9 | 20 11.7 | 49.9 | 317 00.0 | 51.2 | 207 12.3 | 32.6 | | | |
| D 12 | 325 51.5 | 333 12.6 S 4 33.6 | | 35 12.1 S22 49.7 | | 332 01.9 S 3 51.0 | | 222 14.9 N22 32.6 | | Gacrux | 172 32.6 S56 58.4 | |
| A 13 | 340 54.0 | 348 12.2 | 32.3 | 50 12.6 | 49.5 | 347 03.8 | 50.8 | 237 17.4 | 32.6 | Gienah | 176 21.6 S17 24.4 | |
| Y 14 | 355 56.4 | 3 11.8 | 31.0 | 65 13.1 | 49.2 | 2 05.8 | 50.6 | 252 20.0 | 32.6 | Hadar | 149 28.5 S60 15.1 | |
| 15 | 10 58.9 | 18 11.5 ·· | 29.8 | 80 13.5 ·· | 49.0 | 17 07.7 ·· | 50.3 | 267 22.6 ·· | 32.6 | Hamal | 328 33.3 N23 20.8 | |
| 16 | 26 01.4 | 33 11.1 | 28.5 | 95 14.0 | 48.8 | 32 09.6 | 50.1 | 282 25.2 | 32.7 | Kaus Aust. | 84 22.1 S34 23.8 | |
| 17 | 41 03.8 | 48 10.7 | 27.2 | 110 14.4 | 48.5 | 47 11.6 | 49.9 | 297 27.8 | 32.7 | | | |
| 18 | 56 06.3 | 63 10.4 S 4 25.9 | | 125 14.9 S22 48.3 | | 62 13.5 S 3 49.6 | | 312 30.4 N22 32.7 | | Kochab | 137 18.5 N74 15.1 | |
| 19 | 71 08.8 | 78 10.0 | 24.6 | 140 15.4 | 48.1 | 77 15.4 | 49.4 | 327 33.0 | 32.7 | Markab | 14 07.2 N15 04.3 | |
| 20 | 86 11.2 | 93 09.6 | 23.3 | 155 15.8 | 47.8 | 92 17.4 | 49.2 | 342 35.6 | 32.7 | Menkar | 314 45.1 N 3 59.5 | |
| 21 | 101 13.7 | 108 09.3 ·· | 22.1 | 170 16.3 ·· | 47.6 | 107 19.3 ·· | 48.9 | 357 38.1 ·· | 32.7 | Menkent | 148 41.3 S36 14.9 | |
| 22 | 116 16.1 | 123 08.9 | 20.8 | 185 16.7 | 47.4 | 122 21.2 | 48.7 | 12 40.7 | 32.7 | Miaplacidus | 221 44.9 S69 37.1 | |
| 23 | 131 18.6 | 138 08.5 | 19.5 | 200 17.2 | 47.1 | 137 23.2 | 48.5 | 27 43.3 | 32.8 | | | |
| 17 00 | 146 21.1 | 153 08.2 S 4 18.2 | | 215 17.7 S22 46.9 | | 152 25.1 S 3 48.2 | | 42 45.9 N22 32.8 | | Mirfak | 309 21.6 N49 46.6 | |
| 01 | 161 23.5 | 168 07.8 | 16.9 | 230 18.1 | 46.7 | 167 27.0 | 48.0 | 57 48.5 | 32.8 | Nunki | 76 34.1 S26 19.7 | |
| 02 | 176 26.0 | 183 07.5 | 15.6 | 245 18.6 | 46.4 | 182 29.0 | 47.8 | 72 51.1 | 32.8 | Peacock | 54 04.9 S56 48.8 | |
| 03 | 191 28.5 | 198 07.1 ·· | 14.4 | 260 19.0 ·· | 46.2 | 197 30.9 ·· | 47.6 | 87 53.7 ·· | 32.8 | Pollux | 244 02.5 N28 05.1 | |
| 04 | 206 30.9 | 213 06.7 | 13.1 | 275 19.5 | 45.9 | 212 32.8 | 47.3 | 102 56.2 | 32.8 | Procyon | 245 29.5 N 5 17.2 | |
| 05 | 221 33.4 | 228 06.4 | 11.8 | 290 20.0 | 45.7 | 227 34.8 | 47.1 | 117 58.8 | 32.9 | | | |
| 06 | 236 35.9 | 243 06.0 S 4 10.5 | | 305 20.4 S22 45.5 | | 242 36.7 S 3 46.9 | | 133 01.4 N22 32.9 | | Rasalhague | 96 33.3 N12 34.5 | |
| 07 | 251 38.3 | 258 05.6 | 09.2 | 320 20.9 | 45.2 | 257 38.6 | 46.6 | 148 04.0 | 32.9 | Regulus | 208 13.7 N12 05.1 | |
| 08 | 266 40.8 | 273 05.3 | 07.9 | 335 21.3 | 45.0 | 272 40.6 | 46.4 | 163 06.6 | 32.9 | Rigel | 281 39.5 S 8 13.9 | |
| M 09 | 281 43.3 | 288 04.9 ·· | 06.7 | 350 21.8 ·· | 44.7 | 287 42.5 ·· | 46.2 | 178 09.2 ·· | 32.9 | Rigil Kent. | 140 30.8 S60 43.8 | |
| O 10 | 296 45.7 | 303 04.6 | 05.4 | 5 22.3 | 44.5 | 302 44.4 | 45.9 | 193 11.7 | 32.9 | Sabik | 102 45.6 S15 41.7 | |
| N 11 | 311 48.2 | 318 04.2 | 04.1 | 20 22.7 | 44.3 | 317 46.4 | 45.7 | 208 14.3 | 33.0 | | | |
| D 12 | 326 50.6 | 333 03.8 S 4 02.8 | | 35 23.2 S22 44.0 | | 332 48.3 S 3 45.5 | | 223 16.9 N22 33.0 | | Schedar | 350 13.8 N56 24.3 | |
| A 13 | 341 53.1 | 348 03.5 | 01.5 | 50 23.6 | 43.8 | 347 50.2 | 45.2 | 238 19.5 | 33.0 | Shaula | 97 01.1 S37 05.1 | |
| Y 14 | 356 55.6 | 3 03.1 | 4 00.2 | 65 24.1 | 43.5 | 2 52.2 | 45.0 | 253 22.1 | 33.0 | Sirius | 258 58.8 S16 41.1 | |
| 15 | 11 58.0 | 18 02.8 | 3 58.9 | 80 24.6 ·· | 43.3 | 17 54.1 ·· | 44.8 | 268 24.7 ·· | 33.0 | Spica | 159 01.3 S11 02.1 | |
| 16 | 27 00.5 | 33 02.4 | 57.7 | 95 25.0 | 43.0 | 32 56.0 | 44.6 | 283 27.2 | 33.0 | Suhail | 223 13.1 S43 20.1 | |
| 17 | 42 03.0 | 48 02.0 | 56.4 | 110 25.5 | 42.8 | 47 58.0 | 44.3 | 298 29.8 | 33.0 | | | |
| 18 | 57 05.4 | 63 01.7 S 3 55.1 | | 125 25.9 S22 42.6 | | 62 59.9 S 3 44.1 | | 313 32.4 N22 33.1 | | Vega | 80 58.7 N38 45.4 | |
| 19 | 72 07.9 | 78 01.3 | 53.8 | 140 26.4 | 42.3 | 78 01.8 | 43.9 | 328 35.0 | 33.1 | Zuben'ubi | 137 37.2 S15 56.4 | |
| 20 | 87 10.4 | 93 01.0 | 52.5 | 155 26.9 | 42.1 | 93 03.8 | 43.6 | 343 37.6 | 33.1 | | | |
| 21 | 102 12.8 | 108 00.6 ·· | 51.2 | 170 27.3 ·· | 41.8 | 108 05.7 ·· | 43.4 | 358 40.2 ·· | 33.1 | | S.H.A. | Mer. Pass. |
| 22 | 117 15.3 | 123 00.3 | 49.9 | 185 27.8 | 41.6 | 123 07.6 | 43.2 | 13 42.7 | 33.1 | Venus | 7 55.0 | 13 47 |
| 23 | 132 17.7 | 137 59.9 | 48.6 | 200 28.3 | 41.3 | 138 09.5 | 42.9 | 28 45.3 | 33.1 | Mars | 69 44.7 | 9 39 |
| Mer. Pass. 14 16.2 | | v −0.4 d 1.3 | | v 0.5 d 0.2 | | v 1.9 d 0.2 | | v 2.6 d 0.0 | | Jupiter | 6 16.7 | 13 52 |
| | | | | | | | | | | Saturn | 256 21.9 | 21 09 |

Fig. A5.2

FEBRUARY 15, 16, 17 (SAT., SUN., MON.)   41

## SUN / MOON

| G.M.T. | SUN G.H.A. | SUN Dec. | MOON G.H.A. | v | MOON Dec. | d | H.P. |
|---|---|---|---|---|---|---|---|
| d h | ° ′ | ° ′ | ° ′ | ′ | ° ′ | ′ | ′ |
| 15 00 | 176 26.7 | S12 57.8 | 139 52.5 | 15.4 | N 6 39.7 | 10.6 | 54.3 |
| 01 | 191 26.7 | 56.9 | 154 26.9 | 15.3 | 6 50.3 | 10.6 | 54.3 |
| 02 | 206 26.8 | 56.1 | 169 01.2 | 15.3 | 7 00.9 | 10.6 | 54.3 |
| 03 | 221 26.8 | .. 55.2 | 183 35.5 | 15.3 | 7 11.5 | 10.6 | 54.4 |
| 04 | 236 26.8 | 54.4 | 198 09.8 | 15.2 | 7 22.1 | 10.5 | 54.4 |
| 05 | 251 26.8 | 53.5 | 212 44.0 | 15.3 | 7 32.6 | 10.5 | 54.4 |
| 06 | 266 26.9 | S12 52.7 | 227 18.3 | 15.1 | N 7 43.1 | 10.5 | 54.4 |
| S 07 | 281 26.9 | 51.8 | 241 52.4 | 15.2 | 7 53.6 | 10.4 | 54.4 |
| A 08 | 296 26.9 | 51.0 | 256 26.6 | 15.1 | 8 04.0 | 10.4 | 54.4 |
| T 09 | 311 27.0 | .. 50.1 | 271 00.7 | 15.1 | 8 14.5 | 10.4 | 54.4 |
| U 10 | 326 27.0 | 49.3 | 285 34.8 | 15.0 | 8 24.9 | 10.3 | 54.4 |
| R 11 | 341 27.0 | 48.4 | 300 08.8 | 15.0 | 8 35.2 | 10.4 | 54.5 |
| D 12 | 356 27.0 | S12 47.5 | 314 42.8 | 15.0 | N 8 45.6 | 10.3 | 54.5 |
| A 13 | 11 27.1 | 46.7 | 329 16.8 | 14.9 | 8 55.9 | 10.3 | 54.5 |
| Y 14 | 26 27.1 | 45.8 | 343 50.7 | 14.8 | 9 06.2 | 10.2 | 54.5 |
| 15 | 41 27.1 | .. 45.0 | 358 24.5 | 14.9 | 9 16.4 | 10.2 | 54.5 |
| 16 | 56 27.1 | 44.1 | 12 58.4 | 14.8 | 9 26.6 | 10.2 | 54.5 |
| 17 | 71 27.2 | 43.3 | 27 32.2 | 14.7 | 9 36.8 | 10.1 | 54.6 |
| 18 | 86 27.2 | S12 42.4 | 42 05.9 | 14.7 | N 9 46.9 | 10.1 | 54.6 |
| 19 | 101 27.2 | 41.5 | 56 39.6 | 14.7 | 9 57.0 | 10.1 | 54.6 |
| 20 | 116 27.3 | 40.7 | 71 13.3 | 14.6 | 10 07.1 | 10.0 | 54.6 |
| 21 | 131 27.3 | .. 39.8 | 85 46.9 | 14.6 | 10 17.1 | 10.0 | 54.6 |
| 22 | 146 27.3 | 39.0 | 100 20.5 | 14.5 | 10 27.1 | 10.0 | 54.6 |
| 23 | 161 27.4 | 38.1 | 114 54.0 | 14.5 | 10 37.1 | 9.9 | 54.7 |
| 16 00 | 176 27.4 | S12 37.2 | 129 27.5 | 14.4 | N10 47.0 | 9.9 | 54.7 |
| 01 | 191 27.4 | 36.4 | 144 00.9 | 14.4 | 10 56.9 | 9.8 | 54.7 |
| 02 | 206 27.4 | 35.5 | 158 34.3 | 14.3 | 11 06.7 | 9.8 | 54.7 |
| 03 | 221 27.5 | .. 34.7 | 173 07.6 | 14.3 | 11 16.5 | 9.7 | 54.7 |
| 04 | 236 27.5 | 33.8 | 187 40.9 | 14.2 | 11 26.2 | 9.7 | 54.7 |
| 05 | 251 27.5 | 32.9 | 202 14.1 | 14.2 | 11 35.9 | 9.7 | 54.8 |
| 06 | 266 27.6 | S12 32.1 | 216 47.3 | 14.1 | N11 45.6 | 9.6 | 54.8 |
| 07 | 281 27.6 | 31.2 | 231 20.4 | 14.1 | 11 55.2 | 9.6 | 54.8 |
| S 08 | 296 27.6 | 30.4 | 245 53.5 | 14.0 | 12 04.8 | 9.5 | 54.8 |
| U 09 | 311 27.7 | .. 29.5 | 260 26.5 | 14.0 | 12 14.3 | 9.5 | 54.8 |
| N 10 | 326 27.7 | 28.6 | 274 59.5 | 13.9 | 12 23.8 | 9.4 | 54.9 |
| 11 | 341 27.7 | 27.8 | 289 32.4 | 13.8 | 12 33.2 | 9.4 | 54.9 |
| D 12 | 356 27.8 | S12 26.9 | 304 05.2 | 13.8 | N12 42.6 | 9.4 | 54.9 |
| A 13 | 11 27.8 | 26.0 | 318 38.0 | 13.8 | 12 52.0 | 9.3 | 54.9 |
| Y 14 | 26 27.9 | 25.2 | 333 10.8 | 13.7 | 13 01.3 | 9.2 | 54.9 |
| 15 | 41 27.9 | .. 24.3 | 347 43.5 | 13.6 | 13 10.5 | 9.2 | 55.0 |
| 16 | 56 27.9 | 23.4 | 2 16.1 | 13.6 | 13 19.7 | 9.2 | 55.0 |
| 17 | 71 28.0 | 22.6 | 16 48.7 | 13.5 | 13 28.8 | 9.1 | 55.0 |
| 18 | 86 28.0 | S12 21.7 | 31 21.2 | 13.4 | N13 37.9 | 9.0 | 55.0 |
| 19 | 101 28.0 | 20.8 | 45 53.6 | 13.4 | 13 46.9 | 9.0 | 55.0 |
| 20 | 116 28.1 | 20.0 | 60 26.0 | 13.4 | 13 55.9 | 8.9 | 55.1 |
| 21 | 131 28.1 | .. 19.1 | 74 58.4 | 13.2 | 14 04.8 | 8.9 | 55.1 |
| 22 | 146 28.1 | 18.2 | 89 30.6 | 13.2 | 14 13.7 | 8.8 | 55.1 |
| 23 | 161 28.2 | 17.4 | 104 02.8 | 13.2 | 14 22.5 | 8.7 | 55.1 |
| 17 00 | 176 28.2 | S12 16.5 | 118 35.0 | 13.1 | N14 31.2 | 8.7 | 55.2 |
| 01 | 191 28.2 | 15.6 | 133 07.1 | 13.0 | 14 39.9 | 8.7 | 55.2 |
| 02 | 206 28.3 | 14.8 | 147 39.1 | 12.9 | 14 48.6 | 8.5 | 55.2 |
| 03 | 221 28.3 | .. 13.9 | 162 11.0 | 12.9 | 14 57.1 | 8.5 | 55.2 |
| 04 | 236 28.4 | 13.0 | 176 42.9 | 12.8 | 15 05.6 | 8.5 | 55.2 |
| 05 | 251 28.4 | 12.2 | 191 14.7 | 12.8 | 15 14.1 | 8.4 | 55.3 |
| 06 | 266 28.5 | S12 11.3 | 205 46.5 | 12.7 | N15 22.5 | 8.3 | 55.3 |
| 07 | 281 28.5 | 10.4 | 220 18.2 | 12.6 | 15 30.8 | 8.2 | 55.3 |
| 08 | 296 28.5 | 09.5 | 234 49.8 | 12.6 | 15 39.0 | 8.2 | 55.3 |
| M 09 | 311 28.6 | .. 08.7 | 249 21.4 | 12.5 | 15 47.2 | 8.2 | 55.4 |
| O 10 | 326 28.6 | 07.8 | 263 52.9 | 12.4 | 15 55.4 | 8.0 | 55.4 |
| N 11 | 341 28.7 | 06.9 | 278 24.3 | 12.3 | 16 03.4 | 8.0 | 55.4 |
| D 12 | 356 28.7 | S12 06.1 | 292 55.6 | 12.3 | N16 11.4 | 7.9 | 55.4 |
| A 13 | 11 28.8 | 05.2 | 307 26.9 | 12.2 | 16 19.3 | 7.9 | 55.5 |
| Y 14 | 26 28.8 | 04.3 | 321 58.1 | 12.2 | 16 27.2 | 7.8 | 55.5 |
| 15 | 41 28.8 | .. 03.4 | 336 29.3 | 12.1 | 16 35.0 | 7.7 | 55.5 |
| 16 | 56 28.9 | 02.6 | 351 00.4 | 12.0 | 16 42.7 | 7.6 | 55.5 |
| 17 | 71 28.9 | 01.7 | 5 31.4 | 11.9 | 16 50.3 | 7.6 | 55.6 |
| 18 | 86 29.0 | S12 00.8 | 20 02.3 | 11.9 | N16 57.9 | 7.5 | 55.6 |
| 19 | 101 29.0 | 11 59.9 | 34 33.2 | 11.7 | 17 05.4 | 7.4 | 55.6 |
| 20 | 116 29.1 | 59.1 | 49 03.9 | 11.8 | 17 12.8 | 7.3 | 55.7 |
| 21 | 131 29.1 | .. 58.2 | 63 34.7 | 11.6 | 17 20.1 | 7.3 | 55.7 |
| 22 | 146 29.2 | 57.3 | 78 05.3 | 11.6 | 17 27.4 | 7.1 | 55.7 |
| 23 | 161 29.2 | 56.4 | 92 35.9 | 11.5 | 17 34.5 | 7.2 | 55.7 |
| | S.D. 16.2  d 0.9 | | S.D. 14.8 | 15.0 | | | 15.1 |

## Twilight / Sunrise / Moonrise

| Lat. | Naut. | Civil | Sunrise | Moonrise 15 | 16 | 17 | 18 |
|---|---|---|---|---|---|---|---|
| ° | h m | h m | h m | h m | h m | h m | h m |
| N 72 | 06 13 | 07 33 | 08 52 | 07 13 | 06 54 | 06 28 | □ |
| N 70 | 06 12 | 07 24 | 08 32 | 07 24 | 07 14 | 07 02 | 06 42 |
| 68 | 06 10 | 07 16 | 08 17 | 07 33 | 07 30 | 07 27 | 07 24 |
| 66 | 06 09 | 07 09 | 08 05 | 07 41 | 07 43 | 07 46 | 07 53 |
| 64 | 06 08 | 07 03 | 07 54 | 07 47 | 07 53 | 08 02 | 08 15 |
| 62 | 06 06 | 06 58 | 07 45 | 07 53 | 08 02 | 08 15 | 08 32 |
| 60 | 06 05 | 06 54 | 07 37 | 07 58 | 08 10 | 08 26 | 08 47 |
| N 58 | 06 04 | 06 50 | 07 31 | 08 03 | 08 17 | 08 36 | 08 59 |
| 56 | 06 03 | 06 46 | 07 25 | 08 06 | 08 23 | 08 44 | 09 10 |
| 54 | 06 01 | 06 43 | 07 19 | 08 10 | 08 29 | 08 52 | 09 20 |
| 52 | 06 00 | 06 40 | 07 15 | 08 13 | 08 34 | 08 58 | 09 28 |
| 50 | 05 59 | 06 37 | 07 10 | 08 16 | 08 39 | 09 05 | 09 36 |
| 45 | 05 56 | 06 30 | 07 01 | 08 23 | 08 48 | 09 18 | 09 52 |
| N 40 | 05 53 | 06 25 | 06 53 | 08 28 | 08 57 | 09 29 | 10 06 |
| 35 | 05 50 | 06 20 | 06 46 | 08 33 | 09 04 | 09 38 | 10 17 |
| 30 | 05 47 | 06 15 | 06 40 | 08 37 | 09 10 | 09 47 | 10 28 |
| 20 | 05 41 | 06 07 | 06 29 | 08 44 | 09 21 | 10 01 | 10 45 |
| N 10 | 05 33 | 05 58 | 06 20 | 08 50 | 09 31 | 10 14 | 11 00 |
| 0 | 05 25 | 05 50 | 06 11 | 08 56 | 09 40 | 10 26 | 11 15 |
| S 10 | 05 15 | 05 40 | 06 02 | 09 02 | 09 49 | 10 38 | 11 29 |
| 20 | 05 02 | 05 29 | 05 52 | 09 09 | 09 59 | 10 51 | 11 44 |
| 30 | 04 46 | 05 16 | 05 41 | 09 16 | 10 10 | 11 05 | 12 02 |
| 35 | 04 36 | 05 08 | 05 34 | 09 20 | 10 17 | 11 14 | 12 12 |
| 40 | 04 23 | 04 58 | 05 26 | 09 25 | 10 24 | 11 24 | 12 24 |
| 45 | 04 08 | 04 46 | 05 18 | 09 31 | 10 33 | 11 35 | 12 39 |
| S 50 | 03 47 | 04 32 | 05 07 | 09 38 | 10 43 | 11 50 | 12 56 |
| 52 | 03 37 | 04 25 | 05 02 | 09 41 | 10 48 | 11 56 | 13 04 |
| 54 | 03 26 | 04 17 | 04 57 | 09 45 | 10 54 | 12 03 | 13 13 |
| 56 | 03 12 | 04 08 | 04 50 | 09 49 | 11 00 | 12 12 | 13 23 |
| 58 | 02 56 | 03 58 | 04 43 | 09 53 | 11 06 | 12 21 | 13 35 |
| S 60 | 02 36 | 03 46 | 04 36 | 09 58 | 11 14 | 12 32 | 13 49 |

## Sunset / Twilight / Moonset

| Lat. | Sunset | Civil | Naut. | Moonset 15 | 16 | 17 | 18 |
|---|---|---|---|---|---|---|---|
| ° | h m | h m | h m | h m | h m | h m | h m |
| N 72 | 15 38 | 16 57 | 18 17 | 23 43 | 25 43 | 01 43 | □ |
| N 70 | 15 58 | 17 06 | 18 18 | 23 25 | 25 10 | 01 10 | 03 09 |
| 68 | 16 13 | 17 14 | 18 20 | 23 10 | 24 47 | 00 47 | 02 28 |
| 66 | 16 25 | 17 21 | 18 21 | 22 59 | 24 28 | 00 28 | 02 00 |
| 64 | 16 35 | 17 26 | 18 22 | 22 49 | 24 14 | 00 14 | 01 39 |
| 62 | 16 44 | 17 31 | 18 23 | 22 41 | 24 01 | 00 01 | 01 22 |
| 60 | 16 52 | 17 36 | 18 25 | 22 34 | 23 51 | 25 08 | 01 08 |
| N 58 | 16 59 | 17 40 | 18 26 | 22 28 | 23 42 | 24 56 | 00 56 |
| 56 | 17 04 | 17 43 | 18 27 | 22 22 | 23 34 | 24 46 | 00 46 |
| 54 | 17 10 | 17 46 | 18 28 | 22 18 | 23 27 | 24 37 | 00 37 |
| 52 | 17 15 | 17 49 | 18 29 | 22 13 | 23 21 | 24 28 | 00 28 |
| 50 | 17 19 | 17 52 | 18 30 | 22 09 | 23 15 | 24 21 | 00 21 |
| 45 | 17 28 | 17 59 | 18 33 | 22 01 | 23 03 | 24 06 | 00 06 |
| N 40 | 17 36 | 18 04 | 18 36 | 21 53 | 22 53 | 23 53 | 24 53 |
| 35 | 17 43 | 18 09 | 18 38 | 21 47 | 22 44 | 23 42 | 24 41 |
| 30 | 17 49 | 18 13 | 18 42 | 21 42 | 22 36 | 23 32 | 24 30 |
| 20 | 17 59 | 18 22 | 18 48 | 21 33 | 22 24 | 23 16 | 24 11 |
| N 10 | 18 09 | 18 30 | 18 55 | 21 25 | 22 12 | 23 02 | 23 54 |
| 0 | 18 18 | 18 39 | 19 03 | 21 17 | 22 02 | 22 49 | 23 39 |
| S 10 | 18 27 | 18 48 | 19 13 | 21 09 | 21 51 | 22 36 | 23 24 |
| 20 | 18 36 | 18 59 | 19 25 | 21 01 | 21 40 | 22 22 | 23 07 |
| 30 | 18 47 | 19 12 | 19 42 | 20 52 | 21 27 | 22 05 | 22 49 |
| 35 | 18 54 | 19 20 | 19 52 | 20 47 | 21 20 | 21 56 | 22 38 |
| 40 | 19 01 | 19 30 | 20 04 | 20 41 | 21 11 | 21 45 | 22 25 |
| 45 | 19 10 | 19 41 | 20 19 | 20 34 | 21 01 | 21 33 | 22 11 |
| S 50 | 19 21 | 19 55 | 20 39 | 20 26 | 20 50 | 21 18 | 21 53 |
| 52 | 19 25 | 20 02 | 20 49 | 20 22 | 20 44 | 21 11 | 21 44 |
| 54 | 19 31 | 20 10 | 21 00 | 20 18 | 20 38 | 21 03 | 21 35 |
| 56 | 19 37 | 20 18 | 21 13 | 20 13 | 20 32 | 20 54 | 21 24 |
| 58 | 19 43 | 20 28 | 21 29 | 20 08 | 20 25 | 20 45 | 21 12 |
| S 60 | 19 51 | 20 40 | 21 48 | 20 02 | 20 16 | 20 33 | 20 58 |

## SUN / MOON

| Day | SUN Eqn. of Time 00h | 12h | Mer. Pass. | MOON Mer. Pass. Upper | Lower | Age | Phase |
|---|---|---|---|---|---|---|---|
| | m s | m s | h m | h m | h m | d | |
| 15 | 14 13 | 14 12 | 12 14 | 15 07 | 02 45 | 04 | |
| 16 | 14 11 | 14 09 | 12 14 | 15 51 | 03 28 | 05 | |
| 17 | 14 07 | 14 05 | 12 14 | 16 37 | 04 14 | 06 | ● |

Fig. A5.3

102  MAY 19, 20, 21 (MON., TUES., WED.)

| G.M.T. | ARIES G.H.A. | VENUS −3.7 G.H.A. | Dec. | MARS +1.0 G.H.A. | Dec. | JUPITER −1.7 G.H.A. | Dec. | SATURN +0.4 G.H.A. | Dec. |
|---|---|---|---|---|---|---|---|---|---|
| **19 (MON) 00** | 236 02.7 | 134 41.2 | N25 35.2 | 237 01.4 | S 2 10.4 | 222 33.8 | N 4 31.9 | 129 09.4 | N22 24.4 |
| 01 | 251 05.1 | 149 40.6 | 35.1 | 252 02.1 | 09.6 | 237 35.8 | 32.1 | 144 11.6 | 24.4 |
| 02 | 266 07.6 | 164 40.0 | 34.9 | 267 02.8 | 08.9 | 252 37.8 | 32.3 | 159 13.8 | 24.3 |
| 03 | 281 10.1 | 179 39.4 | ·· 34.7 | 282 03.6 | ·· 08.2 | 267 39.8 | ·· 32.5 | 174 16.0 | ·· 24.3 |
| 04 | 296 12.5 | 194 38.8 | 34.5 | 297 04.3 | 07.4 | 282 41.8 | 32.7 | 189 18.2 | 24.3 |
| 05 | 311 15.0 | 209 38.2 | 34.3 | 312 05.0 | 06.7 | 297 43.8 | 32.9 | 204 20.4 | 24.3 |
| 06 | 326 17.5 | 224 37.6 | N25 34.1 | 327 05.8 | S 2 06.0 | 312 45.7 | N 4 33.1 | 219 22.6 | N22 24.2 |
| 07 | 341 19.9 | 239 37.1 | 33.9 | 342 06.5 | 05.2 | 327 47.7 | 33.3 | 234 24.7 | 24.2 |
| 08 | 356 22.4 | 254 36.5 | 33.7 | 357 07.2 | 04.5 | 342 49.7 | 33.5 | 249 26.9 | 24.2 |
| M 09 | 11 24.8 | 269 35.9 | ·· 33.5 | 12 08.0 | ·· 03.7 | 357 51.7 | ·· 33.7 | 264 29.1 | ·· 24.2 |
| O 10 | 26 27.3 | 284 35.3 | 33.3 | 27 08.7 | 03.0 | 12 53.7 | 33.8 | 279 31.3 | 24.1 |
| N 11 | 41 29.8 | 299 34.7 | 33.1 | 42 09.4 | 02.3 | 27 55.7 | 34.0 | 294 33.5 | 24.1 |
| D 12 | 56 32.2 | 314 34.1 | N25 32.9 | 57 10.2 | S 2 01.5 | 42 57.4 | N 4 34.2 | 309 35.7 | N22 24.1 |
| A 13 | 71 34.7 | 329 33.6 | 32.7 | 72 10.9 | 00.8 | 57 59.4 | 34.4 | 324 37.9 | 24.1 |
| Y 14 | 86 37.2 | 344 33.0 | 32.5 | 87 11.6 | 2 00.1 | 73 01.6 | 34.6 | 339 40.1 | 24.0 |
| 15 | 101 39.6 | 359 32.4 | ·· 32.3 | 102 12.4 | 1 59.3 | 88 03.6 | ·· 34.8 | 354 42.3 | ·· 24.0 |
| 16 | 116 42.1 | 14 31.8 | 32.1 | 117 13.1 | 58.6 | 103 05.6 | 35.0 | 9 44.5 | 24.0 |
| 17 | 131 44.6 | 29 31.2 | 31.9 | 132 13.8 | 57.8 | 118 07.6 | 35.2 | 24 46.7 | 24.0 |
| 18 | 146 47.0 | 44 30.7 | N25 31.7 | 147 14.6 | S 1 57.1 | 133 09.6 | N 4 35.4 | 39 48.9 | N22 23.9 |
| 19 | 161 49.5 | 59 30.1 | 31.5 | 162 15.3 | 56.4 | 148 11.5 | 35.6 | 54 51.0 | 23.9 |
| 20 | 176 52.0 | 74 29.5 | 31.3 | 177 16.0 | 55.6 | 163 13.5 | 35.8 | 69 53.2 | 23.9 |
| 21 | 191 54.4 | 89 28.9 | ·· 31.1 | 192 16.8 | ·· 54.9 | 178 15.5 | ·· 36.0 | 84 55.4 | ·· 23.9 |
| 22 | 206 56.9 | 104 28.3 | 30.9 | 207 17.5 | 54.2 | 193 17.5 | 36.2 | 99 57.6 | 23.8 |
| 23 | 221 59.3 | 119 27.8 | 30.7 | 222 18.2 | 53.4 | 208 19.5 | 36.4 | 114 59.8 | 23.8 |
| **20 (TUES) 00** | 237 01.8 | 134 27.2 | N25 30.5 | 237 19.0 | S 1 52.7 | 223 21.5 | N 4 36.6 | 130 02.0 | N22 23.8 |
| 01 | 252 04.3 | 149 26.6 | 30.3 | 252 19.7 | 51.9 | 238 23.5 | 36.8 | 145 04.2 | 23.8 |
| 02 | 267 06.7 | 164 26.0 | 30.0 | 267 20.4 | 51.2 | 253 25.4 | 36.9 | 160 06.4 | 23.7 |
| 03 | 282 09.2 | 179 25.5 | ·· 29.8 | 282 21.2 | ·· 50.5 | 268 27.4 | ·· 37.1 | 175 08.6 | ·· 23.7 |
| 04 | 297 11.7 | 194 24.9 | 29.6 | 297 21.9 | 49.7 | 283 29.4 | 37.3 | 190 10.8 | 23.7 |
| 05 | 312 14.1 | 209 24.3 | 29.4 | 312 22.6 | 49.0 | 298 31.4 | 37.5 | 205 12.9 | 23.7 |
| 06 | 327 16.6 | 224 23.7 | N25 29.2 | 327 23.4 | S 1 48.3 | 313 33.4 | N 4 37.7 | 220 15.1 | N22 23.6 |
| 07 | 342 19.1 | 239 23.2 | 29.0 | 342 24.1 | 47.5 | 328 35.4 | 37.9 | 235 17.3 | 23.6 |
| 08 | 357 21.5 | 254 22.6 | 28.7 | 357 24.8 | 46.8 | 343 37.4 | 38.1 | 250 19.5 | 23.6 |
| T 09 | 12 24.0 | 269 22.0 | ·· 28.5 | 12 25.6 | ·· 46.0 | 358 39.4 | ·· 38.3 | 265 21.7 | ·· 23.6 |
| U 10 | 27 26.4 | 284 21.5 | 28.3 | 27 26.3 | 45.3 | 13 41.3 | 38.5 | 280 23.9 | 23.5 |
| E 11 | 42 28.9 | 299 20.9 | 28.1 | 42 27.0 | 44.6 | 28 43.3 | 38.7 | 295 26.1 | 23.5 |
| S 12 | 57 31.4 | 314 20.3 | N25 27.8 | 57 27.8 | S 1 43.8 | 43 45.3 | N 4 38.9 | 310 28.3 | N22 23.4 |
| D 13 | 72 33.8 | 329 19.8 | 27.6 | 72 28.5 | 43.1 | 58 47.3 | 39.1 | 325 30.5 | 23.4 |
| A 14 | 87 36.3 | 344 19.2 | 27.4 | 87 29.2 | 42.4 | 73 49.3 | 39.3 | 340 32.6 | 23.4 |
| Y 15 | 102 38.8 | 359 18.6 | ·· 27.2 | 102 30.0 | ·· 41.6 | 88 51.3 | ·· 39.5 | 355 34.8 | ·· 23.4 |
| 16 | 117 41.2 | 14 18.1 | 26.9 | 117 30.7 | 40.9 | 103 53.3 | 39.6 | 10 37.0 | 23.4 |
| 17 | 132 43.7 | 29 17.5 | 26.7 | 132 31.4 | 40.1 | 118 55.3 | 39.8 | 25 39.2 | 23.3 |
| 18 | 147 46.2 | 44 16.9 | N25 26.5 | 147 32.2 | S 1 39.4 | 133 57.2 | N 4 40.0 | 40 41.4 | N22 23.3 |
| 19 | 162 48.6 | 59 16.4 | 26.2 | 162 32.9 | 38.7 | 148 59.2 | 40.2 | 55 43.6 | 23.3 |
| 20 | 177 51.1 | 74 15.8 | 26.0 | 177 33.7 | 37.9 | 164 01.2 | 40.4 | 70 45.8 | 23.3 |
| 21 | 192 53.6 | 89 15.2 | ·· 25.8 | 192 34.4 | ·· 37.2 | 179 03.2 | ·· 40.6 | 85 48.0 | ·· 23.2 |
| 22 | 207 56.0 | 104 14.7 | 25.5 | 207 35.1 | 36.5 | 194 05.2 | 40.8 | 100 50.2 | 23.2 |
| 23 | 222 58.5 | 119 14.1 | 25.3 | 222 35.9 | 35.7 | 209 07.2 | 41.0 | 115 52.3 | 23.2 |
| **21 (WED) 00** | 238 00.9 | 134 13.5 | N25 25.1 | 237 36.6 | S 1 35.0 | 224 09.2 | N 4 41.2 | 130 54.5 | N22 23.2 |
| 01 | 253 03.4 | 149 13.0 | 24.8 | 252 37.3 | 34.2 | 239 11.2 | 41.4 | 145 56.7 | 23.1 |
| 02 | 268 05.9 | 164 12.4 | 24.6 | 267 38.1 | 33.5 | 254 13.2 | 41.6 | 160 58.9 | 23.1 |
| 03 | 283 08.3 | 179 11.9 | ·· 24.3 | 282 38.8 | ·· 32.8 | 269 15.1 | ·· 41.8 | 176 01.1 | ·· 23.1 |
| 04 | 298 10.8 | 194 11.3 | 24.1 | 297 39.5 | 32.0 | 284 17.1 | 42.0 | 191 03.3 | 23.1 |
| 05 | 313 13.3 | 209 10.7 | 23.8 | 312 40.3 | 31.3 | 299 19.1 | 42.1 | 206 05.5 | 23.0 |
| 06 | 328 15.7 | 224 10.2 | N25 23.6 | 327 41.0 | S 1 30.6 | 314 21.1 | N 4 42.3 | 221 07.7 | N22 23.0 |
| W 07 | 343 18.2 | 239 09.6 | 23.4 | 342 41.7 | 29.8 | 329 23.1 | 42.5 | 236 09.8 | 23.0 |
| E 08 | 358 20.7 | 254 09.1 | 23.1 | 357 42.5 | 29.1 | 344 25.1 | 42.7 | 251 12.0 | 23.0 |
| D 09 | 13 23.1 | 269 08.5 | ·· 22.9 | 12 43.2 | ·· 28.3 | 359 27.1 | ·· 42.9 | 266 14.2 | ·· 22.9 |
| N 10 | 28 25.6 | 284 08.0 | 22.6 | 27 44.0 | 27.6 | 14 29.1 | 43.1 | 281 16.4 | 22.9 |
| E 11 | 43 28.0 | 299 07.4 | 22.4 | 42 44.7 | 26.9 | 29 31.1 | 43.3 | 296 18.6 | 22.9 |
| S 12 | 58 30.5 | 314 06.9 | N25 22.1 | 57 45.4 | S 1 26.1 | 44 33.1 | N 4 43.5 | 311 20.8 | N22 22.8 |
| D 13 | 73 33.0 | 329 06.3 | 21.9 | 72 46.2 | 25.4 | 59 35.0 | 43.7 | 326 23.0 | 22.8 |
| A 14 | 88 35.4 | 344 05.7 | 21.6 | 87 46.9 | 24.7 | 74 37.0 | 43.9 | 341 25.1 | 22.8 |
| Y 15 | 103 37.9 | 359 05.2 | ·· 21.4 | 102 47.6 | ·· 23.9 | 89 39.0 | ·· 44.1 | 356 27.3 | ·· 22.8 |
| 16 | 118 40.4 | 14 04.6 | 21.1 | 117 48.4 | 23.2 | 104 41.0 | 44.2 | 11 29.5 | 22.7 |
| 17 | 133 42.8 | 29 04.1 | 20.8 | 132 49.1 | 22.4 | 119 43.0 | 44.4 | 26 31.7 | 22.7 |
| 18 | 148 45.3 | 44 03.5 | N25 20.6 | 147 49.8 | S 1 21.7 | 134 45.0 | N 4 44.6 | 41 33.9 | N22 22.7 |
| 19 | 163 47.8 | 59 03.0 | 20.3 | 162 50.6 | 21.0 | 149 47.0 | 44.8 | 56 36.1 | 22.7 |
| 20 | 178 50.2 | 74 02.4 | 20.1 | 177 51.3 | 20.2 | 164 49.0 | 45.0 | 71 38.3 | 22.6 |
| 21 | 193 52.7 | 89 01.9 | ·· 19.8 | 192 52.1 | ·· 19.5 | 179 51.0 | ·· 45.2 | 86 40.4 | ·· 22.6 |
| 22 | 208 55.2 | 104 01.3 | 19.5 | 207 52.8 | 18.8 | 194 53.0 | 45.4 | 101 42.6 | 22.6 |
| 23 | 223 57.6 | 119 00.8 | 19.3 | 222 53.5 | 18.0 | 209 55.0 | 45.6 | 116 44.8 | 22.6 |
| Mer. Pass. | 8 10.5 | v −0.6 | d 0.2 | v 0.7 | d 0.7 | v 2.0 | d 0.2 | v 2.2 | d 0.0 |

### STARS

| Name | S.H.A. | Dec. |
|---|---|---|
| Acamar | 315 40.4 | S40 24.1 |
| Achernar | 335 48.4 | S57 21.5 |
| Acrux | 173 40.9 | S62 58.1 |
| Adhara | 255 35.2 | S28 56.5 |
| Aldebaran | 291 22.5 | N16 27.6 |
| Alioth | 166 45.3 | N56 05.7 |
| Alkaid | 153 20.9 | N49 26.2 |
| Al Na'ir | 28 19.5 | S47 04.5 |
| Alnilam | 276 15.7 | S 1 13.1 |
| Alphard | 218 24.2 | S 8 33.3 |
| Alphecca | 126 34.8 | N26 47.8 |
| Alpheratz | 358 13.3 | N28 57.2 |
| Altair | 62 35.9 | N 8 48.1 |
| Ankaa | 353 44.1 | S42 26.2 |
| Antares | 113 00.9 | S26 22.7 |
| Arcturus | 146 21.5 | N19 18.5 |
| Atria | 108 27.9 | S68 59.0 |
| Avior | 234 30.0 | S59 26.2 |
| Bellatrix | 279 03.0 | N 6 19.6 |
| Betelgeuse | 271 32.5 | N 7 24.1 |
| Canopus | 264 09.3 | S52 41.2 |
| Capella | 281 17.1 | N45 58.4 |
| Deneb | 49 50.8 | N45 11.4 |
| Denebola | 183 02.6 | N14 42.5 |
| Diphda | 349 24.7 | S18 07.2 |
| Dubhe | 194 26.4 | N61 53.2 |
| Elnath | 278 49.1 | N28 35.2 |
| Eltanin | 90 58.9 | N51 29.4 |
| Enif | 34 15.1 | N 9 45.7 |
| Fomalhaut | 15 55.5 | S29 45.0 |
| Gacrux | 172 32.4 | S56 58.9 |
| Gienah | 176 21.5 | S17 24.6 |
| Hadar | 149 27.9 | S60 15.5 |
| Hamal | 328 33.3 | N23 20.7 |
| Kaus Aust. | 84 21.3 | S34 23.7 |
| Kochab | 137 17.6 | N74 15.4 |
| Markab | 14 06.9 | N15 04.3 |
| Menkar | 314 45.2 | N 3 59.6 |
| Menkent | 148 40.9 | S36 15.2 |
| Miaplacidus | 221 45.9 | S69 37.4 |
| Mirfak | 309 21.8 | N49 46.4 |
| Nunki | 76 33.4 | S26 19.6 |
| Peacock | 54 03.8 | S56 48.6 |
| Pollux | 244 02.8 | N28 05.2 |
| Procyon | 245 29.8 | N 5 17.2 |
| Rasalhague | 96 32.6 | N12 34.6 |
| Regulus | 208 13.9 | N12 05.2 |
| Rigel | 281 39.8 | S 8 13.9 |
| Rigil Kent. | 140 30.1 | S60 44.2 |
| Sabik | 102 45.0 | S15 41.7 |
| Schedar | 350 13.5 | N56 24.0 |
| Shaula | 97 00.3 | S37 05.2 |
| Sirius | 258 59.2 | S16 41.1 |
| Spica | 159 01.1 | S11 02.2 |
| Suhail | 223 13.6 | S43 20.3 |
| Vega | 80 58.0 | N38 45.5 |
| Zuben'ubi | 137 36.7 | S15 56.5 |

| | S.H.A. | Mer. Pass. |
|---|---|---|
| Venus | 257 25.4 | 15 03 |
| Mars | 0 17.2 | 8 10 |
| Jupiter | 346 19.7 | 9 05 |
| Saturn | 253 00.2 | 15 18 |

Fig. A5.4

MAY 19, 20, 21 (MON., TUES., WED.)          103

| G.M.T. | SUN G.H.A. | Dec. | MOON G.H.A. | v | Dec. | d | H.P. |
|---|---|---|---|---|---|---|---|
| **19 00** | 180 54.3 | N19 35.1 | 81 14.3 | 10.2 | N 4 48.5 | 12.6 | 59.4 |
| 01 | 195 54.2 | 35.6 | 95 43.5 | 10.2 | 4 35.9 | 12.7 | 59.4 |
| 02 | 210 54.2 | 36.2 | 110 12.7 | 10.2 | 4 23.2 | 12.7 | 59.4 |
| 03 | 225 54.2 · · | 36.7 | 124 41.9 | 10.2 | 4 10.5 | 12.7 | 59.4 |
| 04 | 240 54.2 | 37.3 | 139 11.1 | 10.2 | 3 57.8 | 12.8 | 59.4 |
| 05 | 255 54.1 | 37.8 | 153 40.3 | 10.2 | 3 45.0 | 12.8 | 59.4 |
| 06 | 270 54.1 | N19 38.4 | 168 09.5 | 10.2 | N 3 32.2 | 12.8 | 59.4 |
| 07 | 285 54.1 | 38.9 | 182 38.7 | 10.2 | 3 19.4 | 12.8 | 59.4 |
| 08 | 300 54.1 | 39.4 | 197 07.9 | 10.2 | 3 06.6 | 12.8 | 59.4 |
| M 09 | 315 54.0 · · | 40.0 | 211 37.1 | 10.3 | 2 53.8 | 12.9 | 59.4 |
| O 10 | 330 54.0 | 40.5 | 226 06.4 | 10.2 | 2 40.9 | 12.9 | 59.4 |
| N 11 | 345 54.0 | 41.1 | 240 35.6 | 10.2 | 2 28.1 | 12.9 | 59.4 |
| D 12 | 0 53.9 | N19 41.6 | 255 04.8 | 10.3 | N 2 15.2 | 12.9 | 59.4 |
| A 13 | 15 53.9 | 42.1 | 269 34.1 | 10.2 | 2 02.3 | 13.0 | 59.4 |
| Y 14 | 30 53.9 | 42.7 | 284 03.3 | 10.3 | 1 49.3 | 12.9 | 59.4 |
| 15 | 45 53.9 · · | 43.2 | 298 32.6 | 10.3 | 1 36.4 | 13.0 | 59.5 |
| 16 | 60 53.8 | 43.8 | 313 01.8 | 10.2 | 1 23.4 | 12.9 | 59.5 |
| 17 | 75 53.8 | 44.3 | 327 31.0 | 10.3 | 1 10.5 | 13.0 | 59.5 |
| 18 | 90 53.8 | N19 44.8 | 342 00.3 | 10.2 | N 0 57.5 | 13.0 | 59.5 |
| 19 | 105 53.8 | 45.4 | 356 29.5 | 10.2 | 0 44.5 | 13.0 | 59.5 |
| 20 | 120 53.7 | 45.9 | 10 58.7 | 10.3 | 0 31.5 | 12.9 | 59.5 |
| 21 | 135 53.7 · · | 46.4 | 25 28.0 | 10.2 | 0 18.6 | 13.0 | 59.5 |
| 22 | 150 53.7 | 47.0 | 39 57.2 | 10.2 | N 0 05.6 | 13.0 | 59.5 |
| 23 | 165 53.6 | 47.5 | 54 26.4 | 10.2 | S 0 07.4 | 13.0 | 59.5 |
| **20 00** | 180 53.6 | N19 48.1 | 68 55.6 | 10.2 | S 0 20.4 | 13.0 | 59.5 |
| 01 | 195 53.6 | 48.6 | 83 24.8 | 10.2 | 0 33.4 | 13.0 | 59.5 |
| 02 | 210 53.5 | 49.1 | 97 54.0 | 10.2 | 0 46.4 | 13.0 | 59.5 |
| 03 | 225 53.5 · · | 49.6 | 112 23.2 | 10.2 | 0 59.4 | 13.0 | 59.5 |
| 04 | 240 53.5 | 50.2 | 126 52.4 | 10.1 | 1 12.4 | 13.0 | 59.5 |
| 05 | 255 53.5 | 50.7 | 141 21.5 | 10.2 | 1 25.4 | 13.0 | 59.5 |
| 06 | 270 53.4 | N19 51.2 | 155 50.7 | 10.1 | S 1 38.4 | 13.0 | 59.5 |
| 07 | 285 53.4 | 51.8 | 170 19.8 | 10.1 | 1 51.4 | 12.9 | 59.5 |
| T 08 | 300 53.4 | 52.3 | 184 48.9 | 10.1 | 2 04.3 | 13.0 | 59.5 |
| U 09 | 315 53.3 · · | 52.8 | 199 18.0 | 10.1 | 2 17.3 | 12.9 | 59.5 |
| E 10 | 330 53.3 | 53.4 | 213 47.1 | 10.1 | 2 30.2 | 13.0 | 59.5 |
| S 11 | 345 53.3 | 53.9 | 228 16.2 | 10.1 | 2 43.2 | 12.9 | 59.5 |
| D 12 | 0 53.2 | N19 54.4 | 242 45.3 | 10.0 | S 2 56.1 | 12.9 | 59.5 |
| A 13 | 15 53.2 | 54.9 | 257 14.3 | 10.1 | 3 09.0 | 12.9 | 59.5 |
| Y 14 | 30 53.2 | 55.5 | 271 43.4 | 10.0 | 3 21.9 | 12.9 | 59.5 |
| 15 | 45 53.1 · · | 56.0 | 286 12.4 | 10.0 | 3 34.8 | 12.8 | 59.5 |
| 16 | 60 53.1 | 56.5 | 300 41.4 | 10.0 | 3 47.6 | 12.8 | 59.5 |
| 17 | 75 53.1 | 57.0 | 315 10.4 | 9.9 | 4 00.4 | 12.8 | 59.5 |
| 18 | 90 53.0 | N19 57.6 | 329 39.3 | 9.9 | S 4 13.2 | 12.8 | 59.5 |
| 19 | 105 53.0 | 58.1 | 344 08.2 | 10.0 | 4 26.0 | 12.8 | 59.5 |
| 20 | 120 53.0 | 58.6 | 358 37.2 | 9.8 | 4 38.8 | 12.7 | 59.5 |
| 21 | 135 52.9 · · | 59.1 | 13 06.0 | 9.9 | 4 51.5 | 12.7 | 59.5 |
| 22 | 150 52.9 | 19 59.6 | 27 34.9 | 9.9 | 5 04.2 | 12.7 | 59.5 |
| 23 | 165 52.9 | 20 00.2 | 42 03.8 | 9.8 | 5 16.9 | 12.7 | 59.5 |
| **21 00** | 180 52.8 | N20 00.7 | 56 32.6 | 9.8 | S 5 29.6 | 12.6 | 59.5 |
| 01 | 195 52.8 | 01.2 | 71 01.4 | 9.7 | 5 42.2 | 12.6 | 59.5 |
| 02 | 210 52.8 | 01.7 | 85 30.1 | 9.8 | 5 54.8 | 12.5 | 59.5 |
| 03 | 225 52.7 · · | 02.2 | 99 58.9 | 9.7 | 6 07.3 | 12.6 | 59.5 |
| 04 | 240 52.7 | 02.8 | 114 27.6 | 9.7 | 6 19.9 | 12.4 | 59.5 |
| 05 | 255 52.6 | 03.3 | 128 56.3 | 9.6 | 6 32.3 | 12.5 | 59.5 |
| 06 | 270 52.6 | N20 03.8 | 143 24.9 | 9.7 | S 6 44.8 | 12.4 | 59.5 |
| 07 | 285 52.6 | 04.3 | 157 53.6 | 9.6 | 6 57.2 | 12.4 | 59.5 |
| W 08 | 300 52.5 | 04.8 | 172 22.2 | 9.5 | 7 09.6 | 12.3 | 59.5 |
| E 09 | 315 52.5 · · | 05.3 | 186 50.7 | 9.6 | 7 21.9 | 12.3 | 59.5 |
| D 10 | 330 52.5 | 05.8 | 201 19.3 | 9.5 | 7 34.2 | 12.2 | 59.5 |
| N 11 | 345 52.4 | 06.4 | 215 47.8 | 9.5 | 7 46.4 | 12.2 | 59.5 |
| E 12 | 0 52.4 | N20 06.9 | 230 16.3 | 9.4 | S 7 58.6 | 12.1 | 59.5 |
| S 13 | 15 52.4 | 07.4 | 244 44.7 | 9.4 | 8 10.7 | 12.1 | 59.5 |
| D 14 | 30 52.3 | 07.9 | 259 13.1 | 9.4 | 8 22.8 | 12.1 | 59.5 |
| A 15 | 45 52.3 · · | 08.4 | 273 41.5 | 9.4 | 8 34.9 | 12.0 | 59.5 |
| Y 16 | 60 52.2 | 08.9 | 288 09.9 | 9.3 | 8 46.9 | 11.9 | 59.5 |
| 17 | 75 52.2 | 09.4 | 302 38.2 | 9.3 | 8 58.8 | 11.9 | 59.5 |
| 18 | 90 52.2 | N20 09.9 | 317 06.5 | 9.2 | S 9 10.7 | 11.8 | 59.5 |
| 19 | 105 52.1 | 10.4 | 331 34.7 | 9.2 | 9 22.5 | 11.8 | 59.5 |
| 20 | 120 52.1 | 10.9 | 346 02.9 | 9.2 | 9 34.3 | 11.7 | 59.5 |
| 21 | 135 52.0 · · | 11.5 | 0 31.1 | 9.1 | 9 46.0 | 11.7 | 59.5 |
| 22 | 150 52.0 | 12.0 | 14 59.2 | 9.2 | 9 57.7 | 11.6 | 59.5 |
| 23 | 165 52.0 | 12.5 | 29 27.4 | 9.1 | 10 09.3 | 11.6 | 59.5 |
| | S.D. 15.8 | d 0.5 | S.D. 16.2 | | 16.2 | | 16.2 |

| Lat. | Twilight Naut. | Civil | Sunrise | Moonrise 19 | 20 | 21 | 22 |
|---|---|---|---|---|---|---|---|
| | h m | h m | h m | h m | h m | h m | h m |
| N 72 | ☐ | ☐ | ☐ | 12 37 | 14 40 | 16 47 | 19 05 |
| N 70 | ☐ | ☐ | ☐ | 12 40 | 14 35 | 16 32 | 18 35 |
| 68 | //// | //// | 01 21 | 12 42 | 14 30 | 16 21 | 18 13 |
| 66 | //// | //// | 02 05 | 12 44 | 14 27 | 16 11 | 17 56 |
| 64 | //// | 00 27 | 02 34 | 12 45 | 14 24 | 16 03 | 17 43 |
| 62 | //// | 01 32 | 02 55 | 12 47 | 14 21 | 15 56 | 17 31 |
| 60 | //// | 02 05 | 03 13 | 12 48 | 14 19 | 15 50 | 17 21 |
| N 58 | 00 24 | 02 29 | 03 27 | 12 49 | 14 17 | 15 45 | 17 13 |
| 56 | 01 23 | 02 48 | 03 39 | 12 50 | 14 15 | 15 40 | 17 05 |
| 54 | 01 54 | 03 04 | 03 50 | 12 51 | 14 13 | 15 36 | 16 59 |
| 52 | 02 16 | 03 17 | 04 00 | 12 52 | 14 12 | 15 33 | 16 53 |
| 50 | 02 34 | 03 28 | 04 09 | 12 53 | 14 11 | 15 29 | 16 47 |
| 45 | 03 07 | 03 52 | 04 28 | 12 54 | 14 08 | 15 22 | 16 36 |
| N 40 | 03 32 | 04 10 | 04 41 | 12 55 | 14 05 | 15 16 | 16 26 |
| 35 | 03 51 | 04 25 | 04 53 | 12 57 | 14 03 | 15 11 | 16 18 |
| 30 | 04 06 | 04 38 | 05 04 | 12 58 | 14 02 | 15 06 | 16 11 |
| 20 | 04 30 | 04 59 | 05 22 | 12 59 | 13 59 | 14 58 | 15 59 |
| N 10 | 04 49 | 05 16 | 05 38 | 13 01 | 13 56 | 14 52 | 15 48 |
| 0 | 05 05 | 05 31 | 05 53 | 13 02 | 13 54 | 14 45 | 15 39 |
| S 10 | 05 19 | 05 45 | 06 07 | 13 04 | 13 51 | 14 39 | 15 29 |
| 20 | 05 33 | 05 59 | 06 23 | 13 06 | 13 49 | 14 32 | 15 18 |
| 30 | 05 46 | 06 15 | 06 40 | 13 07 | 13 46 | 14 25 | 15 07 |
| 35 | 05 52 | 06 23 | 06 50 | 13 08 | 13 44 | 14 21 | 15 00 |
| 40 | 06 00 | 06 33 | 07 02 | 13 10 | 13 42 | 14 16 | 14 52 |
| 45 | 06 07 | 06 43 | 07 16 | 13 11 | 13 40 | 14 10 | 14 43 |
| S 50 | 06 16 | 06 56 | 07 32 | 13 13 | 13 38 | 14 04 | 14 33 |
| 52 | 06 20 | 07 02 | 07 40 | 13 13 | 13 36 | 14 01 | 14 28 |
| 54 | 06 24 | 07 08 | 07 49 | 13 14 | 13 35 | 13 57 | 14 22 |
| 56 | 06 29 | 07 15 | 07 58 | 13 15 | 13 34 | 13 54 | 14 16 |
| 58 | 06 33 | 07 23 | 08 10 | 13 16 | 13 32 | 13 50 | 14 10 |
| S 60 | 06 39 | 07 31 | 08 22 | 13 17 | 13 31 | 13 45 | 14 02 |

| Lat. | Sunset | Twilight Civil | Naut. | Moonset 19 | 20 | 21 | 22 |
|---|---|---|---|---|---|---|---|
| ° | h m | h m | h m | h m | h m | h m | h m |
| N 72 | ☐ | ☐ | ☐ | 01 32 | 01 17 | 01 02 | 00 44 |
| N 70 | ☐ | ☐ | ☐ | 01 26 | 01 18 | 01 10 | 01 01 |
| 68 | 22 37 | //// | //// | 01 21 | 01 19 | 01 17 | 01 15 |
| 66 | 21 51 | //// | //// | 01 17 | 01 20 | 01 23 | 01 26 |
| 64 | 21 22 | 23 50 | //// | 01 14 | 01 20 | 01 27 | 01 35 |
| 62 | 20 59 | 22 25 | //// | 01 11 | 01 21 | 01 31 | 01 43 |
| 60 | 20 42 | 21 50 | //// | 01 08 | 01 21 | 01 35 | 01 50 |
| N 58 | 20 27 | 21 26 | 23 49 | 01 06 | 01 22 | 01 38 | 01 57 |
| 56 | 20 14 | 21 07 | 22 33 | 01 03 | 01 22 | 01 41 | 02 02 |
| 54 | 20 03 | 20 51 | 22 01 | 01 01 | 01 23 | 01 44 | 02 07 |
| 52 | 19 54 | 20 37 | 21 39 | 01 00 | 01 23 | 01 46 | 02 12 |
| 50 | 19 45 | 20 26 | 21 21 | 00 58 | 01 23 | 01 48 | 02 16 |
| 45 | 19 27 | 20 02 | 20 47 | 00 55 | 01 24 | 01 53 | 02 25 |
| N 40 | 19 12 | 19 43 | 20 22 | 00 52 | 01 24 | 01 57 | 02 32 |
| 35 | 19 00 | 19 28 | 20 03 | 00 49 | 01 25 | 02 01 | 02 38 |
| 30 | 18 49 | 19 15 | 19 47 | 00 47 | 01 25 | 02 04 | 02 44 |
| 20 | 18 31 | 18 54 | 19 23 | 00 43 | 01 26 | 02 09 | 02 54 |
| N 10 | 18 15 | 18 37 | 19 04 | 00 39 | 01 26 | 02 14 | 03 02 |
| 0 | 18 00 | 18 22 | 18 48 | 00 36 | 01 27 | 02 18 | 03 10 |
| S 10 | 17 45 | 18 08 | 18 33 | 00 32 | 01 27 | 02 22 | 03 19 |
| 20 | 17 30 | 17 53 | 18 20 | 00 28 | 01 28 | 02 27 | 03 27 |
| 30 | 17 12 | 17 38 | 18 07 | 00 24 | 01 28 | 02 32 | 03 37 |
| 35 | 17 02 | 17 29 | 18 00 | 00 22 | 01 28 | 02 35 | 03 43 |
| 40 | 16 51 | 17 20 | 17 53 | 00 19 | 01 29 | 02 39 | 03 49 |
| 45 | 16 37 | 17 09 | 17 45 | 00 16 | 01 29 | 02 43 | 03 57 |
| S 50 | 16 20 | 16 57 | 17 36 | 00 12 | 01 30 | 02 48 | 04 06 |
| 52 | 16 12 | 16 51 | 17 32 | 00 10 | 01 30 | 02 50 | 04 11 |
| 54 | 16 04 | 16 44 | 17 28 | 00 08 | 01 30 | 02 53 | 04 15 |
| 56 | 15 54 | 16 37 | 17 24 | 00 06 | 01 30 | 02 55 | 04 20 |
| 58 | 15 43 | 16 29 | 17 19 | 00 03 | 01 31 | 02 58 | 04 26 |
| S 60 | 15 30 | 16 21 | 17 14 | 00 00 | 01 31 | 03 02 | 04 33 |

| Day | SUN Eqn. of Time 00ʰ | 12ʰ | Mer. Pass. | MOON Mer. Pass. Upper | Lower | Age | Phase |
|---|---|---|---|---|---|---|---|
| | m s | m s | h m | h m | h m | d | |
| 19 | 03 37 | 03 36 | 11 56 | 19 15 | 06 49 | 08 | ◖ |
| 20 | 03 34 | 03 33 | 11 56 | 20 06 | 07 40 | 09 | |
| 21 | 03 31 | 03 30 | 11 57 | 20 58 | 08 32 | 10 | |

Fig. A5.5

170                                AUGUST 29, 30, 31 (FRI., SAT., SUN.)

| G.M.T. | ARIES G.H.A. | VENUS −3.3 G.H.A. | Dec. | MARS +0.3 G.H.A. | Dec. | JUPITER −2.3 G.H.A. | Dec. | SATURN +0.4 G.H.A. | Dec. |
|---|---|---|---|---|---|---|---|---|---|
| 29 00 | 336 34.8 | 184 55.3 N 2 | 33.7 | 269 43.2 N20 | 37.9 | 313 26.8 N 8 | 02.0 | 216 28.4 N20 | 35.3 |
| 01 | 351 37.3 | 199 59.2 | 34.1 | 284 44.1 | 38.1 | 328 29.4 | 02.0 | 231 30.6 | 35.3 |
| 02 | 6 39.8 | 215 03.2 | 34.6 | 299 45.1 | 38.4 | 343 32.0 | 01.9 | 246 32.8 | 35.2 |
| 03 | 21 42.2 | 230 07.1 ·· | 35.1 | 314 46.1 ·· | 38.6 | 358 34.5 ·· | 01.9 | 261 34.9 ·· | 35.2 |
| 04 | 36 44.7 | 245 11.0 | 35.5 | 329 47.0 | 38.9 | 13 37.1 | 01.8 | 276 37.1 | 35.1 |
| 05 | 51 47.2 | 260 14.9 | 36.0 | 344 48.0 | 39.2 | 28 39.7 | 01.8 | 291 39.3 | 35.1 |
| 06 | 66 49.6 | 275 18.8 N 2 | 36.5 | 359 49.0 N20 | 39.4 | 43 42.3 N 8 | 01.7 | 306 41.4 N20 | 35.0 |
| 07 | 81 52.1 | 290 22.8 | 36.9 | 14 49.9 | 39.7 | 58 44.8 | 01.7 | 321 43.6 | 35.0 |
| 08 | 96 54.6 | 305 26.7 | 37.4 | 29 50.9 | 40.0 | 73 47.4 | 01.6 | 336 45.8 | 34.9 |
| F 09 | 111 57.0 | 320 30.6 ·· | 37.9 | 44 51.9 ·· | 40.2 | 88 50.0 ·· | 01.6 | 351 47.9 ·· | 34.8 |
| R 10 | 126 59.5 | 335 34.5 | 38.3 | 59 52.8 | 40.5 | 103 52.6 | 01.5 | 6 50.1 | 34.8 |
| I 11 | 142 01.9 | 350 38.4 | 38.8 | 74 53.8 | 40.7 | 118 55.1 | 01.4 | 21 52.3 | 34.7 |
| D 12 | 157 04.4 | 5 42.3 N 2 | 39.3 | 89 54.8 N20 | 41.0 | 133 57.7 N 8 | 01.4 | 36 54.4 N20 | 34.7 |
| A 13 | 172 06.9 | 20 46.2 | 39.8 | 104 55.7 | 41.3 | 149 00.3 | 01.3 | 51 56.6 | 34.6 |
| Y 14 | 187 09.3 | 35 50.1 | 40.2 | 119 56.7 | 41.5 | 164 02.8 | 01.3 | 66 58.8 | 34.6 |
| 15 | 202 11.8 | 50 54.0 ·· | 40.7 | 134 57.7 ·· | 41.8 | 179 05.4 ·· | 01.2 | 82 01.0 ·· | 34.5 |
| 16 | 217 14.3 | 65 58.0 | 41.2 | 149 58.6 | 42.0 | 194 08.0 | 01.2 | 97 03.1 | 34.5 |
| 17 | 232 16.7 | 81 01.9 | 41.7 | 164 59.6 | 42.3 | 209 10.6 | 01.1 | 112 05.3 | 34.4 |
| 18 | 247 19.2 | 96 05.8 N 2 | 42.2 | 180 00.6 N20 | 42.6 | 224 13.1 N 8 | 01.1 | 127 07.5 N20 | 34.4 |
| 19 | 262 21.7 | 111 09.7 | 42.7 | 195 01.5 | 42.8 | 239 15.7 | 01.0 | 142 09.6 | 34.3 |
| 20 | 277 24.1 | 126 13.6 | 43.1 | 210 02.5 | 43.1 | 254 18.3 | 01.0 | 157 11.8 | 34.3 |
| 21 | 292 26.6 | 141 17.5 ·· | 43.6 | 225 03.5 ·· | 43.3 | 269 20.9 ·· | 00.9 | 172 14.0 ·· | 34.2 |
| 22 | 307 29.1 | 156 21.4 | 44.1 | 240 04.5 | 43.6 | 284 23.4 | 00.9 | 187 16.2 | 34.2 |
| 23 | 322 31.5 | 171 25.3 | 44.6 | 255 05.4 | 43.8 | 299 26.0 | 00.8 | 202 18.3 | 34.1 |
| 30 00 | 337 34.0 | 186 29.2 N 2 | 45.1 | 270 06.4 N20 | 44.1 | 314 28.6 N 8 | 00.7 | 217 20.5 N20 | 34.1 |
| 01 | 352 36.4 | 201 33.0 | 45.6 | 285 07.4 | 44.4 | 329 31.2 | 00.7 | 232 22.7 | 34.0 |
| 02 | 7 38.9 | 216 36.9 | 46.1 | 300 08.4 | 44.6 | 344 33.8 | 00.6 | 247 24.8 | 34.0 |
| 03 | 22 41.4 | 231 40.8 ·· | 46.5 | 315 09.3 ·· | 44.9 | 359 36.3 ·· | 00.6 | 262 27.0 ·· | 33.9 |
| 04 | 37 43.8 | 246 44.7 | 47.0 | 330 10.3 | 45.1 | 14 38.9 | 00.5 | 277 29.2 | 33.9 |
| 05 | 52 46.3 | 261 48.6 | 47.5 | 345 11.3 | 45.4 | 29 41.5 | 00.5 | 292 31.4 | 33.8 |
| 06 | 67 48.8 | 276 52.5 N 2 | 48.0 | 0 12.2 N20 | 45.7 | 44 44.1 N 8 | 00.4 | 307 33.5 N20 | 33.7 |
| 07 | 82 51.2 | 291 56.4 | 48.5 | 15 13.2 | 45.9 | 59 46.7 | 00.4 | 322 35.7 | 33.7 |
| S 08 | 97 53.7 | 307 00.3 | 49.0 | 30 14.2 | 46.2 | 74 49.2 | 00.3 | 337 37.9 | 33.6 |
| A 09 | 112 56.2 | 322 04.1 ·· | 49.5 | 45 15.2 ·· | 46.4 | 89 51.8 ·· | 00.3 | 352 40.0 ·· | 33.6 |
| T 10 | 127 58.6 | 337 08.0 | 50.0 | 60 16.1 | 46.7 | 104 54.4 | 00.2 | 7 42.2 | 33.5 |
| U 11 | 143 01.1 | 352 11.9 | 50.5 | 75 17.1 | 46.9 | 119 57.0 | 00.1 | 22 44.4 | 33.5 |
| R 12 | 158 03.6 | 7 15.8 N 2 | 51.0 | 90 18.1 N20 | 47.2 | 134 59.6 N 8 | 00.1 | 37 46.6 N20 | 33.4 |
| D 13 | 173 06.0 | 22 19.7 | 51.5 | 105 19.1 | 47.4 | 150 02.1 | 00.0 | 52 48.7 | 33.4 |
| A 14 | 188 08.5 | 37 23.5 | 52.0 | 120 20.1 | 47.7 | 165 04.7 8 | 00.0 | 67 50.9 | 33.3 |
| Y 15 | 203 10.9 | 52 27.4 ·· | 52.5 | 135 21.0 ·· | 48.0 | 180 07.3 7 | 59.9 | 82 53.1 ·· | 33.3 |
| 16 | 218 13.4 | 67 31.3 | 53.0 | 150 22.0 | 48.2 | 195 09.9 | 59.9 | 97 55.2 | 33.2 |
| 17 | 233 15.9 | 82 35.1 | 53.5 | 165 23.0 | 48.5 | 210 12.5 | 59.8 | 112 57.4 | 33.2 |
| 18 | 248 18.3 | 97 39.0 N 2 | 54.0 | 180 24.0 N20 | 48.7 | 225 15.0 N 7 | 59.7 | 127 59.6 N20 | 33.1 |
| 19 | 263 20.8 | 112 42.9 | 54.5 | 195 24.9 | 49.0 | 240 17.6 | 59.7 | 143 01.8 | 33.1 |
| 20 | 278 23.3 | 127 46.7 | 55.0 | 210 25.9 | 49.2 | 255 20.2 | 59.6 | 158 03.9 | 33.0 |
| 21 | 293 25.7 | 142 50.6 ·· | 55.5 | 225 26.9 ·· | 49.5 | 270 22.8 ·· | 59.6 | 173 06.1 ·· | 33.0 |
| 22 | 308 28.2 | 157 54.5 | 56.1 | 240 27.9 | 49.7 | 285 25.4 | 59.5 | 188 08.3 | 32.9 |
| 23 | 323 30.7 | 172 58.3 | 56.6 | 255 28.9 | 50.0 | 300 28.0 | 59.5 | 203 10.5 | 32.9 |
| 31 00 | 338 33.1 | 188 02.2 N 2 | 57.1 | 270 29.8 N20 | 50.2 | 315 30.6 N 7 | 59.4 | 218 12.6 N20 | 32.8 |
| 01 | 353 35.6 | 203 06.0 | 57.6 | 285 30.8 | 50.5 | 330 33.1 | 59.3 | 233 14.8 | 32.8 |
| 02 | 8 38.0 | 218 09.9 | 58.1 | 300 31.8 | 50.7 | 345 35.7 | 59.3 | 248 17.0 | 32.7 |
| 03 | 23 40.5 | 233 13.7 ·· | 58.6 | 315 32.8 ·· | 51.0 | 0 38.3 ·· | 59.2 | 263 19.1 ·· | 32.7 |
| 04 | 38 43.0 | 248 17.6 | 59.1 | 330 33.8 | 51.2 | 15 40.9 | 59.2 | 278 21.3 | 32.6 |
| 05 | 53 45.4 | 263 21.4 2 | 59.6 | 345 34.8 | 51.5 | 30 43.5 | 59.1 | 293 23.5 | 32.6 |
| 06 | 68 47.9 | 278 25.3 N 3 | 00.1 | 0 35.7 N20 | 51.7 | 45 46.1 N 7 | 59.1 | 308 25.7 N20 | 32.5 |
| 07 | 83 50.4 | 293 29.1 | 00.7 | 15 36.7 | 52.0 | 60 48.7 | 59.0 | 323 27.8 | 32.4 |
| 08 | 98 52.8 | 308 33.0 | 01.2 | 30 37.7 | 52.2 | 75 51.2 | 58.9 | 338 30.0 | 32.4 |
| S 09 | 113 55.3 | 323 36.8 ·· | 01.7 | 45 38.7 ·· | 52.5 | 90 53.8 ·· | 58.9 | 353 32.2 ·· | 32.3 |
| U 10 | 128 57.8 | 338 40.6 | 02.2 | 60 39.7 | 52.7 | 105 56.4 | 58.8 | 8 34.4 | 32.3 |
| N 11 | 144 00.2 | 353 44.5 | 02.7 | 75 40.7 | 53.0 | 120 59.0 | 58.8 | 23 36.5 | 32.2 |
| D 12 | 159 02.7 | 8 48.3 N 3 | 03.3 | 90 41.6 N20 | 53.2 | 136 01.6 N 7 | 58.7 | 38 38.7 N20 | 32.2 |
| A 13 | 174 05.2 | 23 52.1 | 03.8 | 105 42.6 | 53.5 | 151 04.2 | 58.6 | 53 40.9 | 32.1 |
| Y 14 | 189 07.6 | 38 56.0 | 04.3 | 120 43.6 | 53.7 | 166 06.8 | 58.6 | 68 43.1 | 32.1 |
| 15 | 204 10.1 | 53 59.8 ·· | 04.8 | 135 44.6 ·· | 54.0 | 181 09.4 ·· | 58.5 | 83 45.2 ·· | 32.0 |
| 16 | 219 12.5 | 69 03.6 | 05.4 | 150 45.6 | 54.2 | 196 12.0 | 58.5 | 98 47.4 | 32.0 |
| 17 | 234 15.0 | 84 07.4 | 05.9 | 165 46.6 | 54.5 | 211 14.5 | 58.4 | 113 49.6 | 31.9 |
| 18 | 249 17.5 | 99 11.3 N 3 | 06.4 | 180 47.6 N20 | 54.7 | 226 17.1 N 7 | 58.4 | 128 51.8 N20 | 31.9 |
| 19 | 264 19.9 | 114 15.1 | 06.9 | 195 48.5 | 55.0 | 241 19.7 | 58.3 | 143 53.9 | 31.8 |
| 20 | 279 22.4 | 129 18.9 | 07.5 | 210 49.5 | 55.2 | 256 22.3 | 58.2 | 158 56.1 | 31.8 |
| 21 | 294 24.9 | 144 22.7 ·· | 08.0 | 225 50.5 ·· | 55.5 | 271 24.9 ·· | 58.2 | 173 58.3 ·· | 31.7 |
| 22 | 309 27.3 | 159 26.5 | 08.5 | 240 51.5 | 55.7 | 286 27.5 | 58.1 | 189 00.5 | 31.7 |
| 23 | 324 29.8 | 174 30.4 | 09.0 | 255 52.5 | 56.0 | 301 30.1 | 58.1 | 204 02.6 | 31.6 |
| Mer. Pass. | h m 1 29.5 | v 3.9 | d 0.5 | v 1.0 | d 0.3 | v 2.6 | d 0.1 | v 2.2 | d 0.1 |

**STARS**

| Name | S.H.A. | Dec. |
|---|---|---|
| Acamar | 315 39.7 | S40 23.8 |
| Achernar | 335 47.4 | S57 21.3 |
| Acrux | 173 41.6 | S62 58.0 |
| Adhara | 255 35.0 | S28 56.2 |
| Aldebaran | 291 21.9 | N16 27.7 |
| Alioth | 166 45.9 | N56 05.7 |
| Alkaid | 153 21.5 | N49 26.3 |
| Al Na'ir | 28 18.7 | S47 04.6 |
| Alnilam | 276 15.2 | S 1 12.9 |
| Alphard | 218 24.2 | S 8 33.1 |
| Alphecca | 126 35.1 | N26 48.0 |
| Alpheratz | 358 12.5 | N28 57.5 |
| Altair | 62 35.6 | N 8 48.5 |
| Ankaa | 353 43.2 | S42 26.0 |
| Antares | 113 01.0 | S26 22.7 |
| Arcturus | 146 21.7 | N19 18.7 |
| Atria | 108 28.2 | S68 59.3 |
| Avior | 234 30.1 | S59 25.8 |
| Bellatrix | 279 02.5 | N 6 19.8 |
| Betelgeuse | 271 32.1 | N 7 24.2 |
| Canopus | 264 09.0 | S52 40.7 |
| Capella | 281 16.4 | N45 58.3 |
| Deneb | 49 50.4 | N45 11.9 |
| Denebola | 183 02.8 | N14 42.5 |
| Diphda | 349 24.0 | S18 06.9 |
| Dubhe | 194 27.0 | N61 53.0 |
| Elnath | 278 48.5 | N28 35.2 |
| Eltanin | 90 59.1 | N51 29.9 |
| Enif | 34 14.6 | N 9 46.0 |
| Fomalhaut | 15 54.8 | S29 44.8 |
| Gacrux | 172 33.0 | S56 58.8 |
| Gienah | 176 21.8 | S17 24.4 |
| Hadar | 149 28.5 | S60 15.6 |
| Hamal | 328 32.6 | N23 20.9 |
| Kaus Aust. | 84 21.2 | S34 23.8 |
| Kochab | 137 19.3 | N74 15.6 |
| Markab | 14 06.2 | N15 04.7 |
| Menkar | 314 44.6 | N 3 59.8 |
| Menkent | 148 41.2 | S36 15.2 |
| Miaplacidus | 221 46.5 | S69 37.0 |
| Mirfak | 309 20.9 | N49 46.4 |
| Nunki | 76 33.2 | S26 19.6 |
| Peacock | 54 03.2 | S56 48.8 |
| Pollux | 244 02.6 | N28 05.1 |
| Procyon | 245 29.6 | N 5 17.3 |
| Rasalhague | 96 32.6 | N12 34.9 |
| Regulus | 208 13.9 | N12 05.2 |
| Rigel | 281 39.4 | S 8 13.6 |
| Rigil Kent. | 140 30.7 | S60 44.3 |
| Sabik | 102 45.0 | S15 41.7 |
| Schedar | 350 12.4 | N56 24.3 |
| Shaula | 97 00.3 | S37 05.3 |
| Sirius | 258 58.9 | S16 40.8 |
| Spica | 159 01.4 | S11 02.1 |
| Suhail | 223 13.7 | S43 20.0 |
| Vega | 80 57.9 | N38 46.0 |
| Zuben'ubi | 137 36.9 | S15 56.5 |

| | S.H.A. | Mer. Pass. |
|---|---|---|
| Venus | 208 55.2 | h m 11 31 |
| Mars | 292 32.4 | 5 59 |
| Jupiter | 336 54.6 | 3 02 |
| Saturn | 239 46.5 | 9 29 |

Fig. A5.6

AUGUST 29, 30, 31 (FRI., SAT., SUN.)     171

| G.M.T. | SUN G.H.A. | SUN Dec. | MOON G.H.A. | v | MOON Dec. | d | H.P. |
|---|---|---|---|---|---|---|---|
| 29 00 | 179 41.9 | N 9 39.6 | 285 08.4 | 11.1 | N18 51.7 | 4.9 | 55.5 |
| 01 | 194 42.1 | 38.8 | 299 38.5 | 11.1 | 18 56.6 | 4.9 | 55.5 |
| 02 | 209 42.3 | 37.9 | 314 08.6 | 11.0 | 19 01.5 | 4.8 | 55.5 |
| 03 | 224 42.5 | .. 37.0 | 328 38.6 | 11.0 | 19 06.3 | 4.7 | 55.6 |
| 04 | 239 42.6 | 36.1 | 343 08.6 | 10.9 | 19 11.0 | 4.6 | 55.6 |
| 05 | 254 42.8 | 35.2 | 357 38.5 | 10.8 | 19 15.6 | 4.5 | 55.6 |
| 06 | 269 43.0 | N 9 34.3 | 12 08.3 | 10.8 | N19 20.1 | 4.4 | 55.6 |
| 07 | 284 43.2 | 33.5 | 26 38.1 | 10.7 | 19 24.5 | 4.4 | 55.7 |
| 08 | 299 43.4 | 32.6 | 41 07.8 | 10.6 | 19 28.9 | 4.2 | 55.7 |
| F 09 | 314 43.6 | .. 31.7 | 55 37.4 | 10.6 | 19 33.1 | 4.1 | 55.7 |
| R 10 | 329 43.8 | 30.8 | 70 07.0 | 10.5 | 19 37.2 | 4.1 | 55.8 |
| I 11 | 344 43.9 | 29.9 | 84 36.5 | 10.5 | 19 41.3 | 3.9 | 55.8 |
| D 12 | 359 44.1 | N 9 29.0 | 99 06.0 | 10.4 | N19 45.2 | 3.9 | 55.8 |
| A 13 | 14 44.3 | 28.1 | 113 35.4 | 10.3 | 19 49.1 | 3.7 | 55.8 |
| Y 14 | 29 44.5 | 27.3 | 128 04.7 | 10.3 | 19 52.8 | 3.7 | 55.9 |
| 15 | 44 44.7 | .. 26.4 | 142 34.0 | 10.2 | 19 56.5 | 3.5 | 55.9 |
| 16 | 59 44.9 | 25.5 | 157 03.2 | 10.2 | 20 00.0 | 3.5 | 55.9 |
| 17 | 74 45.1 | 24.6 | 171 32.4 | 10.1 | 20 03.5 | 3.3 | 56.0 |
| 18 | 89 45.3 | N 9 23.7 | 186 01.5 | 10.0 | N20 06.8 | 3.3 | 56.0 |
| 19 | 104 45.4 | 22.8 | 200 30.5 | 10.0 | 20 10.1 | 3.1 | 56.0 |
| 20 | 119 45.6 | 21.9 | 214 59.5 | 9.9 | 20 13.2 | 3.1 | 56.1 |
| 21 | 134 45.8 | .. 21.0 | 229 28.4 | 9.8 | 20 16.3 | 2.9 | 56.1 |
| 22 | 149 46.0 | 20.1 | 243 57.2 | 9.8 | 20 19.2 | 2.8 | 56.1 |
| 23 | 164 46.2 | 19.3 | 258 26.0 | 9.7 | 20 22.0 | 2.8 | 56.2 |
| 30 00 | 179 46.4 | N 9 18.4 | 272 54.7 | 9.7 | N20 24.8 | 2.6 | 56.2 |
| 01 | 194 46.6 | 17.5 | 287 23.4 | 9.6 | 20 27.4 | 2.5 | 56.2 |
| 02 | 209 46.8 | 16.6 | 301 52.0 | 9.6 | 20 29.9 | 2.5 | 56.3 |
| 03 | 224 46.9 | .. 15.7 | 316 20.6 | 9.5 | 20 32.4 | 2.3 | 56.3 |
| 04 | 239 47.1 | 14.8 | 330 49.1 | 9.4 | 20 34.7 | 2.2 | 56.3 |
| 05 | 254 47.3 | 13.9 | 345 17.5 | 9.4 | 20 36.9 | 2.1 | 56.4 |
| 06 | 269 47.5 | N 9 13.0 | 359 45.9 | 9.3 | N20 39.0 | 1.9 | 56.4 |
| 07 | 284 47.7 | 12.1 | 14 14.2 | 9.3 | 20 40.9 | 1.9 | 56.4 |
| S 08 | 299 47.9 | 11.2 | 28 42.5 | 9.2 | 20 42.8 | 1.8 | 56.5 |
| A 09 | 314 48.1 | .. 10.3 | 43 10.7 | 9.2 | 20 44.6 | 1.6 | 56.5 |
| T 10 | 329 48.3 | 09.5 | 57 38.9 | 9.1 | 20 46.2 | 1.6 | 56.5 |
| U 11 | 344 48.5 | 08.6 | 72 07.0 | 9.0 | 20 47.8 | 1.4 | 56.6 |
| R 12 | 359 48.6 | N 9 07.7 | 86 35.0 | 9.0 | N20 49.2 | 1.3 | 56.6 |
| D 13 | 14 48.8 | 06.8 | 101 03.0 | 9.0 | 20 50.5 | 1.2 | 56.6 |
| A 14 | 29 49.0 | 05.9 | 115 31.0 | 8.8 | 20 51.7 | 1.1 | 56.7 |
| Y 15 | 44 49.2 | .. 05.0 | 129 58.8 | 8.9 | 20 52.8 | 1.0 | 56.7 |
| 16 | 59 49.4 | 04.1 | 144 26.7 | 8.8 | 20 53.8 | 0.9 | 56.7 |
| 17 | 74 49.6 | 03.2 | 158 54.5 | 8.7 | 20 54.7 | 0.7 | 56.8 |
| 18 | 89 49.8 | N 9 02.3 | 173 22.2 | 8.7 | N20 55.4 | 0.6 | 56.8 |
| 19 | 104 50.0 | 01.4 | 187 49.9 | 8.6 | 20 56.0 | 0.5 | 56.9 |
| 20 | 119 50.2 | 9 00.5 | 202 17.5 | 8.6 | 20 56.5 | 0.4 | 56.9 |
| 21 | 134 50.4 | 8 59.6 | 216 45.1 | 8.5 | 20 56.9 | 0.3 | 56.9 |
| 22 | 149 50.5 | 58.7 | 231 12.6 | 8.5 | 20 57.2 | 0.2 | 57.0 |
| 23 | 164 50.7 | 57.8 | 245 40.1 | 8.4 | 20 57.4 | 0.0 | 57.0 |
| 31 00 | 179 50.9 | N 8 56.9 | 260 07.5 | 8.4 | N20 57.4 | 0.1 | 57.0 |
| 01 | 194 51.1 | 56.0 | 274 34.9 | 8.4 | 20 57.3 | 0.2 | 57.1 |
| 02 | 209 51.3 | 55.1 | 289 02.3 | 8.3 | 20 57.1 | 0.4 | 57.1 |
| 03 | 224 51.5 | .. 54.2 | 303 29.6 | 8.2 | 20 56.8 | 0.4 | 57.2 |
| 04 | 239 51.7 | 53.3 | 317 56.8 | 8.2 | 20 56.4 | 0.6 | 57.2 |
| 05 | 254 51.9 | 52.4 | 332 24.0 | 8.2 | 20 55.8 | 0.7 | 57.2 |
| 06 | 269 52.1 | N 8 51.5 | 346 51.2 | 8.1 | N20 55.1 | 0.8 | 57.3 |
| 07 | 284 52.3 | 50.6 | 1 18.3 | 8.1 | 20 54.3 | 0.9 | 57.3 |
| 08 | 299 52.5 | 49.8 | 15 45.4 | 8.1 | 20 53.4 | 1.1 | 57.3 |
| S 09 | 314 52.7 | .. 48.9 | 30 12.5 | 8.0 | 20 52.3 | 1.1 | 57.4 |
| U 10 | 329 52.8 | 48.0 | 44 39.5 | 7.9 | 20 51.2 | 1.3 | 57.4 |
| N 11 | 344 53.0 | 47.1 | 59 06.4 | 7.9 | 20 49.9 | 1.5 | 57.5 |
| D 12 | 359 53.2 | N 8 46.2 | 73 33.3 | 7.9 | N20 48.4 | 1.5 | 57.5 |
| A 13 | 14 53.4 | 45.3 | 88 00.2 | 7.9 | 20 46.9 | 1.7 | 57.5 |
| Y 14 | 29 53.6 | 44.4 | 102 27.1 | 7.8 | 20 45.2 | 1.8 | 57.6 |
| 15 | 44 53.8 | .. 43.5 | 116 53.9 | 7.8 | 20 43.4 | 1.9 | 57.6 |
| 16 | 59 54.0 | 42.6 | 131 20.7 | 7.7 | 20 41.5 | 2.0 | 57.7 |
| 17 | 74 54.2 | 41.7 | 145 47.4 | 7.7 | 20 39.5 | 2.2 | 57.7 |
| 18 | 89 54.4 | N 8 40.8 | 160 14.1 | 7.7 | N20 37.3 | 2.3 | 57.7 |
| 19 | 104 54.6 | 39.9 | 174 40.8 | 7.6 | 20 35.0 | 2.4 | 57.8 |
| 20 | 119 54.8 | 39.0 | 189 07.4 | 7.6 | 20 32.6 | 2.6 | 57.8 |
| 21 | 134 55.0 | .. 38.1 | 203 34.0 | 7.6 | 20 30.0 | 2.6 | 57.9 |
| 22 | 149 55.2 | 37.2 | 218 00.6 | 7.5 | 20 27.4 | 2.8 | 57.9 |
| 23 | 164 55.4 | 36.3 | 232 27.1 | 7.6 | 20 24.6 | 3.0 | 57.9 |
| S.D. | 15.9 | d 0.9 | S.D. 15.2 | | 15.4 | | 15.7 |

### Twilight / Sunrise / Moonrise

| Lat. | Naut. | Civil | Sunrise | 29 | 30 | 31 | 1 |
|---|---|---|---|---|---|---|---|
| N 72 | //// | 02 09 | 03 47 | □ | □ | □ | □ |
| N 70 | //// | 02 43 | 04 03 | 17 44 | □ | □ | 21 50 |
| 68 | 00 59 | 03 07 | 04 16 | 19 20 | 19 50 | 20 59 | 22 39 |
| 66 | 01 51 | 03 26 | 04 26 | 19 59 | 20 38 | 21 42 | 23 10 |
| 64 | 02 22 | 03 40 | 04 35 | 20 26 | 21 08 | 22 11 | 23 33 |
| 62 | 02 44 | 03 52 | 04 42 | 20 47 | 21 31 | 22 33 | 23 51 |
| 60 | 03 02 | 04 02 | 04 48 | 21 04 | 21 50 | 22 51 | 24 06 |
| N 58 | 03 16 | 04 11 | 04 54 | 21 19 | 22 05 | 23 06 | 24 19 |
| 56 | 03 28 | 04 19 | 04 59 | 21 31 | 22 19 | 23 18 | 24 30 |
| 54 | 03 38 | 04 25 | 05 03 | 21 42 | 22 30 | 23 29 | 24 40 |
| 52 | 03 47 | 04 31 | 05 07 | 21 52 | 22 40 | 23 39 | 24 48 |
| 50 | 03 55 | 04 37 | 05 11 | 22 00 | 22 49 | 23 48 | 24 56 |
| 45 | 04 11 | 04 48 | 05 18 | 22 19 | 23 08 | 24 06 | 00 06 |
| N 40 | 04 24 | 04 57 | 05 25 | 22 33 | 23 24 | 24 22 | 00 22 |
| 35 | 04 34 | 05 05 | 05 30 | 22 46 | 23 37 | 24 34 | 00 34 |
| 30 | 04 42 | 05 11 | 05 35 | 22 57 | 23 49 | 24 45 | 00 45 |
| 20 | 04 55 | 05 21 | 05 44 | 23 16 | 24 08 | 00 08 | 01 04 |
| N 10 | 05 05 | 05 30 | 05 51 | 23 33 | 24 25 | 00 25 | 01 21 |
| 0 | 05 12 | 05 36 | 05 58 | 23 48 | 24 42 | 00 42 | 01 37 |
| S 10 | 05 18 | 05 43 | 06 04 | 24 04 | 00 04 | 00 58 | 01 52 |
| 20 | 05 23 | 05 49 | 06 11 | 24 21 | 00 21 | 01 15 | 02 09 |
| 30 | 05 27 | 05 54 | 06 19 | 24 40 | 00 40 | 01 35 | 02 28 |
| 35 | 05 28 | 05 57 | 06 23 | 24 51 | 00 51 | 01 46 | 02 39 |
| 40 | 05 29 | 06 00 | 06 28 | 00 07 | 01 04 | 02 00 | 02 52 |
| 45 | 05 30 | 06 04 | 06 33 | 00 21 | 01 20 | 02 15 | 03 07 |
| S 50 | 05 30 | 06 07 | 06 40 | 00 38 | 01 38 | 02 35 | 03 25 |
| 52 | 05 30 | 06 09 | 06 43 | 00 46 | 01 47 | 02 44 | 03 34 |
| 54 | 05 30 | 06 11 | 06 47 | 00 55 | 01 57 | 02 54 | 03 43 |
| 56 | 05 30 | 06 13 | 06 50 | 01 05 | 02 09 | 03 06 | 03 54 |
| 58 | 05 30 | 06 15 | 06 55 | 01 16 | 02 22 | 03 19 | 04 07 |
| S 60 | 05 29 | 06 17 | 06 59 | 01 30 | 02 37 | 03 35 | 04 21 |

### Sunset / Twilight / Moonset

| Lat. | Sunset | Civil | Naut. | 29 | 30 | 31 | 1 |
|---|---|---|---|---|---|---|---|
| N 72 | 20 11 | 21 46 | //// | □ | □ | □ | 18 55 |
| N 70 | 19 56 | 21 14 | //// | 17 20 | 17 04 | 17 49 | 18 06 |
| 68 | 19 44 | 20 51 | 22 51 | 15 45 | 16 17 | 17 06 | 17 35 |
| 66 | 19 34 | 20 33 | 22 04 | 15 06 | 16 17 | 17 06 | 17 35 |
| 64 | 19 25 | 20 19 | 21 35 | 14 39 | 15 46 | 16 37 | 17 11 |
| 62 | 19 18 | 20 08 | 21 14 | 14 19 | 15 23 | 16 14 | 16 52 |
| 60 | 19 12 | 19 57 | 20 57 | 14 02 | 15 04 | 15 56 | 16 37 |
| N 58 | 19 06 | 19 49 | 20 44 | 13 47 | 14 49 | 15 41 | 16 24 |
| 56 | 19 02 | 19 41 | 20 32 | 13 35 | 14 36 | 15 29 | 16 12 |
| 54 | 18 57 | 19 35 | 20 22 | 13 24 | 14 24 | 15 17 | 16 02 |
| 52 | 18 53 | 19 29 | 20 13 | 13 15 | 14 14 | 15 07 | 15 54 |
| 50 | 18 50 | 19 24 | 20 05 | 13 07 | 14 05 | 14 59 | 15 46 |
| 45 | 18 42 | 19 13 | 19 49 | 12 49 | 13 46 | 14 40 | 15 28 |
| N 40 | 18 36 | 19 04 | 19 37 | 12 34 | 13 31 | 14 24 | 15 14 |
| 35 | 18 31 | 18 56 | 19 27 | 12 22 | 13 18 | 14 11 | 15 02 |
| 30 | 18 26 | 18 50 | 19 19 | 12 11 | 13 06 | 14 00 | 14 52 |
| 20 | 18 18 | 18 40 | 19 06 | 11 53 | 12 47 | 13 41 | 14 34 |
| N 10 | 18 11 | 18 32 | 18 57 | 11 37 | 12 30 | 13 24 | 14 18 |
| 0 | 18 04 | 18 25 | 18 49 | 11 22 | 12 14 | 13 08 | 14 03 |
| S 10 | 17 58 | 18 19 | 18 43 | 11 07 | 11 58 | 12 52 | 13 49 |
| 20 | 17 51 | 18 14 | 18 39 | 10 51 | 11 41 | 12 35 | 13 33 |
| 30 | 17 43 | 18 08 | 18 35 | 10 32 | 11 21 | 12 15 | 13 14 |
| 35 | 17 39 | 18 05 | 18 34 | 10 21 | 11 10 | 12 03 | 13 03 |
| 40 | 17 34 | 18 02 | 18 33 | 10 10 | 10 56 | 11 50 | 12 51 |
| 45 | 17 29 | 17 58 | 18 32 | 09 55 | 10 41 | 11 35 | 12 37 |
| S 50 | 17 22 | 17 55 | 18 32 | 09 38 | 10 22 | 11 15 | 12 19 |
| 52 | 17 19 | 17 53 | 18 32 | 09 29 | 10 13 | 11 06 | 12 10 |
| 54 | 17 16 | 17 52 | 18 33 | 09 20 | 10 03 | 10 56 | 12 01 |
| 56 | 17 12 | 17 50 | 18 33 | 09 10 | 09 51 | 10 44 | 11 50 |
| 58 | 17 08 | 17 48 | 18 34 | 08 58 | 09 38 | 10 31 | 11 38 |
| S 60 | 17 03 | 17 46 | 18 34 | 08 44 | 09 23 | 10 15 | 11 24 |

| Day | SUN Eqn. of Time 00ʰ | SUN Eqn. of Time 12ʰ | Mer. Pass. | MOON Mer. Pass. Upper | MOON Mer. Pass. Lower | Age | Phase |
|---|---|---|---|---|---|---|---|
| 29 | 01 13 | 01 04 | 12 01 | 05 10 | 17 35 | 22 | |
| 30 | 00 55 | 00 46 | 12 01 | 06 01 | 18 28 | 23 | |
| 31 | 00 37 | 00 27 | 12 00 | 06 55 | 19 22 | 24 | ◖ |

Fig. A5.7

276

# POLARIS (POLE STAR) TABLES,
## FOR DETERMINING LATITUDE FROM SEXTANT ALTITUDE AND FOR AZIMUTH

| L.H.A. ARIES | 240°–249° | 250°–259° | 260°–269° | 270°–279° | 280°–289° | 290°–299° | 300°–309° | 310°–319° | 320°–329° | 330°–339° | 340°–349° | 350°–359° |
|---|---|---|---|---|---|---|---|---|---|---|---|---|
| | $a_0$ | $a_0$ | $a_0$ | $a_0$ | $a_0$ | $a_0$ | $a_0$ | $a_0$ | $a_0$ | $a_0$ | $a_0$ | $a_0$ |
| 0 | 1 43·8 | 1 39·1 | 1 33·1 | 1 26·1 | 1 18·3 | 1 09·9 | 1 01·1 | 0 52·3 | 0 43·6 | 0 35·4 | 0 27·9 | 0 21·3 |
| 1 | 43·4 | 38·5 | 32·5 | 25·4 | 17·5 | 09·0 | 1 00·2 | 51·4 | 42·8 | 34·6 | 27·2 | 20·7 |
| 2 | 43·0 | 38·0 | 31·8 | 24·6 | 16·7 | 08·2 | 0 59·4 | 50·5 | 41·9 | 33·8 | 26·5 | 20·1 |
| 3 | 42·5 | 37·4 | 31·1 | 23·9 | 15·8 | 07·3 | 58·5 | 49·6 | 41·1 | 33·1 | 25·8 | 19·6 |
| 4 | 42·1 | 36·8 | 30·4 | 23·1 | 15·0 | 06·4 | 57·6 | 48·8 | 40·3 | 32·3 | 25·1 | 19·0 |
| 5 | 1 41·6 | 1 36·2 | 1 29·7 | 1 22·3 | 1 14·2 | 1 05·5 | 0 56·7 | 0 47·9 | 0 39·4 | 0 31·5 | 0 24·5 | 0 18·5 |
| 6 | 41·1 | 35·6 | 29·0 | 21·5 | 13·3 | 04·7 | 55·8 | 47·0 | 38·6 | 30·8 | 23·8 | 17·9 |
| 7 | 40·6 | 35·0 | 28·3 | 20·7 | 12·5 | 03·8 | 54·9 | 46·2 | 37·8 | 30·0 | 23·2 | 17·4 |
| 8 | 40·1 | 34·4 | 27·6 | 19·9 | 11·6 | 02·9 | 54·0 | 45·3 | 37·0 | 29·3 | 22·5 | 16·9 |
| 9 | 39·6 | 33·8 | 26·9 | 19·1 | 10·8 | 02·0 | 53·2 | 44·5 | 36·2 | 28·6 | 21·9 | 16·4 |
| 10 | 1 39·1 | 1 33·1 | 1 26·1 | 1 18·3 | 1 09·9 | 1 01·1 | 0 52·3 | 0 43·6 | 0 35·4 | 0 27·9 | 0 21·3 | 0 15·9 |
| Lat. | $a_1$ | $a_1$ | $a_1$ | $a_1$ | $a_1$ | $a_1$ | $a_1$ | $a_1$ | $a_1$ | $a_1$ | $a_1$ | $a_1$ |
| 0 | 0·5 | 0·4 | 0·3 | 0·2 | 0·2 | 0·2 | 0·2 | 0·2 | 0·2 | 0·3 | 0·4 | 0·4 |
| 10 | ·5 | ·4 | ·4 | ·3 | ·3 | ·2 | ·2 | ·2 | ·3 | ·3 | ·4 | ·5 |
| 20 | ·5 | ·5 | ·4 | ·4 | ·3 | ·3 | ·3 | ·3 | ·3 | ·4 | ·4 | ·5 |
| 30 | ·5 | ·5 | ·5 | ·4 | ·4 | ·4 | ·4 | ·4 | ·4 | ·4 | ·5 | ·5 |
| 40 | 0·6 | 0·5 | 0·5 | 0·5 | 0·5 | 0·5 | 0·5 | 0·5 | 0·5 | 0·5 | 0·5 | 0·6 |
| 45 | ·6 | ·6 | ·6 | ·5 | ·5 | ·5 | ·5 | ·5 | ·5 | ·5 | ·6 | ·6 |
| 50 | ·6 | ·6 | ·6 | ·6 | ·6 | ·6 | ·6 | ·6 | ·6 | ·6 | ·6 | ·6 |
| 55 | ·6 | ·6 | ·7 | ·7 | ·7 | ·7 | ·7 | ·7 | ·7 | ·7 | ·6 | ·6 |
| 60 | ·7 | ·7 | ·7 | ·8 | ·8 | ·8 | ·8 | ·8 | ·8 | ·7 | ·7 | ·7 |
| 62 | 0·7 | 0·7 | 0·8 | 0·8 | 0·8 | 0·9 | 0·9 | 0·8 | 0·8 | 0·8 | 0·7 | 0·7 |
| 64 | ·7 | ·7 | ·8 | ·9 | 0·9 | 0·9 | 0·9 | 0·9 | ·9 | ·8 | ·8 | ·7 |
| 66 | ·7 | ·8 | ·9 | 0·9 | 1·0 | 1·0 | 1·0 | 1·0 | 0·9 | ·9 | ·8 | ·7 |
| 68 | 0·7 | 0·8 | 0·9 | 1·0 | 1·0 | 1·1 | 1·1 | 1·1 | 1·0 | 0·9 | 0·9 | 0·8 |
| Month | $a_2$ | $a_2$ | $a_2$ | $a_2$ | $a_2$ | $a_2$ | $a_2$ | $a_2$ | $a_2$ | $a_2$ | $a_2$ | $a_2$ |
| Jan. | 0·4 | 0·4 | 0·4 | 0·5 | 0·5 | 0·5 | 0·6 | 0·6 | 0·6 | 0·7 | 0·7 | 0·7 |
| Feb. | ·3 | ·3 | ·3 | ·3 | ·3 | ·4 | ·4 | ·4 | ·5 | ·5 | ·6 | ·6 |
| Mar. | ·3 | ·3 | ·3 | ·3 | ·3 | ·3 | ·3 | ·3 | ·3 | ·4 | ·4 | ·5 |
| Apr. | 0·4 | 0·4 | 0·3 | 0·3 | 0·3 | 0·2 | 0·2 | 0·2 | 0·2 | 0·3 | 0·3 | 0·3 |
| May | ·6 | ·5 | ·5 | ·4 | ·3 | ·3 | ·3 | ·2 | ·2 | ·2 | ·2 | ·2 |
| June | ·7 | ·7 | ·6 | ·5 | ·5 | ·4 | ·4 | ·3 | ·3 | ·3 | ·2 | ·2 |
| July | 0·8 | 0·8 | 0·8 | 0·7 | 0·6 | 0·6 | 0·5 | 0·5 | 0·4 | 0·4 | 0·3 | 0·3 |
| Aug. | ·9 | ·9 | ·9 | ·8 | ·8 | ·8 | ·7 | ·7 | ·6 | ·5 | ·5 | ·4 |
| Sept. | ·9 | ·9 | ·9 | ·9 | ·9 | ·9 | ·9 | ·8 | ·8 | ·7 | ·7 | ·6 |
| Oct. | 0·8 | 0·8 | 0·9 | 0·9 | 0·9 | 0·9 | 0·9 | 0·9 | 0·9 | 0·9 | 0·9 | 0·8 |
| Nov. | ·6 | ·7 | ·8 | ·8 | ·9 | ·9 | 1·0 | 1·0 | 1·0 | 1·0 | 1·0 | 1·0 |
| Dec. | 0·5 | 0·5 | 0·6 | 0·7 | 0·8 | 0·9 | 0·9 | 1·0 | 1·0 | 1·0 | 1·1 | 1·1 |
| Lat. | | | | | | AZIMUTH | | | | | | |
| 0 | 0·5 | 0·6 | 0·7 | 0·8 | 0·8 | 0·8 | 0·8 | 0·8 | 0·8 | 0·7 | 0·6 | 0·5 |
| 20 | 0·5 | 0·6 | 0·7 | 0·8 | 0·9 | 0·9 | 0·9 | 0·9 | 0·8 | 0·8 | 0·7 | 0·5 |
| 40 | 0·6 | 0·7 | 0·9 | 1·0 | 1·1 | 1·1 | 1·1 | 1·1 | 1·0 | 0·9 | 0·8 | 0·7 |
| 50 | 0·7 | 0·9 | 1·0 | 1·2 | 1·3 | 1·3 | 1·3 | 1·3 | 1·2 | 1·1 | 1·0 | 0·8 |
| 55 | 0·8 | 1·0 | 1·2 | 1·3 | 1·4 | 1·5 | 1·5 | 1·4 | 1·4 | 1·3 | 1·1 | 0·9 |
| 60 | 0·9 | 1·1 | 1·3 | 1·5 | 1·6 | 1·7 | 1·7 | 1·7 | 1·6 | 1·4 | 1·3 | 1·0 |
| 65 | 1·1 | 1·3 | 1·6 | 1·8 | 1·9 | 2·0 | 2·0 | 2·0 | 1·9 | 1·7 | 1·5 | 1·2 |

Latitude = Apparent altitude (corrected for refraction) $- 1° + a_0 + a_1 + a_2$

**Fig. A5.8**

The table is entered with L.H.A. Aries to determine the column to be used; each column refers to a range of 10°. $a_0$ is taken, with mental interpolation, from the upper table with the units of L.H.A. Aries in degrees as argument; $a_1$, $a_2$ are taken, without interpolation, from the second and third tables with arguments latitude and month respectively. $a_0$, $a_1$, $a_2$ are always positive. The final table gives the azimuth of *Polaris*.

## CONVERSION OF ARC TO TIME

| 0°–59° | | 60°–119° | | 120°–179° | | 180°–239° | | 240°–299° | | 300°–359° | | ′ | 0′.00 | 0′.25 | 0′.50 | 0′.75 |
|---|---|---|---|---|---|---|---|---|---|---|---|---|---|---|---|---|
| ° | h m | ° | h m | ° | h m | ° | h m | ° | h m | ° | h m | ′ | m s | m s | m s | m s |
| 0 | 0 00 | 60 | 4 00 | 120 | 8 00 | 180 | 12 00 | 240 | 16 00 | 300 | 20 00 | 0 | 0 00 | 0 01 | 0 02 | 0 03 |
| 1 | 0 04 | 61 | 4 04 | 121 | 8 04 | 181 | 12 04 | 241 | 16 04 | 301 | 20 04 | 1 | 0 04 | 0 05 | 0 06 | 0 07 |
| 2 | 0 08 | 62 | 4 08 | 122 | 8 08 | 182 | 12 08 | 242 | 16 08 | 302 | 20 08 | 2 | 0 08 | 0 09 | 0 10 | 0 11 |
| 3 | 0 12 | 63 | 4 12 | 123 | 8 12 | 183 | 12 12 | 243 | 16 12 | 303 | 20 12 | 3 | 0 12 | 0 13 | 0 14 | 0 15 |
| 4 | 0 16 | 64 | 4 16 | 124 | 8 16 | 184 | 12 16 | 244 | 16 16 | 304 | 20 16 | 4 | 0 16 | 0 17 | 0 18 | 0 19 |
| 5 | 0 20 | 65 | 4 20 | 125 | 8 20 | 185 | 12 20 | 245 | 16 20 | 305 | 20 20 | 5 | 0 20 | 0 21 | 0 22 | 0 23 |
| 6 | 0 24 | 66 | 4 24 | 126 | 8 24 | 186 | 12 24 | 246 | 16 24 | 306 | 20 24 | 6 | 0 24 | 0 25 | 0 26 | 0 27 |
| 7 | 0 28 | 67 | 4 28 | 127 | 8 28 | 187 | 12 28 | 247 | 16 28 | 307 | 20 28 | 7 | 0 28 | 0 29 | 0 30 | 0 31 |
| 8 | 0 32 | 68 | 4 32 | 128 | 8 32 | 188 | 12 32 | 248 | 16 32 | 308 | 20 32 | 8 | 0 32 | 0 33 | 0 34 | 0 35 |
| 9 | 0 36 | 69 | 4 36 | 129 | 8 36 | 189 | 12 36 | 249 | 16 36 | 309 | 20 36 | 9 | 0 36 | 0 37 | 0 38 | 0 39 |
| 10 | 0 40 | 70 | 4 40 | 130 | 8 40 | 190 | 12 40 | 250 | 16 40 | 310 | 20 40 | 10 | 0 40 | 0 41 | 0 42 | 0 43 |
| 11 | 0 44 | 71 | 4 44 | 131 | 8 44 | 191 | 12 44 | 251 | 16 44 | 311 | 20 44 | 11 | 0 44 | 0 45 | 0 46 | 0 47 |
| 12 | 0 48 | 72 | 4 48 | 132 | 8 48 | 192 | 12 48 | 252 | 16 48 | 312 | 20 48 | 12 | 0 48 | 0 49 | 0 50 | 0 51 |
| 13 | 0 52 | 73 | 4 52 | 133 | 8 52 | 193 | 12 52 | 253 | 16 52 | 313 | 20 52 | 13 | 0 52 | 0 53 | 0 54 | 0 55 |
| 14 | 0 56 | 74 | 4 56 | 134 | 8 56 | 194 | 12 56 | 254 | 16 56 | 314 | 20 56 | 14 | 0 56 | 0 57 | 0 58 | 0 59 |
| 15 | 1 00 | 75 | 5 00 | 135 | 9 00 | 195 | 13 00 | 255 | 17 00 | 315 | 21 00 | 15 | 1 00 | 1 01 | 1 02 | 1 03 |
| 16 | 1 04 | 76 | 5 04 | 136 | 9 04 | 196 | 13 04 | 256 | 17 04 | 316 | 21 04 | 16 | 1 04 | 1 05 | 1 06 | 1 07 |
| 17 | 1 08 | 77 | 5 08 | 137 | 9 08 | 197 | 13 08 | 257 | 17 08 | 317 | 21 08 | 17 | 1 08 | 1 09 | 1 10 | 1 11 |
| 18 | 1 12 | 78 | 5 12 | 138 | 9 12 | 198 | 13 12 | 258 | 17 12 | 318 | 21 12 | 18 | 1 12 | 1 13 | 1 14 | 1 15 |
| 19 | 1 16 | 79 | 5 16 | 139 | 9 16 | 199 | 13 16 | 259 | 17 16 | 319 | 21 16 | 19 | 1 16 | 1 17 | 1 18 | 1 19 |
| 20 | 1 20 | 80 | 5 20 | 140 | 9 20 | 200 | 13 20 | 260 | 17 20 | 320 | 21 20 | 20 | 1 20 | 1 21 | 1 22 | 1 23 |
| 21 | 1 24 | 81 | 5 24 | 141 | 9 24 | 201 | 13 24 | 261 | 17 24 | 321 | 21 24 | 21 | 1 24 | 1 25 | 1 26 | 1 27 |
| 22 | 1 28 | 82 | 5 28 | 142 | 9 28 | 202 | 13 28 | 262 | 17 28 | 322 | 21 28 | 22 | 1 28 | 1 29 | 1 30 | 1 31 |
| 23 | 1 32 | 83 | 5 32 | 143 | 9 32 | 203 | 13 32 | 263 | 17 32 | 323 | 21 32 | 23 | 1 32 | 1 33 | 1 34 | 1 35 |
| 24 | 1 36 | 84 | 5 36 | 144 | 9 36 | 204 | 13 36 | 264 | 17 36 | 324 | 21 36 | 24 | 1 36 | 1 37 | 1 38 | 1 39 |
| 25 | 1 40 | 85 | 5 40 | 145 | 9 40 | 205 | 13 40 | 265 | 17 40 | 325 | 21 40 | 25 | 1 40 | 1 41 | 1 42 | 1 43 |
| 26 | 1 44 | 86 | 5 44 | 146 | 9 44 | 206 | 13 44 | 266 | 17 44 | 326 | 21 44 | 26 | 1 44 | 1 45 | 1 46 | 1 47 |
| 27 | 1 48 | 87 | 5 48 | 147 | 9 48 | 207 | 13 48 | 267 | 17 48 | 327 | 21 48 | 27 | 1 48 | 1 49 | 1 50 | 1 51 |
| 28 | 1 52 | 88 | 5 52 | 148 | 9 52 | 208 | 13 52 | 268 | 17 52 | 328 | 21 52 | 28 | 1 52 | 1 53 | 1 54 | 1 55 |
| 29 | 1 56 | 89 | 5 56 | 149 | 9 56 | 209 | 13 56 | 269 | 17 56 | 329 | 21 56 | 29 | 1 56 | 1 57 | 1 58 | 1 59 |
| 30 | 2 00 | 90 | 6 00 | 150 | 10 00 | 210 | 14 00 | 270 | 18 00 | 330 | 22 00 | 30 | 2 00 | 2 01 | 2 02 | 2 03 |
| 31 | 2 04 | 91 | 6 04 | 151 | 10 04 | 211 | 14 04 | 271 | 18 04 | 331 | 22 04 | 31 | 2 04 | 2 05 | 2 06 | 2 07 |
| 32 | 2 08 | 92 | 6 08 | 152 | 10 08 | 212 | 14 08 | 272 | 18 08 | 332 | 22 08 | 32 | 2 08 | 2 09 | 2 10 | 2 11 |
| 33 | 2 12 | 93 | 6 12 | 153 | 10 12 | 213 | 14 12 | 273 | 18 12 | 333 | 22 12 | 33 | 2 12 | 2 13 | 2 14 | 2 15 |
| 34 | 2 16 | 94 | 6 16 | 154 | 10 16 | 214 | 14 16 | 274 | 18 16 | 334 | 22 16 | 34 | 2 16 | 2 17 | 2 18 | 2 19 |
| 35 | 2 20 | 95 | 6 20 | 155 | 10 20 | 215 | 14 20 | 275 | 18 20 | 335 | 22 20 | 35 | 2 20 | 2 21 | 2 22 | 2 23 |
| 36 | 2 24 | 96 | 6 24 | 156 | 10 24 | 216 | 14 24 | 276 | 18 24 | 336 | 22 24 | 36 | 2 24 | 2 25 | 2 26 | 2 27 |
| 37 | 2 28 | 97 | 6 28 | 157 | 10 28 | 217 | 14 28 | 277 | 18 28 | 337 | 22 28 | 37 | 2 28 | 2 29 | 2 30 | 2 31 |
| 38 | 2 32 | 98 | 6 32 | 158 | 10 32 | 218 | 14 32 | 278 | 18 32 | 338 | 22 32 | 38 | 2 32 | 2 33 | 2 34 | 2 35 |
| 39 | 2 36 | 99 | 6 36 | 159 | 10 36 | 219 | 14 36 | 279 | 18 36 | 339 | 22 36 | 39 | 2 36 | 2 37 | 2 38 | 2 39 |
| 40 | 2 40 | 100 | 6 40 | 160 | 10 40 | 220 | 14 40 | 280 | 18 40 | 340 | 22 40 | 40 | 2 40 | 2 41 | 2 42 | 2 43 |
| 41 | 2 44 | 101 | 6 44 | 161 | 10 44 | 221 | 14 44 | 281 | 18 44 | 341 | 22 44 | 41 | 2 44 | 2 45 | 2 46 | 2 47 |
| 42 | 2 48 | 102 | 6 48 | 162 | 10 48 | 222 | 14 48 | 282 | 18 48 | 342 | 22 48 | 42 | 2 48 | 2 49 | 2 50 | 2 51 |
| 43 | 2 52 | 103 | 6 52 | 163 | 10 52 | 223 | 14 52 | 283 | 18 52 | 343 | 22 52 | 43 | 2 52 | 2 53 | 2 54 | 2 55 |
| 44 | 2 56 | 104 | 6 56 | 164 | 10 56 | 224 | 14 56 | 284 | 18 56 | 344 | 22 56 | 44 | 2 56 | 2 57 | 2 58 | 2 59 |
| 45 | 3 00 | 105 | 7 00 | 165 | 11 00 | 225 | 15 00 | 285 | 19 00 | 345 | 23 00 | 45 | 3 00 | 3 01 | 3 02 | 3 03 |
| 46 | 3 04 | 106 | 7 04 | 166 | 11 04 | 226 | 15 04 | 286 | 19 04 | 346 | 23 04 | 46 | 3 04 | 3 05 | 3 06 | 3 07 |
| 47 | 3 08 | 107 | 7 08 | 167 | 11 08 | 227 | 15 08 | 287 | 19 08 | 347 | 23 08 | 47 | 3 08 | 3 09 | 3 10 | 3 11 |
| 48 | 3 12 | 108 | 7 12 | 168 | 11 12 | 228 | 15 12 | 288 | 19 12 | 348 | 23 12 | 48 | 3 12 | 3 13 | 3 14 | 3 15 |
| 49 | 3 16 | 109 | 7 16 | 169 | 11 16 | 229 | 15 16 | 289 | 19 16 | 349 | 23 16 | 49 | 3 16 | 3 17 | 3 18 | 3 19 |
| 50 | 3 20 | 110 | 7 20 | 170 | 11 20 | 230 | 15 20 | 290 | 19 20 | 350 | 23 20 | 50 | 3 20 | 3 21 | 3 22 | 3 23 |
| 51 | 3 24 | 111 | 7 24 | 171 | 11 24 | 231 | 15 24 | 291 | 19 24 | 351 | 23 24 | 51 | 3 24 | 3 25 | 3 26 | 3 27 |
| 52 | 3 28 | 112 | 7 28 | 172 | 11 28 | 232 | 15 28 | 292 | 19 28 | 352 | 23 28 | 52 | 3 28 | 3 29 | 3 30 | 3 31 |
| 53 | 3 32 | 113 | 7 32 | 173 | 11 32 | 233 | 15 32 | 293 | 19 32 | 353 | 23 32 | 53 | 3 32 | 3 33 | 3 34 | 3 35 |
| 54 | 3 36 | 114 | 7 36 | 174 | 11 36 | 234 | 15 36 | 294 | 19 36 | 354 | 23 36 | 54 | 3 36 | 3 37 | 3 38 | 3 39 |
| 55 | 3 40 | 115 | 7 40 | 175 | 11 40 | 235 | 15 40 | 295 | 19 40 | 355 | 23 40 | 55 | 3 40 | 3 41 | 3 42 | 3 43 |
| 56 | 3 44 | 116 | 7 44 | 176 | 11 44 | 236 | 15 44 | 296 | 19 44 | 356 | 23 44 | 56 | 3 44 | 3 45 | 3 46 | 3 47 |
| 57 | 3 48 | 117 | 7 48 | 177 | 11 48 | 237 | 15 48 | 297 | 19 48 | 357 | 23 48 | 57 | 3 48 | 3 49 | 3 50 | 3 51 |
| 58 | 3 52 | 118 | 7 52 | 178 | 11 52 | 238 | 15 52 | 298 | 19 52 | 358 | 23 52 | 58 | 3 52 | 3 53 | 3 54 | 3 55 |
| 59 | 3 56 | 119 | 7 56 | 179 | 11 56 | 239 | 15 56 | 299 | 19 56 | 359 | 23 56 | 59 | 3 56 | 3 57 | 3 58 | 3 59 |

The above table is for converting expressions in arc to their equivalent in time ; its main use in this Almanac is for the conversion of longitude for application to L.M.T. (*added* if *west*, *subtracted* if *east*) to give G.M.T. or vice versa, particularly in the case of sunrise, sunset, etc.

Fig. A5.9

**52ᵐ**      INCREMENTS AND CORRECTIONS      **53ᵐ**

| 52 | SUN PLANETS | ARIES | MOON | $v$ or Corrⁿ $d$ | | $v$ or Corrⁿ $d$ | | $v$ or Corrⁿ $d$ | |
|---|---|---|---|---|---|---|---|---|---|
| s | ° ′ | ° ′ | ° ′ | ′ | ′ | ′ | ′ | ′ | ′ |
| 00 | 13 00·0 | 13 02·1 | 12 24·5 | 0·0 | 0·0 | 6·0 | 5·3 | 12·0 | 10·5 |
| 01 | 13 00·3 | 13 02·4 | 12 24·7 | 0·1 | 0·1 | 6·1 | 5·3 | 12·1 | 10·6 |
| 02 | 13 00·5 | 13 02·6 | 12 24·9 | 0·2 | 0·2 | 6·2 | 5·4 | 12·2 | 10·7 |
| 03 | 13 00·8 | 13 02·9 | 12 25·2 | 0·3 | 0·3 | 6·3 | 5·5 | 12·3 | 10·8 |
| 04 | 13 01·0 | 13 03·1 | 12 25·4 | 0·4 | 0·4 | 6·4 | 5·6 | 12·4 | 10·9 |
| 05 | 13 01·3 | 13 03·4 | 12 25·7 | 0·5 | 0·4 | 6·5 | 5·7 | 12·5 | 10·9 |
| 06 | 13 01·5 | 13 03·6 | 12 25·9 | 0·6 | 0·5 | 6·6 | 5·8 | 12·6 | 11·0 |
| 07 | 13 01·8 | 13 03·9 | 12 26·1 | 0·7 | 0·6 | 6·7 | 5·9 | 12·7 | 11·1 |
| 08 | 13 02·0 | 13 04·1 | 12 26·4 | 0·8 | 0·7 | 6·8 | 6·0 | 12·8 | 11·2 |
| 09 | 13 02·3 | 13 04·4 | 12 26·6 | 0·9 | 0·8 | 6·9 | 6·0 | 12·9 | 11·3 |
| 10 | 13 02·5 | 13 04·6 | 12 26·9 | 1·0 | 0·9 | 7·0 | 6·1 | 13·0 | 11·4 |
| 11 | 13 02·8 | 13 04·9 | 12 27·1 | 1·1 | 1·0 | 7·1 | 6·2 | 13·1 | 11·5 |
| 12 | 13 03·0 | 13 05·1 | 12 27·3 | 1·2 | 1·1 | 7·2 | 6·3 | 13·2 | 11·6 |
| 13 | 13 03·3 | 13 05·4 | 12 27·6 | 1·3 | 1·1 | 7·3 | 6·4 | 13·3 | 11·6 |
| 14 | 13 03·5 | 13 05·6 | 12 27·8 | 1·4 | 1·2 | 7·4 | 6·5 | 13·4 | 11·7 |
| 15 | 13 03·8 | 13 05·9 | 12 28·0 | 1·5 | 1·3 | 7·5 | 6·6 | 13·5 | 11·8 |
| 16 | 13 04·0 | 13 06·1 | 12 28·3 | 1·6 | 1·4 | 7·6 | 6·7 | 13·6 | 11·9 |
| 17 | 13 04·3 | 13 06·4 | 12 28·5 | 1·7 | 1·5 | 7·7 | 6·7 | 13·7 | 12·0 |
| 18 | 13 04·5 | 13 06·6 | 12 28·8 | 1·8 | 1·6 | 7·8 | 6·8 | 13·8 | 12·1 |
| 19 | 13 04·8 | 13 06·9 | 12 29·0 | 1·9 | 1·7 | 7·9 | 6·9 | 13·9 | 12·2 |
| 20 | 13 05·0 | 13 07·1 | 12 29·2 | 2·0 | 1·8 | 8·0 | 7·0 | 14·0 | 12·3 |
| 21 | 13 05·3 | 13 07·4 | 12 29·5 | 2·1 | 1·8 | 8·1 | 7·1 | 14·1 | 12·3 |
| 22 | 13 05·5 | 13 07·7 | 12 29·7 | 2·2 | 1·9 | 8·2 | 7·2 | 14·2 | 12·4 |
| 23 | 13 05·8 | 13 07·9 | 12 30·0 | 2·3 | 2·0 | 8·3 | 7·3 | 14·3 | 12·5 |
| 24 | 13 06·0 | 13 08·2 | 12 30·2 | 2·4 | 2·1 | 8·4 | 7·4 | 14·4 | 12·6 |
| 25 | 13 06·3 | 13 08·4 | 12 30·4 | 2·5 | 2·2 | 8·5 | 7·4 | 14·5 | 12·7 |
| 26 | 13 06·5 | 13 08·7 | 12 30·7 | 2·6 | 2·3 | 8·6 | 7·5 | 14·6 | 12·8 |
| 27 | 13 06·8 | 13 08·9 | 12 30·9 | 2·7 | 2·4 | 8·7 | 7·6 | 14·7 | 12·9 |
| 28 | 13 07·0 | 13 09·2 | 12 31·1 | 2·8 | 2·5 | 8·8 | 7·7 | 14·8 | 13·0 |
| 29 | 13 07·3 | 13 09·4 | 12 31·4 | 2·9 | 2·5 | 8·9 | 7·8 | 14·9 | 13·0 |
| 30 | 13 07·5 | 13 09·7 | 12 31·6 | 3·0 | 2·6 | 9·0 | 7·9 | 15·0 | 13·1 |
| 31 | 13 07·8 | 13 09·9 | 12 31·9 | 3·1 | 2·7 | 9·1 | 8·0 | 15·1 | 13·2 |
| 32 | 13 08·0 | 13 10·2 | 12 32·1 | 3·2 | 2·8 | 9·2 | 8·1 | 15·2 | 13·3 |
| 33 | 13 08·3 | 13 10·4 | 12 32·3 | 3·3 | 2·9 | 9·3 | 8·1 | 15·3 | 13·4 |
| 34 | 13 08·5 | 13 10·7 | 12 32·6 | 3·4 | 3·0 | 9·4 | 8·2 | 15·4 | 13·5 |
| 35 | 13 08·8 | 13 10·9 | 12 32·8 | 3·5 | 3·1 | 9·5 | 8·3 | 15·5 | 13·6 |
| 36 | 13 09·0 | 13 11·2 | 12 33·1 | 3·6 | 3·2 | 9·6 | 8·4 | 15·6 | 13·7 |
| 37 | 13 09·3 | 13 11·4 | 12 33·3 | 3·7 | 3·2 | 9·7 | 8·5 | 15·7 | 13·7 |
| 38 | 13 09·5 | 13 11·7 | 12 33·5 | 3·8 | 3·3 | 9·8 | 8·6 | 15·8 | 13·8 |
| 39 | 13 09·8 | 13 11·9 | 12 33·8 | 3·9 | 3·4 | 9·9 | 8·7 | 15·9 | 13·9 |
| 40 | 13 10·0 | 13 12·2 | 12 34·0 | 4·0 | 3·5 | 10·0 | 8·8 | 16·0 | 14·0 |
| 41 | 13 10·3 | 13 12·4 | 12 34·2 | 4·1 | 3·6 | 10·1 | 8·8 | 16·1 | 14·1 |
| 42 | 13 10·5 | 13 12·7 | 12 34·5 | 4·2 | 3·7 | 10·2 | 8·9 | 16·2 | 14·2 |
| 43 | 13 10·8 | 13 12·9 | 12 34·7 | 4·3 | 3·8 | 10·3 | 9·0 | 16·3 | 14·3 |
| 44 | 13 11·0 | 13 13·2 | 12 35·0 | 4·4 | 3·9 | 10·4 | 9·1 | 16·4 | 14·4 |
| 45 | 13 11·3 | 13 13·4 | 12 35·2 | 4·5 | 3·9 | 10·5 | 9·2 | 16·5 | 14·4 |
| 46 | 13 11·5 | 13 13·7 | 12 35·4 | 4·6 | 4·0 | 10·6 | 9·3 | 16·6 | 14·5 |
| 47 | 13 11·8 | 13 13·9 | 12 35·7 | 4·7 | 4·1 | 10·7 | 9·4 | 16·7 | 14·6 |
| 48 | 13 12·0 | 13 14·2 | 12 35·9 | 4·8 | 4·2 | 10·8 | 9·5 | 16·8 | 14·7 |
| 49 | 13 12·3 | 13 14·4 | 12 36·2 | 4·9 | 4·3 | 10·9 | 9·5 | 16·9 | 14·8 |
| 50 | 13 12·5 | 13 14·7 | 12 36·4 | 5·0 | 4·4 | 11·0 | 9·6 | 17·0 | 14·9 |
| 51 | 13 12·8 | 13 14·9 | 12 36·6 | 5·1 | 4·5 | 11·1 | 9·7 | 17·1 | 15·0 |
| 52 | 13 13·0 | 13 15·2 | 12 36·9 | 5·2 | 4·6 | 11·2 | 9·8 | 17·2 | 15·1 |
| 53 | 13 13·3 | 13 15·4 | 12 37·1 | 5·3 | 4·6 | 11·3 | 9·9 | 17·3 | 15·1 |
| 54 | 13 13·5 | 13 15·7 | 12 37·4 | 5·4 | 4·7 | 11·4 | 10·0 | 17·4 | 15·2 |
| 55 | 13 13·8 | 13 15·9 | 12 37·6 | 5·5 | 4·8 | 11·5 | 10·1 | 17·5 | 15·3 |
| 56 | 13 14·0 | 13 16·2 | 12 37·8 | 5·6 | 4·9 | 11·6 | 10·2 | 17·6 | 15·4 |
| 57 | 13 14·3 | 13 16·4 | 12 38·1 | 5·7 | 5·0 | 11·7 | 10·2 | 17·7 | 15·5 |
| 58 | 13 14·5 | 13 16·7 | 12 38·3 | 5·8 | 5·1 | 11·8 | 10·3 | 17·8 | 15·6 |
| 59 | 13 14·8 | 13 16·9 | 12 38·5 | 5·9 | 5·2 | 11·9 | 10·4 | 17·9 | 15·7 |
| 60 | 13 15·0 | 13 17·2 | 12 38·8 | 6·0 | 5·3 | 12·0 | 10·5 | 18·0 | 15·8 |

| 53 | SUN PLANETS | ARIES | MOON | $v$ or Corrⁿ $d$ | | $v$ or Corrⁿ $d$ | | $v$ or Corrⁿ $d$ | |
|---|---|---|---|---|---|---|---|---|---|
| s | ° ′ | ° ′ | ° ′ | ′ | ′ | ′ | ′ | ′ | ′ |
| 00 | 13 15·0 | 13 17·2 | 12 38·8 | 0·0 | 0·0 | 6·0 | 5·4 | 12·0 | 10·7 |
| 01 | 13 15·3 | 13 17·4 | 12 39·0 | 0·1 | 0·1 | 6·1 | 5·4 | 12·1 | 10·8 |
| 02 | 13 15·5 | 13 17·7 | 12 39·3 | 0·2 | 0·2 | 6·2 | 5·5 | 12·2 | 10·9 |
| 03 | 13 15·8 | 13 17·9 | 12 39·5 | 0·3 | 0·3 | 6·3 | 5·6 | 12·3 | 11·0 |
| 04 | 13 16·0 | 13 18·2 | 12 39·7 | 0·4 | 0·4 | 6·4 | 5·7 | 12·4 | 11·1 |
| 05 | 13 16·3 | 13 18·4 | 12 40·0 | 0·5 | 0·4 | 6·5 | 5·8 | 12·5 | 11·1 |
| 06 | 13 16·5 | 13 18·7 | 12 40·2 | 0·6 | 0·5 | 6·6 | 5·9 | 12·6 | 11·2 |
| 07 | 13 16·8 | 13 18·9 | 12 40·5 | 0·7 | 0·6 | 6·7 | 6·0 | 12·7 | 11·3 |
| 08 | 13 17·0 | 13 19·2 | 12 40·7 | 0·8 | 0·7 | 6·8 | 6·1 | 12·8 | 11·4 |
| 09 | 13 17·3 | 13 19·4 | 12 40·9 | 0·9 | 0·8 | 6·9 | 6·2 | 12·9 | 11·5 |
| 10 | 13 17·5 | 13 19·7 | 12 41·2 | 1·0 | 0·9 | 7·0 | 6·2 | 13·0 | 11·6 |
| 11 | 13 17·8 | 13 19·9 | 12 41·4 | 1·1 | 1·0 | 7·1 | 6·3 | 13·1 | 11·7 |
| 12 | 13 18·0 | 13 20·2 | 12 41·6 | 1·2 | 1·1 | 7·2 | 6·4 | 13·2 | 11·8 |
| 13 | 13 18·3 | 13 20·4 | 12 41·9 | 1·3 | 1·2 | 7·3 | 6·5 | 13·3 | 11·9 |
| 14 | 13 18·5 | 13 20·7 | 12 42·1 | 1·4 | 1·2 | 7·4 | 6·6 | 13·4 | 11·9 |
| 15 | 13 18·8 | 13 20·9 | 12 42·4 | 1·5 | 1·3 | 7·5 | 6·7 | 13·5 | 12·0 |
| 16 | 13 19·0 | 13 21·2 | 12 42·6 | 1·6 | 1·4 | 7·6 | 6·8 | 13·6 | 12·1 |
| 17 | 13 19·3 | 13 21·4 | 12 42·8 | 1·7 | 1·5 | 7·7 | 6·9 | 13·7 | 12·2 |
| 18 | 13 19·5 | 13 21·7 | 12 43·1 | 1·8 | 1·6 | 7·8 | 7·0 | 13·8 | 12·3 |
| 19 | 13 19·8 | 13 21·9 | 12 43·3 | 1·9 | 1·7 | 7·9 | 7·0 | 13·9 | 12·4 |
| 20 | 13 20·0 | 13 22·2 | 12 43·6 | 2·0 | 1·8 | 8·0 | 7·1 | 14·0 | 12·5 |
| 21 | 13 20·3 | 13 22·4 | 12 43·8 | 2·1 | 1·9 | 8·1 | 7·2 | 14·1 | 12·6 |
| 22 | 13 20·5 | 13 22·7 | 12 44·0 | 2·2 | 2·0 | 8·2 | 7·3 | 14·2 | 12·7 |
| 23 | 13 20·8 | 13 22·9 | 12 44·3 | 2·3 | 2·1 | 8·3 | 7·4 | 14·3 | 12·8 |
| 24 | 13 21·0 | 13 23·2 | 12 44·5 | 2·4 | 2·1 | 8·4 | 7·5 | 14·4 | 12·8 |
| 25 | 13 21·3 | 13 23·4 | 12 44·7 | 2·5 | 2·2 | 8·5 | 7·6 | 14·5 | 12·9 |
| 26 | 13 21·5 | 13 23·7 | 12 45·0 | 2·6 | 2·3 | 8·6 | 7·7 | 14·6 | 13·0 |
| 27 | 13 21·8 | 13 23·9 | 12 45·2 | 2·7 | 2·4 | 8·7 | 7·8 | 14·7 | 13·1 |
| 28 | 13 22·0 | 13 24·2 | 12 45·5 | 2·8 | 2·5 | 8·8 | 7·8 | 14·8 | 13·2 |
| 29 | 13 22·3 | 13 24·4 | 12 45·7 | 2·9 | 2·6 | 8·9 | 7·9 | 14·9 | 13·3 |
| 30 | 13 22·5 | 13 24·7 | 12 45·9 | 3·0 | 2·7 | 9·0 | 8·0 | 15·0 | 13·4 |
| 31 | 13 22·8 | 13 24·9 | 12 46·2 | 3·1 | 2·8 | 9·1 | 8·1 | 15·1 | 13·5 |
| 32 | 13 23·0 | 13 25·2 | 12 46·4 | 3·2 | 2·9 | 9·2 | 8·2 | 15·2 | 13·6 |
| 33 | 13 23·3 | 13 25·4 | 12 46·7 | 3·3 | 2·9 | 9·3 | 8·3 | 15·3 | 13·6 |
| 34 | 13 23·5 | 13 25·7 | 12 46·9 | 3·4 | 3·0 | 9·4 | 8·4 | 15·4 | 13·7 |
| 35 | 13 23·8 | 13 26·0 | 12 47·1 | 3·5 | 3·1 | 9·5 | 8·5 | 15·5 | 13·8 |
| 36 | 13 24·0 | 13 26·2 | 12 47·4 | 3·6 | 3·2 | 9·6 | 8·6 | 15·6 | 13·9 |
| 37 | 13 24·3 | 13 26·5 | 12 47·6 | 3·7 | 3·3 | 9·7 | 8·6 | 15·7 | 14·0 |
| 38 | 13 24·5 | 13 26·7 | 12 47·9 | 3·8 | 3·4 | 9·8 | 8·7 | 15·8 | 14·1 |
| 39 | 13 24·8 | 13 27·0 | 12 48·1 | 3·9 | 3·5 | 9·9 | 8·8 | 15·9 | 14·2 |
| 40 | 13 25·0 | 13 27·2 | 12 48·3 | 4·0 | 3·6 | 10·0 | 8·9 | 16·0 | 14·3 |
| 41 | 13 25·3 | 13 27·5 | 12 48·6 | 4·1 | 3·7 | 10·1 | 9·0 | 16·1 | 14·4 |
| 42 | 13 25·5 | 13 27·7 | 12 48·8 | 4·2 | 3·7 | 10·2 | 9·1 | 16·2 | 14·4 |
| 43 | 13 25·8 | 13 28·0 | 12 49·0 | 4·3 | 3·8 | 10·3 | 9·2 | 16·3 | 14·5 |
| 44 | 13 26·0 | 13 28·2 | 12 49·3 | 4·4 | 3·9 | 10·4 | 9·3 | 16·4 | 14·6 |
| 45 | 13 26·3 | 13 28·5 | 12 49·5 | 4·5 | 4·0 | 10·5 | 9·4 | 16·5 | 14·7 |
| 46 | 13 26·5 | 13 28·7 | 12 49·8 | 4·6 | 4·1 | 10·6 | 9·5 | 16·6 | 14·8 |
| 47 | 13 26·8 | 13 29·0 | 12 50·0 | 4·7 | 4·2 | 10·7 | 9·5 | 16·7 | 14·9 |
| 48 | 13 27·0 | 13 29·2 | 12 50·2 | 4·8 | 4·3 | 10·8 | 9·6 | 16·8 | 15·0 |
| 49 | 13 27·3 | 13 29·5 | 12 50·5 | 4·9 | 4·4 | 10·9 | 9·7 | 16·9 | 15·1 |
| 50 | 13 27·5 | 13 29·7 | 12 50·7 | 5·0 | 4·5 | 11·0 | 9·8 | 17·0 | 15·2 |
| 51 | 13 27·8 | 13 30·0 | 12 51·0 | 5·1 | 4·5 | 11·1 | 9·9 | 17·1 | 15·2 |
| 52 | 13 28·0 | 13 30·2 | 12 51·2 | 5·2 | 4·6 | 11·2 | 10·0 | 17·2 | 15·3 |
| 53 | 13 28·3 | 13 30·5 | 12 51·4 | 5·3 | 4·7 | 11·3 | 10·1 | 17·3 | 15·4 |
| 54 | 13 28·5 | 13 30·7 | 12 51·7 | 5·4 | 4·8 | 11·4 | 10·2 | 17·4 | 15·5 |
| 55 | 13 28·8 | 13 31·0 | 12 51·9 | 5·5 | 4·9 | 11·5 | 10·3 | 17·5 | 15·6 |
| 56 | 13 29·0 | 13 31·2 | 12 52·1 | 5·6 | 5·0 | 11·6 | 10·3 | 17·6 | 15·7 |
| 57 | 13 29·3 | 13 31·5 | 12 52·4 | 5·7 | 5·1 | 11·7 | 10·4 | 17·7 | 15·8 |
| 58 | 13 29·5 | 13 31·7 | 12 52·6 | 5·8 | 5·2 | 11·8 | 10·5 | 17·8 | 15·9 |
| 59 | 13 29·8 | 13 32·0 | 12 52·9 | 5·9 | 5·3 | 11·9 | 10·6 | 17·9 | 16·0 |
| 60 | 13 30·0 | 13 32·2 | 12 53·1 | 6·0 | 5·4 | 12·0 | 10·7 | 18·0 | 16·1 |

**Fig. A5.10**

## INCREMENTS AND CORRECTIONS

### 54ᵐ

| 54 s | SUN PLANETS | ARIES | MOON | v or d | Corrn | v or d | Corrn | v or d | Corrn |
|---|---|---|---|---|---|---|---|---|---|
| 00 | 13 30·0 | 13 32·2 | 12 53·1 | 0·0 | 0·0 | 6·0 | 5·5 | 12·0 | 10·9 |
| 01 | 13 30·3 | 13 32·5 | 12 53·3 | 0·1 | 0·1 | 6·1 | 5·5 | 12·1 | 11·0 |
| 02 | 13 30·5 | 13 32·7 | 12 53·6 | 0·2 | 0·2 | 6·2 | 5·6 | 12·2 | 11·1 |
| 03 | 13 30·8 | 13 33·0 | 12 53·8 | 0·3 | 0·3 | 6·3 | 5·7 | 12·3 | 11·2 |
| 04 | 13 31·0 | 13 33·2 | 12 54·1 | 0·4 | 0·4 | 6·4 | 5·8 | 12·4 | 11·3 |
| 05 | 13 31·3 | 13 33·5 | 12 54·3 | 0·5 | 0·5 | 6·5 | 5·9 | 12·5 | 11·4 |
| 06 | 13 31·5 | 13 33·7 | 12 54·5 | 0·6 | 0·5 | 6·6 | 6·0 | 12·6 | 11·4 |
| 07 | 13 31·8 | 13 34·0 | 12 54·8 | 0·7 | 0·6 | 6·7 | 6·1 | 12·7 | 11·5 |
| 08 | 13 32·0 | 13 34·2 | 12 55·0 | 0·8 | 0·7 | 6·8 | 6·2 | 12·8 | 11·6 |
| 09 | 13 32·3 | 13 34·5 | 12 55·2 | 0·9 | 0·8 | 6·9 | 6·3 | 12·9 | 11·7 |
| 10 | 13 32·5 | 13 34·7 | 12 55·5 | 1·0 | 0·9 | 7·0 | 6·4 | 13·0 | 11·8 |
| 11 | 13 32·8 | 13 35·0 | 12 55·7 | 1·1 | 1·0 | 7·1 | 6·4 | 13·1 | 11·9 |
| 12 | 13 33·0 | 13 35·2 | 12 56·0 | 1·2 | 1·1 | 7·2 | 6·5 | 13·2 | 12·0 |
| 13 | 13 33·3 | 13 35·5 | 12 56·2 | 1·3 | 1·2 | 7·3 | 6·6 | 13·3 | 12·1 |
| 14 | 13 33·5 | 13 35·7 | 12 56·4 | 1·4 | 1·3 | 7·4 | 6·7 | 13·4 | 12·2 |
| 15 | 13 33·8 | 13 36·0 | 12 56·7 | 1·5 | 1·4 | 7·5 | 6·8 | 13·5 | 12·3 |
| 16 | 13 34·0 | 13 36·2 | 12 56·9 | 1·6 | 1·5 | 7·6 | 6·9 | 13·6 | 12·4 |
| 17 | 13 34·3 | 13 36·5 | 12 57·2 | 1·7 | 1·5 | 7·7 | 7·0 | 13·7 | 12·4 |
| 18 | 13 34·5 | 13 36·7 | 12 57·4 | 1·8 | 1·6 | 7·8 | 7·1 | 13·8 | 12·5 |
| 19 | 13 34·8 | 13 37·0 | 12 57·6 | 1·9 | 1·7 | 7·9 | 7·2 | 13·9 | 12·6 |
| 20 | 13 35·0 | 13 37·2 | 12 57·9 | 2·0 | 1·8 | 8·0 | 7·3 | 14·0 | 12·7 |
| 21 | 13 35·3 | 13 37·5 | 12 58·1 | 2·1 | 1·9 | 8·1 | 7·4 | 14·1 | 12·8 |
| 22 | 13 35·5 | 13 37·7 | 12 58·3 | 2·2 | 2·0 | 8·2 | 7·4 | 14·2 | 12·9 |
| 23 | 13 35·8 | 13 38·0 | 12 58·6 | 2·3 | 2·1 | 8·3 | 7·5 | 14·3 | 13·0 |
| 24 | 13 36·0 | 13 38·2 | 12 58·8 | 2·4 | 2·2 | 8·4 | 7·6 | 14·4 | 13·1 |
| 25 | 13 36·3 | 13 38·5 | 12 59·1 | 2·5 | 2·3 | 8·5 | 7·7 | 14·5 | 13·2 |
| 26 | 13 36·5 | 13 38·7 | 12 59·3 | 2·6 | 2·4 | 8·6 | 7·8 | 14·6 | 13·3 |
| 27 | 13 36·8 | 13 39·0 | 12 59·5 | 2·7 | 2·5 | 8·7 | 7·9 | 14·7 | 13·4 |
| 28 | 13 37·0 | 13 39·2 | 12 59·8 | 2·8 | 2·5 | 8·8 | 8·0 | 14·8 | 13·4 |
| 29 | 13 37·3 | 13 39·5 | 13 00·0 | 2·9 | 2·6 | 8·9 | 8·1 | 14·9 | 13·5 |
| 30 | 13 37·5 | 13 39·7 | 13 00·3 | 3·0 | 2·7 | 9·0 | 8·2 | 15·0 | 13·6 |
| 31 | 13 37·8 | 13 40·0 | 13 00·5 | 3·1 | 2·8 | 9·1 | 8·3 | 15·1 | 13·7 |
| 32 | 13 38·0 | 13 40·2 | 13 00·7 | 3·2 | 2·9 | 9·2 | 8·4 | 15·2 | 13·8 |
| 33 | 13 38·3 | 13 40·5 | 13 01·0 | 3·3 | 3·0 | 9·3 | 8·4 | 15·3 | 13·9 |
| 34 | 13 38·5 | 13 40·7 | 13 01·2 | 3·4 | 3·1 | 9·4 | 8·5 | 15·4 | 14·0 |
| 35 | 13 38·8 | 13 41·0 | 13 01·5 | 3·5 | 3·2 | 9·5 | 8·6 | 15·5 | 14·1 |
| 36 | 13 39·0 | 13 41·2 | 13 01·7 | 3·6 | 3·3 | 9·6 | 8·7 | 15·6 | 14·2 |
| 37 | 13 39·3 | 13 41·5 | 13 01·9 | 3·7 | 3·4 | 9·7 | 8·8 | 15·7 | 14·3 |
| 38 | 13 39·5 | 13 41·7 | 13 02·2 | 3·8 | 3·5 | 9·8 | 8·9 | 15·8 | 14·4 |
| 39 | 13 39·8 | 13 42·0 | 13 02·4 | 3·9 | 3·5 | 9·9 | 9·0 | 15·9 | 14·4 |
| 40 | 13 40·0 | 13 42·2 | 13 02·6 | 4·0 | 3·6 | 10·0 | 9·1 | 16·0 | 14·5 |
| 41 | 13 40·3 | 13 42·5 | 13 02·9 | 4·1 | 3·7 | 10·1 | 9·2 | 16·1 | 14·6 |
| 42 | 13 40·5 | 13 42·7 | 13 03·1 | 4·2 | 3·8 | 10·2 | 9·3 | 16·2 | 14·7 |
| 43 | 13 40·8 | 13 43·0 | 13 03·4 | 4·3 | 3·9 | 10·3 | 9·4 | 16·3 | 14·8 |
| 44 | 13 41·0 | 13 43·2 | 13 03·6 | 4·4 | 4·0 | 10·4 | 9·4 | 16·4 | 14·9 |
| 45 | 13 41·3 | 13 43·5 | 13 03·8 | 4·5 | 4·1 | 10·5 | 9·5 | 16·5 | 15·0 |
| 46 | 13 41·5 | 13 43·7 | 13 04·1 | 4·6 | 4·2 | 10·6 | 9·6 | 16·6 | 15·1 |
| 47 | 13 41·8 | 13 44·0 | 13 04·3 | 4·7 | 4·3 | 10·7 | 9·7 | 16·7 | 15·2 |
| 48 | 13 42·0 | 13 44·3 | 13 04·6 | 4·8 | 4·4 | 10·8 | 9·8 | 16·8 | 15·3 |
| 49 | 13 42·3 | 13 44·5 | 13 04·8 | 4·9 | 4·5 | 10·9 | 9·9 | 16·9 | 15·4 |
| 50 | 13 42·5 | 13 44·8 | 13 05·0 | 5·0 | 4·5 | 11·0 | 10·0 | 17·0 | 15·4 |
| 51 | 13 42·8 | 13 45·0 | 13 05·3 | 5·1 | 4·6 | 11·1 | 10·1 | 17·1 | 15·5 |
| 52 | 13 43·0 | 13 45·3 | 13 05·5 | 5·2 | 4·7 | 11·2 | 10·2 | 17·2 | 15·6 |
| 53 | 13 43·3 | 13 45·5 | 13 05·7 | 5·3 | 4·8 | 11·3 | 10·3 | 17·3 | 15·7 |
| 54 | 13 43·5 | 13 45·8 | 13 06·0 | 5·4 | 4·9 | 11·4 | 10·4 | 17·4 | 15·8 |
| 55 | 13 43·8 | 13 46·0 | 13 06·2 | 5·5 | 5·0 | 11·5 | 10·4 | 17·5 | 15·9 |
| 56 | 13 44·0 | 13 46·3 | 13 06·5 | 5·6 | 5·1 | 11·6 | 10·5 | 17·6 | 16·0 |
| 57 | 13 44·3 | 13 46·5 | 13 06·7 | 5·7 | 5·2 | 11·7 | 10·6 | 17·7 | 16·1 |
| 58 | 13 44·5 | 13 46·8 | 13 06·9 | 5·8 | 5·3 | 11·8 | 10·7 | 17·8 | 16·2 |
| 59 | 13 44·8 | 13 47·0 | 13 07·2 | 5·9 | 5·4 | 11·9 | 10·8 | 17·9 | 16·3 |
| 60 | 13 45·0 | 13 47·3 | 13 07·4 | 6·0 | 5·5 | 12·0 | 10·9 | 18·0 | 16·4 |

### 55ᵐ

| 55 s | SUN PLANETS | ARIES | MOON | v or d | Corrn | v or d | Corrn | v or d | Corrn |
|---|---|---|---|---|---|---|---|---|---|
| 00 | 13 45·0 | 13 47·3 | 13 07·4 | 0·0 | 0·0 | 6·0 | 5·6 | 12·0 | 11·1 |
| 01 | 13 45·3 | 13 47·5 | 13 07·7 | 0·1 | 0·1 | 6·1 | 5·6 | 12·1 | 11·2 |
| 02 | 13 45·5 | 13 47·8 | 13 07·9 | 0·2 | 0·2 | 6·2 | 5·7 | 12·2 | 11·3 |
| 03 | 13 45·8 | 13 48·0 | 13 08·1 | 0·3 | 0·3 | 6·3 | 5·8 | 12·3 | 11·4 |
| 04 | 13 46·0 | 13 48·3 | 13 08·4 | 0·4 | 0·4 | 6·4 | 5·9 | 12·4 | 11·5 |
| 05 | 13 46·3 | 13 48·5 | 13 08·6 | 0·5 | 0·5 | 6·5 | 6·0 | 12·5 | 11·6 |
| 06 | 13 46·5 | 13 48·8 | 13 08·8 | 0·6 | 0·6 | 6·6 | 6·1 | 12·6 | 11·7 |
| 07 | 13 46·8 | 13 49·0 | 13 09·1 | 0·7 | 0·6 | 6·7 | 6·2 | 12·7 | 11·7 |
| 08 | 13 47·0 | 13 49·3 | 13 09·3 | 0·8 | 0·7 | 6·8 | 6·3 | 12·8 | 11·8 |
| 09 | 13 47·3 | 13 49·5 | 13 09·6 | 0·9 | 0·8 | 6·9 | 6·4 | 12·9 | 11·9 |
| 10 | 13 47·5 | 13 49·8 | 13 09·8 | 1·0 | 0·9 | 7·0 | 6·5 | 13·0 | 12·0 |
| 11 | 13 47·8 | 13 50·0 | 13 10·0 | 1·1 | 1·0 | 7·1 | 6·6 | 13·1 | 12·1 |
| 12 | 13 48·0 | 13 50·3 | 13 10·3 | 1·2 | 1·1 | 7·2 | 6·7 | 13·2 | 12·2 |
| 13 | 13 48·3 | 13 50·5 | 13 10·5 | 1·3 | 1·2 | 7·3 | 6·8 | 13·3 | 12·3 |
| 14 | 13 48·5 | 13 50·8 | 13 10·8 | 1·4 | 1·3 | 7·4 | 6·8 | 13·4 | 12·4 |
| 15 | 13 48·8 | 13 51·0 | 13 11·0 | 1·5 | 1·4 | 7·5 | 6·9 | 13·5 | 12·5 |
| 16 | 13 49·0 | 13 51·3 | 13 11·2 | 1·6 | 1·5 | 7·6 | 7·0 | 13·6 | 12·6 |
| 17 | 13 49·3 | 13 51·5 | 13 11·5 | 1·7 | 1·6 | 7·7 | 7·1 | 13·7 | 12·7 |
| 18 | 13 49·5 | 13 51·8 | 13 11·7 | 1·8 | 1·7 | 7·8 | 7·2 | 13·8 | 12·8 |
| 19 | 13 49·8 | 13 52·0 | 13 12·0 | 1·9 | 1·8 | 7·9 | 7·3 | 13·9 | 12·9 |
| 20 | 13 50·0 | 13 52·3 | 13 12·2 | 2·0 | 1·9 | 8·0 | 7·4 | 14·0 | 13·0 |
| 21 | 13 50·3 | 13 52·5 | 13 12·4 | 2·1 | 1·9 | 8·1 | 7·5 | 14·1 | 13·0 |
| 22 | 13 50·5 | 13 52·8 | 13 12·7 | 2·2 | 2·0 | 8·2 | 7·6 | 14·2 | 13·1 |
| 23 | 13 50·8 | 13 53·0 | 13 12·9 | 2·3 | 2·1 | 8·3 | 7·7 | 14·3 | 13·2 |
| 24 | 13 51·0 | 13 53·3 | 13 13·1 | 2·4 | 2·2 | 8·4 | 7·8 | 14·4 | 13·3 |
| 25 | 13 51·3 | 13 53·5 | 13 13·4 | 2·5 | 2·3 | 8·5 | 7·9 | 14·5 | 13·4 |
| 26 | 13 51·5 | 13 53·8 | 13 13·6 | 2·6 | 2·4 | 8·6 | 8·0 | 14·6 | 13·5 |
| 27 | 13 51·8 | 13 54·0 | 13 13·9 | 2·7 | 2·5 | 8·7 | 8·0 | 14·7 | 13·6 |
| 28 | 13 52·0 | 13 54·3 | 13 14·1 | 2·8 | 2·6 | 8·8 | 8·1 | 14·8 | 13·7 |
| 29 | 13 52·3 | 13 54·5 | 13 14·3 | 2·9 | 2·7 | 8·9 | 8·2 | 14·9 | 13·8 |
| 30 | 13 52·5 | 13 54·8 | 13 14·6 | 3·0 | 2·8 | 9·0 | 8·3 | 15·0 | 13·9 |
| 31 | 13 52·8 | 13 55·0 | 13 14·8 | 3·1 | 2·9 | 9·1 | 8·4 | 15·1 | 14·0 |
| 32 | 13 53·0 | 13 55·3 | 13 15·1 | 3·2 | 3·0 | 9·2 | 8·5 | 15·2 | 14·1 |
| 33 | 13 53·3 | 13 55·5 | 13 15·3 | 3·3 | 3·1 | 9·3 | 8·6 | 15·3 | 14·2 |
| 34 | 13 53·5 | 13 55·8 | 13 15·5 | 3·4 | 3·1 | 9·4 | 8·7 | 15·4 | 14·2 |
| 35 | 13 53·8 | 13 56·0 | 13 15·8 | 3·5 | 3·2 | 9·5 | 8·8 | 15·5 | 14·3 |
| 36 | 13 54·0 | 13 56·3 | 13 16·0 | 3·6 | 3·3 | 9·6 | 8·9 | 15·6 | 14·4 |
| 37 | 13 54·3 | 13 56·5 | 13 16·2 | 3·7 | 3·4 | 9·7 | 9·0 | 15·7 | 14·5 |
| 38 | 13 54·5 | 13 56·8 | 13 16·5 | 3·8 | 3·5 | 9·8 | 9·1 | 15·8 | 14·6 |
| 39 | 13 54·8 | 13 57·0 | 13 16·7 | 3·9 | 3·6 | 9·9 | 9·2 | 15·9 | 14·7 |
| 40 | 13 55·0 | 13 57·3 | 13 17·0 | 4·0 | 3·7 | 10·0 | 9·3 | 16·0 | 14·8 |
| 41 | 13 55·3 | 13 57·5 | 13 17·2 | 4·1 | 3·8 | 10·1 | 9·3 | 16·1 | 14·9 |
| 42 | 13 55·5 | 13 57·8 | 13 17·4 | 4·2 | 3·9 | 10·2 | 9·4 | 16·2 | 15·0 |
| 43 | 13 55·8 | 13 58·0 | 13 17·7 | 4·3 | 4·0 | 10·3 | 9·5 | 16·3 | 15·1 |
| 44 | 13 56·0 | 13 58·3 | 13 17·9 | 4·4 | 4·1 | 10·4 | 9·6 | 16·4 | 15·2 |
| 45 | 13 56·3 | 13 58·5 | 13 18·2 | 4·5 | 4·2 | 10·5 | 9·7 | 16·5 | 15·3 |
| 46 | 13 56·5 | 13 58·8 | 13 18·4 | 4·6 | 4·3 | 10·6 | 9·8 | 16·6 | 15·4 |
| 47 | 13 56·8 | 13 59·0 | 13 18·6 | 4·7 | 4·3 | 10·7 | 9·9 | 16·7 | 15·4 |
| 48 | 13 57·0 | 13 59·3 | 13 18·9 | 4·8 | 4·4 | 10·8 | 10·0 | 16·8 | 15·5 |
| 49 | 13 57·3 | 13 59·5 | 13 19·1 | 4·9 | 4·5 | 10·9 | 10·1 | 16·9 | 15·6 |
| 50 | 13 57·5 | 13 59·8 | 13 19·3 | 5·0 | 4·6 | 11·0 | 10·2 | 17·0 | 15·7 |
| 51 | 13 57·8 | 14 00·0 | 13 19·6 | 5·1 | 4·7 | 11·1 | 10·3 | 17·1 | 15·8 |
| 52 | 13 58·0 | 14 00·3 | 13 19·8 | 5·2 | 4·8 | 11·2 | 10·4 | 17·2 | 15·9 |
| 53 | 13 58·3 | 14 00·5 | 13 20·1 | 5·3 | 4·9 | 11·3 | 10·5 | 17·3 | 16·0 |
| 54 | 13 58·5 | 14 00·8 | 13 20·3 | 5·4 | 5·0 | 11·4 | 10·5 | 17·4 | 16·1 |
| 55 | 13 58·8 | 14 01·0 | 13 20·5 | 5·5 | 5·1 | 11·5 | 10·6 | 17·5 | 16·2 |
| 56 | 13 59·0 | 14 01·3 | 13 20·8 | 5·6 | 5·2 | 11·6 | 10·7 | 17·6 | 16·3 |
| 57 | 13 59·3 | 14 01·5 | 13 21·0 | 5·7 | 5·3 | 11·7 | 10·8 | 17·7 | 16·4 |
| 58 | 13 59·5 | 14 01·8 | 13 21·3 | 5·8 | 5·4 | 11·8 | 10·9 | 17·8 | 16·5 |
| 59 | 13 59·8 | 14 02·0 | 13 21·5 | 5·9 | 5·5 | 11·9 | 11·0 | 17·9 | 16·6 |
| 60 | 14 00·0 | 14 02·3 | 13 21·7 | 6·0 | 5·6 | 12·0 | 11·1 | 18·0 | 16·7 |

Fig. A5.11

## ALTITUDE CORRECTION TABLES 0°–35°—MOON

| App. Alt. | 0°–4° Corrⁿ | 5°–9° Corrⁿ | 10°–14° Corrⁿ | 15°–19° Corrⁿ | 20°–24° Corrⁿ | 25°–29° Corrⁿ | 30°–34° Corrⁿ | 35°–39° Corrⁿ | App. Alt. |
|---|---|---|---|---|---|---|---|---|---|
| 00 | 0° 33·8 | 5° 58·2 | 10° 62·1 | 15° 62·8 | 20° 62·2 | 25° 60·8 | 30° 58·9 | 35° 56·5 | 00 |
| 10 | 35·9 | 58·5 | 62·2 | 62·8 | 62·1 | 60·8 | 58·8 | 56·4 | 10 |
| 20 | 37·8 | 58·7 | 62·2 | 62·8 | 62·1 | 60·7 | 58·8 | 56·3 | 20 |
| 30 | 39·6 | 58·9 | 62·3 | 62·8 | 62·1 | 60·7 | 58·7 | 56·2 | 30 |
| 40 | 41·2 | 59·1 | 62·3 | 62·8 | 62·0 | 60·6 | 58·6 | 56·2 | 40 |
| 50 | 42·6 | 59·3 | 62·4 | 62·7 | 62·0 | 60·6 | 58·5 | 56·1 | 50 |
| 00 | 1° 44·0 | 6° 59·5 | 11° 62·4 | 16° 62·7 | 21° 62·0 | 26° 60·5 | 31° 58·5 | 36° 56·0 | 00 |
| 10 | 45·2 | 59·7 | 62·4 | 62·7 | 61·9 | 60·4 | 58·4 | 55·9 | 10 |
| 20 | 46·3 | 59·9 | 62·5 | 62·7 | 61·9 | 60·4 | 58·3 | 55·8 | 20 |
| 30 | 47·3 | 60·0 | 62·5 | 62·7 | 61·9 | 60·3 | 58·2 | 55·7 | 30 |
| 40 | 48·3 | 60·2 | 62·6 | 62·7 | 61·8 | 60·3 | 58·2 | 55·6 | 40 |
| 50 | 49·2 | 60·3 | 62·6 | 62·7 | 61·8 | 60·2 | 58·1 | 55·5 | 50 |
| 00 | 2° 50·0 | 7° 60·5 | 12° 62·6 | 17° 62·7 | 22° 61·7 | 27° 60·1 | 32° 58·0 | 37° 55·4 | 00 |
| 10 | 50·8 | 60·6 | 62·6 | 62·6 | 61·7 | 60·1 | 57·9 | 55·3 | 10 |
| 20 | 51·4 | 60·7 | 62·6 | 62·6 | 61·6 | 60·0 | 57·8 | 55·2 | 20 |
| 30 | 52·1 | 60·9 | 62·7 | 62·6 | 61·6 | 59·9 | 57·8 | 55·1 | 30 |
| 40 | 52·7 | 61·0 | 62·7 | 62·6 | 61·5 | 59·9 | 57·7 | 55·0 | 40 |
| 50 | 53·3 | 61·1 | 62·7 | 62·6 | 61·5 | 59·8 | 57·6 | 55·0 | 50 |
| 00 | 3° 53·8 | 8° 61·2 | 13° 62·7 | 18° 62·5 | 23° 61·5 | 28° 59·7 | 33° 57·5 | 38° 54·9 | 00 |
| 10 | 54·3 | 61·3 | 62·7 | 62·5 | 61·4 | 59·7 | 57·4 | 54·8 | 10 |
| 20 | 54·8 | 61·4 | 62·7 | 62·5 | 61·4 | 59·6 | 57·4 | 54·7 | 20 |
| 30 | 55·2 | 61·5 | 62·8 | 62·5 | 61·3 | 59·6 | 57·3 | 54·6 | 30 |
| 40 | 55·6 | 61·6 | 62·8 | 62·4 | 61·3 | 59·5 | 57·2 | 54·5 | 40 |
| 50 | 56·0 | 61·6 | 62·8 | 62·4 | 61·2 | 59·4 | 57·1 | 54·4 | 50 |
| 00 | 4° 56·4 | 9° 61·7 | 14° 62·8 | 19° 62·4 | 24° 61·2 | 29° 59·3 | 34° 57·0 | 39° 54·3 | 00 |
| 10 | 56·7 | 61·8 | 62·8 | 62·3 | 61·1 | 59·3 | 56·9 | 54·2 | 10 |
| 20 | 57·1 | 61·9 | 62·8 | 62·3 | 61·1 | 59·2 | 56·9 | 54·1 | 20 |
| 30 | 57·4 | 61·9 | 62·8 | 62·3 | 61·0 | 59·1 | 56·8 | 54·0 | 30 |
| 40 | 57·7 | 62·0 | 62·8 | 62·2 | 60·9 | 59·1 | 56·7 | 53·9 | 40 |
| 50 | 57·9 | 62·1 | 62·8 | 62·2 | 60·9 | 59·0 | 56·6 | 53·8 | 50 |

| H.P. | L U | L U | L U | L U | L U | L U | L U | L U | H.P. |
|---|---|---|---|---|---|---|---|---|---|
| 54·0 | 0·3 0·9 | 0·3 0·9 | 0·4 1·0 | 0·5 1·1 | 0·6 1·2 | 0·7 1·3 | 0·9 1·5 | 1·1 1·7 | 54·0 |
| 54·3 | 0·7 1·1 | 0·7 1·2 | 0·7 1·2 | 0·8 1·3 | 0·9 1·4 | 1·1 1·5 | 1·2 1·7 | 1·4 1·8 | 54·3 |
| 54·6 | 1·1 1·4 | 1·1 1·4 | 1·1 1·4 | 1·2 1·5 | 1·3 1·6 | 1·4 1·7 | 1·5 1·8 | 1·7 2·0 | 54·6 |
| 54·9 | 1·4 1·6 | 1·5 1·6 | 1·5 1·6 | 1·6 1·7 | 1·6 1·8 | 1·8 1·9 | 1·9 2·0 | 2·0 2·2 | 54·9 |
| 55·2 | 1·8 1·8 | 1·8 1·8 | 1·9 1·9 | 1·9 1·9 | 2·0 2·0 | 2·1 2·1 | 2·2 2·2 | 2·3 2·3 | 55·2 |
| 55·5 | 2·2 2·0 | 2·2 2·0 | 2·3 2·1 | 2·3 2·1 | 2·4 2·2 | 2·4 2·3 | 2·5 2·4 | 2·7 2·5 | 55·5 |
| 55·8 | 2·6 2·2 | 2·6 2·2 | 2·6 2·3 | 2·7 2·3 | 2·7 2·4 | 2·8 2·4 | 2·9 2·5 | 3·0 2·6 | 55·8 |
| 56·1 | 3·0 2·4 | 3·0 2·5 | 3·0 2·5 | 3·0 2·5 | 3·1 2·6 | 3·1 2·6 | 3·2 2·7 | 3·3 2·8 | 56·1 |
| 56·4 | 3·4 2·7 | 3·4 2·7 | 3·4 2·7 | 3·4 2·7 | 3·4 2·8 | 3·5 2·8 | 3·5 2·9 | 3·6 2·9 | 56·4 |
| 56·7 | 3·7 2·9 | 3·8 2·9 | 3·8 2·9 | 3·8 2·9 | 3·8 3·0 | 3·8 3·0 | 3·9 3·0 | 3·9 3·1 | 56·7 |
| 57·0 | 4·1 3·1 | 4·1 3·1 | 4·1 3·1 | 4·1 3·1 | 4·2 3·1 | 4·2 3·2 | 4·2 3·2 | 4·3 3·2 | 57·0 |
| 57·3 | 4·5 3·3 | 4·5 3·3 | 4·5 3·3 | 4·5 3·3 | 4·5 3·3 | 4·5 3·4 | 4·6 3·4 | 4·6 3·4 | 57·3 |
| 57·6 | 4·9 3·5 | 4·9 3·5 | 4·9 3·5 | 4·9 3·5 | 4·9 3·5 | 4·9 3·6 | 4·9 3·6 | 4·9 3·6 | 57·6 |
| 57·9 | 5·3 3·8 | 5·3 3·8 | 5·2 3·8 | 5·2 3·7 | 5·2 3·7 | 5·2 3·7 | 5·2 3·7 | 5·2 3·7 | 57·9 |
| 58·2 | 5·6 4·0 | 5·6 4·0 | 5·6 4·0 | 5·6 4·0 | 5·6 3·9 | 5·6 3·9 | 5·6 3·9 | 5·5 3·9 | 58·2 |
| 58·5 | 6·0 4·2 | 6·0 4·2 | 6·0 4·2 | 6·0 4·2 | 6·0 4·1 | 5·9 4·1 | 5·9 4·1 | 5·9 4·0 | 58·5 |
| 58·8 | 6·4 4·4 | 6·4 4·4 | 6·4 4·4 | 6·3 4·4 | 6·3 4·3 | 6·3 4·3 | 6·2 4·2 | 6·2 4·2 | 58·8 |
| 59·1 | 6·8 4·6 | 6·8 4·6 | 6·7 4·6 | 6·7 4·6 | 6·7 4·5 | 6·6 4·5 | 6·5 4·4 | 6·5 4·3 | 59·1 |
| 59·4 | 7·2 4·8 | 7·1 4·8 | 7·1 4·8 | 7·1 4·8 | 7·0 4·7 | 7·0 4·7 | 6·9 4·6 | 6·8 4·5 | 59·4 |
| 59·7 | 7·5 5·1 | 7·5 5·0 | 7·5 5·0 | 7·5 5·0 | 7·4 4·9 | 7·3 4·8 | 7·2 4·7 | 7·1 4·6 | 59·7 |
| 60·0 | 7·9 5·3 | 7·9 5·3 | 7·9 5·2 | 7·8 5·2 | 7·8 5·1 | 7·7 5·0 | 7·6 4·9 | 7·5 4·8 | 60·0 |
| 60·3 | 8·3 5·5 | 8·3 5·5 | 8·2 5·4 | 8·2 5·4 | 8·1 5·3 | 8·0 5·2 | 7·9 5·1 | 7·8 5·0 | 60·3 |
| 60·6 | 8·7 5·7 | 8·7 5·7 | 8·6 5·6 | 8·6 5·6 | 8·5 5·5 | 8·4 5·4 | 8·2 5·3 | 8·1 5·1 | 60·6 |
| 60·9 | 9·1 5·9 | 9·0 5·9 | 9·0 5·9 | 8·9 5·8 | 8·8 5·7 | 8·7 5·6 | 8·6 5·4 | 8·4 5·3 | 60·9 |
| 61·2 | 9·5 6·2 | 9·4 6·1 | 9·4 6·1 | 9·3 6·0 | 9·2 5·9 | 9·1 5·8 | 8·9 5·6 | 8·7 5·4 | 61·2 |
| 61·5 | 9·8 6·4 | 9·8 6·3 | 9·7 6·3 | 9·7 6·2 | 9·5 6·1 | 9·4 5·9 | 9·2 5·8 | 9·1 5·6 | 61·5 |

### DIP

| Ht. of Eye m | ft | Corrⁿ | Ht. of Eye m | ft | Corrⁿ |
|---|---|---|---|---|---|
| 2·4 | 8·0 | −2·8 | 9·5 | 31·5 | −5·5 |
| 2·6 | 8·6 | −2·9 | 9·9 | 32·7 | −5·6 |
| 2·8 | 9·2 | −3·0 | 10·3 | 33·9 | −5·7 |
| 3·0 | 9·8 | −3·1 | 10·6 | 35·1 | −5·8 |
| 3·2 | 10·5 | −3·2 | 11·0 | 36·3 | −5·9 |
| 3·4 | 11·2 | −3·3 | 11·4 | 37·6 | −6·0 |
| 3·6 | 11·9 | −3·4 | 11·8 | 38·9 | −6·1 |
| 3·8 | 12·6 | −3·5 | 12·2 | 40·1 | −6·2 |
| 4·0 | 13·3 | −3·6 | 12·6 | 41·5 | −6·3 |
| 4·3 | 14·1 | −3·7 | 13·0 | 42·8 | −6·4 |
| 4·5 | 14·9 | −3·8 | 13·4 | 44·2 | −6·5 |
| 4·7 | 15·7 | −3·9 | 13·8 | 45·5 | −6·6 |
| 5·0 | 16·5 | −4·0 | 14·2 | 46·9 | −6·7 |
| 5·2 | 17·4 | −4·1 | 14·7 | 48·4 | −6·8 |
| 5·5 | 18·3 | −4·2 | 15·1 | 49·8 | −6·9 |
| 5·8 | 19·1 | −4·3 | 15·5 | 51·3 | −7·0 |
| 6·1 | 20·1 | −4·4 | 16·0 | 52·8 | −7·1 |
| 6·3 | 21·0 | −4·5 | 16·5 | 54·3 | −7·2 |
| 6·6 | 22·0 | −4·6 | 16·9 | 55·8 | −7·3 |
| 6·9 | 22·9 | −4·7 | 17·4 | 57·4 | −7·4 |
| 7·2 | 23·9 | −4·8 | 17·9 | 58·9 | −7·5 |
| 7·5 | 24·9 | −4·9 | 18·4 | 60·5 | −7·6 |
| 7·9 | 26·0 | −5·0 | 18·8 | 62·1 | −7·7 |
| 8·2 | 27·1 | −5·1 | 19·3 | 63·8 | −7·8 |
| 8·5 | 28·1 | −5·2 | 19·8 | 65·4 | −7·9 |
| 8·8 | 29·2 | −5·3 | 20·4 | 67·1 | −8·0 |
| 9·2 | 30·4 | −5·4 | 20·9 | 68·8 | −8·1 |
| 9·5 | 31·5 | | 21·4 | 70·5 | |

### MOON CORRECTION TABLE

The correction is in two parts; the first correction is taken from the upper part of the table with argument apparent altitude, and the second from the lower part, with argument H.P., in the same column as that from which the first correction was taken. Separate corrections are given in the lower part for lower (L) and upper (U) limbs. All corrections are to be **added** to apparent altitude, *but 30′ is to be subtracted from the altitude of the upper limb.*

For corrections for pressure and temperature see page A4.

For bubble sextant observations ignore dip, take the mean of upper and lower limb corrections and subtract 15′ from the altitude.

App. Alt. = Apparent altitude = Sextant altitude corrected for index error and dip.

Fig. A5.12

# Appendix 6

# Sight Reduction Tables, Extracts from AP 3270

| LHA γ | Hc Zn | Hc Zn | Hc Zn | Hc Zn | Hc Zn | Hc Zn | Hc Zn |
|---|---|---|---|---|---|---|---|
| | ◆Mirfak | Alpheratz | ◆ALTAIR | Rasalhague | ◆ARCTURUS | Alkaid | Kochab |
| 270 | 15 18 025 | 20 42 069 | 42 56 142 | 52 12 190 | 36 06 257 | 50 18 295 | 58 49 337 |
| 271 | 15 35 026 | 21 18 070 | 43 20 143 | 52 04 192 | 35 29 257 | 49 43 295 | 58 34 337 |
| 272 | 15 52 026 | 21 54 071 | 43 43 144 | 51 55 194 | 34 51 258 | 49 08 295 | 58 19 337 |
| 273 | 16 09 027 | 22 31 071 | 44 05 145 | 51 46 195 | 34 13 259 | 48 33 296 | 58 04 337 |
| 274 | 16 27 028 | 23 07 072 | 44 27 147 | 51 35 197 | 33 35 260 | 47 59 296 | 57 49 337 |
| 275 | 16 45 028 | 23 44 073 | 44 48 148 | 51 24 198 | 32 57 261 | 47 24 297 | 57 33 336 |
| 276 | 17 03 029 | 24 21 073 | 45 08 149 | 51 11 200 | 32 19 262 | 46 50 297 | 57 18 336 |
| 277 | 17 22 029 | 24 58 074 | 45 27 151 | 50 58 201 | 31 41 262 | 46 15 298 | 57 02 336 |
| 278 | 17 41 030 | 25 35 075 | 45 45 152 | 50 43 203 | 31 03 263 | 45 41 298 | 56 47 336 |
| 279 | 18 00 031 | 26 12 075 | 46 03 153 | 50 28 204 | 30 24 264 | 45 07 299 | 56 31 336 |
| 280 | 18 20 031 | 26 50 076 | 46 20 155 | 50 11 206 | 29 46 265 | 44 34 299 | 56 15 336 |
| 281 | 18 40 032 | 27 27 077 | 46 36 156 | 49 54 207 | 29 08 266 | 44 00 299 | 55 59 336 |
| 282 | 19 01 032 | 28 05 077 | 46 51 157 | 49 36 209 | 28 29 266 | 43 26 300 | 55 43 336 |
| 283 | 19 21 033 | 28 42 078 | 47 06 159 | 49 17 210 | 27 51 267 | 42 53 300 | 55 27 335 |
| 284 | 19 42 033 | 29 20 079 | 47 19 160 | 48 57 211 | 27 12 268 | 42 20 301 | 55 11 335 |
| | ◆Mirfak | Alpheratz | ◆ALTAIR | Rasalhague | ◆ARCTURUS | Alkaid | Kochab |
| 285 | 20 04 034 | 29 58 080 | 47 32 162 | 48 37 213 | 26 34 269 | 41 47 301 | 54 55 335 |
| 286 | 20 25 035 | 30 36 080 | 47 43 163 | 48 16 214 | 25 55 270 | 41 14 302 | 54 39 335 |
| 287 | 20 47 035 | 31 14 081 | 47 54 165 | 47 54 216 | 25 16 270 | 40 41 302 | 54 23 335 |
| 288 | 21 10 036 | 31 52 082 | 48 04 166 | 47 31 217 | 24 38 271 | 40 09 303 | 54 07 335 |
| 289 | 21 32 036 | 32 30 082 | 48 13 168 | 47 07 218 | 23 59 272 | 39 36 303 | 53 50 335 |
| 290 | 21 55 037 | 33 09 083 | 48 21 169 | 46 43 220 | 23 21 273 | 39 04 304 | 53 34 335 |
| 291 | 22 19 037 | 33 47 084 | 48 28 170 | 46 18 221 | 22 42 273 | 38 32 304 | 53 18 335 |
| 292 | 22 42 038 | 34 25 084 | 48 33 172 | 45 53 222 | 22 04 274 | 38 00 305 | 53 02 335 |
| 293 | 23 06 038 | 35 04 085 | 48 38 173 | 45 26 223 | 21 25 275 | 37 29 305 | 52 45 335 |
| 294 | 23 30 039 | 35 42 086 | 48 42 175 | 45 00 225 | 20 47 276 | 36 57 306 | 52 29 335 |
| 295 | 23 55 040 | 36 21 087 | 48 45 176 | 44 32 226 | 20 09 276 | 36 26 306 | 52 13 335 |
| 296 | 24 19 040 | 36 59 087 | 48 47 178 | 44 04 227 | 19 30 277 | 35 55 307 | 51 57 335 |
| 297 | 24 44 041 | 37 38 088 | 48 48 179 | 43 36 228 | 18 52 278 | 35 24 307 | 51 40 335 |
| 298 | 25 10 041 | 38 16 089 | 48 48 181 | 43 07 229 | 18 14 279 | 34 54 308 | 51 24 335 |
| 299 | 25 35 042 | 38 55 090 | 48 47 182 | 42 37 230 | 17 36 279 | 34 23 308 | 51 08 335 |
| | CAPELLA | ◆Alpheratz | Enif | ALTAIR | ◆Rasalhague | Alphecca | ◆Kochab |
| 300 | 12 25 028 | 39 33 090 | 44 28 143 | 48 45 184 | 42 07 232 | 34 59 271 | 50 52 335 |
| 301 | 12 44 029 | 40 12 091 | 44 51 144 | 48 42 185 | 41 37 233 | 34 20 272 | 50 36 335 |
| 302 | 13 02 029 | 40 51 092 | 45 13 146 | 48 37 187 | 41 06 234 | 33 42 273 | 50 19 335 |
| 303 | 13 21 030 | 41 29 093 | 45 34 147 | 48 32 188 | 40 35 235 | 33 03 274 | 50 03 335 |
| 304 | 13 41 031 | 42 08 094 | 45 55 148 | 48 26 190 | 40 03 236 | 32 25 274 | 49 47 335 |
| 305 | 14 01 031 | 42 46 094 | 46 15 150 | 48 19 191 | 39 31 237 | 31 46 275 | 49 31 336 |
| 306 | 14 21 032 | 43 25 095 | 46 34 151 | 48 11 193 | 38 58 238 | 31 08 276 | 49 15 336 |
| 307 | 14 41 032 | 44 03 096 | 46 52 152 | 48 02 194 | 38 25 239 | 30 30 276 | 48 59 336 |
| 308 | 15 02 033 | 44 41 097 | 47 09 154 | 47 52 196 | 37 52 240 | 29 51 277 | 48 44 336 |
| 309 | 15 23 034 | 45 19 098 | 47 26 155 | 47 41 197 | 37 18 241 | 29 13 278 | 48 28 336 |
| 310 | 15 45 034 | 45 58 099 | 47 42 157 | 47 29 199 | 36 44 242 | 28 35 279 | 48 12 336 |
| 311 | 16 07 035 | 46 36 099 | 47 57 158 | 47 16 200 | 36 10 243 | 27 57 279 | 47 56 336 |
| 312 | 16 29 036 | 47 14 100 | 48 11 159 | 47 03 201 | 35 36 244 | 27 19 280 | 47 41 336 |
| 313 | 16 52 036 | 47 52 101 | 48 24 161 | 46 48 203 | 35 01 245 | 26 41 281 | 47 25 336 |
| 314 | 17 15 037 | 48 29 102 | 48 36 162 | 46 33 204 | 34 26 246 | 26 03 281 | 47 10 336 |
| | CAPELLA | ◆Hamal | Alpheratz | Enif | ◆ALTAIR | VEGA | ◆Kochab |
| 315 | 17 38 037 | 26 14 084 | 49 07 103 | 48 47 164 | 46 16 206 | 62 17 260 | 46 55 337 |
| 316 | 18 01 038 | 26 52 085 | 49 45 104 | 48 57 165 | 45 58 207 | 61 39 261 | 46 39 337 |

**Fig. A6.1** Vol 1: Selected Stars.

# DECLINATION (0°-14°)

| LHA | 0° Hc | d | Z | 1° Hc | d | Z | 2° Hc | d | Z | 3° Hc | d | Z | 4° Hc | d | Z | 5° Hc | d | Z | 6° Hc | d | Z |
|---|---|---|---|---|---|---|---|---|---|---|---|---|---|---|---|---|---|---|---|---|---|
| 0 | 40 00 | +60 | 180 | 41 00 | +60 | 180 | 42 00 | +60 | 180 | 43 00 | +60 | 180 | 44 00 | +60 | 180 | 45 00 | +60 | 180 | 46 00 | +60 | 180 |
| 1 | 40 00 | 60 | 179 | 41 00 | 60 | 179 | 42 00 | 60 | 179 | 43 00 | 60 | 179 | 44 00 | 60 | 179 | 45 00 | 60 | 179 | 46 00 | 60 | 179 |
| 2 | 39 58 | 60 | 177 | 40 58 | 60 | 177 | 41 58 | 60 | 177 | 42 58 | 60 | 177 | 43 58 | 60 | 177 | 44 58 | 60 | 177 | 45 58 | 60 | 177 |
| 3 | 39 56 | 60 | 176 | 40 56 | 60 | 176 | 41 56 | 60 | 176 | 42 56 | 60 | 176 | 43 56 | 60 | 176 | 44 56 | 60 | 176 | 45 56 | 60 | 176 |
| 4 | 39 53 | 60 | 175 | 40 53 | 60 | 175 | 41 53 | 60 | 175 | 42 53 | 60 | 175 | 43 53 | 59 | 175 | 44 52 | 60 | 174 | 45 52 | 60 | 174 |
| 5 | 39 49 | +60 | 174 | 40 49 | +60 | 173 | 41 49 | +60 | 173 | 42 49 | +59 | 173 | 43 48 | +60 | 173 | 44 48 | +60 | 173 | 45 48 | +60 | 173 |
| 6 | 39 44 | 60 | 172 | 40 44 | 60 | 172 | 41 44 | 59 | 172 | 42 44 | 59 | 172 | 43 43 | 60 | 172 | 44 43 | 60 | 172 | 45 43 | 59 | 171 |
| 7 | 39 39 | 59 | 171 | 40 38 | 60 | 171 | 41 38 | 60 | 171 | 42 38 | 59 | 171 | 43 37 | 60 | 170 | 44 37 | 60 | 170 | 45 37 | 59 | 170 |
| 8 | 39 32 | 60 | 170 | 40 32 | 59 | 170 | 41 31 | 60 | 169 | 42 31 | 59 | 169 | 43 30 | 60 | 169 | 44 30 | 59 | 169 | 45 29 | 60 | 169 |
| 9 | 39 25 | 59 | 168 | 40 24 | 60 | 168 | 41 24 | 59 | 168 | 42 23 | 60 | 168 | 43 23 | 59 | 168 | 44 22 | 59 | 167 | 45 21 | 60 | 167 |
| 10 | 39 16 | +60 | 167 | 40 16 | +59 | 167 | 41 15 | +59 | 167 | 42 14 | +60 | 167 | 43 14 | +59 | 166 | 44 13 | +59 | 166 | 45 12 | +59 | 166 |
| 11 | 39 07 | 60 | 166 | 40 07 | 59 | 166 | 41 06 | 59 | 165 | 42 05 | 59 | 165 | 43 04 | 59 | 165 | 44 03 | 59 | 165 | 45 02 | 59 | 164 |
| 12 | 38 57 | 60 | 165 | 39 57 | 59 | 164 | 40 56 | 59 | 164 | 41 55 | 59 | 164 | 42 54 | 59 | 164 | 43 53 | 59 | 163 | 44 52 | 59 | 163 |
| 13 | 38 47 | 59 | 163 | 39 46 | 59 | 163 | 40 45 | 59 | 163 | 41 44 | 58 | 163 | 42 42 | 59 | 162 | 43 41 | 59 | 162 | 44 40 | 59 | 162 |
| 14 | 38 35 | 59 | 162 | 39 34 | 59 | 162 | 40 33 | 58 | 161 | 41 31 | 59 | 161 | 42 30 | 59 | 161 | 43 29 | 58 | 161 | 44 27 | 59 | 160 |
| 15 | 38 23 | +59 | 161 | 39 22 | +59 | 160 | 40 20 | +59 | 160 | 41 19 | +58 | 160 | 42 17 | +59 | 160 | 43 16 | +58 | 159 | 44 14 | +58 | 159 |
| 16 | 38 10 | 58 | 160 | 39 08 | 59 | 159 | 40 07 | 58 | 159 | 41 05 | 58 | 159 | 42 03 | 58 | 158 | 43 01 | 59 | 158 | 44 00 | 58 | 158 |
| 17 | 37 56 | 58 | 158 | 38 54 | 58 | 158 | 39 52 | 58 | 158 | 40 50 | 57 | 157 | 41 49 | 58 | 157 | 42 47 | 57 | 156 | 43 45 | 57 | 156 |
| 18 | 37 41 | 58 | 157 | 38 39 | 58 | 157 | 39 37 | 58 | 156 | 40 35 | 58 | 156 | 41 33 | 58 | 156 | 42 31 | 58 | 155 | 43 29 | 57 | 155 |
| 19 | 37 26 | 58 | 156 | 38 24 | 57 | 156 | 39 21 | 58 | 155 | 40 19 | 58 | 155 | 41 17 | 57 | 154 | 42 14 | 58 | 154 | 43 12 | 57 | 154 |
| 20 | 37 10 | +57 | 155 | 38 07 | +58 | 154 | 39 05 | +57 | 154 | 40 02 | +58 | 154 | 41 00 | +57 | 153 | 41 57 | +57 | 153 | 42 54 | +58 | 152 |
| 21 | 36 53 | 57 | 153 | 37 50 | 57 | 153 | 38 47 | 57 | 153 | 39 45 | 57 | 152 | 40 42 | 57 | 152 | 41 39 | 57 | 152 | 42 36 | 57 | 151 |
| 22 | 36 35 | 57 | 152 | 37 32 | 57 | 152 | 38 29 | 57 | 151 | 39 26 | 57 | 151 | 40 23 | 57 | 151 | 41 20 | 57 | 150 | 42 17 | 57 | 150 |
| 23 | 36 17 | 57 | 151 | 37 14 | 57 | 151 | 38 11 | 56 | 150 | 39 07 | 57 | 150 | 40 04 | 57 | 149 | 41 01 | 56 | 149 | 41 57 | 57 | 149 |
| 24 | 35 58 | 56 | 150 | 36 54 | 57 | 149 | 37 51 | 56 | 149 | 38 48 | 56 | 149 | 39 44 | 56 | 148 | 40 40 | 57 | 148 | 41 37 | 56 | 147 |
| 25 | 35 38 | +56 | 149 | 36 34 | +57 | 148 | 37 31 | +56 | 148 | 38 27 | +56 | 147 | 39 23 | +57 | 147 | 40 20 | +56 | 147 | 41 16 | +55 | 146 |
| 26 | 35 18 | 56 | 148 | 36 14 | 56 | 147 | 37 10 | 56 | 147 | 38 06 | 56 | 146 | 39 02 | 56 | 146 | 39 58 | 56 | 145 | 40 54 | 55 | 145 |
| 27 | 34 56 | 57 | 146 | 35 53 | 56 | 146 | 36 48 | 56 | 146 | 37 44 | 56 | 145 | 38 40 | 56 | 145 | 39 36 | 55 | 144 | 40 31 | 56 | 144 |
| 28 | 34 35 | 56 | 145 | 35 31 | 55 | 145 | 36 26 | 56 | 144 | 37 22 | 55 | 144 | 38 17 | 56 | 143 | 39 13 | 55 | 143 | 40 08 | 55 | 142 |
| 29 | 34 13 | 55 | 144 | 35 08 | 55 | 144 | 36 03 | 56 | 143 | 36 59 | 55 | 143 | 37 54 | 55 | 142 | 38 49 | 55 | 142 | 39 44 | 55 | 141 |
| 30 | 33 50 | +55 | 143 | 34 45 | +55 | 143 | 35 40 | +55 | 142 | 36 35 | +55 | 142 | 37 30 | +55 | 141 | 38 25 | +54 | 141 | 39 19 | +55 | 140 |
| 31 | 33 26 | 55 | 142 | 34 21 | 55 | 141 | 35 16 | 55 | 141 | 36 11 | 54 | 140 | 37 05 | 55 | 140 | 38 00 | 54 | 139 | 38 54 | 55 | 139 |
| 32 | 33 02 | 55 | 141 | 33 57 | 54 | 140 | 34 51 | 55 | 140 | 35 46 | 54 | 139 | 36 40 | 55 | 139 | 37 35 | 54 | 138 | 38 29 | 54 | 138 |
| 33 | 32 37 | 55 | 140 | 33 32 | 54 | 139 | 34 26 | 55 | 139 | 35 21 | 54 | 138 | 36 15 | 54 | 138 | 37 09 | 53 | 137 | 38 02 | 54 | 137 |
| 34 | 32 12 | 54 | 139 | 33 06 | 55 | 138 | 34 01 | 54 | 138 | 34 55 | 53 | 137 | 35 48 | 54 | 137 | 36 42 | 54 | 136 | 37 36 | 53 | 135 |
| 35 | 31 46 | +54 | 138 | 32 40 | +54 | 137 | 33 34 | +54 | 137 | 34 28 | +54 | 136 | 35 22 | +53 | 135 | 36 15 | +53 | 135 | 37 08 | +53 | 134 |
| 36 | 31 20 | 54 | 137 | 32 14 | 54 | 136 | 33 07 | 54 | 136 | 34 01 | 54 | 135 | 34 54 | 53 | 134 | 35 47 | 53 | 134 | 36 40 | 53 | 133 |
| 37 | 30 53 | 54 | 136 | 31 47 | 53 | 135 | 32 40 | 53 | 134 | 33 33 | 53 | 134 | 34 26 | 53 | 133 | 35 19 | 53 | 133 | 36 12 | 53 | 132 |
| 38 | 30 26 | 53 | 134 | 31 19 | 54 | 134 | 32 12 | 53 | 133 | 33 05 | 53 | 133 | 33 58 | 53 | 132 | 34 51 | 52 | 132 | 35 43 | 53 | 131 |
| 39 | 29 58 | 53 | 133 | 30 51 | 53 | 133 | 31 44 | 53 | 132 | 32 37 | 52 | 132 | 33 29 | 53 | 131 | 34 22 | 52 | 131 | 35 14 | 52 | 130 |
| 40 | 29 30 | +53 | 132 | 30 23 | +52 | 132 | 31 15 | +53 | 131 | 32 08 | +52 | 131 | 33 00 | +52 | 130 | 33 52 | +52 | 130 | 34 44 | +52 | 129 |
| 41 | 29 01 | 53 | 131 | 29 54 | 52 | 131 | 30 46 | 52 | 130 | 31 38 | 52 | 130 | 32 30 | 52 | 129 | 33 22 | 52 | 129 | 34 14 | 51 | 128 |
| 42 | 28 32 | 52 | 130 | 29 24 | 52 | 130 | 30 16 | 52 | 129 | 31 08 | 52 | 129 | 32 00 | 52 | 128 | 32 52 | 51 | 128 | 33 43 | 52 | 127 |
| 43 | 28 03 | 52 | 129 | 28 55 | 51 | 129 | 29 46 | 52 | 128 | 30 38 | 51 | 128 | 31 30 | 51 | 127 | 32 21 | 51 | 127 | 33 12 | 51 | 126 |
| 44 | 27 33 | 51 | 128 | 28 24 | 52 | 128 | 29 16 | 51 | 127 | 30 07 | 52 | 127 | 30 59 | 51 | 126 | 31 50 | 51 | 126 | 32 41 | 51 | 125 |
| 45 | 27 02 | +52 | 128 | 27 54 | +51 | 127 | 28 45 | +51 | 126 | 29 36 | +51 | 126 | 30 27 | +51 | 125 | 31 18 | +51 | 125 | 32 09 | +50 | 124 |
| 46 | 26 31 | 52 | 127 | 27 23 | 51 | 126 | 28 14 | 51 | 125 | 29 05 | 51 | 125 | 29 56 | 50 | 124 | 30 46 | 51 | 124 | 31 37 | 50 | 123 |
| 47 | 26 00 | 51 | 126 | 26 51 | 51 | 125 | 27 42 | 51 | 124 | 28 33 | 50 | 124 | 29 23 | 51 | 123 | 30 14 | 50 | 123 | 31 04 | 50 | 122 |
| 48 | 25 29 | 50 | 125 | 26 19 | 51 | 124 | 27 10 | 50 | 123 | 28 01 | 50 | 123 | 28 51 | 50 | 122 | 29 41 | 50 | 122 | 30 31 | 50 | 121 |
| 49 | 24 57 | 50 | 124 | 25 47 | 51 | 124 | 26 38 | 50 | 123 | 27 28 | 50 | 122 | 28 18 | 50 | 121 | 29 08 | 50 | 121 | 29 58 | 50 | 120 |
| 50 | 24 24 | +51 | 123 | 25 15 | +50 | 122 | 26 05 | +50 | 122 | 26 55 | +50 | 121 | 27 45 | +50 | 120 | 28 35 | +49 | 120 | 29 24 | +50 | 119 |
| 51 | 23 52 | 50 | 122 | 24 42 | 50 | 122 | 25 32 | 50 | 121 | 26 22 | 50 | 120 | 27 12 | 49 | 119 | 28 01 | 49 | 119 | 28 50 | 50 | 118 |
| 52 | 23 19 | 50 | 121 | 24 09 | 50 | 120 | 24 59 | 49 | 120 | 25 48 | 50 | 119 | 26 38 | 49 | 118 | 27 27 | 49 | 118 | 28 16 | 49 | 117 |
| 53 | 22 46 | 49 | 120 | 23 35 | 50 | 120 | 24 25 | 49 | 119 | 25 14 | 50 | 119 | 26 04 | 49 | 118 | 26 53 | 49 | 117 | 27 42 | 49 | 116 |
| 54 | 22 12 | 50 | 119 | 23 02 | 49 | 119 | 23 51 | 49 | 118 | 24 40 | 49 | 117 | 25 29 | 49 | 117 | 26 18 | 49 | 116 | 27 07 | 49 | 115 |
| 55 | 21 38 | +50 | 118 | 22 28 | +49 | 118 | 23 17 | +49 | 117 | 24 06 | +49 | 116 | 24 55 | +49 | 116 | 25 44 | +48 | 115 | 26 32 | +49 | 114 |
| 56 | 21 04 | 49 | 117 | 21 53 | 49 | 117 | 22 42 | 49 | 116 | 23 31 | 49 | 116 | 24 20 | 48 | 115 | 25 08 | 49 | 114 | 25 57 | 48 | 114 |
| 57 | 20 30 | 49 | 116 | 21 19 | 48 | 116 | 22 07 | 49 | 115 | 22 56 | 49 | 115 | 23 45 | 48 | 114 | 24 33 | 48 | 113 | 25 21 | 48 | 113 |
| 58 | 19 55 | 49 | 115 | 20 44 | 48 | 115 | 21 32 | 49 | 114 | 22 21 | 48 | 114 | 23 09 | 49 | 113 | 23 58 | 48 | 112 | 24 46 | 48 | 112 |
| 59 | 19 20 | 49 | 115 | 20 09 | 48 | 114 | 20 57 | 49 | 114 | 21 46 | 48 | 113 | 22 34 | 48 | 112 | 23 22 | 48 | 112 | 24 10 | 48 | 111 |
| 60 | 18 45 | +48 | 114 | 19 33 | +49 | 113 | 20 22 | +48 | 113 | 21 10 | +48 | 112 | 21 58 | +49 | 111 | 22 46 | +48 | 111 | 23 34 | +47 | 110 |
| 61 | 18 09 | 49 | 113 | 18 58 | 48 | 112 | 19 46 | 48 | 112 | 20 34 | 48 | 111 | 21 22 | 48 | 111 | 22 10 | 47 | 110 | 22 57 | 48 | 109 |
| 62 | 17 34 | 48 | 112 | 18 22 | 48 | 112 | 19 10 | 48 | 111 | 19 58 | 48 | 110 | 20 46 | 47 | 110 | 21 33 | 48 | 109 | 22 21 | 47 | 108 |
| 63 | 16 58 | 48 | 111 | 17 46 | 48 | 111 | 18 34 | 47 | 110 | 19 22 | 47 | 109 | 20 09 | 48 | 109 | 20 57 | 47 | 108 | 21 44 | 47 | 108 |
| 64 | 16 22 | 48 | 111 | 17 10 | 48 | 110 | 17 58 | 47 | 109 | 18 45 | 48 | 109 | 19 33 | 47 | 108 | 20 20 | 47 | 107 | 21 07 | 47 | 107 |
| 65 | 15 46 | +48 | 110 | 16 34 | +47 | 109 | 17 21 | +48 | 108 | 18 09 | +47 | 108 | 18 56 | +47 | 107 | 19 43 | +47 | 106 | 20 30 | +47 | 106 |
| 66 | 15 09 | 48 | 109 | 15 57 | 47 | 108 | 16 44 | 48 | 108 | 17 32 | 47 | 107 | 18 19 | 47 | 106 | 19 06 | 47 | 106 | 19 53 | 46 | 105 |
| 67 | 14 33 | 47 | 108 | 15 20 | 48 | 107 | 16 08 | 47 | 107 | 16 55 | 46 | 106 | 17 42 | 47 | 105 | 18 29 | 47 | 105 | 19 16 | 46 | 104 |
| 68 | 13 56 | 47 | 107 | 14 43 | 48 | 107 | 15 31 | 47 | 106 | 16 18 | 47 | 105 | 17 05 | 46 | 105 | 17 51 | 47 | 104 | 18 38 | 47 | 103 |
| 69 | 13 19 | 47 | 106 | 14 06 | 47 | 106 | 14 53 | 47 | 105 | 15 40 | 47 | 105 | 16 27 | 47 | 104 | 17 14 | 47 | 103 | 18 01 | 46 | 103 |

# DECLINATION (0°-14°)

**Fig. A6.2** Extracts from Vol. 3.

SAME NAME AS LATITUDE                                           LAT 50°

LAT 50°

| 7° Hc d Z | 8° Hc d Z | 9° Hc d Z | 10° Hc d Z | 11° Hc d Z | 12° Hc d Z | 13° Hc d Z | 14° Hc d Z | LHA |
|---|---|---|---|---|---|---|---|---|
| 47 00 +60 180 | 48 00 +60 180 | 49 00 +60 180 | 50 00 +60 180 | 51 00 +60 180 | 52 00 +60 180 | 53 00 +60 180 | 54 00 +60 180 | 360 |
| 47 00 60 179 | 48 00 60 179 | 49 00 60 179 | 50 00 60 179 | 51 00 60 178 | 52 00 60 178 | 53 00 59 178 | 53 59 60 178 | 359 |
| 46 58 60 177 | 47 58 60 177 | 48 58 60 177 | 49 58 60 177 | 50 58 60 177 | 51 58 60 177 | 52 58 60 177 | 53 58 60 177 | 358 |
| 46 56 60 176 | 47 56 60 176 | 48 55 60 175 | 49 55 60 175 | 50 55 60 175 | 51 55 60 175 | 52 55 60 175 | 53 55 60 175 | 357 |
| 46 52 60 174 | 47 52 60 174 | 48 52 60 174 | 49 52 60 174 | 50 52 60 174 | 51 52 59 174 | 52 51 60 174 | 53 51 60 173 | 356 |
| 46 48 +60 173 | 47 48 +59 173 | 48 47 +60 173 | 49 47 +60 172 | 50 47 +60 172 | 51 47 +59 172 | 52 46 +60 172 | 53 46 +60 172 | 355 |
| 46 42 60 171 | 47 42 60 171 | 48 42 60 171 | 49 42 59 171 | 50 41 60 171 | 51 41 60 171 | 52 41 59 170 | 53 40 60 170 | 354 |
| 46 36 60 170 | 47 36 59 170 | 48 35 60 170 | 49 35 59 169 | 50 34 60 169 | 51 34 60 169 | 52 34 59 169 | 53 33 59 169 | 353 |
| 46 29 58 168 | 47 28 60 168 | 48 28 59 168 | 49 27 60 168 | 50 27 59 168 | 51 26 59 167 | 52 25 60 167 | 53 25 59 167 | 352 |
| 46 21 59 167 | 47 20 59 167 | 48 19 60 167 | 49 19 59 166 | 50 18 59 166 | 51 17 59 166 | 52 16 59 166 | 53 16 59 165 | 351 |
| 46 12 +59 166 | 47 11 59 165 | 48 10 +59 165 | 49 09 +59 165 | 50 08 +59 165 | 51 07 +59 164 | 52 06 +59 164 | 53 05 +59 164 | 350 |
| 46 01 60 164 | 47 01 59 164 | 48 00 59 164 | 48 59 58 163 | 49 57 59 163 | 50 56 59 163 | 51 55 59 163 | 52 54 59 162 | 349 |
| 45 51 58 163 | 46 49 59 163 | 47 48 59 162 | 48 47 59 162 | 49 46 58 162 | 50 44 59 161 | 51 43 59 161 | 52 42 58 161 | 348 |
| 45 39 58 161 | 46 37 59 161 | 47 36 59 161 | 48 35 58 160 | 49 33 59 160 | 50 32 58 160 | 51 30 59 159 | 52 28 58 159 | 347 |
| 45 26 58 160 | 46 24 59 160 | 47 23 58 159 | 48 21 59 159 | 49 20 59 159 | 50 19 58 158 | 51 17 58 158 | 52 14 59 158 | 346 |
| 45 12 +59 159 | 46 11 +58 158 | 47 09 +58 158 | 48 07 +58 158 | 49 05 +58 157 | 50 03 +58 157 | 51 01 +58 156 | 51 59 +57 156 | 345 |
| 44 58 58 157 | 45 56 58 157 | 46 54 58 157 | 47 52 58 156 | 48 50 57 156 | 49 47 58 155 | 50 45 57 155 | 51 42 58 154 | 344 |
| 44 42 58 156 | 45 40 58 156 | 46 38 58 155 | 47 36 57 155 | 48 33 58 154 | 49 31 57 154 | 50 28 57 153 | 51 25 58 153 | 343 |
| 44 26 58 155 | 45 24 57 154 | 46 21 58 154 | 47 19 57 153 | 48 16 57 153 | 49 13 57 152 | 50 10 57 152 | 51 07 57 152 | 342 |
| 44 09 58 153 | 45 07 57 153 | 46 04 57 152 | 47 01 57 152 | 47 58 57 152 | 48 55 57 151 | 49 52 57 151 | 50 49 56 150 | 341 |
| 43 52 +57 152 | 44 49 +57 152 | 45 46 +57 151 | 46 43 +56 151 | 47 39 +57 150 | 48 36 +56 150 | 49 32 +57 149 | 50 29 +56 149 | 340 |
| 43 33 57 151 | 44 30 57 150 | 45 27 56 150 | 46 23 57 149 | 47 20 56 149 | 48 16 56 148 | 49 12 56 148 | 50 08 56 147 | 339 |
| 43 14 56 149 | 44 10 57 149 | 45 07 56 148 | 46 03 56 148 | 46 59 56 147 | 47 55 56 147 | 48 51 56 146 | 49 47 56 146 | 338 |
| 42 54 56 148 | 43 50 56 148 | 44 46 56 147 | 45 42 56 147 | 46 38 56 146 | 47 34 55 146 | 48 29 56 145 | 49 25 55 144 | 337 |
| 42 33 56 147 | 43 29 56 146 | 44 25 56 146 | 45 21 56 145 | 46 16 56 145 | 47 12 55 144 | 48 07 55 144 | 49 02 55 143 | 336 |
| 42 11 +56 146 | 43 07 +56 145 | 44 03 +55 145 | 44 58 +56 144 | 45 54 +55 143 | 46 49 +55 143 | 47 44 +54 142 | 48 38 +55 142 | 335 |
| 41 49 56 144 | 42 45 55 144 | 43 40 55 143 | 44 35 55 143 | 45 30 55 142 | 46 25 55 142 | 47 20 54 141 | 48 14 54 140 | 334 |
| 41 26 56 143 | 42 22 55 143 | 43 17 54 142 | 44 11 55 141 | 45 06 55 141 | 46 01 54 140 | 46 55 54 140 | 47 49 54 139 | 333 |
| 41 03 55 142 | 41 58 55 141 | 42 53 54 141 | 43 47 55 140 | 44 42 54 140 | 45 36 54 139 | 46 30 54 138 | 47 24 53 138 | 332 |
| 40 39 54 141 | 41 33 55 140 | 42 28 54 140 | 43 22 54 139 | 44 16 54 138 | 45 10 54 138 | 46 04 53 137 | 46 57 54 136 | 331 |
| 40 14 +54 140 | 41 08 +54 139 | 42 02 +54 138 | 42 56 +54 138 | 43 50 +54 137 | 44 44 +53 137 | 45 37 +53 136 | 46 30 +53 135 | 330 |
| 39 49 54 138 | 40 43 54 138 | 41 37 53 137 | 42 30 54 137 | 43 24 53 136 | 44 17 53 135 | 45 10 53 135 | 46 03 53 134 | 329 |
| 39 23 53 137 | 40 16 54 137 | 41 10 53 136 | 42 03 54 135 | 42 57 53 135 | 43 50 52 134 | 44 42 53 133 | 45 35 52 133 | 328 |
| 38 56 53 136 | 39 50 53 135 | 40 43 53 135 | 41 36 53 134 | 42 29 53 134 | 43 22 52 133 | 44 14 52 132 | 45 06 52 132 | 327 |
| 38 29 53 135 | 39 22 53 134 | 40 15 53 134 | 41 08 53 133 | 42 01 52 132 | 42 53 52 132 | 43 45 52 131 | 44 37 52 130 | 326 |
| 38 01 +53 134 | 38 54 +53 133 | 39 47 +53 133 | 40 40 +52 130 | 41 32 +52 131 | 42 24 +52 131 | 43 16 +52 131 | 44 08 +51 129 | 325 |
| 37 33 53 133 | 38 26 52 132 | 39 18 52 131 | 40 11 52 131 | 41 03 52 130 | 41 55 51 129 | 42 46 51 129 | 43 37 51 128 | 324 |
| 37 05 52 132 | 37 57 52 131 | 38 49 52 130 | 39 41 52 130 | 40 33 51 129 | 41 24 51 128 | 42 16 51 128 | 43 07 51 127 | 323 |
| 36 36 52 130 | 37 28 52 130 | 38 20 51 129 | 39 11 52 129 | 40 03 51 128 | 40 54 51 127 | 41 45 51 127 | 42 36 50 126 | 322 |
| 36 06 52 129 | 36 58 51 129 | 37 49 52 128 | 38 41 51 127 | 39 32 51 127 | 40 23 51 126 | 41 14 50 125 | 42 04 50 125 | 321 |
| 35 36 +52 128 | 36 27 +52 128 | 37 19 +51 127 | 38 10 +51 126 | 39 01 +51 126 | 39 52 +50 125 | 40 42 +50 124 | 41 32 +50 124 | 320 |
| 35 05 52 127 | 35 57 51 127 | 36 48 51 126 | 37 39 50 125 | 38 29 51 125 | 39 20 50 124 | 40 10 50 123 | 41 00 49 123 | 319 |
| 34 35 51 126 | 35 26 50 126 | 36 16 51 125 | 37 07 50 124 | 37 57 51 124 | 38 48 50 123 | 39 38 49 122 | 40 27 50 121 | 318 |
| 34 03 51 125 | 34 54 51 125 | 35 45 50 124 | 36 35 50 123 | 37 25 50 123 | 38 15 50 122 | 39 05 49 121 | 39 54 49 120 | 317 |
| 33 32 50 124 | 34 22 50 124 | 35 12 51 123 | 36 03 50 122 | 36 52 50 122 | 37 42 50 121 | 38 31 49 120 | 39 21 49 119 | 316 |
| 32 59 +51 123 | 33 50 +50 123 | 34 40 +50 122 | 35 30 +49 121 | 36 19 +50 121 | 37 09 +49 120 | 37 58 +49 119 | 38 47 +48 118 | 315 |
| 32 27 50 122 | 33 17 50 122 | 34 07 50 121 | 34 57 49 120 | 35 46 49 120 | 36 35 49 119 | 37 24 49 118 | 38 13 48 117 | 314 |
| 31 54 50 121 | 32 44 50 121 | 33 34 49 120 | 34 23 49 119 | 35 12 49 119 | 36 01 49 118 | 36 50 48 117 | 37 38 49 116 | 313 |
| 31 21 50 120 | 32 11 49 120 | 33 00 49 119 | 33 49 49 118 | 34 38 49 118 | 35 27 48 117 | 36 15 49 116 | 37 04 48 115 | 312 |
| 30 48 49 119 | 31 37 49 119 | 32 26 49 118 | 33 15 49 117 | 34 04 48 117 | 34 52 49 116 | 35 41 48 115 | 36 29 47 114 | 311 |
| 30 14 +49 118 | 31 03 +49 118 | 31 52 +49 117 | 32 41 +48 116 | 33 29 +49 116 | 34 18 +48 115 | 35 06 +47 114 | 35 53 +48 113 | 310 |
| 29 40 49 117 | 30 29 48 117 | 31 17 49 116 | 32 06 48 115 | 32 54 48 115 | 33 42 48 114 | 34 30 47 113 | 35 18 47 113 | 309 |
| 29 05 49 117 | 29 54 48 116 | 30 43 48 115 | 31 31 48 114 | 32 19 48 114 | 33 07 48 113 | 33 55 47 112 | 34 42 47 112 | 308 |
| 28 31 48 116 | 29 19 49 115 | 30 08 48 114 | 30 56 48 114 | 31 44 48 113 | 32 32 47 112 | 33 19 47 111 | 34 06 47 111 | 307 |
| 27 56 48 114 | 28 44 48 114 | 29 32 48 113 | 30 20 48 112 | 31 08 48 112 | 31 56 47 111 | 32 43 47 111 | 33 30 47 110 | 306 |
| 27 21 +48 114 | 28 09 +48 113 | 28 57 +48 112 | 29 45 +47 112 | 30 32 +48 111 | 31 20 +47 110 | 32 07 +47 110 | 32 54 +46 109 | 305 |
| 26 45 48 113 | 27 33 48 112 | 28 21 48 112 | 29 09 47 111 | 29 56 47 110 | 30 43 47 109 | 31 30 47 109 | 32 17 46 108 | 304 |
| 26 09 48 112 | 26 57 48 111 | 27 45 48 111 | 28 33 47 110 | 29 20 47 109 | 30 07 47 109 | 30 54 46 108 | 31 40 46 107 | 303 |
| 25 34 47 111 | 26 21 48 110 | 27 09 47 110 | 27 56 47 109 | 28 43 47 108 | 29 30 47 108 | 30 17 46 107 | 31 03 46 106 | 302 |
| 24 58 47 110 | 25 45 47 110 | 26 32 47 109 | 27 20 47 108 | 28 07 46 108 | 28 53 47 107 | 29 40 46 106 | 30 26 46 105 | 301 |
| 24 21 +48 109 | 25 09 +47 109 | 25 56 +47 108 | 26 43 +47 107 | 27 30 +46 107 | 28 16 +47 106 | 29 03 +46 105 | 29 49 +46 104 | 300 |
| 23 45 47 109 | 24 32 47 108 | 25 19 47 107 | 26 06 47 106 | 26 53 46 106 | 27 39 46 105 | 28 25 46 104 | 29 11 46 103 | 299 |
| 23 08 47 108 | 23 55 47 107 | 24 42 47 106 | 25 29 46 106 | 26 15 47 105 | 27 02 46 104 | 27 48 46 104 | 28 34 46 103 | 298 |
| 22 31 47 107 | 23 18 47 106 | 24 05 47 105 | 24 52 46 105 | 25 38 46 104 | 26 24 46 103 | 27 10 46 103 | 27 56 46 102 | 297 |
| 21 54 47 106 | 22 41 47 105 | 23 28 46 105 | 24 14 47 104 | 25 01 46 103 | 25 47 46 103 | 26 33 45 102 | 27 18 46 101 | 296 |
| 21 17 +47 105 | 22 04 +46 104 | 22 50 +47 104 | 23 37 +46 103 | 24 23 +46 102 | 25 09 +46 102 | 25 55 +45 101 | 26 40 +46 100 | 295 |
| 20 40 47 104 | 21 26 47 104 | 22 13 46 103 | 22 59 46 102 | 23 45 46 102 | 24 31 46 101 | 25 17 45 100 | 26 02 46 99 | 294 |
| 20 02 47 104 | 20 49 46 103 | 21 35 46 102 | 22 21 46 101 | 23 07 46 101 | 23 53 46 100 | 24 39 45 99 | 25 24 46 99 | 293 |
| 19 25 46 103 | 20 11 46 102 | 20 57 47 101 | 21 44 46 101 | 22 30 46 100 | 23 15 46 99 | 24 01 45 99 | 24 46 45 98 | 292 |
| 18 47 46 102 | 19 33 47 101 | 20 20 46 101 | 21 06 45 100 | 21 51 46 99 | 22 37 46 98 | 23 23 45 98 | 24 08 45 97 | 291 |

| 7° | 8° | 9° | 10° | 11° | 12° | 13° | 14° | |

SAME NAME AS LATITUDE

N. Lat. {LHA greater than 180°........ Zn=Z
{LHA less than 180°...... Zn=360−Z

## DECLINATION (0°-14°)

| LHA | 0° Hc | d | Z | 1° Hc | d | Z | 2° Hc | d | Z | 3° Hc | d | Z | 4° Hc | d | Z | 5° Hc | d | Z | 6° Hc | d | Z |
|---|---|---|---|---|---|---|---|---|---|---|---|---|---|---|---|---|---|---|---|---|---|
| 70 | 12 42 | +47 | 106 | 13 29 | +47 | 105 | 14 16 | +47 | 104 | 15 03 | +47 | 104 | 15 50 | +46 | 103 | 16 36 | +47 | 102 | 17 23 | +46 | 102 |
| 71 | 12 05 | 47 | 105 | 12 52 | 47 | 104 | 13 39 | 46 | 104 | 14 25 | 47 | 103 | 15 12 | 47 | 102 | 15 59 | 46 | 102 | 16 45 | 46 | 101 |
| 72 | 11 27 | 47 | 104 | 12 14 | 47 | 103 | 13 01 | 47 | 103 | 13 48 | 46 | 102 | 14 34 | 47 | 101 | 15 21 | 46 | 101 | 16 07 | 46 | 100 |
| 73 | 10 50 | 47 | 103 | 11 37 | 46 | 103 | 12 23 | 47 | 102 | 13 10 | 46 | 101 | 13 56 | 47 | 101 | 14 43 | 46 | 100 | 15 29 | 46 | 99 |
| 74 | 10 12 | 47 | 102 | 10 59 | 47 | 102 | 11 46 | 46 | 101 | 12 32 | 47 | 101 | 13 19 | 46 | 100 | 14 05 | 46 | 99 | 14 51 | 46 | 99 |
| 75 | 09 35 | +46 | 102 | 10 21 | +47 | 101 | 11 08 | +46 | 100 | 11 54 | +46 | 100 | 12 40 | +47 | 99 | 13 27 | +46 | 98 | 14 13 | +46 | 98 |
| 76 | 08 57 | 46 | 101 | 09 43 | 47 | 100 | 10 30 | 46 | 100 | 11 16 | 46 | 99 | 12 02 | 47 | 98 | 12 49 | 46 | 98 | 13 35 | 46 | 97 |
| 77 | 08 19 | 46 | 100 | 09 05 | 47 | 99 | 09 52 | 46 | 99 | 10 38 | 46 | 98 | 11 24 | 46 | 97 | 12 10 | 46 | 97 | 12 56 | 46 | 96 |
| 78 | 07 41 | 46 | 99 | 08 27 | 46 | 99 | 09 13 | 47 | 98 | 10 00 | 46 | 97 | 10 46 | 46 | 97 | 11 32 | 46 | 96 | 12 18 | 46 | 95 |
| 79 | 07 03 | 46 | 99 | 07 49 | 46 | 98 | 08 35 | 46 | 97 | 09 21 | 47 | 97 | 10 08 | 46 | 96 | 10 54 | 45 | 95 | 11 39 | 46 | 95 |
| 80 | 06 25 | +46 | 98 | 07 11 | +46 | 97 | 07 57 | +46 | 96 | 08 43 | +46 | 96 | 09 29 | +46 | 95 | 10 15 | +46 | 95 | 11 01 | +46 | 94 |
| 81 | 05 46 | 46 | 97 | 06 32 | 47 | 96 | 07 19 | 46 | 96 | 08 05 | 46 | 95 | 08 51 | 46 | 94 | 09 37 | 46 | 94 | 10 23 | 45 | 93 |
| 82 | 05 08 | 46 | 96 | 05 54 | 46 | 96 | 06 40 | 46 | 95 | 07 26 | 46 | 94 | 08 12 | 46 | 94 | 08 58 | 46 | 93 | 09 44 | 46 | 92 |
| 83 | 04 30 | 46 | 95 | 05 16 | 46 | 95 | 06 02 | 46 | 94 | 06 48 | 46 | 93 | 07 34 | 46 | 93 | 08 20 | 45 | 92 | 09 05 | 46 | 92 |
| 84 | 03 51 | 46 | 95 | 04 37 | 46 | 94 | 05 23 | 46 | 93 | 06 09 | 46 | 93 | 06 55 | 46 | 92 | 07 41 | 46 | 91 | 08 27 | 46 | 91 |
| 85 | 03 13 | +46 | 94 | 03 59 | +46 | 93 | 04 45 | +46 | 93 | 05 31 | +46 | 92 | 06 17 | +45 | 91 | 07 02 | +46 | 91 | 07 48 | +46 | 90 |
| 86 | 02 34 | 46 | 93 | 03 20 | 46 | 92 | 04 06 | 46 | 92 | 04 52 | 46 | 91 | 05 38 | 46 | 91 | 06 24 | 46 | 90 | 07 10 | 45 | 89 |
| 87 | 01 56 | 46 | 92 | 02 42 | 46 | 92 | 03 28 | 46 | 91 | 04 14 | 45 | 90 | 04 59 | 46 | 90 | 05 45 | 46 | 89 | 06 31 | 46 | 88 |
| 88 | 01 17 | 46 | 92 | 02 03 | 46 | 91 | 02 49 | 46 | 90 | 03 35 | 46 | 90 | 04 21 | 46 | 89 | 05 07 | 46 | 88 | 05 53 | 45 | 88 |
| 89 | 00 39 | 46 | 91 | 01 25 | 45 | 90 | 02 10 | 46 | 89 | 02 56 | 46 | 89 | 03 42 | 46 | 88 | 04 28 | 46 | 88 | 05 14 | 46 | 87 |
| 90 | 00 00 | +46 | 90 | 00 46 | +46 | 89 | 01 32 | +46 | 89 | 02 18 | +46 | 88 | 03 04 | +46 | 87 | 03 50 | +46 | 87 | 04 36 | +45 | 86 |
| 91 | −0 39 | 46 | 89 | 00 07 | 46 | 89 | 00 53 | 46 | 88 | 01 39 | 46 | 87 | 02 25 | 46 | 87 | 03 11 | 46 | 86 | 03 57 | 46 | 85 |
| 92 | −1 17 | 46 | 88 | −0 31 | 46 | 88 | 00 15 | 46 | 87 | 01 01 | 46 | 87 | 01 47 | 46 | 86 | 02 33 | 46 | 85 | 03 19 | 46 | 85 |
| 93 | −1 56 | 46 | 88 | −1 10 | 46 | 87 | −0 24 | 46 | 86 | 00 22 | 46 | 86 | 01 08 | 46 | 85 | 01 54 | 46 | 84 | 02 40 | 46 | 84 |
| 94 | −2 34 | 46 | 87 | −1 48 | 46 | 86 | −1 02 | 46 | 86 | −0 16 | 46 | 85 | 00 30 | 46 | 85 | 01 16 | 46 | 84 | 02 02 | 46 | 83 |
| 95 | −3 13 | +46 | 86 | −2 27 | +46 | 86 | −1 41 | +46 | 85 | −0 55 | +47 | 84 | −0 08 | +46 | 84 | 00 38 | +46 | 83 | 01 24 | +46 | 82 |
| 96 | −3 51 | 46 | 85 | −3 05 | 46 | 85 | −2 19 | 46 | 84 | −1 33 | 46 | 83 | −0 47 | 46 | 83 | −0 01 | 47 | 82 | 00 46 | 46 | 82 |
| 97 | −4 30 | 47 | 85 | −3 43 | 46 | 84 | −2 57 | 46 | 83 | −2 11 | 46 | 83 | −1 25 | 46 | 82 | −0 39 | 46 | 81 | 00 07 | 47 | 81 |
| 98 | −5 08 | 46 | 84 | −4 22 | 46 | 83 | −3 36 | 46 | 82 | −2 49 | 46 | 82 | −2 03 | 46 | 81 | −1 17 | 46 | 81 | −0 31 | 47 | 80 |
| 99 | −5 46 | 46 | 83 | −5 00 | 46 | 82 | −4 14 | 46 | 82 | −3 28 | 46 | 81 | −2 41 | 46 | 81 | −1 55 | 46 | 80 | −1 09 | 47 | 79 |
| 100 | | | | −5 38 | +46 | 82 | −4 52 | +46 | 81 | −4 06 | +47 | 80 | −3 19 | +46 | 80 | −2 33 | +47 | 79 | −1 46 | +46 | 78 |
| 101 | | | | | | | −5 30 | 46 | 80 | −4 44 | 47 | 80 | −3 57 | 46 | 79 | −3 11 | 47 | 78 | −2 24 | 46 | 78 |
| 102 | | | | | | | −6 08 | 47 | 79 | −5 21 | 46 | 79 | −4 35 | 47 | 78 | −3 48 | 47 | 78 | −3 02 | 47 | 77 |
| 103 | | | | | | | | | | −5 59 | 46 | 78 | −5 13 | 47 | 77 | −4 26 | 47 | 77 | −3 39 | 47 | 76 |
| 104 | | | | | | | | | | | | | −5 50 | 47 | 77 | −5 03 | 46 | 76 | −4 17 | 47 | 75 |
| 105 | | | | | | | | | | | | | | | | −5 41 | +47 | 75 | −4 54 | +47 | 75 |
| 106 | | | | | | | | | | | | | | | | | | | −5 31 | 47 | 74 |
| 107 | | | | | | | | | | | | | | | | | | | −6 08 | 47 | 73 |

108

S. Lat. {LHA greater than 180°...... Zn=180−Z
{LHA less than 180°...... Zn=180+Z

| 0° | 1° | 2° | 3° | 4° | 5° | 6° |
|---|---|---|---|---|---|---|

## DECLINATION (0°-14°)

**Fig. A6.3** Extracts from Vol. 3.

SAME NAME AS LATITUDE

| 7° | | | 8° | | | 9° | | | 10° | | | 11° | | | 12° | | | 13° | | | 14° | | | |
|---|---|---|---|---|---|---|---|---|---|---|---|---|---|---|---|---|---|---|---|---|---|---|---|---|
| Hc | d | Z | Hc | d | Z | Hc | d | Z | Hc | d | Z | Hc | d | Z | Hc | d | Z | Hc | d | Z | Hc | d | Z | LHA |
| ° ′ | ′ | ° | ° ′ | ′ | ° | ° ′ | ′ | ° | ° ′ | ′ | ° | ° ′ | ′ | ° | ° ′ | ′ | ° | ° ′ | ′ | ° | ° ′ | ′ | ° | |
| 18 09 | +47 | 101 | 18 56 | +46 | 100 | 19 42 | +46 | 100 | 20 28 | +45 | 99 | 21 13 | +46 | 98 | 21 59 | +45 | 98 | 22 44 | +46 | 97 | 23 30 | +45 | 96 | 290 |
| 17 31 | 47 | 100 | 18 18 | 46 | 100 | 19 04 | 45 | 99 | 19 49 | 46 | 98 | 20 35 | 46 | 98 | 21 21 | 45 | 97 | 22 06 | 45 | 96 | 22 51 | 45 | 95 | 289 |
| 16 53 | 46 | 99 | 17 39 | 46 | 99 | 18 25 | 46 | 98 | 19 11 | 46 | 97 | 19 57 | 45 | 97 | 20 42 | 46 | 96 | 21 28 | 45 | 95 | 22 13 | 45 | 95 | 288 |
| 16 15 | 46 | 99 | 17 01 | 46 | 98 | 17 47 | 46 | 97 | 18 33 | 46 | 97 | 19 19 | 45 | 96 | 20 04 | 45 | 95 | 20 49 | 45 | 95 | 21 34 | 45 | 94 | 287 |
| 15 37 | 46 | 98 | 16 23 | 46 | 97 | 17 09 | 46 | 97 | 17 55 | 45 | 96 | 18 40 | 46 | 95 | 19 26 | 45 | 94 | 20 11 | 45 | 94 | 20 56 | 45 | 93 | 286 |
| 14 59 | +46 | 97 | 15 45 | +46 | 96 | 16 31 | +45 | 96 | 17 16 | +46 | 95 | 18 02 | +45 | 94 | 18 47 | +45 | 94 | 19 32 | +45 | 93 | 20 17 | +45 | 92 | 285 |
| 14 21 | 45 | 96 | 15 06 | 46 | 96 | 15 52 | 46 | 95 | 16 38 | 45 | 94 | 17 23 | 46 | 94 | 18 09 | 45 | 93 | 18 54 | 45 | 92 | 19 39 | 45 | 92 | 284 |
| 13 42 | 46 | 95 | 14 28 | 46 | 95 | 15 14 | 45 | 94 | 15 59 | 46 | 94 | 16 45 | 45 | 93 | 17 30 | 45 | 93 | 18 15 | 45 | 91 | 19 00 | 45 | 91 | 283 |
| 13 04 | 46 | 95 | 13 50 | 45 | 94 | 14 35 | 46 | 93 | 15 21 | 45 | 93 | 16 06 | 45 | 92 | 16 51 | 46 | 91 | 17 37 | 45 | 91 | 18 22 | 45 | 90 | 282 |
| 12 25 | 46 | 94 | 13 11 | 46 | 93 | 13 57 | 45 | 93 | 14 42 | 46 | 92 | 15 28 | 45 | 91 | 16 13 | 45 | 91 | 16 58 | 45 | 90 | 17 43 | 45 | 89 | 281 |
| 11 47 | +46 | 93 | 12 33 | +45 | 93 | 13 18 | +46 | 92 | 14 04 | +45 | 91 | 14 49 | +45 | 91 | 15 34 | +46 | 90 | 16 20 | +45 | 89 | 17 05 | +44 | 88 | 280 |
| 11 08 | 46 | 92 | 11 54 | 46 | 92 | 12 40 | 45 | 91 | 13 25 | 46 | 90 | 14 11 | 45 | 90 | 14 56 | 45 | 89 | 15 41 | 45 | 88 | 16 26 | 45 | 88 | 279 |
| 10 30 | 45 | 92 | 11 15 | 46 | 91 | 12 01 | 46 | 90 | 12 47 | 45 | 90 | 13 32 | 45 | 89 | 14 17 | 45 | 88 | 15 02 | 45 | 88 | 15 47 | 45 | 87 | 278 |
| 09 51 | 46 | 91 | 10 37 | 45 | 90 | 11 22 | 46 | 90 | 12 08 | 45 | 89 | 12 53 | 46 | 88 | 13 39 | 45 | 88 | 14 24 | 45 | 87 | 15 09 | 45 | 86 | 277 |
| 09 13 | 45 | 90 | 09 58 | 46 | 89 | 10 44 | 45 | 89 | 11 29 | 46 | 88 | 12 15 | 45 | 87 | 13 00 | 45 | 87 | 13 45 | 46 | 86 | 14 31 | 45 | 85 | 276 |
| 08 34 | +46 | 89 | 09 20 | +45 | 89 | 10 05 | +46 | 88 | 10 51 | +45 | 87 | 11 36 | +46 | 87 | 12 22 | +45 | 86 | 13 07 | +45 | 85 | 13 52 | +45 | 85 | 275 |
| 07 55 | 46 | 89 | 08 41 | 46 | 88 | 09 27 | 45 | 87 | 10 12 | 46 | 87 | 10 58 | 45 | 86 | 11 43 | 46 | 85 | 12 29 | 45 | 84 | 13 14 | 45 | 84 | 274 |
| 07 17 | 46 | 88 | 08 03 | 45 | 87 | 08 48 | 46 | 87 | 09 34 | 45 | 86 | 10 19 | 46 | 85 | 11 05 | 45 | 85 | 11 50 | 45 | 84 | 12 35 | 46 | 83 | 273 |
| 06 38 | 46 | 87 | 07 24 | 46 | 86 | 08 10 | 45 | 86 | 08 55 | 46 | 85 | 09 41 | 45 | 84 | 10 26 | 46 | 84 | 11 12 | 45 | 83 | 11 57 | 45 | 82 | 272 |
| 06 00 | 46 | 86 | 06 46 | 45 | 86 | 07 31 | 46 | 85 | 08 17 | 45 | 84 | 09 03 | 45 | 84 | 09 48 | 46 | 83 | 10 34 | 45 | 82 | 11 19 | 45 | 82 | 271 |
| 05 21 | +46 | 86 | 06 07 | +46 | 85 | 06 53 | +46 | 84 | 07 39 | +45 | 84 | 08 24 | +46 | 83 | 09 10 | +45 | 82 | 09 55 | +46 | 82 | 10 41 | +45 | 81 | 270 |
| 04 43 | 46 | 85 | 05 29 | 46 | 84 | 06 15 | 45 | 83 | 07 00 | 46 | 83 | 07 46 | 45 | 82 | 08 32 | 45 | 82 | 09 17 | 46 | 81 | 10 03 | 45 | 80 | 269 |
| 04 05 | 45 | 84 | 04 50 | 46 | 83 | 05 36 | 46 | 83 | 06 22 | 46 | 82 | 07 08 | 45 | 81 | 07 54 | 45 | 81 | 08 39 | 46 | 80 | 09 25 | 45 | 79 | 268 |
| 03 26 | 46 | 83 | 04 12 | 46 | 83 | 04 58 | 46 | 82 | 05 44 | 46 | 81 | 06 30 | 46 | 81 | 07 16 | 45 | 80 | 08 01 | 46 | 79 | 08 47 | 46 | 79 | 267 |
| 02 48 | 46 | 82 | 03 34 | 46 | 82 | 04 20 | 46 | 81 | 05 06 | 46 | 81 | 05 52 | 46 | 80 | 06 38 | 45 | 79 | 07 23 | 46 | 79 | 08 09 | 46 | 78 | 266 |
| 02 10 | +47 | 82 | 02 57 | +46 | 81 | 03 42 | +46 | 80 | 04 28 | +46 | 80 | 05 14 | +46 | 79 | 06 00 | +46 | 79 | 06 46 | +46 | 78 | 07 32 | +45 | 77 | 265 |
| 01 32 | 46 | 81 | 02 18 | 46 | 80 | 03 04 | 46 | 80 | 03 50 | 46 | 79 | 04 36 | 46 | 78 | 05 22 | 46 | 78 | 06 08 | 46 | 77 | 06 54 | 46 | 76 | 264 |
| 00 54 | 46 | 80 | 01 40 | 46 | 80 | 02 26 | 46 | 79 | 03 12 | 46 | 78 | 03 58 | 46 | 78 | 04 44 | 47 | 77 | 05 31 | 46 | 76 | 06 17 | 46 | 76 | 263 |
| 00 16 | 46 | 79 | 01 02 | 46 | 79 | 01 48 | 46 | 78 | 02 34 | 47 | 77 | 03 21 | 46 | 77 | 04 07 | 46 | 76 | 04 53 | 46 | 75 | 05 39 | 46 | 75 | 262 |
| −0 22 | 46 | 79 | 00 24 | 47 | 78 | 01 11 | 46 | 77 | 01 57 | 46 | 77 | 02 43 | 47 | 76 | 03 30 | 46 | 76 | 04 16 | 46 | 75 | 05 02 | 46 | 74 | 261 |
| −1 00 | +47 | 78 | −0 13 | +46 | 77 | 00 33 | +46 | 77 | 01 19 | +47 | 76 | 02 06 | +46 | 75 | 02 52 | +47 | 75 | 03 39 | +46 | 74 | 04 25 | +46 | 73 | 260 |
| −1 38 | 47 | 77 | −0 51 | 47 | 76 | −0 04 | 46 | 76 | 00 42 | 47 | 75 | 01 29 | 46 | 75 | 02 15 | 47 | 74 | 03 02 | 46 | 73 | 03 48 | 47 | 73 | 259 |
| −2 15 | 46 | 76 | −1 28 | 46 | 76 | −0 42 | 47 | 75 | 00 05 | 47 | 74 | 00 52 | 46 | 74 | 01 38 | 47 | 73 | 02 25 | 46 | 73 | 03 11 | 47 | 72 | 258 |
| −2 53 | 47 | 76 | −2 06 | 47 | 75 | −1 19 | 47 | 74 | −0 32 | 47 | 74 | 00 15 | 46 | 73 | 01 01 | 47 | 72 | 01 48 | 47 | 72 | 02 35 | 47 | 71 | 257 |
| −3 30 | 47 | 75 | −2 43 | 47 | 74 | −1 56 | 47 | 74 | −1 09 | 47 | 73 | −0 22 | 47 | 72 | 00 25 | 47 | 72 | 01 12 | 46 | 71 | 01 58 | 47 | 70 | 256 |
| −4 07 | +47 | 74 | −3 20 | +47 | 73 | −2 33 | +47 | 73 | −1 46 | +47 | 72 | −0 59 | +47 | 71 | −0 12 | +47 | 71 | 00 35 | +47 | 70 | 01 22 | +47 | 70 | 255 |
| −4 44 | 47 | 73 | −3 57 | 47 | 73 | −3 10 | 47 | 72 | −2 23 | 48 | 71 | −1 35 | 47 | 71 | −0 48 | 47 | 70 | −0 01 | 47 | 69 | 00 46 | 47 | 69 | 254 |
| −5 21 | 47 | 72 | −4 34 | 48 | 72 | −3 46 | 47 | 71 | −2 59 | 47 | 71 | −2 12 | 47 | 70 | −1 24 | 47 | 69 | −0 37 | 47 | 69 | 00 10 | 48 | 68 | 253 |
| −5 58 | 48 | 72 | −5 10 | 47 | 71 | −4 23 | 48 | 70 | −3 35 | 47 | 70 | −2 48 | 48 | 69 | −2 00 | 47 | 69 | −1 13 | 48 | 68 | −0 25 | 47 | 67 | 252 |
| | | 109 | −5 47 | 48 | 70 | −4 59 | 48 | 70 | −4 11 | 47 | 69 | −3 24 | 48 | 68 | −2 36 | 47 | 68 | −1 49 | 48 | 67 | −1 01 | 48 | 67 | 251 |
| | | | | | 110 | −5 35 | +48 | 69 | −4 47 | +47 | 68 | −4 00 | +48 | 68 | −3 12 | +48 | 67 | −2 24 | +48 | 66 | −1 36 | +48 | 66 | 250 |
| | | | | | 111 | −6 11 | 48 | 68 | −5 23 | 48 | 67 | −4 35 | 48 | 67 | −3 47 | 48 | 66 | −2 59 | 48 | 66 | −2 11 | 48 | 65 | 249 |
| | | | | | | | | 112 | −5 59 | 48 | 67 | −5 11 | 49 | 66 | −4 22 | 48 | 65 | −3 34 | 48 | 65 | −2 46 | 48 | 64 | 248 |
| | | | | | | | | | | | 113 | −5 46 | 49 | 65 | −4 57 | 48 | 65 | −4 09 | 48 | 64 | −3 21 | 49 | 63 | 247 |
| | | | | | | | | | | | | | | 114 | −5 32 | 48 | 64 | −4 44 | 49 | 63 | −3 55 | 49 | 63 | 246 |
| | | | | | | | | | | | | | | 115 | −6 07 | +49 | 63 | −5 18 | +49 | 62 | −4 29 | +48 | 62 | 245 |
| | | | | | | | | | | | | | | | | | 116 | −5 52 | 49 | 62 | −5 03 | 49 | 61 | 244 |
| | | | | | | | | | | | | | | | | | | | | 117 | −5 37 | 49 | 60 | 243 |

| 7° | 8° | 9° | 10° | 11° | 12° | 13° | 14° | LAT 50° |

SAME NAME AS LATITUDE LAT 50°

LAT 50°

N. Lat. { LHA greater than 180°...... Zn=Z / LHA less than 180°......... Zn=360—Z }

## DECLINATION (0°-14°)

| LHA | 0° Hc | d | Z | 1° Hc | d | Z | 2° Hc | d | Z | 3° Hc | d | Z | 4° Hc | d | Z | 5° Hc | d | Z | 6° Hc | d | Z |
|---|---|---|---|---|---|---|---|---|---|---|---|---|---|---|---|---|---|---|---|---|---|
| 69 | 13 19 | 47 | 106 | 12 32 | 48 | 107 | 11 44 | 47 | 108 | 10 57 | 47 | 108 | 10 10 | 48 | 109 | 09 22 | 48 | 110 | 08 34 | 47 | 110 |
| 68 | 13 56 | 47 | 107 | 13 09 | 48 | 108 | 12 21 | 47 | 109 | 11 34 | 48 | 109 | 10 46 | 48 | 110 | 09 58 | 48 | 110 | 09 10 | 47 | 111 |
| 67 | 14 33 | 48 | 108 | 13 45 | 47 | 109 | 12 58 | 48 | 109 | 12 10 | 48 | 110 | 11 22 | 48 | 111 | 10 34 | 48 | 111 | 09 46 | 48 | 112 |
| 66 | 15 09 | 47 | 109 | 14 22 | 48 | 110 | 13 34 | 48 | 110 | 12 46 | 48 | 111 | 11 58 | 48 | 111 | 11 10 | 48 | 112 | 10 22 | 48 | 113 |
| 65 | 15 46 | 48 | 110 | 14 58 | 48 | 110 | 14 10 | 48 | 111 | 13 22 | 48 | 112 | 12 34 | 48 | 112 | 11 46 | 48 | 113 | 10 58 | 49 | 113 |
| 64 | 16 22 | 48 | 111 | 15 34 | 48 | 111 | 14 46 | 48 | 112 | 13 58 | 48 | 112 | 13 10 | 49 | 113 | 12 21 | 48 | 114 | 11 33 | 49 | 114 |
| 63 | 16 58 | 48 | 111 | 16 10 | 48 | 112 | 15 22 | 49 | 113 | 14 33 | 48 | 113 | 13 45 | 49 | 114 | 12 56 | 48 | 114 | 12 08 | 49 | 115 |
| 62 | 17 34 | 48 | 112 | 16 46 | 49 | 113 | 15 57 | 48 | 113 | 15 09 | 49 | 114 | 14 20 | 49 | 115 | 13 32 | 49 | 115 | 12 43 | 49 | 116 |
| 61 | 18 09 | 48 | 113 | 17 21 | 48 | 114 | 16 33 | 49 | 114 | 15 44 | 49 | 115 | 14 55 | 49 | 116 | 14 06 | 49 | 116 | 13 17 | 49 | 117 |
| 60 | 18 45 | 49 | 114 | 17 56 | 48 | 115 | 17 08 | 49 | 115 | 16 19 | 49 | 116 | 15 30 | 49 | 116 | 14 41 | 49 | 117 | 13 52 | 50 | 118 |
| 59 | 19 20 | 49 | 115 | 18 31 | 49 | 115 | 17 42 | 49 | 116 | 16 53 | 49 | 117 | 16 04 | 49 | 117 | 15 15 | 49 | 118 | 14 26 | 50 | 118 |
| 58 | 19 55 | 49 | 116 | 19 06 | 49 | 116 | 18 17 | 49 | 117 | 17 28 | 50 | 117 | 16 38 | 49 | 119 | 15 49 | 49 | 119 | 15 00 | 50 | 119 |
| 57 | 20 30 | 50 | 116 | 19 40 | 49 | 117 | 18 51 | 49 | 118 | 18 02 | 50 | 118 | 17 12 | 49 | 119 | 16 23 | 50 | 119 | 15 33 | 50 | 120 |
| 56 | 21 04 | 49 | 117 | 20 15 | 50 | 118 | 19 25 | 49 | 119 | 18 36 | 50 | 119 | 17 46 | 50 | 120 | 16 56 | 50 | 120 | 16 06 | 50 | 121 |
| 55 | 21 38 | 49 | 118 | 20 49 | 50 | 119 | 19 59 | 50 | 119 | 19 09 | 50 | 120 | 18 19 | 50 | 121 | 17 29 | 50 | 121 | 16 39 | 50 | 121 |
| 54 | 22 12 | 50 | 119 | 21 22 | 50 | 120 | 20 32 | 50 | 120 | 19 42 | 50 | 121 | 18 52 | 50 | 122 | 18 02 | 50 | 122 | 17 12 | 50 | 123 |
| 53 | 22 46 | 50 | 120 | 21 56 | 50 | 121 | 21 06 | 51 | 121 | 20 15 | 50 | 122 | 19 25 | 50 | 122 | 18 35 | 51 | 123 | 17 44 | 50 | 124 |
| 52 | 23 19 | 50 | 121 | 22 29 | 51 | 122 | 21 38 | 50 | 122 | 20 48 | 50 | 123 | 19 58 | 51 | 123 | 19 07 | 51 | 124 | 18 16 | 51 | 124 |
| 51 | 23 52 | 51 | 122 | 23 01 | 50 | 122 | 22 11 | 51 | 123 | 21 20 | 50 | 124 | 20 30 | 51 | 124 | 19 39 | 51 | 125 | 18 48 | 51 | 125 |
| 50 | 24 24 | 50 | 123 | 23 34 | 51 | 123 | 22 43 | 51 | 124 | 21 52 | 51 | 125 | 21 01 | 51 | 125 | 20 10 | 51 | 126 | 19 19 | 51 | 126 |
| 49 | 24 57 | 51 | 124 | 24 06 | 51 | 124 | 23 15 | 51 | 125 | 22 24 | 51 | 126 | 21 33 | 51 | 126 | 20 42 | 52 | 127 | 19 50 | 51 | 127 |
| 48 | 25 29 | 51 | 125 | 24 38 | 52 | 125 | 23 46 | 51 | 126 | 22 55 | 51 | 126 | 22 04 | 52 | 127 | 21 12 | 51 | 127 | 20 21 | 52 | 128 |
| 47 | 26 00 | 51 | 126 | 25 09 | 51 | 126 | 24 18 | 52 | 127 | 23 26 | 52 | 127 | 22 34 | 51 | 128 | 21 43 | 52 | 128 | 20 51 | 52 | 129 |
| 46 | 26 31 | 51 | 127 | 25 40 | 52 | 127 | 24 48 | 51 | 128 | 23 57 | 52 | 128 | 23 05 | 52 | 129 | 22 13 | 52 | 129 | 21 21 | 52 | 130 |
| 45 | 27 02 | 52 | 128 | 26 10 | 51 | 128 | 25 19 | 52 | 129 | 24 27 | 52 | 129 | 23 35 | 53 | 130 | 22 42 | 52 | 130 | 21 50 | 52 | 131 |
| 44 | 27 33 | 52 | 128 | 26 41 | 52 | 129 | 25 49 | 53 | 130 | 24 56 | 52 | 130 | 24 04 | 52 | 131 | 23 12 | 53 | 131 | 22 19 | 52 | 132 |
| 43 | 28 03 | 53 | 129 | 27 10 | 52 | 130 | 26 18 | 52 | 131 | 25 26 | 53 | 131 | 24 33 | 52 | 132 | 23 41 | 53 | 132 | 22 48 | 53 | 133 |
| 42 | 28 32 | 52 | 130 | 27 40 | 53 | 131 | 26 47 | 52 | 132 | 25 55 | 53 | 132 | 25 02 | 53 | 133 | 24 09 | 53 | 133 | 23 16 | 53 | 134 |
| 41 | 29 01 | 52 | 131 | 28 09 | 53 | 132 | 27 16 | 53 | 133 | 26 23 | 53 | 133 | 25 30 | 54 | 134 | 24 37 | 53 | 134 | 23 44 | 54 | 135 |
| 40 | 29 30 | 53 | 132 | 28 37 | 53 | 133 | 27 44 | 53 | 134 | 26 51 | 53 | 134 | 25 58 | 54 | 135 | 25 04 | 53 | 135 | 24 11 | 54 | 136 |
| 39 | 29 58 | 53 | 133 | 29 05 | 53 | 134 | 28 12 | 54 | 135 | 27 18 | 53 | 135 | 26 25 | 54 | 136 | 25 31 | 54 | 136 | 24 38 | 54 | 137 |
| 38 | 30 26 | 54 | 134 | 29 33 | 54 | 135 | 28 39 | 53 | 136 | 27 46 | 54 | 136 | 26 52 | 54 | 137 | 25 58 | 54 | 137 | 25 04 | 54 | 138 |
| 37 | 30 53 | 53 | 136 | 30 00 | 54 | 136 | 29 06 | 54 | 137 | 28 12 | 54 | 137 | 27 18 | 54 | 138 | 26 24 | 54 | 138 | 25 30 | 54 | 139 |
| 36 | 31 20 | 54 | 137 | 30 26 | 54 | 137 | 29 32 | 54 | 138 | 28 38 | 54 | 138 | 27 44 | 54 | 139 | 26 50 | 55 | 139 | 25 55 | 54 | 140 |
| 35 | 31 46 | 54 | 138 | 30 52 | 54 | 138 | 29 58 | 54 | 139 | 29 04 | 54 | 139 | 28 09 | 54 | 140 | 27 15 | 54 | 140 | 26 20 | 55 | 141 |
| 34 | 32 12 | 54 | 139 | 31 18 | 55 | 139 | 30 23 | 54 | 140 | 29 29 | 55 | 140 | 28 34 | 55 | 141 | 27 39 | 55 | 141 | 26 44 | 55 | 142 |
| 33 | 32 37 | 54 | 140 | 31 43 | 55 | 140 | 30 48 | 55 | 141 | 29 53 | 55 | 141 | 28 58 | 55 | 142 | 28 03 | 55 | 142 | 27 08 | 55 | 143 |
| 32 | 33 02 | 55 | 141 | 32 07 | 55 | 141 | 31 12 | 55 | 142 | 30 17 | 55 | 142 | 29 22 | 55 | 143 | 28 27 | 56 | 143 | 27 31 | 55 | 144 |
| 31 | 33 26 | 55 | 142 | 32 31 | 55 | 142 | 31 36 | 56 | 143 | 30 40 | 55 | 143 | 29 45 | 56 | 144 | 28 49 | 55 | 144 | 27 54 | 56 | 145 |
| 30 | 33 50 | 56 | 143 | 32 54 | 55 | 144 | 31 59 | 56 | 144 | 31 03 | 55 | 144 | 30 08 | 56 | 145 | 29 12 | 56 | 145 | 28 16 | 56 | 146 |
| 29 | 34 13 | 56 | 144 | 33 17 | 56 | 145 | 32 21 | 56 | 145 | 31 25 | 56 | 145 | 30 29 | 56 | 146 | 29 33 | 56 | 146 | 28 37 | 56 | 147 |
| 28 | 34 35 | 56 | 145 | 33 39 | 56 | 146 | 32 43 | 56 | 146 | 31 47 | 56 | 147 | 30 51 | 56 | 147 | 29 55 | 57 | 147 | 28 58 | 56 | 148 |
| 27 | 34 56 | 56 | 146 | 34 00 | 56 | 147 | 33 04 | 56 | 147 | 32 08 | 56 | 148 | 31 12 | 57 | 148 | 30 15 | 56 | 148 | 29 19 | 57 | 149 |
| 26 | 35 18 | 57 | 148 | 34 21 | 56 | 148 | 33 25 | 57 | 148 | 32 28 | 56 | 149 | 31 32 | 57 | 149 | 30 35 | 57 | 150 | 29 38 | 57 | 150 |
| 25 | 35 38 | 57 | 149 | 34 41 | 56 | 149 | 33 45 | 57 | 150 | 32 48 | 57 | 150 | 31 51 | 57 | 150 | 30 54 | 57 | 151 | 29 57 | 57 | 151 |
| 24 | 35 58 | 57 | 150 | 35 01 | 57 | 150 | 34 04 | 57 | 151 | 33 07 | 57 | 151 | 32 10 | 57 | 151 | 31 13 | 57 | 152 | 30 16 | 58 | 152 |
| 23 | 36 17 | 57 | 151 | 35 20 | 57 | 151 | 34 22 | 57 | 152 | 33 25 | 57 | 152 | 32 28 | 57 | 153 | 31 31 | 58 | 153 | 30 33 | 57 | 153 |
| 22 | 36 35 | 57 | 152 | 35 38 | 58 | 153 | 34 40 | 57 | 153 | 33 43 | 57 | 153 | 32 46 | 58 | 154 | 31 48 | 58 | 154 | 30 50 | 57 | 154 |
| 21 | 36 53 | 58 | 153 | 35 55 | 57 | 154 | 34 58 | 58 | 154 | 34 00 | 58 | 154 | 33 02 | 57 | 155 | 32 05 | 58 | 155 | 31 07 | 58 | 155 |
| 20 | 37 10 | 58 | 155 | 36 12 | 58 | 155 | 35 14 | 58 | 155 | 34 16 | 58 | 156 | 33 18 | 57 | 156 | 32 21 | 58 | 156 | 31 23 | 58 | 157 |
| 19 | 37 26 | 58 | 156 | 36 28 | 58 | 156 | 35 30 | 58 | 156 | 34 32 | 58 | 157 | 33 34 | 58 | 157 | 32 36 | 58 | 157 | 31 38 | 59 | 158 |
| 18 | 37 41 | 58 | 157 | 36 43 | 58 | 157 | 35 45 | 58 | 158 | 34 47 | 59 | 158 | 33 48 | 58 | 158 | 32 50 | 58 | 159 | 31 52 | 58 | 159 |
| 17 | 37 56 | 58 | 158 | 36 58 | 59 | 159 | 35 59 | 58 | 159 | 35 01 | 59 | 159 | 34 02 | 58 | 159 | 33 04 | 59 | 160 | 32 05 | 58 | 160 |
| 16 | 38 10 | 59 | 160 | 37 11 | 58 | 160 | 36 13 | 59 | 160 | 35 14 | 59 | 160 | 34 16 | 59 | 161 | 33 17 | 59 | 161 | 32 18 | 58 | 161 |
| 15 | 38 23 | 59 | 161 | 37 24 | 58 | 161 | 36 26 | 59 | 161 | 35 27 | 59 | 162 | 34 28 | 59 | 162 | 33 29 | 58 | 162 | 32 31 | 59 | 162 |
| 14 | 38 35 | 59 | 162 | 37 36 | 59 | 162 | 36 38 | 59 | 163 | 35 39 | 59 | 163 | 34 40 | 59 | 163 | 33 41 | 59 | 163 | 32 42 | 59 | 163 |
| 13 | 38 47 | 59 | 163 | 37 48 | 59 | 164 | 36 49 | 59 | 164 | 35 50 | 59 | 164 | 34 51 | 59 | 164 | 33 52 | 59 | 164 | 32 53 | 60 | 165 |
| 12 | 38 57 | 59 | 165 | 37 58 | 59 | 165 | 36 59 | 59 | 165 | 36 00 | 59 | 165 | 35 01 | 59 | 165 | 34 02 | 60 | 166 | 33 02 | 59 | 166 |
| 11 | 39 07 | 59 | 166 | 38 08 | 59 | 166 | 37 09 | 59 | 166 | 36 10 | 60 | 166 | 35 10 | 59 | 167 | 34 11 | 59 | 167 | 33 12 | 60 | 167 |
| 10 | 39 16 | 59 | 167 | 38 17 | 59 | 168 | 37 18 | 60 | 167 | 36 18 | 59 | 168 | 35 19 | 60 | 168 | 34 19 | 59 | 168 | 33 20 | 60 | 168 |
| 9 | 39 25 | 60 | 168 | 38 25 | 59 | 169 | 37 26 | 60 | 169 | 36 26 | 60 | 169 | 35 27 | 60 | 169 | 34 27 | 59 | 169 | 33 28 | 60 | 169 |
| 8 | 39 32 | 60 | 170 | 38 32 | 59 | 170 | 37 33 | 60 | 170 | 36 33 | 59 | 170 | 35 34 | 60 | 170 | 34 34 | 60 | 170 | 33 34 | 59 | 170 |
| 7 | 39 39 | 60 | 171 | 38 39 | 60 | 171 | 37 39 | 59 | 171 | 36 40 | 60 | 171 | 35 40 | 60 | 171 | 34 40 | 60 | 172 | 33 40 | 59 | 172 |
| 6 | 39 44 | 59 | 172 | 38 45 | 60 | 172 | 37 45 | 60 | 172 | 36 45 | 60 | 173 | 35 45 | 60 | 173 | 34 45 | 59 | 173 | 33 46 | 60 | 173 |
| 5 | 39 49 | 60 | 174 | 38 49 | 60 | 174 | 37 49 | 59 | 174 | 36 50 | 60 | 174 | 35 50 | 60 | 174 | 34 50 | 60 | 174 | 33 50 | 60 | 174 |
| 4 | 39 53 | 60 | 175 | 38 53 | 60 | 175 | 37 53 | 60 | 175 | 36 53 | 60 | 175 | 35 53 | 59 | 175 | 34 54 | 60 | 175 | 33 54 | 60 | 175 |
| 3 | 39 56 | 60 | 176 | 38 56 | 60 | 176 | 37 56 | 60 | 176 | 36 56 | 60 | 176 | 35 56 | 60 | 176 | 34 56 | 60 | 176 | 33 56 | 60 | 176 |
| 2 | 39 58 | 60 | 177 | 38 58 | 60 | 177 | 37 58 | 60 | 178 | 36 58 | 60 | 178 | 35 58 | 60 | 178 | 34 58 | 60 | 178 | 33 58 | 60 | 178 |
| 1 | 40 00 | 60 | 179 | 39 00 | 60 | 179 | 38 00 | 60 | 179 | 37 00 | 60 | 179 | 36 00 | 60 | 179 | 35 00 | 60 | 179 | 34 00 | 60 | 179 |
| 0 | 40 00 | 60 | 180 | 39 00 | 60 | 180 | 38 00 | 60 | 180 | 37 00 | 60 | 180 | 36 00 | 60 | 180 | 35 00 | 60 | 180 | 34 00 | 60 | 180 |

S. Lat. { LHA greater than 180°...... Zn=180—Z / LHA less than 180°......... Zn=180+Z }

## DECLINATION (0°-14°)

**Fig. A6.4** Extracts from Vol. 3.

## CONTRARY NAME TO LATITUDE — LAT 50°

| 7° Hc | d | Z | 8° Hc | d | Z | 9° Hc | d | Z | 10° Hc | d | Z | 11° Hc | d | Z | 12° Hc | d | Z | 13° Hc | d | Z | 14° Hc | d | Z | LHA |
|---|---|---|---|---|---|---|---|---|---|---|---|---|---|---|---|---|---|---|---|---|---|---|---|---|
| 0747 | 48 | 111 | 0659 | 48 | 111 | 0611 | 48 | 112 | 0523 | 48 | 113 | 0435 | 48 | 113 | 0347 | 48 | 114 | 0259 | 48 | 114 | 0211 | 48 | 115 | 291 |
| 0823 | 48 | 112 | 0735 | 48 | 112 | 0647 | 48 | 113 | 0559 | 48 | 113 | 0511 | 49 | 114 | 0422 | 48 | 115 | 0334 | 48 | 115 | 0246 | 48 | 116 | 292 |
| 0858 | 48 | 112 | 0810 | 48 | 113 | 0722 | 48 | 114 | 0634 | 48 | 114 | 0546 | 49 | 115 | 0457 | 48 | 115 | 0409 | 48 | 116 | 0321 | 49 | 117 | 293 |
| 0934 | 48 | 113 | 0846 | 49 | 114 | 0757 | 48 | 114 | 0709 | 48 | 115 | 0621 | 49 | 116 | 0532 | 48 | 116 | 0444 | 49 | 117 | 0355 | 48 | 117 | 294 |
| 1009 | -48 | 114 | 0921 | -49 | 115 | 0832 | -48 | 115 | 0744 | -49 | 116 | 0655 | -48 | 116 | 0607 | -49 | 117 | 0518 | -49 | 118 | 0429 | -48 | 118 | 295 |
| 1044 | 48 | 115 | 0956 | 49 | 115 | 0907 | 49 | 116 | 0818 | 48 | 117 | 0730 | 49 | 117 | 0641 | 49 | 118 | 0552 | 49 | 118 | 0503 | 49 | 119 | 296 |
| 1119 | 48 | 116 | 1031 | 49 | 116 | 0942 | 49 | 117 | 0853 | 49 | 117 | 0804 | 49 | 118 | 0715 | 49 | 119 | 0626 | 49 | 119 | 0537 | 49 | 120 | 297 |
| 1154 | 49 | 116 | 1105 | 49 | 117 | 1016 | 49 | 118 | 0927 | 49 | 118 | 0838 | 49 | 119 | 0749 | 49 | 119 | 0700 | 50 | 120 | 0610 | 49 | 121 | 298 |
| 1228 | 49 | 117 | 1139 | 49 | 118 | 1050 | 49 | 118 | 1001 | 49 | 119 | 0912 | 50 | 120 | 0822 | 49 | 120 | 0733 | 50 | 121 | 0643 | 49 | 121 | 299 |
| 1302 | -49 | 118 | 1213 | -49 | 119 | 1124 | -50 | 119 | 1034 | -49 | 120 | 0945 | -50 | 120 | 0855 | -49 | 121 | 0806 | -50 | 122 | 0716 | -50 | 122 | 300 |
| 1336 | 49 | 119 | 1247 | 50 | 120 | 1157 | 49 | 120 | 1108 | 50 | 121 | 1018 | 50 | 121 | 0928 | 49 | 122 | 0839 | 50 | 122 | 0749 | 50 | 123 | 301 |
| 1410 | 50 | 120 | 1320 | 49 | 120 | 1231 | 50 | 121 | 1141 | 50 | 122 | 1051 | 50 | 122 | 1001 | 50 | 123 | 0911 | 50 | 123 | 0821 | 50 | 124 | 302 |
| 1443 | 50 | 121 | 1353 | 49 | 121 | 1304 | 50 | 122 | 1214 | 51 | 122 | 1123 | 50 | 123 | 1033 | 50 | 123 | 0943 | 50 | 124 | 0853 | 50 | 125 | 303 |
| 1516 | 50 | 122 | 1426 | 50 | 122 | 1336 | 50 | 123 | 1246 | 50 | 123 | 1156 | 51 | 124 | 1105 | 50 | 124 | 1015 | 51 | 125 | 0924 | 50 | 125 | 304 |
| 1549 | -50 | 122 | 1459 | -50 | 123 | 1409 | -51 | 124 | 1318 | -50 | 124 | 1228 | -51 | 125 | 1137 | -51 | 125 | 1046 | -50 | 126 | 0956 | -51 | 126 | 305 |
| 1622 | 51 | 123 | 1531 | 51 | 124 | 1441 | 51 | 124 | 1350 | 51 | 125 | 1259 | 51 | 125 | 1208 | 50 | 126 | 1118 | 51 | 127 | 1027 | 51 | 127 | 306 |
| 1654 | 51 | 124 | 1603 | 51 | 125 | 1512 | 51 | 125 | 1421 | 51 | 126 | 1330 | 51 | 126 | 1239 | 51 | 127 | 1148 | 51 | 127 | 1057 | 51 | 128 | 307 |
| 1725 | 50 | 125 | 1635 | 51 | 126 | 1544 | 51 | 126 | 1453 | 52 | 127 | 1401 | 51 | 127 | 1310 | 51 | 128 | 1219 | 51 | 128 | 1128 | 52 | 129 | 308 |
| 1757 | 51 | 126 | 1706 | 51 | 126 | 1615 | 52 | 127 | 1523 | 51 | 128 | 1432 | 51 | 128 | 1341 | 52 | 129 | 1249 | 52 | 129 | 1157 | 51 | 130 | 309 |
| 1828 | -51 | 127 | 1737 | -52 | 127 | 1645 | -51 | 128 | 1554 | -52 | 128 | 1502 | -51 | 129 | 1411 | -52 | 129 | 1319 | -52 | 130 | 1227 | -52 | 130 | 310 |
| 1859 | 52 | 128 | 1807 | 51 | 129 | 1716 | 52 | 129 | 1624 | 52 | 129 | 1532 | 52 | 130 | 1440 | 52 | 130 | 1348 | 52 | 131 | 1256 | 52 | 131 | 311 |
| 1929 | 52 | 129 | 1837 | 52 | 129 | 1745 | 51 | 130 | 1654 | 52 | 130 | 1601 | 51 | 131 | 1509 | 52 | 131 | 1417 | 52 | 132 | 1325 | 52 | 132 | 312 |
| 1959 | 52 | 129 | 1907 | 52 | 130 | 1815 | 52 | 131 | 1723 | 52 | 131 | 1631 | 53 | 132 | 1538 | 52 | 132 | 1446 | 53 | 133 | 1353 | 52 | 133 | 313 |
| 2029 | 53 | 130 | 1936 | 52 | 131 | 1844 | 53 | 131 | 1752 | 53 | 132 | 1659 | 52 | 132 | 1607 | 53 | 133 | 1514 | 53 | 133 | 1421 | 53 | 134 | 314 |
| 2058 | -53 | 131 | 2005 | -52 | 132 | 1913 | -53 | 132 | 1820 | -52 | 133 | 1728 | -53 | 133 | 1635 | -53 | 134 | 1542 | -53 | 134 | 1449 | -53 | 135 | 315 |
| 2127 | 53 | 132 | 2034 | 53 | 133 | 1941 | 53 | 133 | 1848 | 53 | 134 | 1755 | 53 | 134 | 1702 | 53 | 135 | 1609 | 53 | 135 | 1516 | 53 | 136 | 316 |
| 2155 | 53 | 133 | 2102 | 53 | 134 | 2009 | 53 | 134 | 1916 | 53 | 135 | 1823 | 53 | 135 | 1730 | 54 | 136 | 1636 | 53 | 136 | 1543 | 54 | 137 | 317 |
| 2223 | 54 | 134 | 2130 | 53 | 135 | 2037 | 54 | 135 | 1943 | 53 | 136 | 1850 | 54 | 136 | 1756 | 53 | 137 | 1703 | 54 | 137 | 1609 | 54 | 138 | 318 |
| 2250 | 53 | 135 | 2157 | 54 | 136 | 2104 | 54 | 136 | 2010 | 54 | 137 | 1916 | 53 | 137 | 1823 | 54 | 138 | 1729 | 54 | 138 | 1635 | 54 | 138 | 319 |
| 2317 | -53 | 136 | 2224 | -54 | 137 | 2130 | -54 | 137 | 2036 | -54 | 137 | 1942 | -54 | 138 | 1848 | -54 | 138 | 1754 | -54 | 139 | 1700 | -54 | 139 | 320 |
| 2344 | 54 | 137 | 2250 | 54 | 138 | 2156 | 54 | 138 | 2102 | 54 | 138 | 2008 | 54 | 139 | 1914 | 54 | 139 | 1820 | 55 | 140 | 1725 | 54 | 140 | 321 |
| 2410 | 54 | 138 | 2316 | 54 | 139 | 2222 | 54 | 139 | 2127 | 54 | 139 | 2033 | 54 | 140 | 1939 | 55 | 140 | 1844 | 54 | 141 | 1750 | 55 | 141 | 322 |
| 2436 | 55 | 139 | 2341 | 54 | 139 | 2247 | 55 | 140 | 2152 | 54 | 140 | 2058 | 55 | 141 | 2003 | 55 | 141 | 1908 | 54 | 142 | 1814 | 55 | 142 | 323 |
| 2501 | 55 | 140 | 2406 | 55 | 140 | 2311 | 55 | 141 | 2217 | 55 | 141 | 2122 | 55 | 142 | 2027 | 55 | 142 | 1932 | 55 | 143 | 1837 | 55 | 143 | 324 |
| 2525 | -55 | 141 | 2430 | -54 | 141 | 2336 | -55 | 142 | 2241 | -55 | 142 | 2146 | -56 | 143 | 2050 | -55 | 143 | 1955 | -55 | 144 | 1900 | -55 | 144 | 325 |
| 2549 | 55 | 142 | 2454 | 55 | 142 | 2359 | 55 | 143 | 2304 | 55 | 143 | 2209 | 56 | 144 | 2113 | 55 | 144 | 2018 | 55 | 145 | 1923 | 56 | 145 | 326 |
| 2613 | 55 | 143 | 2518 | 56 | 143 | 2422 | 55 | 144 | 2327 | 56 | 144 | 2231 | 55 | 145 | 2136 | 56 | 145 | 2040 | 56 | 145 | 1944 | 55 | 146 | 327 |
| 2636 | 56 | 144 | 2540 | 55 | 144 | 2445 | 56 | 145 | 2349 | 56 | 145 | 2253 | 56 | 146 | 2158 | 56 | 146 | 2102 | 56 | 146 | 2006 | 56 | 147 | 328 |
| 2658 | 56 | 145 | 2602 | 55 | 145 | 2507 | 56 | 146 | 2411 | 56 | 146 | 2315 | 56 | 147 | 2219 | 56 | 147 | 2123 | 56 | 147 | 2027 | 56 | 148 | 329 |
| 2720 | -56 | 146 | 2624 | -56 | 146 | 2528 | -56 | 147 | 2432 | -56 | 147 | 2336 | -56 | 148 | 2240 | -57 | 148 | 2143 | -56 | 148 | 2047 | -56 | 149 | 330 |
| 2741 | 56 | 147 | 2645 | 56 | 148 | 2549 | 56 | 148 | 2453 | 57 | 148 | 2356 | 56 | 149 | 2300 | 57 | 149 | 2203 | 56 | 149 | 2107 | 57 | 150 | 331 |
| 2802 | 56 | 148 | 2706 | 57 | 149 | 2609 | 56 | 149 | 2513 | 57 | 149 | 2416 | 57 | 150 | 2319 | 56 | 150 | 2223 | 57 | 150 | 2126 | 57 | 151 | 332 |
| 2822 | 57 | 149 | 2725 | 56 | 150 | 2629 | 57 | 150 | 2532 | 57 | 150 | 2435 | 57 | 151 | 2338 | 57 | 151 | 2241 | 57 | 151 | 2144 | 57 | 152 | 333 |
| 2841 | 56 | 150 | 2745 | 57 | 151 | 2648 | 57 | 151 | 2551 | 57 | 151 | 2454 | 57 | 152 | 2357 | 57 | 152 | 2300 | 58 | 152 | 2202 | 57 | 153 | 334 |
| 2900 | -57 | 151 | 2803 | -57 | 152 | 2706 | -57 | 152 | 2609 | -57 | 152 | 2512 | -58 | 153 | 2414 | -57 | 153 | 2317 | -57 | 153 | 2220 | -58 | 154 | 335 |
| 2918 | 57 | 152 | 2821 | 57 | 153 | 2724 | 58 | 153 | 2626 | 57 | 153 | 2529 | 57 | 154 | 2432 | 58 | 154 | 2334 | 57 | 154 | 2237 | 58 | 155 | 336 |
| 2936 | 57 | 154 | 2839 | 58 | 154 | 2741 | 58 | 154 | 2643 | 57 | 155 | 2546 | 58 | 155 | 2448 | 57 | 155 | 2351 | 58 | 155 | 2253 | 58 | 156 | 337 |
| 2953 | 58 | 155 | 2855 | 58 | 155 | 2757 | 57 | 155 | 2700 | 58 | 156 | 2602 | 58 | 156 | 2504 | 58 | 156 | 2406 | 58 | 156 | 2308 | 57 | 157 | 338 |
| 3009 | 58 | 156 | 2911 | 58 | 156 | 2813 | 58 | 156 | 2715 | 58 | 157 | 2617 | 58 | 157 | 2519 | 58 | 157 | 2421 | 58 | 158 | 2323 | 58 | 158 | 339 |
| 3025 | -58 | 157 | 2927 | -59 | 157 | 2828 | -58 | 157 | 2730 | -58 | 158 | 2632 | -58 | 158 | 2534 | -58 | 158 | 2436 | -58 | 159 | 2338 | -59 | 159 | 340 |
| 3039 | 58 | 158 | 2941 | 58 | 159 | 2843 | 58 | 159 | 2745 | 59 | 159 | 2646 | 58 | 159 | 2548 | 58 | 159 | 2450 | 59 | 160 | 2351 | 58 | 160 | 341 |
| 3054 | 59 | 159 | 2955 | 58 | 159 | 2857 | 59 | 160 | 2758 | 58 | 160 | 2700 | 59 | 160 | 2601 | 59 | 160 | 2503 | 59 | 161 | 2404 | 59 | 161 | 342 |
| 3107 | 59 | 160 | 3008 | 58 | 160 | 2910 | 59 | 161 | 2811 | 58 | 161 | 2713 | 59 | 161 | 2614 | 59 | 161 | 2515 | 58 | 162 | 2417 | 59 | 162 | 343 |
| 3120 | 59 | 161 | 3021 | 59 | 162 | 2922 | 59 | 162 | 2823 | 58 | 162 | 2725 | 59 | 162 | 2626 | 59 | 162 | 2527 | 59 | 163 | 2428 | 59 | 163 | 344 |
| 3132 | -59 | 163 | 3033 | -59 | 163 | 2934 | -59 | 163 | 2835 | -59 | 163 | 2736 | -59 | 163 | 2637 | -59 | 164 | 2538 | -59 | 164 | 2439 | -59 | 164 | 345 |
| 3143 | 59 | 164 | 3044 | 59 | 164 | 2945 | 59 | 164 | 2846 | 59 | 164 | 2747 | 59 | 164 | 2648 | 59 | 165 | 2549 | 59 | 165 | 2450 | 60 | 165 | 346 |
| 3153 | 59 | 165 | 3054 | 59 | 165 | 2955 | 59 | 165 | 2856 | 59 | 165 | 2757 | 59 | 166 | 2658 | 60 | 166 | 2558 | 59 | 166 | 2459 | 59 | 166 | 347 |
| 3203 | 59 | 166 | 3104 | 59 | 166 | 3005 | 60 | 166 | 2905 | 59 | 166 | 2806 | 60 | 167 | 2707 | 60 | 167 | 2607 | 59 | 167 | 2508 | 59 | 167 | 348 |
| 3212 | 59 | 167 | 3113 | 60 | 167 | 3013 | 59 | 167 | 2914 | 60 | 168 | 2815 | 60 | 168 | 2715 | 60 | 168 | 2616 | 60 | 168 | 2516 | 59 | 168 | 349 |
| 3220 | -59 | 168 | 3121 | -59 | 168 | 3021 | -59 | 169 | 2922 | -60 | 169 | 2822 | -59 | 169 | 2723 | -60 | 169 | 2623 | -59 | 169 | 2524 | -60 | 169 | 350 |
| 3228 | 60 | 169 | 3128 | 59 | 170 | 3029 | 60 | 170 | 2929 | 59 | 170 | 2830 | 60 | 170 | 2730 | 60 | 170 | 2630 | 59 | 170 | 2531 | 60 | 170 | 351 |
| 3235 | 60 | 171 | 3135 | 60 | 171 | 3035 | 59 | 171 | 2936 | 60 | 171 | 2836 | 60 | 171 | 2736 | 59 | 171 | 2637 | 60 | 171 | 2537 | 60 | 171 | 352 |
| 3241 | 60 | 172 | 3141 | 60 | 172 | 3041 | 60 | 172 | 2941 | 59 | 172 | 2842 | 60 | 172 | 2742 | 60 | 172 | 2642 | 60 | 172 | 2542 | 59 | 173 | 353 |
| 3246 | 60 | 173 | 3146 | 60 | 173 | 3046 | 60 | 173 | 2946 | 60 | 173 | 2846 | 60 | 173 | 2747 | 60 | 173 | 2647 | 60 | 173 | 2547 | 60 | 174 | 354 |
| 3250 | -60 | 174 | 3150 | -60 | 174 | 3050 | -60 | 174 | 2950 | -59 | 174 | 2851 | -60 | 174 | 2751 | -60 | 175 | 2651 | -60 | 175 | 2551 | -60 | 175 | 355 |
| 3254 | 60 | 175 | 3154 | 60 | 175 | 3054 | 60 | 175 | 2954 | 60 | 176 | 2854 | 60 | 176 | 2754 | 60 | 176 | 2654 | 60 | 176 | 2554 | 60 | 176 | 356 |
| 3256 | 60 | 177 | 3157 | 60 | 177 | 3057 | 60 | 177 | 2957 | 60 | 177 | 2857 | 60 | 177 | 2757 | 60 | 177 | 2657 | 60 | 177 | 2557 | 60 | 177 | 357 |
| 3258 | 60 | 178 | 3158 | 60 | 178 | 3058 | 60 | 178 | 2959 | 60 | 178 | 2859 | 60 | 178 | 2759 | 60 | 178 | 2659 | 60 | 178 | 2559 | 60 | 178 | 358 |
| 3300 | 60 | 179 | 3200 | 60 | 179 | 3100 | 60 | 179 | 3000 | 60 | 179 | 2900 | 60 | 179 | 2800 | 60 | 179 | 2700 | 60 | 179 | 2600 | 60 | 179 | 359 |
| 3300 | 60 | 180 | 3200 | 60 | 180 | 3100 | 60 | 180 | 3000 | 60 | 180 | 2900 | -60 | 180 | 2800 | -60 | 180 | 2700 | -60 | 180 | 2600 | 60 | 180 | 360 |

| 7° | 8° | 9° | 10° | 11° | 12° | 13° | 14° | |
|---|---|---|---|---|---|---|---|---|

CONTRARY NAME TO LATITUDE — LAT 50°

N. Lat. {LHA greater than 180°....... Zn=Z / LHA less than 180°......... Zn=360−Z}

## DECLINATION (15°–29°)

| LHA | 15° Hc | d | Z | 16° Hc | d | Z | 17° Hc | d | Z | 18° Hc | d | Z | 19° Hc | d | Z | 20° Hc | d | Z | 21° Hc | d | Z |
|---|---|---|---|---|---|---|---|---|---|---|---|---|---|---|---|---|---|---|---|---|---|
| 69 | 01 23 | 48 | 116 | 00 35 | 48 | 116 | −0 13 | 48 | 117 | −1 01 | 48 | 117 | −1 49 | 48 | 118 | −2 37 | 48 | 119 | −3 25 | 48 | 119 |
| 68 | 01 58 | 48 | 116 | 01 10 | 48 | 117 | 00 22 | 49 | 118 | −0 27 | 48 | 118 | −1 15 | 48 | 119 | −2 03 | 48 | 119 | −2 51 | 48 | 120 |
| 67 | 02 32 | 48 | 117 | 01 44 | 48 | 118 | 00 56 | 49 | 118 | 00 07 | 48 | 119 | −0 41 | 48 | 119 | −1 29 | 49 | 120 | −2 18 | 48 | 121 |
| 66 | 03 07 | 49 | 118 | 02 18 | 48 | 118 | 01 30 | 49 | 119 | 00 41 | 49 | 120 | −0 08 | 48 | 120 | −0 56 | 49 | 121 | −1 45 | 48 | 121 |
| 65 | 03 41 | −49 | 119 | 02 52 | −49 | 119 | 02 03 | −49 | 120 | 01 14 | −48 | 120 | 00 26 | −49 | 121 | −0 23 | −49 | 122 | −1 12 | −49 | 121 |
| 64 | 04 14 | 49 | 119 | 03 25 | 49 | 120 | 02 36 | 48 | 121 | 01 48 | 49 | 121 | 00 59 | 49 | 122 | 00 10 | 49 | 122 | −0 39 | 49 | 123 |
| 63 | 04 48 | 49 | 120 | 03 59 | 49 | 121 | 03 10 | 50 | 121 | 02 20 | 49 | 122 | 01 31 | 49 | 123 | 00 42 | 49 | 123 | −0 07 | 49 | 124 |
| 62 | 05 21 | 49 | 121 | 04 32 | 50 | 122 | 03 42 | 49 | 122 | 02 53 | 49 | 123 | 02 04 | 50 | 123 | 01 14 | 49 | 124 | 00 25 | 50 | 124 |
| 61 | 05 54 | 50 | 122 | 05 04 | 49 | 122 | 04 15 | 50 | 123 | 03 25 | 49 | 124 | 02 36 | 50 | 124 | 01 46 | 50 | 125 | 00 56 | 49 | 125 |
| 60 | 06 26 | −49 | 123 | 05 37 | −50 | 123 | 04 47 | −50 | 124 | 03 57 | −50 | 124 | 03 07 | −49 | 125 | 02 18 | −50 | 125 | 01 28 | −50 | 126 |
| 59 | 06 59 | 50 | 124 | 06 09 | 50 | 124 | 05 19 | 50 | 125 | 04 29 | 50 | 125 | 03 39 | 50 | 126 | 02 49 | 50 | 126 | 01 59 | 50 | 127 |
| 58 | 07 31 | 50 | 124 | 06 41 | 50 | 125 | 05 51 | 51 | 125 | 05 00 | 50 | 126 | 04 10 | 50 | 126 | 03 20 | 51 | .127 | 02 30 | 51 | 128 |
| 57 | 08 03 | 51 | 125 | 07 12 | 50 | 126 | 06 22 | 51 | 126 | 05 31 | 50 | 127 | 04 41 | 51 | 127 | 03 50 | 50 | 128 | 03 00 | 51 | 128 |
| 56 | 08 34 | 51 | 126 | 07 43 | 50 | 127 | 06 53 | 51 | 127 | 06 02 | 51 | 128 | 05 11 | 50 | 128 | 04 21 | 51 | 129 | 03 30 | 51 | 129 |
| 55 | 09 05 | −51 | 127 | 08 14 | −51 | 127 | 07 23 | −50 | 128 | 06 33 | −51 | 128 | 05 42 | −51 | 129 | 04 51 | −51 | 129 | 04 00 | −51 | 130 |
| 54 | 09 36 | 51 | 128 | 08 45 | 51 | 128 | 07 54 | 51 | 129 | 07 03 | 52 | 129 | 06 11 | 51 | 130 | 05 20 | 51 | 130 | 04 29 | 51 | 131 |
| 53 | 10 06 | 51 | 128 | 09 15 | 51 | 129 | 08 24 | 52 | 130 | 07 32 | 51 | 130 | 06 41 | 51 | 131 | 05 50 | 51 | 131 | 04 58 | 52 | 132 |
| 52 | 10 36 | 51 | 129 | 09 45 | 52 | 130 | 08 53 | 51 | 130 | 08 02 | 52 | 131 | 07 10 | 51 | 131 | 06 19 | 52 | 132 | 05 27 | 52 | 132 |
| 51 | 11 06 | 52 | 130 | 10 14 | 51 | 131 | 09 22 | 51 | 131 | 08 31 | 52 | 132 | 07 39 | 52 | 132 | 06 47 | 52 | 133 | 05 55 | 52 | 133 |
| 50 | 11 35 | −52 | 131 | 10 43 | −52 | 132 | 09 51 | −52 | 132 | 08 59 | −52 | 133 | 08 07 | −52 | 133 | 07 15 | −52 | 134 | 06 23 | −52 | 134 |
| 49 | 12 04 | 52 | 132 | 11 12 | 52 | 132 | 10 20 | 52 | 133 | 09 28 | 53 | 133 | 08 35 | 52 | 134 | 07 43 | 52 | 134 | 06 51 | 53 | 135 |
| 48 | 12 33 | 53 | 133 | 11 40 | 52 | 133 | 10 48 | 53 | 134 | 09 55 | 52 | 134 | 09 03 | 53 | 135 | 08 10 | 52 | 135 | 07 18 | 53 | 136 |
| 47 | 13 01 | 53 | 134 | 12 08 | 52 | 134 | 11 16 | 53 | 135 | 10 23 | 53 | 135 | 09 30 | 53 | 136 | 08 37 | 52 | 136 | 07 45 | 53 | 136 |
| 46 | 13 29 | 53 | 134 | 12 36 | 53 | 135 | 11 43 | 53 | 135 | 10 50 | 53 | 136 | 09 57 | 53 | 136 | 09 04 | 53 | 137 | 08 11 | 53 | 137 |
| 45 | 13 56 | −53 | 135 | 13 03 | −53 | 136 | 12 10 | −53 | 136 | 11 17 | −54 | 136 | 10 23 | −53 | 137 | 09 30 | −53 | 138 | 08 37 | −53 | 138 |
| 44 | 14 23 | 53 | 136 | 13 30 | 54 | 137 | 12 36 | 53 | 137 | 11 43 | 54 | 138 | 10 49 | 54 | 138 | 09 56 | 53 | 139 | 09 03 | 54 | 139 |
| 43 | 14 49 | 53 | 137 | 13 56 | 54 | 138 | 13 02 | 53 | 138 | 12 09 | 54 | 138 | 11 15 | 54 | 139 | 10 21 | 53 | 139 | 09 28 | 54 | 140 |
| 42 | 15 15 | 53 | 138 | 14 22 | 54 | 138 | 13 28 | 54 | 139 | 12 34 | 54 | 139 | 11 40 | 54 | 140 | 10 46 | 54 | 140 | 09 52 | 54 | 140 |
| 41 | 15 41 | 54 | 139 | 14 47 | 54 | 139 | 13 53 | 54 | 140 | 12 59 | 54 | 140 | 12 05 | 54 | 141 | 11 11 | 54 | 141 | 10 17 | 55 | 141 |
| 40 | 16 06 | −54 | 140 | 15 12 | −54 | 140 | 14 18 | −55 | 141 | 13 23 | −54 | 141 | 12 29 | −54 | 142 | 11 35 | −55 | 142 | 10 40 | −54 | 142 |
| 39 | 16 31 | 55 | 141 | 15 36 | 54 | 141 | 14 42 | 55 | 142 | 13 47 | 54 | 142 | 12 53 | 55 | 142 | 11 58 | 54 | 143 | 11 04 | 55 | 143 |
| 38 | 16 55 | 55 | 142 | 16 00 | 54 | 142 | 15 06 | 55 | 142 | 14 11 | 55 | 143 | 13 16 | 55 | 143 | 12 21 | 55 | 144 | 11 26 | 54 | 144 |
| 37 | 17 19 | 55 | 143 | 16 24 | 55 | 143 | 15 29 | 55 | 143 | 14 34 | 55 | 144 | 13 39 | 55 | 144 | 12 44 | 55 | 145 | 11 49 | 55 | 145 |
| 36 | 17 42 | 55 | 143 | 16 47 | 55 | 144 | 15 52 | 55 | 145 | 14 57 | 56 | 145 | 14 01 | 55 | 146 | 13 06 | 56 | 146 | 12 11 | 56 | 146 |
| 35 | 18 05 | −56 | 144 | 17 09 | −55 | 145 | 16 14 | −55 | 145 | 15 19 | −56 | 146 | 14 23 | −55 | 146 | 13 28 | −56 | 146 | 12 32 | −55 | 147 |
| 34 | 18 27 | 56 | 145 | 17 31 | 55 | 146 | 16 36 | 56 | 146 | 15 40 | 55 | 147 | 14 45 | 56 | 147 | 13 49 | 56 | 147 | 12 53 | 56 | 148 |
| 33 | 18 49 | 56 | 146 | 17 53 | 56 | 147 | 16 57 | 56 | 147 | 16 01 | 56 | 147 | 15 05 | 56 | 148 | 14 09 | 56 | 148 | 13 13 | 56 | 149 |
| 32 | 19 10 | 56 | 147 | 18 14 | 56 | 148 | 17 18 | 56 | 148 | 16 22 | 56 | 148 | 15 26 | 56 | 149 | 14 30 | 57 | 149 | 13 33 | 56 | 149 |
| 31 | 19 31 | 57 | 148 | 18 34 | 56 | 148 | 17 38 | 56 | 149 | 16 42 | 57 | 149 | 15 45 | 56 | 150 | 14 49 | 56 | 150 | 13 53 | 57 | 150 |
| 30 | 19 51 | −57 | 149 | 18 54 | −56 | 150 | 17 58 | −57 | 150 | 17 01 | −56 | 150 | 16 05 | −57 | 151 | 15 08 | −56 | 151 | 14 12 | −57 | 151 |
| 29 | 20 10 | 56 | 150 | 19 14 | 57 | 150 | 18 17 | 57 | 151 | 17 20 | 57 | 151 | 16 23 | 56 | 151 | 15 27 | 57 | 152 | 14 30 | 57 | 152 |
| 28 | 20 29 | 57 | 151 | 19 32 | 57 | 151 | 18 35 | 57 | 152 | 17 39 | 57 | 152 | 16 42 | 57 | 152 | 15 45 | 57 | 153 | 14 48 | 57 | 153 |
| 27 | 20 47 | 57 | 152 | 19 50 | 57 | 152 | 18 53 | 57 | 153 | 17 56 | 57 | 153 | 16 59 | 57 | 153 | 16 02 | 57 | 154 | 15 05 | 57 | 154 |
| 26 | 21 05 | 57 | 153 | 20 08 | 57 | 153 | 19 11 | 57 | 154 | 18 14 | 57 | 154 | 17 16 | 57 | 154 | 16 19 | 58 | 155 | 15 21 | 57 | 155 |
| 25 | 21 22 | −57 | 154 | 20 25 | −57 | 154 | 19 28 | −58 | 155 | 18 30 | −57 | 155 | 17 33 | −58 | 155 | 16 35 | −57 | 156 | 15 38 | −58 | 156 |
| 24 | 21 39 | 58 | 155 | 20 41 | 57 | 155 | 19 44 | 58 | 156 | 18 46 | 57 | 156 | 17 49 | 58 | 156 | 16 51 | 58 | 157 | 15 53 | 58 | 157 |
| 23 | 21 55 | 58 | 156 | 20 57 | 58 | 156 | 19 59 | 57 | 157 | 19 02 | 58 | 157 | 18 04 | 58 | 157 | 17 06 | 58 | 157 | 16 08 | 58 | 158 |
| 22 | 22 10 | 57 | 157 | 21 12 | 57 | 157 | 20 15 | 58 | 158 | 19 17 | 59 | 158 | 18 18 | 58 | 158 | 17 20 | 58 | 158 | 16 22 | 58 | 159 |
| 21 | 22 25 | 58 | 158 | 21 27 | 58 | 158 | 20 29 | 58 | 159 | 19 31 | 58 | 159 | 18 33 | 59 | 159 | 17 34 | 58 | 159 | 16 36 | 58 | 160 |
| 20 | 22 39 | −58 | 159 | 21 41 | −58 | 159 | 20 43 | −59 | 160 | 19 44 | −58 | 160 | 18 46 | −58 | 160 | 17 48 | −59 | 160 | 16 49 | −58 | 161 |
| 19 | 22 53 | 59 | 160 | 21 54 | 58 | 160 | 20 56 | 59 | 161 | 19 57 | 59 | 161 | 18 59 | 59 | 161 | 18 00 | 59 | 161 | 17 02 | 59 | 162 |
| 18 | 23 06 | 59 | 161 | 22 07 | 59 | 161 | 21 08 | 58 | 162 | 20 10 | 59 | 162 | 19 11 | 59 | 162 | 18 12 | 58 | 162 | 17 14 | 59 | 162 |
| 17 | 23 18 | 59 | 162 | 22 19 | 59 | 162 | 21 20 | 58 | 163 | 20 22 | 59 | 163 | 19 23 | 59 | 163 | 18 24 | 59 | 163 | 17 25 | 59 | 163 |
| 16 | 23 29 | 58 | 163 | 22 30 | 58 | 163 | 21 32 | 59 | 164 | 20 33 | 59 | 164 | 19 34 | 59 | 164 | 18 35 | 59 | 164 | 17 36 | 59 | 164 |
| 15 | 23 40 | 59 | 164 | 22 41 | 59 | 164 | 21 42 | −59 | 165 | 20 43 | −59 | 165 | 19 44 | −59 | 165 | 18 45 | −59 | 165 | 17 46 | −59 | 165 |
| 14 | 23 50 | 59 | 165 | 22 51 | 59 | 165 | 21 52 | 59 | 166 | 20 53 | 59 | 166 | 19 54 | 60 | 166 | 18 55 | 60 | 166 | 17 55 | 60 | 166 |
| 13 | 24 00 | 59 | 166 | 23 01 | 60 | 166 | 22 01 | 59 | 167 | 21 02 | 59 | 167 | 20 03 | 59 | 167 | 19 04 | 60 | 167 | 18 04 | 59 | 167 |
| 12 | 24 09 | 60 | 167 | 23 09 | 60 | 167 | 22 10 | 59 | 168 | 21 11 | 60 | 168 | 20 11 | 59 | 168 | 19 12 | 60 | 168 | 18 12 | 59 | 168 |
| 11 | 24 17 | 60 | 168 | 23 17 | 59 | 169 | 22 18 | 59 | 169 | 21 19 | 60 | 169 | 20 19 | 59 | 169 | 19 20 | 60 | 169 | 18 20 | 59 | 169 |
| 10 | 24 24 | −59 | 169 | 23 25 | −60 | 170 | 22 25 | −59 | 170 | 21 26 | −60 | 170 | 20 26 | −59 | 170 | 19 27 | −60 | 170 | 18 27 | −60 | 170 |
| 9 | 24 31 | 60 | 170 | 23 31 | 59 | 171 | 22 32 | 60 | 171 | 21 32 | 59 | 171 | 20 33 | 60 | 171 | 19 33 | 60 | 171 | 18 33 | 59 | 171 |
| 8 | 24 37 | 60 | 172 | 23 37 | 60 | 172 | 22 38 | 60 | 172 | 21 38 | 60 | 172 | 20 38 | 59 | 172 | 19 39 | 60 | 172 | 18 39 | 60 | 172 |
| 7 | 24 43 | 60 | 173 | 23 43 | 60 | 173 | 22 43 | 60 | 173 | 21 43 | 60 | 173 | 20 43 | 59 | 173 | 19 44 | 60 | 173 | 18 44 | 60 | 173 |
| 6 | 24 47 | 60 | 174 | 23 47 | 60 | 174 | 22 47 | 59 | 174 | 21 48 | 60 | 174 | 20 48 | 60 | 174 | 19 48 | 60 | 174 | 18 48 | 60 | 174 |
| 5 | 24 51 | −60 | 175 | 23 51 | −60 | 175 | 22 51 | −60 | 175 | 21 51 | −59 | 175 | 20 52 | −60 | 175 | 19 52 | −60 | 175 | 18 52 | −60 | 175 |
| 4 | 24 54 | 60 | 176 | 23 54 | 60 | 176 | 22 54 | 59 | 176 | 21 55 | 60 | 176 | 20 55 | 60 | 176 | 19 55 | 60 | 176 | 18 55 | 60 | 176 |
| 3 | 24 57 | 60 | 177 | 23 57 | 60 | 177 | 22 57 | 60 | 177 | 21 57 | 60 | 177 | 20 57 | 60 | 177 | 19 57 | 60 | 177 | 18 57 | 60 | 177 |
| 2 | 24 59 | 60 | 178 | 23 59 | 60 | 178 | 22 59 | 60 | 178 | 21 59 | 60 | 178 | 20 59 | 60 | 178 | 19 59 | 60 | 178 | 18 59 | 60 | 178 |
| 1 | 25 00 | 60 | 179 | 24 00 | 60 | 179 | 23 00 | 60 | 179 | 22 00 | 60 | 179 | 21 00 | 60 | 179 | 20 00 | 60 | 179 | 19 00 | 60 | 179 |
| 0 | 25 00 | −60 | 180 | 24 00 | −60 | 180 | 23 00 | −60 | 180 | 22 00 | −60 | 180 | 21 00 | −60 | 180 | 20 00 | −60 | 180 | 19 00 | −60 | 180 |

15° 16° 17° 18° 19° 20° 21°

S. Lat. {LHA greater than 180°...... Zn=180−Z / LHA less than 180°..........Zn=180+Z}

## DECLINATION (15°–29°)

**Fig. A6.5** Extracts from Vol. 3.

SAME NAME AS LATITUDE      LAT 50°

LAT 50°

| 22° | | | 23° | | | 24° | | | 25° | | | 26° | | | 27° | | | 28° | | | 29° | | | LHA |
|---|---|---|---|---|---|---|---|---|---|---|---|---|---|---|---|---|---|---|---|---|---|---|---|---|
| Hc | d | Z | Hc | d | Z | Hc | d | Z | Hc | d | Z | Hc | d | Z | Hc | d | Z | Hc | d | Z | Hc | d | Z | |
| 62 00 | +60 | 180 | 63 00 | +60 | 180 | 64 00 | +60 | 180 | 65 00 | +60 | 180 | 66 00 | +60 | 180 | 67 00 | +60 | 180 | 68 00 | +60 | 180 | 69 00 | +60 | 180 | 360 |
| 61 59 | 60 | 178 | 62 59 | 60 | 178 | 63 59 | 60 | 178 | 64 59 | 60 | 178 | 65 59 | 60 | 178 | 66 59 | 60 | 178 | 67 59 | 60 | 178 | 68 59 | 60 | 178 | 359 |
| 61 57 | 60 | 176 | 62 57 | 60 | 176 | 63 57 | 60 | 176 | 64 57 | 60 | 176 | 65 57 | 60 | 176 | 66 57 | 60 | 175 | 67 57 | 60 | 175 | 68 57 | 60 | 175 | 358 |
| 61 54 | 60 | 174 | 62 54 | 60 | 174 | 63 54 | 60 | 174 | 64 54 | 59 | 174 | 65 53 | 60 | 173 | 66 53 | 60 | 173 | 67 53 | 60 | 173 | 68 53 | 59 | 173 | 357 |
| 61 49 | 60 | 172 | 62 49 | 60 | 172 | 63 49 | 60 | 172 | 64 49 | 59 | 172 | 65 48 | 60 | 171 | 66 48 | 60 | 171 | 67 47 | 60 | 171 | 68 47 | 59 | 170 | 356 |
| 61 44 | +59 | 170 | 62 43 | +60 | 170 | 63 43 | +59 | 170 | 64 42 | +60 | 169 | 65 42 | +59 | 169 | 66 41 | +59 | 169 | 67 40 | +60 | 168 | 68 40 | +59 | 168 | 355 |
| 61 36 | 60 | 168 | 62 36 | 59 | 168 | 63 35 | 59 | 168 | 64 34 | 60 | 167 | 65 34 | 59 | 167 | 66 33 | 59 | 167 | 67 32 | 59 | 166 | 68 31 | 59 | 166 | 354 |
| 61 28 | 59 | 166 | 62 27 | 59 | 166 | 63 26 | 59 | 166 | 64 25 | 59 | 165 | 65 24 | 59 | 165 | 66 23 | 59 | 164 | 67 22 | 58 | 164 | 68 20 | 59 | 163 | 353 |
| 61 18 | 59 | 164 | 62 17 | 59 | 164 | 63 16 | 59 | 164 | 64 15 | 58 | 163 | 65 13 | 59 | 163 | 66 12 | 58 | 162 | 67 10 | 59 | 162 | 68 09 | 58 | 161 | 352 |
| 61 07 | 59 | 163 | 62 06 | 58 | 162 | 63 04 | 59 | 162 | 64 03 | 58 | 161 | 65 01 | 58 | 161 | 65 59 | 58 | 160 | 66 57 | 58 | 159 | 67 55 | 58 | 159 | 351 |
| 60 55 | +58 | 161 | 61 53 | +58 | 160 | 62 51 | +59 | 160 | 63 50 | +58 | 159 | 64 48 | +57 | 159 | 65 45 | +58 | 158 | 66 43 | +58 | 157 | 67 41 | +57 | 156 | 350 |
| 60 42 | 58 | 159 | 61 40 | 57 | 158 | 62 37 | 58 | 158 | 63 35 | 58 | 158 | 64 33 | 57 | 157 | 65 30 | 57 | 156 | 66 27 | 57 | 155 | 67 24 | 57 | 154 | 349 |
| 60 27 | 58 | 157 | 61 25 | 57 | 156 | 62 22 | 58 | 156 | 63 20 | 57 | 155 | 64 17 | 57 | 155 | 65 14 | 57 | 154 | 66 11 | 56 | 153 | 67 07 | 56 | 152 | 348 |
| 60 11 | 58 | 155 | 61 09 | 57 | 155 | 62 06 | 57 | 154 | 63 03 | 57 | 153 | 64 00 | 56 | 153 | 64 56 | 56 | 152 | 65 52 | 56 | 151 | 66 48 | 56 | 150 | 347 |
| 59 55 | 57 | 153 | 60 52 | 56 | 153 | 61 48 | 57 | 152 | 62 45 | 56 | 151 | 63 41 | 56 | 151 | 64 37 | 56 | 150 | 65 33 | 56 | 149 | 66 29 | 55 | 148 | 346 |
| 59 37 | +56 | 152 | 60 33 | +57 | 151 | 61 30 | +56 | 150 | 62 26 | +56 | 150 | 63 22 | +55 | 149 | 64 17 | +56 | 148 | 65 13 | +54 | 147 | 66 07 | +55 | 146 | 345 |
| 59 18 | 56 | 150 | 60 14 | 56 | 149 | 61 10 | 56 | 149 | 62 06 | 55 | 148 | 63 01 | 55 | 147 | 63 56 | 55 | 146 | 64 51 | 54 | 145 | 65 45 | 54 | 144 | 344 |
| 58 58 | 55 | 148 | 59 54 | 56 | 148 | 60 50 | 55 | 147 | 61 45 | 55 | 146 | 62 40 | 54 | 145 | 63 34 | 54 | 144 | 64 28 | 54 | 143 | 65 22 | 54 | 142 | 343 |
| 58 38 | 55 | 147 | 59 33 | 55 | 146 | 60 28 | 55 | 145 | 61 23 | 54 | 144 | 62 17 | 54 | 143 | 63 11 | 54 | 142 | 64 05 | 53 | 141 | 64 58 | 53 | 140 | 342 |
| 58 16 | 55 | 145 | 59 11 | 54 | 144 | 60 05 | 55 | 143 | 61 00 | 54 | 143 | 61 54 | 53 | 142 | 62 47 | 53 | 141 | 63 40 | 53 | 140 | 64 33 | 52 | 139 | 341 |
| 57 53 | +55 | 143 | 58 48 | +54 | 143 | 59 42 | +54 | 142 | 60 36 | +53 | 141 | 61 29 | +53 | 140 | 62 22 | +53 | 139 | 63 15 | +52 | 138 | 64 07 | +52 | 137 | 340 |
| 57 30 | 54 | 142 | 58 24 | 54 | 140 | 59 18 | 53 | 140 | 60 11 | 53 | 139 | 61 04 | 53 | 138 | 61 57 | 52 | 137 | 62 49 | 51 | 136 | 63 40 | 51 | 135 | 339 |
| 57 06 | 53 | 140 | 57 59 | 54 | 139 | 58 53 | 52 | 139 | 59 45 | 53 | 138 | 60 38 | 52 | 137 | 61 30 | 51 | 136 | 62 21 | 51 | 135 | 63 12 | 51 | 133 | 338 |
| 56 41 | 53 | 139 | 57 34 | 53 | 138 | 58 27 | 52 | 137 | 59 19 | 52 | 136 | 60 11 | 52 | 135 | 61 03 | 51 | 134 | 61 54 | 50 | 133 | 62 44 | 50 | 132 | 337 |
| 56 15 | 53 | 137 | 57 08 | 52 | 136 | 58 00 | 52 | 136 | 58 52 | 51 | 135 | 59 43 | 51 | 134 | 60 34 | 51 | 133 | 61 25 | 50 | 131 | 62 15 | 49 | 130 | 336 |
| 55 48 | +52 | 136 | 56 41 | +52 | 135 | 57 33 | +51 | 134 | 58 24 | +51 | 133 | 59 15 | +51 | 132 | 60 06 | +50 | 130 | 60 56 | +49 | 130 | 61 45 | +49 | 129 | 335 |
| 55 21 | 52 | 134 | 56 13 | 51 | 133 | 57 04 | 52 | 133 | 57 56 | 50 | 132 | 58 46 | 50 | 131 | 59 36 | 50 | 130 | 60 26 | 49 | 128 | 61 15 | 48 | 127 | 334 |
| 54 53 | 52 | 133 | 55 45 | 51 | 132 | 56 36 | 50 | 131 | 57 26 | 51 | 130 | 58 17 | 49 | 129 | 59 06 | 49 | 128 | 59 55 | 49 | 127 | 60 44 | 48 | 126 | 333 |
| 54 25 | 51 | 132 | 55 16 | 50 | 130 | 56 06 | 51 | 130 | 56 57 | 49 | 129 | 57 46 | 49 | 128 | 58 35 | 49 | 127 | 59 24 | 48 | 126 | 60 12 | 47 | 124 | 332 |
| 53 55 | 50 | 130 | 54 46 | 50 | 129 | 55 36 | 50 | 128 | 56 26 | 49 | 127 | 57 15 | 49 | 126 | 58 04 | 48 | 125 | 58 52 | 48 | 124 | 59 40 | 47 | 123 | 331 |
| 53 26 | +50 | 129 | 54 16 | +50 | 127 | 55 06 | +49 | 127 | 55 55 | +49 | 126 | 56 44 | +48 | 125 | 57 32 | +48 | 124 | 58 20 | +47 | 123 | 59 07 | +47 | 122 | 330 |
| 52 55 | 50 | 128 | 53 45 | 50 | 127 | 54 35 | 49 | 126 | 55 24 | 48 | 125 | 56 12 | 48 | 123 | 57 00 | 48 | 123 | 57 48 | 46 | 121 | 58 34 | 46 | 120 | 329 |
| 52 25 | 49 | 126 | 53 14 | 49 | 125 | 54 03 | 49 | 124 | 54 52 | 48 | 123 | 55 40 | 48 | 122 | 56 28 | 46 | 121 | 57 14 | 47 | 120 | 58 01 | 45 | 119 | 328 |
| 51 53 | 49 | 125 | 52 42 | 49 | 124 | 53 31 | 48 | 123 | 54 19 | 48 | 122 | 55 07 | 47 | 121 | 55 54 | 47 | 120 | 56 41 | 46 | 119 | 57 27 | 45 | 118 | 327 |
| 51 21 | 49 | 124 | 52 10 | 49 | 123 | 52 59 | 48 | 122 | 53 47 | 47 | 121 | 54 34 | 47 | 120 | 55 21 | 46 | 119 | 56 07 | 45 | 118 | 56 52 | 45 | 117 | 326 |
| 50 49 | +49 | 123 | 51 38 | +48 | 121 | 52 26 | +47 | 121 | 53 13 | +47 | 120 | 54 00 | +47 | 119 | 54 47 | +46 | 118 | 55 33 | +45 | 117 | 56 18 | +44 | 115 | 325 |
| 50 17 | 48 | 122 | 51 05 | 47 | 121 | 51 52 | 48 | 120 | 52 40 | 46 | 119 | 53 26 | 46 | 118 | 54 12 | 46 | 116 | 54 58 | 45 | 115 | 55 43 | 44 | 114 | 324 |
| 49 43 | 48 | 120 | 50 31 | 48 | 119 | 51 19 | 47 | 118 | 52 06 | 46 | 117 | 52 52 | 46 | 116 | 53 38 | 45 | 115 | 54 23 | 44 | 114 | 55 07 | 44 | 113 | 323 |
| 49 10 | 48 | 119 | 49 58 | 47 | 118 | 50 45 | 46 | 117 | 51 31 | 46 | 116 | 52 17 | 46 | 115 | 53 03 | 45 | 114 | 53 48 | 44 | 113 | 54 32 | 43 | 112 | 322 |
| 48 36 | 47 | 118 | 49 23 | 47 | 117 | 50 10 | 46 | 116 | 50 56 | 46 | 115 | 51 42 | 45 | 114 | 52 27 | 45 | 113 | 53 12 | 44 | 112 | 53 56 | 43 | 111 | 321 |
| 48 02 | +47 | 117 | 48 49 | +46 | 116 | 49 35 | +46 | 115 | 50 21 | +46 | 114 | 51 07 | +45 | 113 | 51 52 | +44 | 112 | 52 36 | +44 | 111 | 53 20 | +43 | 110 | 320 |
| 47 27 | 47 | 116 | 48 14 | 46 | 115 | 49 00 | 46 | 114 | 49 46 | 45 | 113 | 50 31 | 45 | 112 | 51 16 | 44 | 111 | 52 00 | 43 | 110 | 52 43 | 43 | 109 | 319 |
| 46 53 | 46 | 115 | 47 39 | 46 | 114 | 48 25 | 45 | 113 | 49 10 | 45 | 112 | 49 55 | 45 | 111 | 50 40 | 43 | 110 | 51 23 | 44 | 109 | 52 07 | 42 | 108 | 318 |
| 46 17 | 47 | 114 | 47 04 | 45 | 113 | 47 49 | 45 | 112 | 48 34 | 45 | 111 | 49 19 | 44 | 110 | 50 03 | 44 | 109 | 50 47 | 43 | 108 | 51 30 | 42 | 107 | 317 |
| 45 42 | 46 | 113 | 46 28 | 45 | 112 | 47 13 | 45 | 111 | 47 58 | 44 | 110 | 48 43 | 44 | 109 | 49 27 | 43 | 108 | 50 10 | 43 | 107 | 50 53 | 42 | 106 | 316 |
| 45 06 | +46 | 112 | 45 52 | +45 | 111 | 46 37 | +45 | 110 | 47 22 | +44 | 109 | 48 06 | +44 | 108 | 48 50 | +43 | 107 | 49 33 | +42 | 106 | 50 15 | +42 | 105 | 315 |
| 44 30 | 46 | 111 | 45 16 | 45 | 110 | 46 01 | 44 | 109 | 46 45 | 44 | 108 | 47 29 | 44 | 107 | 48 13 | 43 | 106 | 48 56 | 42 | 105 | 49 38 | 42 | 104 | 314 |
| 43 54 | 45 | 110 | 44 39 | 45 | 109 | 45 24 | 44 | 108 | 46 09 | 43 | 107 | 46 52 | 44 | 106 | 47 36 | 42 | 105 | 48 18 | 43 | 104 | 49 01 | 41 | 103 | 313 |
| 43 18 | 45 | 109 | 44 03 | 44 | 108 | 44 47 | 45 | 107 | 45 32 | 43 | 106 | 46 15 | 43 | 105 | 46 58 | 43 | 104 | 47 41 | 42 | 103 | 48 23 | 41 | 102 | 312 |
| 42 41 | 45 | 108 | 43 26 | 44 | 107 | 44 10 | 44 | 106 | 44 54 | 44 | 105 | 45 38 | 43 | 104 | 46 21 | 42 | 103 | 47 03 | 42 | 102 | 47 45 | 41 | 101 | 311 |
| 42 04 | +45 | 107 | 42 49 | +44 | 106 | 43 33 | +44 | 105 | 44 17 | +43 | 104 | 45 00 | +43 | 103 | 45 43 | +42 | 102 | 46 25 | +42 | 101 | 47 07 | +41 | 100 | 310 |
| 41 27 | 45 | 106 | 42 12 | 44 | 105 | 42 56 | 44 | 104 | 43 40 | 43 | 103 | 44 23 | 42 | 102 | 45 05 | 43 | 101 | 45 48 | 41 | 100 | 46 29 | 41 | 99 | 309 |
| 40 50 | 45 | 105 | 41 35 | 43 | 104 | 42 18 | 44 | 103 | 43 02 | 43 | 102 | 43 45 | 43 | 101 | 44 28 | 42 | 100 | 45 10 | 41 | 99 | 45 51 | 41 | 98 | 308 |
| 40 13 | 44 | 104 | 40 57 | 44 | 103 | 41 41 | 43 | 102 | 42 24 | 43 | 101 | 43 07 | 43 | 101 | 43 50 | 41 | 100 | 44 31 | 42 | 99 | 45 13 | 40 | 98 | 307 |
| 39 35 | 44 | 103 | 40 19 | 44 | 102 | 41 03 | 43 | 102 | 41 46 | 43 | 101 | 42 29 | 42 | 100 | 43 11 | 42 | 99 | 43 53 | 42 | 98 | 44 35 | 40 | 97 | 306 |
| 38 58 | +44 | 102 | 39 42 | +43 | 101 | 40 25 | +43 | 101 | 41 08 | +43 | 100 | 41 51 | +42 | 99 | 42 33 | +42 | 98 | 43 15 | +41 | 97 | 43 56 | +41 | 96 | 305 |
| 38 20 | 44 | 102 | 39 04 | 43 | 101 | 39 47 | 44 | 100 | 40 30 | 43 | 99 | 41 13 | 42 | 99 | 41 55 | 42 | 97 | 42 37 | 41 | 96 | 43 18 | 40 | 95 | 304 |
| 37 42 | 44 | 101 | 38 26 | 43 | 100 | 39 09 | 43 | 99 | 39 52 | 43 | 98 | 40 35 | 42 | 97 | 41 17 | 41 | 96 | 41 58 | 41 | 95 | 42 39 | 41 | 94 | 303 |
| 37 04 | 44 | 100 | 37 48 | 42 | 99 | 38 31 | 43 | 98 | 39 14 | 42 | 97 | 39 56 | 42 | 96 | 40 38 | 41 | 95 | 41 20 | 41 | 94 | 42 01 | 40 | 93 | 302 |
| 36 26 | 44 | 99 | 37 10 | 43 | 98 | 37 53 | 43 | 97 | 38 36 | 42 | 96 | 39 18 | 42 | 95 | 40 00 | 41 | 95 | 40 41 | 41 | 94 | 41 22 | 41 | 93 | 301 |
| 35 48 | +44 | 98 | 36 32 | +43 | 97 | 37 15 | +42 | 96 | 37 57 | +43 | 96 | 38 40 | +41 | 95 | 39 21 | +42 | 94 | 40 03 | +41 | 93 | 40 44 | +40 | 92 | 300 |
| 35 10 | 43 | 97 | 35 53 | 43 | 96 | 36 36 | 43 | 96 | 37 19 | 42 | 95 | 38 01 | 42 | 94 | 38 43 | 41 | 93 | 39 24 | 41 | 92 | 40 05 | 41 | 91 | 299 |
| 34 32 | 43 | 97 | 35 15 | 43 | 95 | 35 58 | 42 | 95 | 36 40 | 43 | 94 | 37 23 | 41 | 93 | 38 04 | 42 | 92 | 38 46 | 41 | 91 | 39 27 | 40 | 90 | 298 |
| 33 53 | 43 | 96 | 34 36 | 43 | 95 | 35 19 | 43 | 94 | 36 02 | 42 | 93 | 36 44 | 42 | 92 | 37 26 | 41 | 91 | 38 07 | 41 | 90 | 38 48 | 40 | 90 | 297 |
| 33 15 | 43 | 95 | 33 58 | 43 | 94 | 34 41 | 42 | 93 | 35 23 | 43 | 92 | 36 06 | 41 | 91 | 36 47 | 42 | 91 | 37 29 | 41 | 90 | 38 10 | 40 | 89 | 296 |
| 32 36 | +44 | 94 | 33 20 | +42 | 93 | 34 02 | +43 | 92 | 34 45 | +42 | 92 | 35 27 | +42 | 91 | 36 09 | +41 | 90 | 36 50 | +41 | 89 | 37 31 | +40 | 88 | 295 |
| 31 58 | 43 | 93 | 32 41 | 43 | 92 | 33 24 | 42 | 92 | 34 06 | 42 | 91 | 34 48 | 42 | 90 | 35 30 | 41 | 89 | 36 12 | 40 | 88 | 36 52 | 41 | 87 | 294 |
| 31 19 | 43 | 92 | 32 02 | 42 | 92 | 32 45 | 43 | 91 | 33 28 | 42 | 90 | 34 10 | 42 | 90 | 34 52 | 41 | 88 | 35 33 | 41 | 87 | 36 14 | 41 | 87 | 293 |
| 30 41 | 43 | 92 | 31 24 | 43 | 91 | 32 07 | 42 | 90 | 32 49 | 42 | 89 | 33 31 | 42 | 88 | 34 13 | 41 | 88 | 34 54 | 41 | 87 | 35 35 | 41 | 86 | 292 |
| 30 02 | 43 | 91 | 30 45 | 43 | 90 | 31 28 | 43 | 89 | 32 11 | 42 | 89 | 32 53 | 42 | 88 | 33 35 | 41 | 87 | 34 16 | 41 | 86 | 34 57 | 41 | 85 | 291 |
| **22°** | | | **23°** | | | **24°** | | | **25°** | | | **26°** | | | **27°** | | | **28°** | | | **29°** | | | |

SAME NAME AS LATITUDE

N. Lat. { LHA greater than 180°...... Zn=Z  
LHA less than 180°...... Zn=360−Z }

## DECLINATION (15°–29°)

| LHA | 15° Hc | d | Z | 16° Hc | d | Z | 17° Hc | d | Z | 18° Hc | d | Z | 19° Hc | d | Z | 20° Hc | d | Z | 21° Hc | d | Z |
|---|---|---|---|---|---|---|---|---|---|---|---|---|---|---|---|---|---|---|---|---|---|
| 70 | 24 15 | +45 | 96 | 25 00 | +44 | 95 | 25 44 | +45 | 94 | 26 29 | +44 | 93 | 27 13 | +44 | 93 | 27 57 | +43 | 92 | 28 40 | +44 | 91 |
| 71 | 23 36 | 45 | 95 | 24 21 | 45 | 94 | 25 06 | 44 | 93 | 25 50 | 44 | 93 | 26 34 | 44 | 92 | 27 18 | 44 | 91 | 28 02 | 43 | 90 |
| 72 | 22 58 | 45 | 94 | 23 43 | 44 | 93 | 24 27 | 44 | 92 | 25 11 | 45 | 92 | 25 56 | 43 | 91 | 26 39 | 44 | 90 | 27 23 | 44 | 89 |
| 73 | 22 19 | 45 | 93 | 23 04 | 45 | 92 | 23 49 | 44 | 92 | 24 33 | 44 | 91 | 25 17 | 44 | 90 | 26 01 | 44 | 89 | 26 45 | 43 | 89 |
| 74 | 21 41 | 45 | 92 | 22 26 | 44 | 92 | 23 10 | 44 | 91 | 23 54 | 44 | 90 | 24 38 | 44 | 89 | 25 22 | 44 | 89 | 26 06 | 43 | 88 |
| 75 | 21 02 | +45 | 92 | 21 47 | +44 | 91 | 22 31 | +45 | 90 | 23 16 | +44 | 89 | 24 00 | +44 | 89 | 24 44 | +44 | 88 | 25 28 | +43 | 87 |
| 76 | 20 24 | 44 | 91 | 21 08 | 45 | 90 | 21 53 | 44 | 89 | 22 37 | 44 | 89 | 23 21 | 44 | 88 | 24 05 | 44 | 87 | 24 49 | 43 | 86 |
| 77 | 19 45 | 45 | 90 | 20 30 | 44 | 89 | 21 14 | 45 | 89 | 21 59 | 44 | 88 | 22 43 | 44 | 87 | 23 27 | 44 | 86 | 24 11 | 43 | 86 |
| 78 | 19 07 | 45 | 89 | 19 51 | 45 | 89 | 20 36 | 44 | 88 | 21 20 | 44 | 87 | 22 04 | 44 | 86 | 22 48 | 44 | 86 | 23 32 | 44 | 85 |
| 79 | 18 28 | 45 | 89 | 19 13 | 44 | 88 | 19 57 | 45 | 87 | 20 42 | 44 | 86 | 21 26 | 44 | 86 | 22 10 | 44 | 85 | 22 54 | 43 | 84 |
| 80 | 17 49 | +45 | 88 | 18 34 | +45 | 87 | 19 19 | +44 | 86 | 20 03 | +44 | 86 | 20 47 | +44 | 85 | 21 31 | +44 | 84 | 22 15 | +44 | 83 |
| 81 | 17 11 | 45 | 87 | 17 56 | 45 | 86 | 18 40 | 45 | 86 | 19 25 | 44 | 85 | 20 09 | 44 | 84 | 20 53 | 44 | 83 | 21 37 | 44 | 83 |
| 82 | 16 32 | 45 | 86 | 17 17 | 45 | 86 | 18 02 | 45 | 85 | 18 46 | 45 | 84 | 19 31 | 44 | 83 | 20 15 | 44 | 83 | 20 59 | 44 | 82 |
| 83 | 15 54 | 45 | 86 | 16 39 | 45 | 85 | 17 23 | 45 | 84 | 18 08 | 44 | 83 | 18 52 | 45 | 83 | 19 37 | 44 | 82 | 20 21 | 44 | 81 |
| 84 | 15 16 | 44 | 85 | 16 00 | 45 | 84 | 16 45 | 45 | 83 | 17 30 | 44 | 83 | 18 14 | 44 | 82 | 18 58 | 45 | 81 | 19 43 | 44 | 81 |
| 85 | 14 37 | +45 | 84 | 15 22 | +45 | 83 | 16 07 | +45 | 83 | 16 52 | +44 | 82 | 17 36 | +44 | 81 | 18 20 | +45 | 81 | 19 05 | +44 | 80 |
| 86 | 13 59 | 45 | 83 | 14 44 | 45 | 83 | 15 29 | 44 | 82 | 16 13 | 45 | 81 | 16 58 | 44 | 80 | 17 42 | 45 | 80 | 18 27 | 44 | 79 |
| 87 | 13 21 | 45 | 83 | 14 06 | 45 | 82 | 14 51 | 44 | 81 | 15 35 | 45 | 80 | 16 20 | 45 | 80 | 17 05 | 44 | 79 | 17 49 | 44 | 78 |
| 88 | 12 42 | 45 | 82 | 13 27 | 45 | 81 | 14 12 | 45 | 80 | 14 57 | 44 | 80 | 15 42 | 45 | 79 | 16 27 | 44 | 78 | 17 11 | 45 | 78 |
| 89 | 12 04 | 45 | 81 | 12 49 | 45 | 80 | 13 34 | 45 | 80 | 14 19 | 45 | 79 | 15 04 | 45 | 78 | 15 49 | 45 | 78 | 16 34 | 44 | 77 |
| 90 | 11 26 | +45 | 80 | 12 11 | +46 | 80 | 12 57 | +45 | 79 | 13 42 | +45 | 78 | 14 27 | +44 | 78 | 15 11 | +45 | 77 | 15 56 | +44 | 76 |
| 91 | 10 48 | 46 | 80 | 11 34 | 45 | 79 | 12 19 | 45 | 78 | 13 04 | 45 | 78 | 13 49 | 45 | 77 | 14 34 | 45 | 75 | 15 19 | 44 | 75 |
| 92 | 10 10 | 46 | 79 | 10 56 | 45 | 78 | 11 41 | 45 | 77 | 12 26 | 45 | 77 | 13 11 | 46 | 76 | 13 57 | 44 | 75 | 14 41 | 45 | 75 |
| 93 | 09 33 | 45 | 78 | 10 18 | 46 | 77 | 11 04 | 45 | 77 | 11 49 | 45 | 76 | 12 34 | 45 | 75 | 13 19 | 45 | 75 | 14 04 | 45 | 74 |
| 94 | 08 55 | 45 | 77 | 09 41 | 45 | 77 | 10 26 | 45 | 76 | 11 11 | 46 | 75 | 11 57 | 45 | 75 | 12 42 | 45 | 74 | 13 27 | 45 | 73 |
| 95 | 08 17 | +46 | 77 | 09 03 | +46 | 76 | 09 49 | +46 | 75 | 10 34 | +46 | 75 | 11 20 | +45 | 74 | 12 05 | +45 | 73 | 12 50 | +46 | 73 |
| 96 | 07 40 | 46 | 76 | 08 26 | 45 | 75 | 09 11 | 46 | 75 | 09 57 | 46 | 74 | 10 43 | 45 | 73 | 11 28 | 46 | 73 | 12 14 | 45 | 72 |
| 97 | 07 03 | 46 | 75 | 07 49 | 45 | 74 | 08 34 | 46 | 74 | 09 20 | 46 | 73 | 10 06 | 46 | 72 | 10 52 | 45 | 72 | 11 37 | 46 | 71 |
| 98 | 06 25 | 46 | 74 | 07 11 | 46 | 74 | 07 57 | 46 | 73 | 08 43 | 46 | 72 | 09 29 | 46 | 72 | 10 15 | 46 | 71 | 11 01 | 45 | 70 |
| 99 | 05 48 | 46 | 74 | 06 35 | 46 | 73 | 07 21 | 46 | 72 | 08 07 | 46 | 72 | 08 53 | 46 | 71 | 09 39 | 46 | 70 | 10 25 | 45 | 70 |
| 100 | 05 11 | +47 | 73 | 05 58 | +46 | 72 | 06 44 | +46 | 72 | 07 30 | +46 | 71 | 08 16 | +46 | 70 | 09 02 | +46 | 70 | 09 48 | +46 | 69 |
| 101 | 04 35 | 47 | 72 | 05 21 | 46 | 71 | 06 07 | 47 | 71 | 06 54 | 46 | 70 | 07 40 | 46 | 70 | 08 26 | 47 | 69 | 09 13 | 46 | 68 |
| 102 | 03 58 | 47 | 71 | 04 45 | 46 | 71 | 05 31 | 47 | 70 | 06 18 | 46 | 69 | 07 04 | 46 | 69 | 07 50 | 47 | 68 | 08 37 | 46 | 68 |
| 103 | 03 22 | 47 | 71 | 04 08 | 47 | 70 | 04 55 | 47 | 69 | 05 42 | 46 | 69 | 06 28 | 47 | 68 | 07 15 | 46 | 67 | 08 01 | 47 | 67 |
| 104 | 02 45 | 47 | 70 | 03 32 | 47 | 69 | 04 19 | 47 | 69 | 05 06 | 47 | 68 | 05 53 | 46 | 67 | 06 39 | 47 | 67 | 07 26 | 47 | 66 |
| 105 | 02 09 | +47 | 69 | 02 56 | +47 | 68 | 03 43 | +47 | 68 | 04 30 | +47 | 67 | 05 17 | +47 | 67 | 06 04 | +47 | 66 | 06 51 | +47 | 65 |
| 106 | 01 33 | 47 | 68 | 02 20 | 48 | 68 | 03 08 | 47 | 67 | 03 55 | 47 | 66 | 04 42 | 47 | 66 | 05 29 | 47 | 65 | 06 16 | 47 | 65 |
| 107 | 00 58 | 47 | 68 | 01 45 | 47 | 67 | 02 32 | 47 | 66 | 03 19 | 48 | 66 | 04 07 | 47 | 65 | 04 54 | 47 | 64 | 05 41 | 47 | 64 |
| 108 | 00 22 | 47 | 67 | 01 09 | 48 | 66 | 01 57 | 47 | 66 | 02 44 | 48 | 65 | 03 32 | 47 | 65 | 04 19 | 48 | 64 | 05 07 | 47 | 63 |
| 109 | −0 13 | 47 | 66 | 00 34 | 48 | 65 | 01 22 | 48 | 65 | 02 10 | 47 | 64 | 02 57 | 48 | 64 | 03 45 | 47 | 63 | 04 32 | 48 | 62 |
| 110 | −0 48 | +47 | 65 | −0 01 | +48 | 65 | 00 47 | +48 | 64 | 01 35 | +48 | 63 | 02 23 | +48 | 63 | 03 11 | +47 | 62 | 03 58 | +48 | 62 |
| 111 | −1 23 | 48 | 64 | −0 35 | 48 | 64 | 00 13 | 48 | 63 | 01 01 | 48 | 63 | 01 49 | 48 | 62 | 02 37 | 48 | 61 | 03 25 | 48 | 61 |
| 112 | −1 58 | 48 | 64 | −1 10 | 48 | 63 | −0 22 | 48 | 62 | 00 27 | 48 | 62 | 01 15 | 48 | 61 | 02 03 | 48 | 61 | 02 51 | 48 | 60 |
| 113 | −2 32 | 48 | 63 | −1 44 | 48 | 62 | −0 56 | 49 | 62 | −0 07 | 48 | 61 | 00 41 | 48 | 61 | 01 29 | 49 | 60 | 02 18 | 48 | 59 |
| 114 | −3 07 | 49 | 62 | −2 18 | 48 | 62 | −1 30 | 48 | 61 | −0 41 | 49 | 60 | 00 08 | 48 | 60 | 00 56 | 49 | 59 | 01 45 | 48 | 59 |
| 115 | −3 41 | +49 | 61 | −2 52 | +49 | 61 | −2 03 | +49 | 60 | −1 14 | +48 | 60 | −0 26 | +49 | 59 | 00 23 | +49 | 58 | 01 12 | +49 | 58 |
| 116 | −4 14 | 49 | 61 | −3 25 | 49 | 60 | −2 36 | 48 | 59 | −1 48 | 49 | 59 | −0 59 | 49 | 58 | −0 10 | 49 | 58 | 00 39 | 49 | 57 |
| 117 | −4 48 | 49 | 60 | −3 59 | 49 | 59 | −3 10 | 50 | 59 | −2 20 | 49 | 58 | −1 31 | 49 | 58 | −0 42 | 49 | 57 | 00 07 | 49 | 56 |
| 118 | −5 21 | 49 | 59 | −4 32 | 50 | 58 | −3 42 | 49 | 58 | −2 53 | 49 | 57 | −2 04 | 50 | 57 | −1 14 | 49 | 56 | −0 25 | 50 | 56 |
| 119 | −5 54 | 50 | 58 | −5 04 | 50 | 58 | −4 15 | 50 | 57 | −3 25 | 49 | 56 | −2 36 | 50 | 56 | −1 46 | 50 | 55 | −0 56 | 49 | 55 |
| 120 | | | | −5 37 | +50 | 57 | −4 47 | +50 | 56 | −3 57 | +50 | 56 | −3 07 | +50 | 55 | −2 18 | +50 | 55 | −1 28 | +50 | 54 |
| 121 | | | | | | | −5 19 | 50 | 55 | −4 29 | 50 | 55 | −3 39 | 50 | 54 | −2 49 | 50 | 54 | −1 59 | 50 | 53 |
| 122 | | | | | | | −5 51 | 51 | 55 | −5 00 | 50 | 54 | −4 10 | 50 | 54 | −3 20 | 51 | 53 | −2 30 | 51 | 52 |
| 123 | | | | | | | | | | −5 31 | 50 | 53 | −4 41 | 51 | 53 | −3 50 | 50 | 52 | −3 00 | 51 | 52 |
| 124 | | | | | | | | | | | | | −5 11 | 50 | 52 | −4 21 | 51 | 51 | −3 30 | 51 | 51 |
| 125 | | | | | | | | | | | | | −5 42 | +51 | 51 | −4 51 | +51 | 51 | −4 00 | +51 | 50 |
| 126 | | | | | | | | | | | | | | | | −5 20 | 51 | 50 | −4 29 | 51 | 49 |
| 127 | | | | | | | | | | | | | | | | −5 50 | 52 | 49 | −4 58 | 51 | 48 |
| 128 | | | | | | | | | | | | | | | | | | | −5 27 | 52 | 48 |
| 129 | | | | | | | | | | | | | | | | | | | −5 55 | 52 | 47 |
| 130 | | | | | | | | | | | | | | | | | | | | | |

**Fig. A6.6** Extracts from Vol. 3.

# SAME NAME AS LATITUDE

**LAT 50°**

| LHA | 22° Hc d Z | 23° Hc d Z | 24° Hc d Z | 25° Hc d Z | 26° Hc d Z | 27° Hc d Z | 28° Hc d Z | 29° Hc d Z |
|---|---|---|---|---|---|---|---|---|
| 290 | 29 24 +43 90 | 30 07 +43 89 | 30 50 +42 89 | 31 32 +42 88 | 32 14 +42 87 | 32 56 +42 86 | 33 38 +41 85 | 34 19 +40 84 |
| 289 | 28 45 43 89 | 29 28 43 89 | 30 11 43 88 | 30 54 42 87 | 31 36 42 86 | 32 18 41 85 | 32 59 41 84 | 33 40 41 84 |
| 288 | 28 07 43 89 | 28 50 42 88 | 29 32 42 87 | 30 15 42 86 | 30 57 42 85 | 31 39 42 85 | 32 21 41 84 | 33 02 41 83 |
| 287 | 27 28 43 88 | 28 11 43 87 | 28 54 42 86 | 29 37 42 86 | 30 19 42 85 | 31 01 41 84 | 31 42 42 83 | 32 24 41 82 |
| 286 | 26 49 44 87 | 27 33 43 86 | 28 16 42 86 | 28 58 42 85 | 29 40 42 84 | 30 22 42 83 | 31 04 42 82 | 31 46 41 81 |
| 285 | 26 11 +43 86 | 26 54 +43 86 | 27 37 +43 85 | 28 20 +42 84 | 29 02 +42 83 | 29 44 +42 83 | 30 26 +41 82 | 31 07 +42 81 |
| 284 | 25 32 44 86 | 26 16 43 85 | 26 59 42 84 | 27 41 43 83 | 28 24 42 83 | 29 06 42 82 | 29 48 41 81 | 30 29 42 80 |
| 283 | 24 54 44 85 | 25 37 43 84 | 26 20 43 83 | 27 03 43 83 | 27 46 42 82 | 28 28 42 81 | 29 10 42 80 | 29 52 41 79 |
| 282 | 24 16 44 84 | 24 59 43 83 | 25 42 43 83 | 26 25 43 82 | 27 08 42 81 | 27 50 42 80 | 28 32 42 79 | 29 14 41 79 |
| 281 | 23 37 44 83 | 24 21 43 82 | 25 04 43 82 | 25 47 42 81 | 26 29 43 80 | 27 12 42 80 | 27 54 42 79 | 28 36 41 78 |
| 280 | 22 59 +43 83 | 23 42 +44 82 | 24 26 +43 81 | 25 09 +42 80 | 25 51 +43 80 | 26 34 +42 79 | 27 16 +42 78 | 27 58 +42 77 |
| 279 | 22 21 43 82 | 23 04 44 81 | 23 48 43 80 | 24 31 43 80 | 25 14 42 79 | 25 56 43 78 | 26 39 42 77 | 27 21 42 77 |
| 278 | 21 43 43 81 | 22 26 43 81 | 23 10 43 80 | 23 53 43 79 | 24 36 43 78 | 25 19 42 77 | 26 01 42 77 | 26 43 42 76 |
| 277 | 21 05 43 81 | 21 48 44 80 | 22 32 43 79 | 23 15 43 78 | 23 58 43 78 | 24 41 43 77 | 25 24 42 76 | 26 06 42 75 |
| 276 | 20 27 43 80 | 21 10 44 79 | 21 54 43 78 | 22 37 44 78 | 23 21 43 77 | 24 03 43 76 | 24 46 43 75 | 25 29 42 75 |
| 275 | 19 49 +44 79 | 20 33 +43 78 | 21 16 +44 78 | 22 00 +43 77 | 22 43 +43 76 | 23 26 +43 75 | 24 09 +43 75 | 24 52 +42 74 |
| 274 | 19 11 44 78 | 19 55 44 78 | 20 39 43 77 | 21 22 44 76 | 22 06 43 75 | 22 49 43 75 | 23 32 43 74 | 24 15 42 73 |
| 273 | 18 33 44 78 | 19 17 44 77 | 20 01 44 76 | 20 45 43 75 | 21 28 44 75 | 22 12 43 74 | 22 55 43 73 | 23 38 42 72 |
| 272 | 17 56 44 77 | 18 40 44 76 | 19 24 44 75 | 20 08 43 75 | 20 51 44 74 | 21 35 43 73 | 22 18 43 72 | 23 01 43 72 |
| 271 | 17 18 44 76 | 18 02 44 76 | 18 46 44 75 | 19 30 44 74 | 20 14 44 73 | 20 58 43 73 | 21 41 44 72 | 22 25 43 71 |
| 270 | 16 41 +44 75 | 17 25 +44 75 | 18 09 +44 74 | 18 53 +44 73 | 19 37 +44 73 | 20 21 +44 72 | 21 05 +43 71 | 21 48 +43 70 |
| 269 | 16 03 45 75 | 16 48 44 74 | 17 32 45 73 | 18 17 44 73 | 19 01 44 72 | 19 45 43 71 | 20 28 44 70 | 21 12 43 70 |
| 268 | 15 26 45 74 | 16 11 44 73 | 16 55 44 73 | 17 40 44 72 | 18 24 44 71 | 19 08 44 71 | 19 52 44 70 | 20 36 43 69 |
| 267 | 14 49 45 73 | 15 34 45 73 | 16 19 44 72 | 17 03 44 71 | 17 48 44 71 | 18 32 44 70 | 19 16 44 69 | 20 00 44 68 |
| 266 | 14 12 45 73 | 14 57 45 72 | 15 42 45 71 | 16 27 44 71 | 17 11 45 70 | 17 56 44 69 | 18 40 44 68 | 19 24 44 68 |
| 265 | 13 36 +45 71 | 14 21 +45 71 | 15 06 +45 71 | 15 51 +44 70 | 16 35 +45 69 | 17 20 +44 68 | 18 04 +44 68 | 18 48 +45 67 |
| 264 | 12 59 45 71 | 13 44 45 71 | 14 29 45 70 | 15 14 45 69 | 15 59 45 68 | 16 44 45 68 | 17 29 44 67 | 18 13 45 66 |
| 263 | 12 23 45 70 | 13 08 45 70 | 13 53 45 69 | 14 38 45 68 | 15 24 44 68 | 16 08 45 67 | 16 53 45 66 | 17 38 44 66 |
| 262 | 11 46 46 70 | 12 32 45 69 | 13 17 46 68 | 14 03 45 68 | 14 48 45 67 | 15 33 45 66 | 16 18 45 66 | 17 03 45 65 |
| 261 | 11 10 46 69 | 11 56 46 68 | 12 42 46 68 | 13 27 46 67 | 14 13 45 66 | 14 58 45 66 | 15 43 45 65 | 16 28 45 64 |
| 260 | 10 34 +46 68 | 11 20 +46 68 | 12 06 +46 67 | 12 52 +45 66 | 13 37 +46 66 | 14 23 +45 65 | 15 08 +45 64 | 15 53 +45 64 |
| 259 | 09 59 46 68 | 10 45 46 67 | 11 31 45 66 | 12 16 46 66 | 13 02 46 65 | 13 48 45 64 | 14 33 46 64 | 15 19 45 63 |
| 258 | 09 23 46 67 | 10 09 46 66 | 10 55 46 66 | 11 41 46 65 | 12 27 46 64 | 13 13 46 64 | 13 59 46 63 | 14 45 45 62 |
| 257 | 08 48 46 66 | 09 34 46 65 | 10 20 47 65 | 11 07 46 64 | 11 53 46 64 | 12 39 46 63 | 13 25 46 62 | 14 11 46 62 |
| 256 | 08 13 46 65 | 08 59 47 65 | 09 46 46 64 | 10 32 46 63 | 11 18 46 63 | 12 05 46 62 | 12 51 46 62 | 13 37 46 61 |
| 255 | 07 38 +46 65 | 08 24 +47 64 | 09 11 +47 63 | 09 58 +46 63 | 10 44 +47 62 | 11 31 +46 61 | 12 17 +46 61 | 13 03 +47 60 |
| 254 | 07 03 47 64 | 07 50 47 63 | 08 37 47 63 | 09 24 46 62 | 10 10 47 61 | 10 57 46 61 | 11 43 47 60 | 12 30 46 59 |
| 253 | 06 28 47 63 | 07 15 47 63 | 08 03 47 62 | 08 50 47 61 | 09 37 46 61 | 10 23 47 60 | 11 10 47 59 | 11 57 47 59 |
| 252 | 05 54 47 62 | 06 41 48 62 | 07 29 47 61 | 08 16 47 61 | 09 03 47 60 | 09 50 47 59 | 10 37 47 59 | 11 24 47 58 |
| 251 | 05 20 47 62 | 06 07 48 61 | 06 55 47 61 | 07 42 48 60 | 08 30 47 59 | 09 17 47 59 | 10 04 47 58 | 10 51 48 57 |
| 250 | 04 46 +48 61 | 05 34 +48 60 | 06 22 +47 60 | 07 09 +48 59 | 07 57 +47 59 | 08 44 +48 58 | 09 32 +47 57 | 10 19 +47 57 |
| 249 | 04 13 47 60 | 05 00 48 60 | 05 48 48 59 | 06 36 48 59 | 07 24 48 58 | 08 12 47 57 | 08 59 48 57 | 09 47 48 56 |
| 248 | 03 39 48 59 | 04 27 48 59 | 05 15 48 58 | 06 03 48 58 | 06 51 48 57 | 07 39 48 57 | 08 27 48 56 | 09 15 48 55 |
| 247 | 03 06 48 59 | 03 54 49 58 | 04 43 48 58 | 05 31 48 57 | 06 19 48 57 | 07 07 48 56 | 07 56 48 55 | 08 44 48 55 |
| 246 | 02 33 49 58 | 03 22 49 57 | 04 10 49 57 | 04 59 48 56 | 05 47 49 56 | 06 36 48 55 | 07 24 48 54 | 08 12 49 54 |
| 245 | 02 01 +48 57 | 02 49 +49 57 | 03 38 +49 56 | 04 27 +49 55 | 05 16 +48 55 | 06 04 +49 54 | 06 53 +48 54 | 07 41 +49 53 |
| 244 | 01 28 49 56 | 02 17 49 56 | 03 06 49 55 | 03 55 49 55 | 04 44 49 54 | 05 33 49 54 | 06 22 49 53 | 07 11 48 52 |
| 243 | 00 56 50 56 | 01 46 49 55 | 02 35 49 55 | 03 24 49 54 | 04 13 49 53 | 05 02 49 53 | 05 51 49 52 | 06 40 49 52 |
| 242 | 00 25 49 55 | 01 14 49 54 | 02 03 50 54 | 02 53 49 53 | 03 42 50 53 | 04 32 49 52 | 05 21 49 52 | 06 10 49 51 |
| 241 | -0 07 50 54 | 00 43 50 54 | 01 32 50 53 | 02 22 50 53 | 03 12 49 52 | 04 01 50 51 | 04 51 49 51 | 05 40 50 50 |
| 240 | -0 38 +50 53 | 00 12 +50 53 | 01 02 +50 52 | 01 52 +50 52 | 02 41 +50 51 | 03 31 +50 51 | 04 21 +50 50 | 05 11 +50 50 |
| 239 | -1 09 50 53 | -0 19 50 52 | 00 31 50 52 | 01 21 51 51 | 02 12 50 50 | 03 02 50 50 | 03 52 50 49 | 04 42 50 49 |
| 238 | -1 39 52 52 | -0 49 50 51 | 00 01 51 51 | 00 52 50 50 | 01 42 50 50 | 02 32 51 49 | 03 23 50 49 | 04 13 50 48 |
| 237 | -2 09 51 51 | -1 19 51 51 | -0 28 50 50 | 00 22 51 49 | 01 13 50 49 | 02 03 51 49 | 02 54 50 48 | 03 44 51 47 |
| 236 | -2 39 51 50 | -1 48 50 50 | -0 58 51 49 | -0 07 51 49 | 00 44 51 48 | 01 35 50 48 | 02 25 51 47 | 03 16 51 47 |
| 235 | -3 09 +51 50 | -2 18 +51 49 | -1 27 +51 48 | -0 36 +51 48 | 00 15 +51 47 | 01 06 +51 47 | 01 57 +51 46 | 02 48 +51 46 |
| 234 | -3 38 51 49 | -2 47 51 48 | -1 55 51 48 | -1 04 51 47 | -0 13 51 47 | 00 38 52 46 | 01 30 51 46 | 02 21 51 45 |
| 233 | -4 07 52 48 | -3 15 51 47 | -2 24 52 47 | -1 32 51 47 | -0 41 52 46 | 00 11 51 46 | 01 02 52 45 | 01 54 51 44 |
| 232 | -4 35 52 47 | -3 43 51 47 | -2 52 52 46 | -2 00 52 46 | -1 08 51 45 | -0 17 52 45 | 00 35 52 44 | 01 27 52 44 |
| 231 | -5 03 52 46 | -4 11 52 46 | -3 19 52 45 | -2 27 52 45 | -1 35 52 44 | -0 43 51 44 | 00 08 52 43 | 01 00 53 43 |
| 230 | -5 31 +52 45 | -4 39 +52 45 | -3 47 +53 45 | -2 54 +52 44 | -2 02 +52 44 | -1 10 +52 43 | -0 18 +52 43 | 00 34 +53 42 |
| 229 | 131 | -5 06 53 44 | -4 13 52 44 | -3 21 52 43 | -2 29 53 43 | -1 36 52 42 | -0 44 53 42 | 00 09 52 41 |
| 228 | 132 | -5 33 53 43 | -4 40 53 43 | -3 47 52 43 | -2 55 53 42 | -2 02 53 42 | -1 09 53 41 | -0 16 52 41 |
| 227 | | 133 | -5 06 53 42 | -4 13 53 42 | -3 20 53 41 | -2 27 53 41 | -1 34 53 40 | -0 41 52 40 |
| 226 | | 134 | -5 32 53 41 | -4 39 54 41 | -3 45 53 40 | -2 52 52 40 | -1 59 53 39 | -1 06 53 39 |
| 225 | | | 135 | -5 04 +54 40 | -4 10 +53 40 | -3 17 +54 39 | -2 23 +53 39 | -1 30 +53 38 |
| 224 | | | 136 | -5 28 53 39 | -4 35 54 39 | -3 41 54 38 | -2 47 53 38 | -1 54 54 37 |
| 223 | | | | 137 | -4 58 53 38 | -4 05 54 38 | -3 11 54 37 | -2 17 54 37 |
| 222 | | | | 138 | -5 22 54 37 | -4 28 54 37 | -3 34 54 36 | -2 40 54 36 |
| 221 | | | | 139 | -5 45 54 36 | -4 51 55 36 | -3 56 54 35 | -3 02 54 35 |

| 22° | 23° | 24° | 25° | 26° | 27° | 28° | 29° |
|---|---|---|---|---|---|---|---|

# SAME NAME AS LATITUDE

**LAT 50°**

N. Lat. { LHA greater than 180°...... Zn=Z
{ LHA less than 180°.......... Zn=360−Z

## DECLINATION (15°-29°)

| LHA | 15° Hc | d | Z | 16° Hc | d | Z | 17° Hc | d | Z | 18° Hc | d | Z | 19° Hc | d | Z | 20° Hc | d | Z | 21° Hc | d | Z |
|---|---|---|---|---|---|---|---|---|---|---|---|---|---|---|---|---|---|---|---|---|---|
| 0 | 55 00 | +60 | 180 | 56 00 | +60 | 180 | 57 00 | +60 | 180 | 58 00 | +60 | 180 | 59 00 | +60 | 180 | 60 00 | +60 | 180 | 61 00 | +60 | 180 |
| 1 | 54 59 | 60 | 178 | 55 59 | 60 | 178 | 56 59 | 60 | 178 | 57 59 | 60 | 178 | 58 59 | 60 | 178 | 59 59 | 59 | 178 | 60 59 | 60 | 178 |
| 2 | 54 58 | 60 | 177 | 55 58 | 60 | 177 | 56 58 | 60 | 177 | 57 58 | 60 | 176 | 58 58 | 60 | 176 | 59 58 | 59 | 176 | 60 57 | 59 | 176 |
| 3 | 54 55 | 60 | 175 | 55 55 | 60 | 175 | 56 55 | 60 | 175 | 57 55 | 60 | 175 | 58 54 | 60 | 175 | 59 54 | 59 | 174 | 60 54 | 60 | 173 |
| 4 | 54 51 | 60 | 173 | 55 51 | 60 | 173 | 56 51 | 59 | 173 | 57 50 | 60 | 173 | 58 50 | 60 | 173 | 59 50 | 60 | 173 | 60 50 | 59 | 172 |
| 5 | 54 46 | +60 | 172 | 55 46 | +59 | 171 | 56 45 | +60 | 171 | 57 45 | +60 | 171 | 58 45 | +59 | 171 | 59 44 | 60 | 171 | 60 44 | +60 | 170 |
| 6 | 54 40 | 60 | 170 | 55 39 | 60 | 170 | 56 39 | 59 | 170 | 57 38 | 60 | 169 | 58 38 | 59 | 169 | 59 37 | 60 | 169 | 60 37 | 59 | 169 |
| 7 | 54 32 | 60 | 168 | 55 32 | 59 | 168 | 56 31 | 60 | 168 | 57 31 | 59 | 168 | 58 30 | 59 | 167 | 59 29 | 60 | 167 | 60 29 | 59 | 167 |
| 8 | 54 24 | 60 | 167 | 55 23 | 60 | 166 | 56 23 | 59 | 166 | 57 22 | 59 | 166 | 58 21 | 59 | 166 | 59 20 | 59 | 165 | 60 19 | 59 | 165 |
| 9 | 54 15 | 59 | 165 | 55 14 | 59 | 165 | 56 13 | 59 | 164 | 57 12 | 59 | 164 | 58 11 | 59 | 164 | 59 10 | 58 | 163 | 60 08 | 59 | 163 |
| 10 | 54 04 | +59 | 163 | 55 03 | +59 | 163 | 56 02 | +59 | 163 | 57 01 | +58 | 162 | 57 59 | +59 | 162 | 58 58 | +58 | 160 | 59 56 | +59 | 161 |
| 11 | 53 53 | 58 | 162 | 54 51 | 59 | 161 | 55 50 | 58 | 161 | 56 48 | 59 | 161 | 57 47 | 58 | 160 | 58 45 | 58 | 160 | 59 43 | 59 | 159 |
| 12 | 53 40 | 58 | 160 | 54 38 | 59 | 160 | 55 37 | 58 | 159 | 56 35 | 58 | 159 | 57 33 | 58 | 159 | 58 31 | 58 | 158 | 59 29 | 58 | 158 |
| 13 | 53 26 | 59 | 159 | 54 25 | 58 | 158 | 55 23 | 58 | 158 | 56 21 | 58 | 157 | 57 19 | 57 | 157 | 58 16 | 58 | 156 | 59 14 | 57 | 156 |
| 14 | 53 12 | 58 | 157 | 54 10 | 58 | 157 | 55 08 | 57 | 156 | 56 05 | 58 | 156 | 57 03 | 57 | 155 | 58 00 | 58 | 155 | 58 58 | 57 | 154 |
| 15 | 52 56 | +58 | 156 | 53 54 | +58 | 155 | 54 52 | +57 | 155 | 55 49 | +57 | 154 | 56 46 | +57 | 154 | 57 43 | +57 | 153 | 58 40 | +57 | 152 |
| 16 | 52 40 | 57 | 154 | 53 37 | 57 | 154 | 54 34 | 57 | 153 | 55 32 | 56 | 152 | 56 28 | 57 | 152 | 57 25 | 57 | 151 | 58 22 | 56 | 151 |
| 17 | 52 23 | 57 | 153 | 53 20 | 56 | 152 | 54 16 | 57 | 151 | 55 13 | 57 | 151 | 56 10 | 56 | 150 | 57 06 | 56 | 150 | 58 02 | 56 | 149 |
| 18 | 52 04 | 57 | 151 | 53 01 | 57 | 150 | 53 58 | 56 | 150 | 54 54 | 56 | 149 | 55 50 | 56 | 149 | 56 46 | 56 | 148 | 57 42 | 56 | 147 |
| 19 | 51 45 | 56 | 149 | 52 41 | 57 | 149 | 53 38 | 56 | 148 | 54 34 | 56 | 148 | 55 30 | 55 | 147 | 56 25 | 56 | 146 | 57 21 | 55 | 146 |
| 20 | 51 25 | +56 | 148 | 52 21 | +56 | 147 | 53 17 | +56 | 147 | 54 13 | +55 | 146 | 55 08 | +56 | 146 | 56 04 | +55 | 145 | 56 59 | +54 | 144 |
| 21 | 51 04 | 56 | 147 | 52 00 | 56 | 146 | 52 56 | 55 | 145 | 53 51 | 55 | 145 | 54 46 | 55 | 144 | 55 41 | 55 | 143 | 56 36 | 54 | 143 |
| 22 | 50 43 | 55 | 145 | 51 38 | 55 | 144 | 52 33 | 55 | 144 | 53 28 | 55 | 143 | 54 23 | 54 | 143 | 55 17 | 55 | 142 | 56 12 | 54 | 141 |
| 23 | 50 20 | 55 | 144 | 51 15 | 55 | 143 | 52 10 | 55 | 143 | 53 05 | 54 | 142 | 53 59 | 54 | 141 | 54 53 | 54 | 140 | 55 47 | 54 | 140 |
| 24 | 49 57 | 55 | 142 | 50 52 | 54 | 141 | 51 46 | 54 | 141 | 52 40 | 54 | 140 | 53 34 | 54 | 140 | 54 28 | 54 | 139 | 55 22 | 53 | 138 |
| 25 | 49 33 | +54 | 141 | 50 27 | +55 | 140 | 51 22 | +54 | 140 | 52 16 | +53 | 139 | 53 09 | +53 | 138 | 54 02 | +54 | 137 | 54 56 | +52 | 137 |
| 26 | 49 08 | 54 | 140 | 50 03 | 53 | 139 | 50 56 | 54 | 138 | 51 50 | 53 | 138 | 52 43 | 53 | 137 | 53 36 | 53 | 135 | 54 29 | 52 | 135 |
| 27 | 48 43 | 54 | 138 | 49 37 | 53 | 138 | 50 30 | 53 | 137 | 51 23 | 53 | 136 | 52 16 | 53 | 136 | 53 09 | 52 | 135 | 54 01 | 52 | 134 |
| 28 | 48 17 | 53 | 137 | 49 11 | 53 | 136 | 50 04 | 52 | 136 | 50 56 | 53 | 135 | 51 49 | 52 | 134 | 52 41 | 52 | 133 | 53 33 | 52 | 133 |
| 29 | 47 51 | 53 | 136 | 48 44 | 52 | 135 | 49 36 | 53 | 134 | 50 29 | 52 | 134 | 51 21 | 52 | 133 | 52 13 | 51 | 132 | 53 04 | 51 | 131 |
| 30 | 47 23 | +53 | 135 | 48 16 | +52 | 134 | 49 08 | +53 | 133 | 50 01 | +51 | 132 | 50 52 | +52 | 132 | 51 44 | +51 | 131 | 52 35 | +51 | 130 |
| 31 | 46 56 | 52 | 133 | 47 48 | 52 | 133 | 48 40 | 52 | 132 | 49 32 | 51 | 131 | 50 23 | 51 | 130 | 51 14 | 51 | 129 | 52 05 | 50 | 129 |
| 32 | 46 27 | 52 | 132 | 47 19 | 52 | 131 | 48 11 | 51 | 131 | 49 02 | 51 | 130 | 49 53 | 51 | 129 | 50 44 | 51 | 128 | 51 35 | 50 | 127 |
| 33 | 45 58 | 52 | 131 | 46 50 | 51 | 130 | 47 41 | 51 | 129 | 48 32 | 51 | 128 | 49 23 | 51 | 128 | 50 14 | 50 | 127 | 51 04 | 49 | 126 |
| 34 | 45 29 | 51 | 130 | 46 20 | 51 | 129 | 47 11 | 51 | 128 | 48 02 | 50 | 127 | 48 52 | 51 | 127 | 49 43 | 49 | 126 | 50 32 | 49 | 125 |
| 35 | 44 59 | +51 | 128 | 45 50 | +51 | 128 | 46 41 | +50 | 127 | 47 31 | +50 | 126 | 48 21 | +50 | 125 | 49 11 | +49 | 125 | 50 00 | +49 | 124 |
| 36 | 44 28 | 51 | 127 | 45 19 | 51 | 127 | 46 10 | 50 | 126 | 47 00 | 50 | 125 | 47 50 | 49 | 124 | 48 39 | 49 | 123 | 49 28 | 49 | 122 |
| 37 | 43 58 | 50 | 126 | 44 48 | 50 | 125 | 45 38 | 50 | 125 | 46 28 | 49 | 124 | 47 17 | 49 | 123 | 48 06 | 49 | 122 | 48 55 | 48 | 121 |
| 38 | 43 26 | 50 | 125 | 44 16 | 50 | 124 | 45 06 | 50 | 124 | 45 56 | 49 | 122 | 46 45 | 49 | 122 | 47 34 | 48 | 122 | 48 22 | 48 | 120 |
| 39 | 42 54 | 50 | 124 | 43 44 | 50 | 123 | 44 34 | 49 | 122 | 45 23 | 49 | 122 | 46 12 | 48 | 121 | 47 00 | 48 | 120 | 47 48 | 48 | 119 |
| 40 | 42 22 | +50 | 123 | 43 12 | +49 | 122 | 44 01 | +49 | 121 | 44 50 | +49 | 121 | 45 39 | +48 | 120 | 46 27 | +48 | 120 | 47 15 | +47 | 119 |
| 41 | 41 50 | 49 | 122 | 42 39 | 49 | 121 | 43 28 | 49 | 120 | 44 17 | 48 | 119 | 45 05 | 48 | 119 | 45 53 | 47 | 118 | 46 40 | 47 | 117 |
| 42 | 41 17 | 49 | 121 | 42 06 | 49 | 120 | 42 54 | 49 | 119 | 43 43 | 48 | 118 | 44 31 | 47 | 118 | 45 18 | 48 | 117 | 46 06 | 47 | 116 |
| 43 | 40 43 | 48 | 120 | 41 32 | 48 | 119 | 42 20 | 49 | 118 | 43 09 | 47 | 117 | 43 56 | 48 | 116 | 44 44 | 47 | 116 | 45 31 | 46 | 115 |
| 44 | 40 10 | 48 | 119 | 40 58 | 48 | 118 | 41 46 | 48 | 117 | 42 34 | 48 | 116 | 43 22 | 47 | 115 | 44 09 | 47 | 115 | 44 56 | 46 | 114 |
| 45 | 39 35 | +49 | 117 | 40 24 | +48 | 117 | 41 12 | +47 | 116 | 41 59 | +48 | 115 | 42 47 | +47 | 114 | 43 34 | +46 | 114 | 44 20 | +46 | 113 |
| 46 | 39 01 | 48 | 117 | 39 49 | 48 | 116 | 40 37 | 47 | 115 | 41 24 | 47 | 114 | 42 11 | 47 | 113 | 42 58 | 46 | 113 | 43 44 | 45 | 112 |
| 47 | 38 27 | 48 | 116 | 39 14 | 48 | 115 | 40 02 | 47 | 114 | 40 49 | 47 | 113 | 41 36 | 46 | 112 | 42 22 | 46 | 112 | 43 08 | 46 | 111 |
| 48 | 37 52 | 47 | 115 | 38 39 | 47 | 114 | 39 27 | 46 | 113 | 40 13 | 47 | 112 | 41 00 | 46 | 111 | 41 46 | 46 | 111 | 42 32 | 46 | 110 |
| 49 | 37 16 | 48 | 114 | 38 04 | 47 | 113 | 38 51 | 47 | 112 | 39 38 | 46 | 111 | 40 24 | 46 | 110 | 41 10 | 46 | 110 | 41 56 | 45 | 109 |
| 50 | 36 41 | +47 | 113 | 37 28 | +47 | 112 | 38 15 | +47 | 111 | 39 02 | +46 | 110 | 39 48 | +46 | 110 | 40 34 | +45 | 109 | 41 19 | +45 | 108 |
| 51 | 36 05 | 47 | 112 | 36 52 | 47 | 111 | 37 39 | 46 | 110 | 38 25 | 46 | 109 | 39 11 | 46 | 109 | 39 57 | 45 | 108 | 40 42 | 45 | 107 |
| 52 | 35 29 | 47 | 111 | 36 16 | 47 | 110 | 37 03 | 46 | 109 | 37 49 | 46 | 108 | 38 35 | 45 | 108 | 39 20 | 45 | 107 | 40 05 | 45 | 106 |
| 53 | 34 53 | 47 | 110 | 35 40 | 46 | 109 | 36 26 | 46 | 108 | 37 12 | 46 | 108 | 37 58 | 45 | 107 | 38 43 | 45 | 106 | 39 28 | 45 | 105 |
| 54 | 34 17 | 46 | 109 | 35 03 | 46 | 108 | 35 49 | 46 | 107 | 36 35 | 46 | 107 | 37 21 | 45 | 106 | 38 06 | 45 | 105 | 38 51 | 44 | 104 |
| 55 | 33 40 | +47 | 108 | 34 27 | +46 | 107 | 35 13 | +45 | 107 | 35 58 | +45 | 106 | 36 44 | +45 | 105 | 37 29 | +44 | 104 | 38 13 | +45 | 103 |
| 56 | 33 03 | 47 | 107 | 33 50 | 45 | 106 | 34 35 | 45 | 106 | 35 21 | 45 | 105 | 36 06 | 44 | 104 | 36 51 | 45 | 103 | 37 36 | 44 | 102 |
| 57 | 32 26 | 47 | 106 | 33 13 | 45 | 106 | 33 58 | 45 | 105 | 34 44 | 45 | 104 | 35 29 | 45 | 103 | 36 14 | 45 | 102 | 36 58 | 44 | 102 |
| 58 | 31 49 | 46 | 105 | 32 35 | 45 | 105 | 33 21 | 45 | 104 | 34 06 | 44 | 103 | 34 51 | 44 | 102 | 35 36 | 44 | 102 | 36 20 | 44 | 101 |
| 59 | 31 12 | 46 | 105 | 31 58 | 45 | 104 | 32 43 | 46 | 103 | 33 29 | 44 | 102 | 34 13 | 45 | 102 | 34 58 | 44 | 101 | 35 42 | 44 | 100 |
| 60 | 30 35 | +45 | 104 | 31 20 | +46 | 103 | 32 06 | +45 | 102 | 32 51 | +45 | 101 | 33 36 | +44 | 101 | 34 20 | +44 | 100 | 35 04 | +44 | 99 |
| 61 | 29 57 | 46 | 103 | 30 43 | 45 | 102 | 31 28 | 45 | 101 | 32 13 | 45 | 101 | 32 58 | 44 | 100 | 33 42 | 44 | 99 | 34 26 | 44 | 98 |
| 62 | 29 20 | 45 | 102 | 30 05 | 45 | 101 | 30 50 | 45 | 101 | 31 35 | 44 | 100 | 32 20 | 44 | 99 | 33 04 | 44 | 98 | 33 48 | 43 | 97 |
| 63 | 28 42 | 45 | 102 | 29 27 | 45 | 100 | 30 12 | 45 | 100 | 30 57 | 44 | 98 | 31 41 | 45 | 98 | 32 26 | 44 | 97 | 33 10 | 43 | 97 |
| 64 | 28 04 | 45 | 100 | 28 49 | 45 | 100 | 29 34 | 45 | 99 | 30 19 | 44 | 98 | 31 03 | 44 | 97 | 31 47 | 44 | 97 | 32 31 | 44 | 96 |
| 65 | 27 26 | +45 | 100 | 28 11 | +45 | 99 | 28 56 | +45 | 98 | 29 41 | +44 | 97 | 30 25 | +44 | 96 | 31 09 | +44 | 96 | 31 53 | +43 | 95 |
| 66 | 26 48 | 45 | 99 | 27 33 | 45 | 98 | 28 18 | 44 | 97 | 29 02 | 45 | 96 | 29 47 | 44 | 96 | 30 31 | 43 | 95 | 31 14 | 44 | 94 |
| 67 | 26 10 | 45 | 98 | 26 55 | 44 | 97 | 27 39 | 45 | 96 | 28 24 | 44 | 96 | 29 08 | 44 | 95 | 29 52 | 44 | 94 | 30 36 | 43 | 93 |
| 68 | 25 31 | 45 | 97 | 26 16 | 45 | 96 | 27 01 | 44 | 96 | 27 45 | 45 | 95 | 28 30 | 44 | 94 | 29 14 | 43 | 93 | 29 57 | 44 | 93 |
| 69 | 24 53 | 45 | 96 | 25 38 | 45 | 96 | 26 23 | 44 | 95 | 27 07 | 44 | 94 | 27 51 | 44 | 93 | 28 35 | 44 | 93 | 29 19 | 43 | 92 |

| | 15° | | | 16° | | | 17° | | | 18° | | | 19° | | | 20° | | | 21° | | |

S. Lat. { LHA greater than 180°.........Zn=180−Z
{ LHA less than 180°.........Zn=180+Z

## DECLINATION (15°-29°)

**Fig. A6.7** Extracts from Vol. 3.

## CONTRARY NAME TO LATITUDE

| 22° Hc | d | Z | 23° Hc | d | Z | 24° Hc | d | Z | 25° Hc | d | Z | 26° Hc | d | Z | 27° Hc | d | Z | 28° Hc | d | Z | 29° Hc | d | Z | LHA |
|---|---|---|---|---|---|---|---|---|---|---|---|---|---|---|---|---|---|---|---|---|---|---|---|---|
| -4 13 | 47 | 120 | -5 00 | 48 | 120 | -5 48 | 48 | 121 | 291 | | | | | | | | | | | | | | | | |
| -3 39 | 48 | 121 | -4 27 | 48 | 121 | -5 15 | 48 | 122 | -6 03 | 48 | 122 | 292 | | | | | | | | | | | | |
| -3 06 | 48 | 121 | -3 54 | 49 | 122 | -4 43 | 48 | 122 | -5 31 | 48 | 123 | 293 | | | | | | | | | | | | |
| -2 33 | 49 | 122 | -3 22 | 48 | 123 | -4 10 | 49 | 123 | -4 59 | 48 | 124 | -5 47 | 49 | 124 | 294 | | | | | | | | | |
| -2 01 | -48 | 123 | -2 49 | -49 | 123 | -3 38 | -49 | 124 | -4 27 | -49 | 125 | -5 16 | -48 | 125 | 295 | | | | | | | | | |
| -1 28 | 49 | 124 | -2 17 | 49 | 124 | -3 06 | 49 | 125 | -3 55 | 49 | 125 | -4 44 | 49 | 126 | -5 33 | 49 | 126 | 296 | | | | | | |
| -0 56 | 50 | 124 | -1 46 | 49 | 125 | -2 35 | 49 | 125 | -3 24 | 49 | 126 | -4 13 | 49 | 127 | -5 02 | 49 | 127 | -5 51 | 49 | 128 | 297 | | | |
| -0 25 | 49 | 125 | -1 14 | 49 | 126 | -2 03 | 50 | 126 | -2 53 | 49 | 127 | -3 42 | 50 | 127 | -4 32 | 49 | 128 | -5 21 | 49 | 128 | 298 | | | |
| 0 07 | 50 | 126 | -0 43 | 49 | 126 | -1 32 | 50 | 127 | -2 22 | 50 | 127 | -3 12 | 49 | 128 | -4 01 | 50 | 129 | -4 51 | 49 | 129 | -5 40 | 50 | 130 | 299 |
| 0 38 | -50 | 127 | -0 12 | -50 | 127 | -1 02 | -50 | 128 | -1 52 | -49 | 128 | -2 41 | -50 | 129 | -3 31 | -50 | 129 | -4 21 | -50 | 130 | -5 11 | -50 | 130 | 300 |
| 01 09 | 50 | 127 | 00 19 | 50 | 128 | -0 31 | 50 | 128 | -1 21 | 51 | 129 | -2 12 | 50 | 130 | -3 02 | 50 | 130 | -3 52 | 50 | 131 | -4 42 | 50 | 131 | 301 |
| 01 39 | 50 | 128 | 00 49 | 50 | 129 | -0 01 | 51 | 129 | -0 52 | 50 | 130 | -1 42 | 50 | 130 | -2 32 | 51 | 131 | -3 23 | 50 | 131 | -4 13 | 50 | 132 | 302 |
| 02 09 | 50 | 129 | 01 19 | 51 | 129 | 00 28 | 50 | 130 | -0 22 | 51 | 131 | -1 13 | 50 | 131 | -2 03 | 51 | 132 | -2 54 | 50 | 132 | -3 44 | 51 | 133 | 303 |
| 02 39 | 51 | 130 | 01 48 | 50 | 130 | 00 58 | 51 | 131 | 00 07 | 51 | 131 | -0 44 | 51 | 132 | -1 35 | 50 | 132 | -2 25 | 51 | 133 | -3 16 | 51 | 133 | 304 |
| 03 09 | -51 | 130 | 02 18 | -51 | 131 | 01 27 | -51 | 132 | 00 36 | -51 | 132 | -0 15 | -51 | 133 | -1 06 | -51 | 133 | -1 57 | -51 | 134 | -2 48 | -51 | 134 | 305 |
| 03 38 | 51 | 131 | 02 47 | 52 | 132 | 01 55 | 51 | 132 | 01 04 | 51 | 133 | 00 13 | 51 | 133 | -0 38 | 52 | 134 | -1 30 | 51 | 134 | -2 21 | 51 | 135 | 306 |
| 04 07 | 52 | 132 | 03 15 | 51 | 133 | 02 24 | 52 | 133 | 01 32 | 51 | 134 | 00 41 | 52 | 134 | -0 11 | 51 | 135 | -1 02 | 52 | 135 | -1 54 | 51 | 136 | 307 |
| 04 35 | 52 | 133 | 03 43 | 51 | 133 | 02 52 | 52 | 134 | 02 00 | 52 | 134 | 01 08 | 51 | 135 | 00 17 | 52 | 135 | -0 35 | 52 | 136 | -1 27 | 51 | 136 | 308 |
| 05 03 | 52 | 134 | 04 11 | 52 | 134 | 03 19 | 52 | 135 | 02 27 | 52 | 135 | 01 35 | 52 | 136 | 00 43 | 51 | 136 | -0 08 | 52 | 137 | -1 00 | 53 | 137 | 309 |
| 05 31 | -52 | 135 | 04 39 | -52 | 135 | 03 47 | -53 | 135 | 02 54 | -52 | 136 | 02 02 | -52 | 136 | 01 10 | -52 | 137 | 00 18 | -52 | 137 | -0 34 | -53 | 138 | 310 |
| 05 58 | 52 | 135 | 05 06 | 53 | 136 | 04 13 | 52 | 136 | 03 21 | 52 | 137 | 02 29 | 53 | 137 | 01 36 | 52 | 138 | 00 44 | 53 | 138 | -0 09 | 52 | 139 | 311 |
| 06 25 | 52 | 136 | 05 33 | 53 | 137 | 04 40 | 53 | 137 | 03 47 | 52 | 138 | 02 55 | 53 | 138 | 02 02 | 53 | 139 | 01 09 | 53 | 139 | 00 16 | 52 | 139 | 312 |
| 06 52 | 53 | 137 | 05 59 | 53 | 137 | 05 06 | 53 | 138 | 04 13 | 53 | 138 | 03 20 | 53 | 139 | 02 27 | 53 | 139 | 01 34 | 52 | 140 | 00 41 | 52 | 140 | 313 |
| 07 18 | 53 | 138 | 06 25 | 53 | 138 | 05 32 | 53 | 139 | 04 39 | 54 | 139 | 03 45 | 53 | 140 | 02 52 | 53 | 140 | 01 59 | 53 | 141 | 01 06 | 53 | 141 | 314 |
| 07 44 | -54 | 139 | 06 50 | -53 | 139 | 05 57 | -53 | 140 | 05 04 | -54 | 140 | 04 10 | -53 | 140 | 03 17 | -54 | 141 | 02 23 | -54 | 141 | 01 30 | -53 | 142 | 315 |
| 08 09 | 54 | 139 | 07 15 | 54 | 140 | 06 22 | 54 | 140 | 05 28 | 53 | 141 | 04 35 | 54 | 141 | 03 41 | 54 | 142 | 02 47 | 53 | 142 | 01 54 | 54 | 143 | 316 |
| 08 34 | 54 | 140 | 07 40 | 54 | 141 | 06 46 | 54 | 141 | 05 52 | 54 | 142 | 04 58 | 54 | 142 | 04 05 | 54 | 142 | 03 11 | 54 | 143 | 02 17 | 54 | 143 | 317 |
| 08 58 | 54 | 141 | 08 04 | 54 | 142 | 07 10 | 54 | 142 | 06 16 | 54 | 142 | 05 22 | 54 | 143 | 04 28 | 54 | 143 | 03 34 | 54 | 144 | 02 40 | 54 | 144 | 318 |
| 09 22 | 54 | 142 | 08 28 | 54 | 142 | 07 34 | 54 | 143 | 06 39 | 54 | 143 | 05 45 | 54 | 144 | 04 51 | 54 | 144 | 03 56 | 54 | 145 | 03 02 | 54 | 145 | 319 |
| 09 46 | -55 | 143 | 08 51 | -54 | 143 | 07 57 | -55 | 144 | 07 02 | -54 | 144 | 06 08 | -55 | 145 | 05 13 | -54 | 145 | 04 19 | -55 | 145 | 03 24 | -55 | 146 | 320 |
| 10 09 | 55 | 144 | 09 14 | 54 | 144 | 08 20 | 55 | 145 | 07 25 | 55 | 145 | 06 30 | 55 | 145 | 05 35 | 55 | 146 | 04 40 | 55 | 146 | 03 45 | 55 | 147 | 321 |
| 10 32 | 55 | 145 | 09 37 | 55 | 145 | 08 42 | 55 | 145 | 07 47 | 55 | 146 | 06 52 | 55 | 146 | 05 57 | 55 | 147 | 05 02 | 55 | 147 | 04 06 | 55 | 147 | 322 |
| 10 54 | 55 | 145 | 09 59 | 56 | 146 | 09 03 | 55 | 146 | 08 08 | 55 | 147 | 07 13 | 55 | 147 | 06 18 | 56 | 147 | 05 22 | 55 | 148 | 04 27 | 55 | 148 | 323 |
| 11 15 | 55 | 146 | 10 20 | 55 | 147 | 09 25 | 56 | 147 | 08 29 | 55 | 147 | 07 34 | 56 | 148 | 06 38 | 55 | 148 | 05 43 | 56 | 149 | 04 47 | 55 | 149 | 324 |
| 11 37 | -56 | 147 | 10 41 | -56 | 148 | 09 45 | -55 | 148 | 08 50 | -56 | 148 | 07 54 | -56 | 149 | 06 58 | -55 | 149 | 06 03 | -56 | 149 | 05 07 | -56 | 150 | 325 |
| 11 57 | 56 | 148 | 11 01 | 56 | 148 | 10 06 | 56 | 149 | 09 10 | 56 | 149 | 08 14 | 56 | 150 | 07 18 | 56 | 150 | 06 22 | 56 | 150 | 05 26 | 56 | 151 | 326 |
| 12 17 | 56 | 149 | 11 21 | 56 | 149 | 10 25 | 56 | 150 | 09 29 | 56 | 150 | 08 33 | 56 | 150 | 07 37 | 56 | 151 | 06 41 | 56 | 151 | 05 45 | 56 | 151 | 327 |
| 12 37 | 56 | 150 | 11 41 | 56 | 150 | 10 45 | 57 | 150 | 09 48 | 56 | 151 | 08 52 | 56 | 151 | 07 56 | 57 | 152 | 06 59 | 56 | 152 | 06 03 | 56 | 152 | 328 |
| 12 56 | 56 | 151 | 12 00 | 57 | 151 | 11 03 | 56 | 151 | 10 07 | 57 | 152 | 09 10 | 56 | 152 | 08 14 | 57 | 152 | 07 17 | 56 | 153 | 06 21 | 57 | 153 | 329 |
| 13 15 | -57 | 152 | 12 18 | -56 | 152 | 11 22 | -57 | 152 | 10 25 | -57 | 153 | 09 28 | -57 | 153 | 08 31 | -56 | 153 | 07 35 | -57 | 154 | 06 38 | -57 | 154 | 330 |
| 13 33 | 57 | 153 | 12 36 | 57 | 153 | 11 39 | 57 | 153 | 10 42 | 56 | 153 | 09 46 | 57 | 154 | 08 49 | 57 | 154 | 07 52 | 57 | 154 | 06 55 | 57 | 155 | 331 |
| 13 51 | 57 | 153 | 12 54 | 57 | 154 | 11 57 | 58 | 154 | 10 59 | 57 | 154 | 10 02 | 57 | 155 | 09 05 | 57 | 155 | 08 08 | 57 | 155 | 07 11 | 57 | 156 | 332 |
| 14 08 | 58 | 154 | 13 10 | 57 | 155 | 12 13 | 57 | 155 | 11 16 | 57 | 155 | 10 19 | 58 | 155 | 09 21 | 57 | 156 | 08 24 | 57 | 156 | 07 27 | 58 | 156 | 333 |
| 14 24 | 57 | 155 | 13 27 | 58 | 156 | 12 29 | 57 | 156 | 11 32 | 58 | 156 | 10 34 | 57 | 156 | 09 37 | 58 | 157 | 08 39 | 57 | 157 | 07 42 | 58 | 157 | 334 |
| 14 40 | -58 | 156 | 13 42 | -57 | 156 | 12 45 | -58 | 157 | 11 47 | -58 | 157 | 10 49 | -57 | 157 | 09 52 | -58 | 158 | 08 54 | -58 | 158 | 07 56 | -57 | 158 | 335 |
| 14 55 | 57 | 157 | 13 58 | 58 | 157 | 13 00 | 58 | 158 | 12 02 | 58 | 158 | 11 04 | 58 | 158 | 10 06 | 58 | 158 | 09 08 | 57 | 159 | 08 11 | 59 | 159 | 336 |
| 15 10 | 58 | 158 | 14 12 | 58 | 158 | 13 14 | 58 | 159 | 12 16 | 58 | 159 | 11 18 | 58 | 159 | 10 20 | 58 | 159 | 09 22 | 58 | 160 | 08 24 | 58 | 160 | 337 |
| 15 24 | 58 | 159 | 14 26 | 58 | 159 | 13 28 | 58 | 159 | 12 30 | 58 | 160 | 11 32 | 58 | 160 | 10 34 | 59 | 160 | 09 35 | 58 | 160 | 08 37 | 58 | 161 | 338 |
| 15 38 | 58 | 160 | 14 40 | 58 | 160 | 13 41 | 58 | 161 | 12 43 | 58 | 161 | 11 45 | 58 | 161 | 10 46 | 58 | 161 | 09 48 | 58 | 161 | 08 50 | 59 | 162 | 339 |
| 15 51 | -59 | 161 | 14 52 | -58 | 161 | 13 54 | -58 | 161 | 12 56 | -58 | 162 | 11 57 | -58 | 162 | 10 59 | -59 | 162 | 10 00 | -58 | 162 | 09 02 | -59 | 162 | 340 |
| 16 03 | 58 | 162 | 15 05 | 59 | 162 | 14 06 | 58 | 162 | 13 08 | 59 | 162 | 12 09 | 59 | 163 | 11 10 | 58 | 163 | 10 12 | 59 | 163 | 09 13 | 59 | 163 | 341 |
| 16 15 | 59 | 163 | 15 16 | 58 | 163 | 14 18 | 59 | 163 | 13 19 | 59 | 163 | 12 20 | 59 | 164 | 11 21 | 58 | 164 | 10 23 | 59 | 164 | 09 24 | 59 | 164 | 342 |
| 16 26 | 59 | 164 | 15 27 | 58 | 164 | 14 29 | 59 | 164 | 13 30 | 59 | 164 | 12 31 | 59 | 164 | 11 32 | 59 | 165 | 10 33 | 59 | 165 | 09 34 | 59 | 165 | 343 |
| 16 37 | 59 | 165 | 15 38 | 59 | 165 | 14 39 | 59 | 165 | 13 40 | 59 | 165 | 12 41 | 59 | 166 | 11 42 | 59 | 166 | 10 43 | 59 | 166 | 09 44 | 59 | 166 | 344 |
| 16 47 | -59 | 166 | 15 48 | -59 | 166 | 14 49 | -59 | 166 | 13 50 | -60 | 166 | 12 50 | -59 | 166 | 11 51 | -59 | 166 | 10 52 | -59 | 167 | 09 53 | -59 | 167 | 345 |
| 16 56 | 59 | 166 | 15 57 | 59 | 167 | 14 58 | 59 | 167 | 13 59 | 60 | 167 | 12 59 | 59 | 167 | 12 00 | 59 | 167 | 11 01 | 59 | 167 | 10 02 | 60 | 168 | 346 |
| 17 05 | 59 | 167 | 16 06 | 60 | 168 | 15 06 | 59 | 168 | 14 07 | 59 | 168 | 13 08 | 60 | 168 | 12 08 | 59 | 168 | 11 09 | 59 | 168 | 10 10 | 60 | 168 | 347 |
| 17 13 | 59 | 168 | 16 14 | 60 | 169 | 15 14 | 59 | 169 | 14 15 | 60 | 169 | 13 15 | 59 | 169 | 12 16 | 59 | 169 | 11 17 | 60 | 169 | 10 17 | 59 | 169 | 348 |
| 17 21 | 60 | 169 | 16 21 | 59 | 170 | 15 22 | 60 | 170 | 14 22 | 60 | 170 | 13 22 | 59 | 170 | 12 23 | 59 | 170 | 11 23 | 59 | 170 | 10 23 | 59 | 170 | 349 |
| 17 27 | -59 | 170 | 16 28 | -60 | 170 | 15 28 | -59 | 171 | 14 29 | -60 | 171 | 13 29 | -60 | 171 | 12 29 | -59 | 171 | 11 30 | -60 | 171 | 10 30 | -59 | 171 | 350 |
| 17 34 | 60 | 171 | 16 34 | 60 | 171 | 15 34 | 59 | 172 | 14 35 | 60 | 172 | 13 35 | 60 | 172 | 12 35 | 60 | 172 | 11 36 | 60 | 172 | 10 36 | 60 | 172 | 351 |
| 17 39 | 60 | 172 | 16 39 | 60 | 172 | 15 40 | 60 | 172 | 14 40 | 60 | 173 | 13 40 | 60 | 173 | 12 40 | 60 | 173 | 11 41 | 60 | 173 | 10 41 | 60 | 173 | 352 |
| 17 44 | 60 | 173 | 16 44 | 60 | 173 | 15 44 | 60 | 173 | 14 45 | 60 | 173 | 13 45 | 60 | 174 | 12 45 | 60 | 174 | 11 45 | 60 | 174 | 10 45 | 59 | 174 | 353 |
| 17 48 | 60 | 174 | 16 48 | 59 | 174 | 15 49 | 60 | 174 | 14 49 | 60 | 174 | 13 49 | 60 | 174 | 12 49 | 60 | 175 | 11 49 | 60 | 175 | 10 49 | 60 | 175 | 354 |
| 17 52 | -60 | 175 | 16 52 | -60 | 175 | 15 52 | -60 | 175 | 14 52 | -60 | 175 | 13 52 | -60 | 175 | 12 52 | -60 | 175 | 11 52 | -59 | 176 | 10 53 | -60 | 176 | 355 |
| 17 55 | 60 | 176 | 16 55 | 60 | 176 | 15 55 | 60 | 176 | 14 55 | 60 | 176 | 13 55 | 60 | 176 | 12 55 | 60 | 176 | 11 55 | 60 | 176 | 10 55 | 60 | 176 | 356 |
| 17 57 | 60 | 177 | 16 57 | 60 | 177 | 15 57 | 60 | 177 | 14 57 | 60 | 177 | 13 57 | 60 | 177 | 12 57 | 60 | 177 | 11 57 | 60 | 177 | 10 57 | 60 | 177 | 357 |
| 17 59 | 60 | 178 | 16 59 | 60 | 178 | 15 59 | 60 | 178 | 14 59 | 60 | 178 | 13 59 | 60 | 178 | 12 59 | 60 | 178 | 11 59 | 60 | 178 | 10 59 | 60 | 178 | 358 |
| 18 00 | 60 | 179 | 17 00 | 60 | 179 | 16 00 | 60 | 179 | 15 00 | 60 | 179 | 14 00 | 60 | 179 | 13 00 | 60 | 179 | 12 00 | 60 | 179 | 11 00 | 60 | 179 | 359 |
| 18 00 | -60 | 180 | 17 00 | -60 | 180 | 16 00 | -60 | 180 | 15 00 | -60 | 180 | 14 00 | -60 | 180 | 13 00 | -60 | 180 | 12 00 | -60 | 180 | 11 00 | -60 | 180 | 360 |

22°   23°   24°   25°   26°   27°   28°   29°

CONTRARY NAME TO LATITUDE    LAT 50°

TABLE 5.—Correction to Tabulated

| d / ' | 1 | 2 | 3 | 4 | 5 | 6 | 7 | 8 | 9 | 10 | 11 | 12 | 13 | 14 | 15 | 16 | 17 | 18 | 19 | 20 | 21 | 22 | 23 | 24 | 25 | 26 | 27 | 28 | 29 | 30 |
|---|---|---|---|---|---|---|---|---|---|---|---|---|---|---|---|---|---|---|---|---|---|---|---|---|---|---|---|---|---|---|
| 0 | 0 | 0 | 0 | 0 | 0 | 0 | 0 | 0 | 0 | 0 | 0 | 0 | 0 | 0 | 0 | 0 | 0 | 0 | 0 | 0 | 0 | 0 | 0 | 0 | 0 | 0 | 0 | 0 | 0 | 0 |
| 1 | 0 | 0 | 0 | 0 | 0 | 0 | 0 | 0 | 0 | 0 | 0 | 0 | 0 | 0 | 0 | 0 | 0 | 0 | 0 | 0 | 0 | 0 | 0 | 0 | 0 | 0 | 0 | 0 | 0 | 0 |
| 2 | 0 | 0 | 0 | 0 | 0 | 0 | 0 | 0 | 0 | 0 | 0 | 0 | 0 | 0 | 0 | 1 | 1 | 1 | 1 | 1 | 1 | 1 | 1 | 1 | 1 | 1 | 1 | 1 | 1 | 1 |
| 3 | 0 | 0 | 0 | 0 | 0 | 0 | 0 | 0 | 0 | 0 | 1 | 1 | 1 | 1 | 1 | 1 | 1 | 1 | 1 | 1 | 1 | 1 | 1 | 1 | 1 | 1 | 1 | 1 | 1 | 2 |
| 4 | 0 | 0 | 0 | 0 | 0 | 0 | 0 | 1 | 1 | 1 | 1 | 1 | 1 | 1 | 1 | 1 | 1 | 1 | 1 | 1 | 1 | 1 | 2 | 2 | 2 | 2 | 2 | 2 | 2 | 2 |
| 5 | 0 | 0 | 0 | 0 | 0 | 0 | 1 | 1 | 1 | 1 | 1 | 1 | 1 | 1 | 2 | 1 | 1 | 2 | 2 | 2 | 2 | 2 | 2 | 2 | 2 | 2 | 2 | 2 | 2 | 2 |
| 6 | 0 | 0 | 0 | 0 | 0 | 1 | 1 | 1 | 1 | 1 | 1 | 1 | 1 | 1 | 2 | 2 | 2 | 2 | 2 | 2 | 2 | 2 | 2 | 2 | 2 | 3 | 3 | 3 | 3 | 3 |
| 7 | 0 | 0 | 0 | 0 | 1 | 1 | 1 | 1 | 1 | 1 | 1 | 1 | 2 | 2 | 2 | 2 | 2 | 2 | 2 | 2 | 2 | 3 | 3 | 3 | 3 | 3 | 3 | 3 | 3 | 4 |
| 8 | 0 | 0 | 0 | 1 | 1 | 1 | 1 | 1 | 1 | 1 | 1 | 2 | 2 | 2 | 2 | 2 | 2 | 2 | 3 | 3 | 3 | 3 | 3 | 3 | 3 | 3 | 4 | 4 | 4 | 4 |
| 9 | 0 | 0 | 0 | 1 | 1 | 1 | 1 | 1 | 1 | 2 | 2 | 2 | 2 | 2 | 2 | 2 | 3 | 3 | 3 | 3 | 3 | 3 | 3 | 4 | 4 | 4 | 4 | 4 | 4 | 4 |
| 10 | 0 | 0 | 0 | 1 | 1 | 1 | 1 | 1 | 2 | 2 | 2 | 2 | 2 | 2 | 2 | 3 | 3 | 3 | 3 | 3 | 4 | 4 | 4 | 4 | 4 | 4 | 4 | 5 | 5 | 5 |
| 11 | 0 | 0 | 1 | 1 | 1 | 1 | 1 | 2 | 2 | 2 | 2 | 2 | 2 | 3 | 3 | 3 | 3 | 3 | 3 | 4 | 4 | 4 | 4 | 4 | 5 | 5 | 5 | 5 | 5 | 6 |
| 12 | 0 | 0 | 1 | 1 | 1 | 1 | 1 | 2 | 2 | 2 | 2 | 2 | 3 | 3 | 3 | 3 | 3 | 4 | 4 | 4 | 4 | 4 | 5 | 5 | 5 | 5 | 5 | 6 | 6 | 6 |
| 13 | 0 | 0 | 1 | 1 | 1 | 1 | 2 | 2 | 2 | 2 | 2 | 3 | 3 | 3 | 3 | 3 | 4 | 4 | 4 | 4 | 5 | 5 | 5 | 5 | 5 | 6 | 6 | 6 | 6 | 6 |
| 14 | 0 | 0 | 1 | 1 | 1 | 1 | 2 | 2 | 2 | 2 | 3 | 3 | 3 | 3 | 4 | 4 | 4 | 4 | 4 | 5 | 5 | 5 | 5 | 6 | 6 | 6 | 6 | 7 | 7 | 7 |
| 15 | 0 | 0 | 1 | 1 | 1 | 2 | 2 | 2 | 2 | 2 | 3 | 3 | 3 | 4 | 4 | 4 | 4 | 4 | 5 | 5 | 5 | 6 | 6 | 6 | 6 | 6 | 7 | 7 | 7 | 8 |
| 16 | 0 | 1 | 1 | 1 | 1 | 2 | 2 | 2 | 2 | 3 | 3 | 3 | 3 | 4 | 4 | 4 | 5 | 5 | 5 | 5 | 6 | 6 | 6 | 7 | 7 | 7 | 7 | 7 | 8 | 8 |
| 17 | 0 | 1 | 1 | 1 | 1 | 2 | 2 | 2 | 3 | 3 | 3 | 3 | 4 | 4 | 4 | 5 | 5 | 5 | 5 | 6 | 6 | 6 | 7 | 7 | 7 | 7 | 8 | 8 | 8 | 8 |
| 18 | 0 | 1 | 1 | 1 | 2 | 2 | 2 | 2 | 3 | 3 | 3 | 4 | 4 | 4 | 4 | 5 | 5 | 5 | 6 | 6 | 6 | 7 | 7 | 7 | 8 | 8 | 8 | 8 | 9 | 9 |
| 19 | 0 | 1 | 1 | 1 | 2 | 2 | 2 | 3 | 3 | 3 | 3 | 4 | 4 | 4 | 5 | 5 | 5 | 6 | 6 | 6 | 7 | 7 | 7 | 8 | 8 | 8 | 9 | 9 | 9 | 10 |
| 20 | 0 | 1 | 1 | 1 | 2 | 2 | 2 | 3 | 3 | 3 | 4 | 4 | 4 | 5 | 5 | 5 | 6 | 6 | 6 | 7 | 7 | 7 | 8 | 8 | 8 | 9 | 9 | 9 | 10 | 10 |
| 21 | 0 | 1 | 1 | 1 | 2 | 2 | 2 | 3 | 3 | 4 | 4 | 4 | 5 | 5 | 5 | 6 | 6 | 6 | 7 | 7 | 7 | 8 | 8 | 8 | 9 | 9 | 9 | 10 | 10 | 10 |
| 22 | 0 | 1 | 1 | 1 | 2 | 2 | 3 | 3 | 3 | 4 | 4 | 4 | 5 | 5 | 6 | 6 | 6 | 7 | 7 | 7 | 8 | 8 | 8 | 9 | 9 | 10 | 10 | 10 | 11 | 11 |
| 23 | 0 | 1 | 1 | 2 | 2 | 2 | 3 | 3 | 3 | 4 | 4 | 5 | 5 | 5 | 6 | 6 | 7 | 7 | 7 | 8 | 8 | 8 | 9 | 9 | 10 | 10 | 10 | 11 | 11 | 11 |
| 24 | 0 | 1 | 1 | 2 | 2 | 2 | 3 | 3 | 4 | 4 | 4 | 5 | 5 | 6 | 6 | 6 | 7 | 7 | 8 | 8 | 8 | 9 | 9 | 10 | 10 | 10 | 11 | 11 | 12 | 12 |
| 25 | 0 | 1 | 1 | 2 | 2 | 2 | 3 | 3 | 4 | 4 | 5 | 5 | 5 | 6 | 6 | 7 | 7 | 8 | 8 | 8 | 9 | 9 | 10 | 10 | 10 | 11 | 11 | 12 | 12 | 12 |
| 26 | 0 | 1 | 1 | 2 | 2 | 3 | 3 | 4 | 4 | 5 | 5 | 5 | 6 | 6 | 6 | 7 | 7 | 8 | 8 | 9 | 9 | 10 | 10 | 10 | 11 | 11 | 12 | 12 | 13 | 13 |
| 27 | 0 | 1 | 1 | 2 | 2 | 3 | 3 | 4 | 4 | 4 | 5 | 5 | 6 | 6 | 7 | 7 | 8 | 8 | 9 | 9 | 9 | 10 | 10 | 11 | 11 | 12 | 12 | 13 | 13 | 14 |
| 28 | 0 | 1 | 1 | 2 | 2 | 3 | 3 | 4 | 4 | 5 | 5 | 6 | 6 | 7 | 7 | 7 | 8 | 8 | 9 | 9 | 10 | 10 | 11 | 11 | 12 | 12 | 13 | 13 | 14 | 14 |
| 29 | 0 | 1 | 1 | 2 | 2 | 3 | 3 | 4 | 4 | 5 | 5 | 6 | 6 | 7 | 7 | 8 | 8 | 9 | 9 | 10 | 10 | 11 | 11 | 12 | 12 | 13 | 13 | 14 | 14 | 14 |
| 30 | 0 | 1 | 2 | 2 | 2 | 3 | 4 | 4 | 4 | 5 | 6 | 6 | 6 | 7 | 8 | 8 | 8 | 9 | 10 | 10 | 10 | 11 | 12 | 12 | 12 | 13 | 14 | 14 | 14 | 15 |
| 31 | 1 | 1 | 2 | 2 | 3 | 3 | 4 | 4 | 5 | 5 | 6 | 6 | 7 | 7 | 8 | 8 | 9 | 9 | 10 | 10 | 11 | 11 | 12 | 12 | 13 | 13 | 14 | 14 | 15 | 16 |
| 32 | 1 | 1 | 2 | 2 | 3 | 3 | 4 | 4 | 5 | 5 | 6 | 6 | 7 | 7 | 8 | 9 | 9 | 10 | 10 | 11 | 11 | 12 | 12 | 13 | 13 | 14 | 14 | 15 | 15 | 16 |
| 33 | 1 | 1 | 2 | 2 | 3 | 3 | 4 | 4 | 5 | 6 | 6 | 7 | 7 | 8 | 8 | 9 | 9 | 10 | 10 | 11 | 12 | 12 | 13 | 13 | 14 | 14 | 15 | 15 | 16 | 16 |
| 34 | 1 | 1 | 2 | 2 | 3 | 3 | 4 | 5 | 5 | 6 | 6 | 7 | 7 | 8 | 8 | 9 | 10 | 10 | 11 | 11 | 12 | 12 | 13 | 14 | 14 | 15 | 15 | 16 | 16 | 17 |
| 35 | 1 | 1 | 2 | 2 | 3 | 4 | 4 | 5 | 5 | 6 | 6 | 7 | 8 | 8 | 9 | 9 | 10 | 10 | 11 | 12 | 12 | 13 | 13 | 14 | 15 | 15 | 16 | 16 | 17 | 18 |
| 36 | 1 | 1 | 2 | 2 | 3 | 4 | 4 | 5 | 5 | 6 | 7 | 7 | 8 | 8 | 9 | 10 | 10 | 11 | 11 | 12 | 13 | 13 | 14 | 14 | 15 | 16 | 16 | 17 | 17 | 18 |
| 37 | 1 | 1 | 2 | 2 | 3 | 4 | 5 | 5 | 6 | 6 | 7 | 7 | 8 | 9 | 9 | 10 | 10 | 11 | 12 | 12 | 13 | 14 | 14 | 15 | 15 | 16 | 17 | 18 | 18 | 19 |
| 38 | 1 | 1 | 2 | 3 | 3 | 4 | 4 | 5 | 6 | 6 | 7 | 8 | 8 | 9 | 10 | 10 | 11 | 11 | 12 | 13 | 13 | 14 | 15 | 15 | 16 | 17 | 17 | 18 | 18 | 19 |
| 39 | 1 | 1 | 2 | 3 | 3 | 4 | 5 | 5 | 6 | 6 | 7 | 8 | 8 | 9 | 10 | 10 | 11 | 12 | 12 | 13 | 14 | 14 | 15 | 16 | 16 | 17 | 18 | 18 | 19 | 20 |
| 40 | 1 | 1 | 2 | 3 | 3 | 4 | 5 | 5 | 6 | 7 | 7 | 8 | 9 | 9 | 10 | 11 | 11 | 12 | 13 | 13 | 14 | 15 | 15 | 16 | 17 | 17 | 18 | 19 | 19 | 20 |
| 41 | 1 | 1 | 2 | 3 | 3 | 4 | 5 | 5 | 6 | 7 | 8 | 8 | 9 | 10 | 10 | 11 | 12 | 12 | 13 | 14 | 14 | 15 | 16 | 16 | 17 | 18 | 18 | 19 | 20 | 20 |
| 42 | 1 | 1 | 2 | 3 | 4 | 4 | 5 | 6 | 6 | 7 | 8 | 8 | 9 | 10 | 10 | 11 | 12 | 13 | 13 | 14 | 15 | 15 | 16 | 17 | 18 | 18 | 19 | 20 | 20 | 21 |
| 43 | 1 | 1 | 2 | 3 | 4 | 4 | 5 | 6 | 6 | 7 | 8 | 9 | 9 | 10 | 11 | 11 | 12 | 13 | 14 | 14 | 15 | 16 | 16 | 17 | 18 | 19 | 19 | 20 | 21 | 22 |
| 44 | 1 | 1 | 2 | 3 | 4 | 4 | 5 | 6 | 7 | 7 | 8 | 9 | 10 | 10 | 11 | 12 | 12 | 13 | 14 | 15 | 15 | 16 | 17 | 18 | 18 | 19 | 20 | 21 | 21 | 22 |
| 45 | 1 | 2 | 2 | 3 | 4 | 4 | 5 | 6 | 7 | 8 | 8 | 9 | 10 | 10 | 11 | 12 | 13 | 14 | 14 | 15 | 16 | 16 | 17 | 18 | 19 | 20 | 20 | 21 | 22 | 22 |
| 46 | 1 | 2 | 2 | 3 | 4 | 5 | 5 | 6 | 7 | 8 | 8 | 9 | 10 | 11 | 12 | 12 | 13 | 14 | 15 | 15 | 16 | 17 | 18 | 18 | 19 | 20 | 21 | 21 | 22 | 23 |
| 47 | 1 | 2 | 2 | 3 | 4 | 5 | 5 | 6 | 7 | 8 | 9 | 9 | 10 | 11 | 12 | 13 | 13 | 14 | 15 | 16 | 16 | 17 | 18 | 19 | 20 | 20 | 21 | 22 | 23 | 24 |
| 48 | 1 | 2 | 2 | 3 | 4 | 5 | 6 | 6 | 7 | 8 | 9 | 10 | 10 | 11 | 12 | 13 | 14 | 14 | 15 | 16 | 17 | 18 | 18 | 19 | 20 | 21 | 22 | 22 | 23 | 24 |
| 49 | 1 | 2 | 2 | 3 | 4 | 5 | 6 | 7 | 7 | 8 | 9 | 10 | 11 | 11 | 12 | 13 | 14 | 15 | 16 | 16 | 17 | 18 | 19 | 20 | 20 | 21 | 22 | 23 | 24 | 24 |
| 50 | 1 | 2 | 2 | 3 | 4 | 5 | 6 | 7 | 8 | 8 | 9 | 10 | 11 | 12 | 12 | 13 | 14 | 15 | 16 | 17 | 18 | 18 | 19 | 20 | 21 | 22 | 22 | 23 | 24 | 25 |
| 51 | 1 | 2 | 3 | 3 | 4 | 5 | 6 | 7 | 8 | 8 | 9 | 10 | 11 | 12 | 13 | 14 | 14 | 15 | 16 | 17 | 18 | 19 | 20 | 20 | 21 | 22 | 23 | 24 | 25 | 26 |
| 52 | 1 | 2 | 3 | 3 | 4 | 5 | 6 | 7 | 8 | 9 | 10 | 10 | 11 | 12 | 13 | 14 | 15 | 16 | 16 | 17 | 18 | 19 | 20 | 21 | 22 | 23 | 23 | 24 | 25 | 26 |
| 53 | 1 | 2 | 3 | 3 | 4 | 5 | 6 | 7 | 8 | 9 | 10 | 11 | 11 | 12 | 13 | 14 | 15 | 16 | 17 | 18 | 19 | 19 | 20 | 21 | 22 | 23 | 24 | 25 | 26 | 26 |
| 54 | 1 | 2 | 3 | 4 | 4 | 5 | 6 | 7 | 8 | 9 | 10 | 11 | 12 | 13 | 14 | 14 | 15 | 16 | 17 | 18 | 19 | 20 | 21 | 22 | 22 | 23 | 24 | 25 | 26 | 27 |
| 55 | 1 | 2 | 3 | 4 | 5 | 6 | 6 | 7 | 8 | 9 | 10 | 11 | 12 | 13 | 14 | 15 | 16 | 16 | 17 | 18 | 19 | 20 | 21 | 22 | 23 | 24 | 25 | 26 | 27 | 28 |
| 56 | 1 | 2 | 3 | 4 | 5 | 6 | 7 | 7 | 8 | 9 | 10 | 11 | 12 | 13 | 14 | 15 | 16 | 17 | 18 | 19 | 20 | 21 | 21 | 22 | 23 | 24 | 25 | 26 | 27 | 28 |
| 57 | 1 | 2 | 3 | 4 | 5 | 6 | 7 | 8 | 9 | 10 | 10 | 11 | 12 | 13 | 14 | 15 | 16 | 17 | 18 | 19 | 20 | 21 | 22 | 23 | 24 | 25 | 26 | 27 | 28 | 28 |
| 58 | 1 | 2 | 3 | 4 | 5 | 6 | 7 | 8 | 9 | 10 | 11 | 12 | 13 | 14 | 14 | 15 | 16 | 17 | 18 | 19 | 20 | 21 | 22 | 23 | 24 | 25 | 26 | 27 | 28 | 29 |
| 59 | 1 | 2 | 3 | 4 | 5 | 6 | 7 | 8 | 9 | 10 | 11 | 12 | 13 | 14 | 15 | 16 | 17 | 18 | 19 | 20 | 21 | 22 | 23 | 24 | 25 | 26 | 27 | 28 | 29 | 30 |

**Fig. A6.8** Extracts from Vol. 3.

## Altitude for Minutes of Declination

| 31 | 32 | 33 | 34 | 35 | 36 | 37 | 38 | 39 | 40 | 41 | 42 | 43 | 44 | 45 | 46 | 47 | 48 | 49 | 50 | 51 | 52 | 53 | 54 | 55 | 56 | 57 | 58 | 59 | 60 | d / |
|---|---|---|---|---|---|---|---|---|---|---|---|---|---|---|---|---|---|---|---|---|---|---|---|---|---|---|---|---|---|---|
| 0 | 0 | 0 | 0 | 0 | 0 | 0 | 0 | 0 | 0 | 0 | 0 | 0 | 0 | 0 | 0 | 0 | 0 | 0 | 0 | 0 | 0 | 0 | 0 | 0 | 0 | 0 | 0 | 0 | 0 | 0 |
| 1 | 1 | 1 | 1 | 1 | 1 | 1 | 1 | 1 | 1 | 1 | 1 | 1 | 1 | 1 | 1 | 1 | 1 | 1 | 1 | 1 | 1 | 1 | 1 | 1 | 1 | 1 | 1 | 1 | 1 | 1 |
| 1 | 1 | 1 | 1 | 1 | 1 | 1 | 1 | 1 | 1 | 1 | 1 | 1 | 1 | 2 | 2 | 2 | 2 | 2 | 2 | 2 | 2 | 2 | 2 | 2 | 2 | 2 | 2 | 2 | 2 | 2 |
| 2 | 2 | 2 | 2 | 2 | 2 | 2 | 2 | 2 | 2 | 2 | 2 | 2 | 2 | 2 | 2 | 2 | 2 | 2 | 2 | 3 | 3 | 3 | 3 | 3 | 3 | 3 | 3 | 3 | 3 | 3 |
| 2 | 2 | 2 | 2 | 2 | 2 | 2 | 3 | 3 | 3 | 3 | 3 | 3 | 3 | 3 | 3 | 3 | 3 | 3 | 3 | 3 | 3 | 4 | 4 | 4 | 4 | 4 | 4 | 4 | 4 | 4 |
| 3 | 3 | 3 | 3 | 3 | 3 | 3 | 3 | 3 | 3 | 3 | 4 | 4 | 4 | 4 | 4 | 4 | 4 | 4 | 4 | 4 | 4 | 4 | 4 | 5 | 5 | 5 | 5 | 5 | 5 | 5 |
| 3 | 3 | 3 | 3 | 4 | 4 | 4 | 4 | 4 | 4 | 4 | 4 | 4 | 4 | 4 | 5 | 5 | 5 | 5 | 5 | 5 | 5 | 5 | 5 | 6 | 6 | 6 | 6 | 6 | 6 | 6 |
| 4 | 4 | 4 | 4 | 4 | 4 | 4 | 4 | 5 | 5 | 5 | 5 | 5 | 5 | 5 | 5 | 5 | 6 | 6 | 6 | 6 | 6 | 6 | 6 | 6 | 7 | 7 | 7 | 7 | 7 | 7 |
| 4 | 4 | 4 | 5 | 5 | 5 | 5 | 5 | 5 | 5 | 5 | 6 | 6 | 6 | 6 | 6 | 6 | 6 | 7 | 7 | 7 | 7 | 7 | 7 | 7 | 7 | 8 | 8 | 8 | 8 | 8 |
| 5 | 5 | 5 | 5 | 5 | 5 | 6 | 6 | 6 | 6 | 6 | 6 | 6 | 7 | 7 | 7 | 7 | 7 | 7 | 8 | 8 | 8 | 8 | 8 | 8 | 8 | 9 | 9 | 9 | 9 | 9 |
| 5 | 5 | 6 | 6 | 6 | 6 | 6 | 6 | 6 | 7 | 7 | 7 | 7 | 7 | 8 | 8 | 8 | 8 | 8 | 8 | 8 | 9 | 9 | 9 | 9 | 9 | 10 | 10 | 10 | 10 | 10 |
| 6 | 6 | 6 | 6 | 6 | 7 | 7 | 7 | 7 | 7 | 8 | 8 | 8 | 8 | 8 | 8 | 9 | 9 | 9 | 9 | 9 | 10 | 10 | 10 | 10 | 10 | 10 | 11 | 11 | 11 | 11 |
| 6 | 6 | 7 | 7 | 7 | 7 | 7 | 8 | 8 | 8 | 8 | 8 | 9 | 9 | 9 | 9 | 9 | 10 | 10 | 10 | 10 | 10 | 11 | 11 | 11 | 11 | 11 | 12 | 12 | 12 | 12 |
| 7 | 7 | 7 | 7 | 8 | 8 | 8 | 8 | 8 | 9 | 9 | 9 | 9 | 10 | 10 | 10 | 10 | 10 | 11 | 11 | 11 | 11 | 11 | 12 | 12 | 12 | 12 | 13 | 13 | 13 | 13 |
| 7 | 7 | 8 | 8 | 8 | 8 | 9 | 9 | 9 | 9 | 10 | 10 | 10 | 10 | 10 | 11 | 11 | 11 | 11 | 12 | 12 | 12 | 12 | 13 | 13 | 13 | 13 | 14 | 14 | 14 | 14 |
| 8 | 8 | 8 | 8 | 9 | 9 | 9 | 10 | 10 | 10 | 10 | 10 | 11 | 11 | 11 | 12 | 12 | 12 | 12 | 12 | 13 | 13 | 13 | 14 | 14 | 14 | 14 | 14 | 15 | 15 | 15 |
| 8 | 9 | 9 | 9 | 9 | 10 | 10 | 10 | 10 | 11 | 11 | 11 | 11 | 12 | 12 | 12 | 13 | 13 | 13 | 13 | 14 | 14 | 14 | 14 | 15 | 15 | 15 | 15 | 16 | 16 | 16 |
| 9 | 9 | 9 | 10 | 10 | 10 | 10 | 11 | 11 | 11 | 12 | 12 | 12 | 12 | 13 | 13 | 13 | 14 | 14 | 14 | 14 | 15 | 15 | 15 | 16 | 16 | 16 | 16 | 17 | 17 | 17 |
| 9 | 10 | 10 | 10 | 10 | 11 | 11 | 11 | 12 | 12 | 12 | 13 | 13 | 13 | 14 | 14 | 14 | 14 | 15 | 15 | 15 | 16 | 16 | 16 | 16 | 17 | 17 | 17 | 18 | 18 | 18 |
| 10 | 10 | 10 | 11 | 11 | 11 | 12 | 12 | 12 | 13 | 13 | 13 | 14 | 14 | 14 | 15 | 15 | 15 | 16 | 16 | 16 | 16 | 17 | 17 | 17 | 18 | 18 | 18 | 19 | 19 | 19 |
| 10 | 11 | 11 | 11 | 12 | 12 | 12 | 13 | 13 | 13 | 14 | 14 | 14 | 15 | 15 | 15 | 16 | 16 | 16 | 17 | 17 | 17 | 18 | 18 | 18 | 19 | 19 | 19 | 20 | 20 | 20 |
| 11 | 11 | 12 | 12 | 12 | 13 | 13 | 13 | 14 | 14 | 14 | 15 | 15 | 15 | 16 | 16 | 16 | 17 | 17 | 18 | 18 | 18 | 19 | 19 | 19 | 20 | 20 | 20 | 21 | 21 | 21 |
| 11 | 12 | 12 | 12 | 13 | 13 | 14 | 14 | 14 | 15 | 15 | 15 | 16 | 16 | 16 | 17 | 17 | 18 | 18 | 18 | 19 | 19 | 19 | 20 | 20 | 21 | 21 | 21 | 22 | 22 | 22 |
| 12 | 12 | 13 | 13 | 13 | 14 | 14 | 15 | 15 | 15 | 16 | 16 | 16 | 17 | 17 | 18 | 18 | 18 | 19 | 19 | 20 | 20 | 20 | 21 | 21 | 21 | 22 | 22 | 23 | 23 | 23 |
| 12 | 13 | 13 | 14 | 14 | 14 | 15 | 15 | 16 | 16 | 16 | 17 | 17 | 18 | 18 | 18 | 19 | 19 | 20 | 20 | 20 | 21 | 21 | 22 | 22 | 22 | 23 | 23 | 24 | 24 | 24 |
| 13 | 13 | 14 | 14 | 15 | 15 | 15 | 16 | 16 | 17 | 17 | 18 | 18 | 18 | 19 | 19 | 20 | 20 | 20 | 21 | 21 | 22 | 22 | 22 | 23 | 23 | 24 | 24 | 25 | 25 | 25 |
| 13 | 14 | 14 | 15 | 15 | 16 | 16 | 16 | 17 | 17 | 18 | 18 | 19 | 19 | 20 | 20 | 20 | 21 | 21 | 22 | 22 | 23 | 23 | 23 | 24 | 24 | 25 | 25 | 26 | 26 | 26 |
| 14 | 14 | 15 | 15 | 16 | 16 | 17 | 17 | 18 | 18 | 18 | 19 | 19 | 20 | 20 | 21 | 21 | 22 | 22 | 22 | 23 | 23 | 24 | 24 | 25 | 25 | 26 | 26 | 27 | 27 | 27 |
| 14 | 15 | 15 | 16 | 16 | 17 | 17 | 18 | 18 | 19 | 19 | 20 | 20 | 21 | 21 | 21 | 22 | 22 | 23 | 23 | 24 | 24 | 25 | 25 | 26 | 26 | 27 | 27 | 28 | 28 | 28 |
| 15 | 15 | 16 | 16 | 17 | 17 | 18 | 18 | 19 | 19 | 20 | 20 | 21 | 21 | 22 | 22 | 23 | 23 | 24 | 24 | 25 | 25 | 26 | 26 | 27 | 27 | 28 | 28 | 29 | 29 | 29 |
| 16 | 16 | 16 | 17 | 18 | 18 | 18 | 19 | 20 | 20 | 20 | 21 | 22 | 22 | 22 | 23 | 24 | 24 | 24 | 25 | 26 | 26 | 26 | 27 | 28 | 28 | 28 | 29 | 30 | 30 | 30 |
| 16 | 17 | 17 | 18 | 18 | 19 | 19 | 20 | 20 | 21 | 21 | 22 | 22 | 23 | 23 | 24 | 24 | 25 | 25 | 26 | 26 | 27 | 27 | 28 | 28 | 29 | 29 | 30 | 30 | 31 | 31 |
| 17 | 17 | 18 | 18 | 19 | 19 | 20 | 20 | 21 | 21 | 22 | 22 | 23 | 23 | 24 | 25 | 25 | 26 | 26 | 27 | 27 | 28 | 28 | 29 | 29 | 30 | 30 | 31 | 31 | 32 | 32 |
| 17 | 18 | 18 | 19 | 19 | 20 | 20 | 21 | 21 | 22 | 23 | 23 | 24 | 24 | 25 | 25 | 26 | 26 | 27 | 28 | 28 | 29 | 29 | 30 | 30 | 31 | 31 | 32 | 32 | 33 | 33 |
| 18 | 18 | 19 | 19 | 20 | 20 | 21 | 22 | 22 | 23 | 23 | 24 | 24 | 25 | 26 | 26 | 27 | 27 | 28 | 28 | 29 | 29 | 30 | 31 | 31 | 32 | 32 | 33 | 33 | 34 | 34 |
| 18 | 19 | 19 | 20 | 20 | 21 | 22 | 22 | 23 | 23 | 24 | 24 | 25 | 26 | 26 | 27 | 27 | 28 | 29 | 29 | 30 | 30 | 31 | 32 | 32 | 33 | 33 | 34 | 34 | 35 | 35 |
| 19 | 19 | 20 | 20 | 21 | 22 | 22 | 23 | 23 | 24 | 25 | 25 | 26 | 26 | 27 | 28 | 28 | 29 | 29 | 30 | 31 | 31 | 32 | 32 | 33 | 34 | 34 | 35 | 35 | 36 | 36 |
| 19 | 20 | 20 | 21 | 22 | 22 | 23 | 23 | 24 | 25 | 25 | 26 | 27 | 27 | 28 | 28 | 29 | 30 | 30 | 31 | 31 | 32 | 33 | 33 | 34 | 35 | 35 | 36 | 36 | 37 | 37 |
| 20 | 20 | 21 | 22 | 22 | 23 | 23 | 24 | 25 | 25 | 26 | 27 | 27 | 28 | 28 | 29 | 30 | 30 | 31 | 32 | 32 | 33 | 34 | 34 | 35 | 35 | 36 | 37 | 37 | 38 | 38 |
| 20 | 21 | 21 | 22 | 23 | 23 | 24 | 25 | 25 | 26 | 27 | 27 | 28 | 29 | 29 | 30 | 31 | 31 | 32 | 32 | 33 | 34 | 34 | 35 | 36 | 36 | 37 | 38 | 38 | 39 | 39 |
| 21 | 21 | 22 | 23 | 23 | 24 | 25 | 25 | 26 | 27 | 27 | 28 | 29 | 29 | 30 | 31 | 31 | 32 | 33 | 33 | 34 | 35 | 35 | 36 | 37 | 37 | 38 | 39 | 39 | 40 | 40 |
| 21 | 22 | 23 | 23 | 24 | 25 | 25 | 26 | 27 | 27 | 28 | 29 | 29 | 30 | 31 | 31 | 32 | 33 | 33 | 34 | 35 | 36 | 36 | 37 | 38 | 38 | 39 | 40 | 40 | 41 | 41 |
| 22 | 22 | 23 | 24 | 24 | 25 | 26 | 27 | 27 | 28 | 29 | 29 | 30 | 31 | 32 | 32 | 33 | 34 | 34 | 35 | 36 | 36 | 37 | 38 | 38 | 39 | 40 | 41 | 41 | 42 | 42 |
| 22 | 23 | 24 | 24 | 25 | 26 | 27 | 27 | 28 | 29 | 29 | 30 | 31 | 32 | 32 | 33 | 34 | 34 | 35 | 36 | 37 | 37 | 38 | 39 | 39 | 40 | 41 | 42 | 42 | 43 | 43 |
| 23 | 23 | 24 | 25 | 26 | 26 | 27 | 28 | 29 | 29 | 30 | 31 | 32 | 32 | 33 | 34 | 34 | 35 | 36 | 37 | 37 | 38 | 39 | 40 | 40 | 41 | 42 | 43 | 43 | 44 | 44 |
| 23 | 24 | 25 | 26 | 26 | 27 | 28 | 28 | 29 | 30 | 31 | 32 | 32 | 33 | 34 | 34 | 35 | 36 | 37 | 38 | 38 | 39 | 40 | 40 | 41 | 42 | 43 | 44 | 44 | 45 | 45 |
| 24 | 25 | 25 | 26 | 27 | 28 | 28 | 29 | 30 | 31 | 31 | 32 | 33 | 34 | 34 | 35 | 36 | 37 | 38 | 38 | 39 | 40 | 41 | 41 | 42 | 43 | 44 | 44 | 45 | 46 | 46 |
| 24 | 25 | 26 | 27 | 27 | 28 | 29 | 30 | 31 | 31 | 32 | 33 | 34 | 34 | 35 | 36 | 37 | 38 | 38 | 39 | 40 | 41 | 42 | 42 | 43 | 44 | 45 | 45 | 46 | 47 | 47 |
| 25 | 26 | 26 | 27 | 28 | 29 | 30 | 30 | 31 | 32 | 33 | 34 | 34 | 35 | 36 | 37 | 38 | 38 | 39 | 40 | 41 | 42 | 42 | 43 | 44 | 45 | 46 | 46 | 47 | 48 | 48 |
| 25 | 26 | 27 | 28 | 29 | 29 | 30 | 31 | 32 | 33 | 33 | 34 | 35 | 36 | 37 | 38 | 38 | 39 | 40 | 41 | 42 | 42 | 43 | 44 | 45 | 46 | 47 | 47 | 48 | 49 | 49 |
| 26 | 27 | 28 | 28 | 29 | 30 | 31 | 32 | 32 | 33 | 34 | 35 | 36 | 37 | 38 | 38 | 39 | 40 | 41 | 42 | 42 | 43 | 44 | 45 | 46 | 47 | 48 | 48 | 49 | 50 | 50 |
| 26 | 27 | 28 | 29 | 30 | 31 | 31 | 32 | 33 | 34 | 35 | 36 | 37 | 37 | 38 | 39 | 40 | 41 | 42 | 42 | 43 | 44 | 45 | 46 | 47 | 48 | 48 | 49 | 50 | 51 | 51 |
| 27 | 28 | 29 | 29 | 30 | 31 | 32 | 33 | 34 | 35 | 36 | 36 | 37 | 38 | 39 | 40 | 41 | 42 | 42 | 43 | 44 | 45 | 46 | 47 | 48 | 49 | 49 | 50 | 51 | 52 | 52 |
| 27 | 28 | 29 | 30 | 31 | 32 | 33 | 34 | 34 | 35 | 36 | 37 | 38 | 39 | 40 | 41 | 42 | 42 | 43 | 44 | 45 | 46 | 47 | 48 | 49 | 49 | 50 | 51 | 52 | 53 | 53 |
| 28 | 29 | 30 | 31 | 32 | 32 | 33 | 34 | 35 | 36 | 37 | 38 | 39 | 40 | 40 | 41 | 42 | 43 | 44 | 45 | 46 | 47 | 48 | 49 | 50 | 50 | 51 | 52 | 53 | 54 | 54 |
| 28 | 29 | 30 | 31 | 32 | 33 | 34 | 35 | 36 | 37 | 38 | 38 | 39 | 40 | 41 | 42 | 43 | 44 | 45 | 46 | 47 | 48 | 49 | 50 | 50 | 51 | 52 | 53 | 54 | 55 | 55 |
| 29 | 30 | 31 | 32 | 33 | 34 | 35 | 35 | 36 | 37 | 38 | 39 | 40 | 41 | 42 | 43 | 44 | 45 | 46 | 47 | 48 | 49 | 49 | 50 | 51 | 52 | 53 | 54 | 55 | 56 | 56 |
| 29 | 30 | 31 | 32 | 33 | 34 | 35 | 36 | 37 | 38 | 39 | 40 | 41 | 42 | 43 | 44 | 45 | 46 | 47 | 48 | 48 | 49 | 50 | 51 | 52 | 53 | 54 | 55 | 56 | 57 | 57 |
| 30 | 31 | 32 | 33 | 34 | 35 | 36 | 37 | 38 | 39 | 40 | 41 | 42 | 43 | 44 | 44 | 45 | 46 | 47 | 48 | 49 | 50 | 51 | 52 | 53 | 54 | 55 | 56 | 57 | 58 | 58 |
| 30 | 31 | 32 | 33 | 34 | 35 | 36 | 37 | 38 | 39 | 40 | 41 | 42 | 43 | 44 | 45 | 46 | 47 | 48 | 49 | 50 | 51 | 52 | 53 | 54 | 55 | 56 | 57 | 58 | 59 | 59 |

# Glossary of Terms

**Amplitude** The sun's true bearing at sunrise or sunset, measured from E (on rising) or from W (on setting) towards N when sun's declination is N, towards S when declination is S.

**Azimuth** a bearing measured through 360°.

**Azimuth Angle** The bearing of a heavenly body measured from N or S.

**Calculated altitude** The altitude a body would be if measured at a given latitude and longitude (usually the EP) found by calculation (not by sight reduction tables).

**Chosen position** A chosen latitude and longitude, normally within $\frac{1}{2}$° of the boat's EP, used to find the tabulated altitude for comparison with the true altitude at the actual position.

**DR** Dead reckoning position arrived at by reference only to course steered and distance through the water. No allowance for tidal stream, current or leeway.

**Declination** The angular distance between a body and the celestial equator, equivalent to the latitude of the body's GP.

**Departure** The distance, measured in miles, between the meridians passing through two places, or the miles which one place is E or W of another. The number of minutes of longitude of the departure depends on the latitude of the position.

**Deviation** The number of degrees and direction by which the compass bearing or course differs from the magnetic bearing or course. If present, this 'error' will vary according to the boat's heading when the compass is read.

**Dip** The angle between a line drawn from the observer's eye to the visible horizon and a line at right angles the observer's zenith. Varies only with height of eye.

**Estimated Position** A position arrived at by applying the effects of tidal stream or current, and leeway, to the position found by DR. It is the best possible estimate of the boat's position by reference to course steered and distance run, tidal stream or current and leeway since the last OP or EP.

**Fix** A position found by observations of landmarks.

**Geographical Position (GP)** The point on the earth's surface where a heavenly body is exactly overhead – on the observer's zenith. It is defined by the body's declination ( = Lat) and GHA ( = Long) at a given moment.

**Great Circle** Any circle on whose plane lies the centre of the earth. Any great circle bisects the earth into two equal halves. A portion of a great circle which passes through two positions is the shortest distance between them. It cuts every meridian at a different angle (except when it is part of a meridian, or the equator), and appears as a curve, bowed away from the equator, on a mercator chart. It is a straight line on a gnomonic projection chart.

**Greenwich Hour Angle (GHA)** The longitude of a body's GP at a given moment, always measured westward from 0°. It is the angle at the pole between the Greenwich meridian and the meridian on which the body's GP is at a given moment. It can also be measured along the equator.

**Horizon** The line where sea and sky appear to meet.

**Intercept** The distance between the chosen position and a point through which the (true) position line runs.

**Local Hour Angle (LHA)** The angle between the meridian on which the chosen position (or the observer) lies and the meridian on which the body's GP lies at a given moment. It may be measured at the pole or along the equator, always measured westward *from* CP or observer *to* the body's GP.

**Limb** The upper or lower edge of the sun or moon.

**Magnitude** The relative brightness of a star or planet. The lower the number (or the greater the minus number) the brighter the body.

**Meridian** Any great circle passing through both N and S poles.

**Meridian altitude** Any body is at its greatest altitude when it crosses the observer's meridian. It is then always bearing due N or S (T°).

**Observed position (OP)** A position found by observations of heavenly bodies.

**Parallax** The apparent change of an object's position when viewed from a different position.

**Prime meridian** The meridian on which Greenwich lies, 0°.

**Prime vertical** A vertical circle passing through E and W points on the horizon. A body is crossing the prime vertical when it bears exactly due E or W. Its Zn is then 90° or 270° T.

**Rhumb line** A straight line drawn between two points on a Mercator projection chart. It cuts every meridian at the same angle, and is not the shortest distance. (See Gt Circle.)

**Semi-diameter (SD)** Half the angular diameter of sun or moon at a given time. The moon's SD changes markedly; the sun's much less.

**Tabulated altitude (Tab alt)** The altitude a body would be if measured at the chosen position, given by sight reduction tables.

**True altitude (True alt)** The altitude a body is, as measured at the boat, after all corrections have been applied. Found by sextant.

**Transit** The passage of a body across the observer's meridian, then at the body's highest altitude, and bearing due N or S.

**Twilight** When the sun is below the horizon but indirectly still gives some light. Times of beginning (at am) and ending (pm) of twilights are listed in the *Nautical Almanac* every third day. *Nautical twilight* is when the sun is 12° below the horizon. *Civil twilight* is when the sun is 6° below the horizon. Star sights are best taken around civil twilight.

**Variation** The difference at any place between the true bearing or course and the magnetic bearing or course as shown by a compass without any deviation.

**Zenith** The point in the heavens exactly vertically above the observer.

**Zenith Distance (ZD)** The angular distance between an observer's zenith and a body. It is the body's altitude subtracted from 90°.

# Index